DOWN GIRL

DOWN GIRL

The Logic of Misogyny

Kate Manne

OXFORD
UNIVERSITY PRESS

OXFORD
UNIVERSITY PRESS

Oxford University Press is a department of the University of Oxford. It furthers
the University's objective of excellence in research, scholarship, and education
by publishing worldwide. Oxford is a registered trade mark of Oxford University
Press in the UK and certain other countries.

Published in the United States of America by Oxford University Press
198 Madison Avenue, New York, NY 10016, United States of America.

CIP data is on file at the Library of Congress
ISBN 978–0–19–060498–1

12

Printed by Sheridan Books, Inc., United States of America

Moses describeth a woman thus: "At the first beginning," saith he, "a woman was made to be a helper unto man." And so they are indeed, for she helpeth to spend and consume that which man painfully getteth. He also saith that they were made of the rib of a man, and that their froward [difficult] nature showeth; for a rib is a crooked thing good for nothing else, and women are crooked by nature, for small occasion will cause them to be angry.

The Arraignment of Lewde, Idle, Froward, and Unconstant Women, Joseph Swetnam, 1615

Guiltie, guiltie, guiltie. Guiltie of woman-slander, and defamation.

Swetnam the Woman-Hater, Anonymous, 1618

MR. MANNINGHAM. Admirable, my dear Bella! Admirable! We shall make a great logician of you yet—a Socrates—a John Stuart Mill! You shall go down in history as the shining mind of your day. That is, if your present history does not altogether submerge you—take you away from your fellow creatures. And there is a danger of that, you know, in more ways than one. [*Puts milk on the mantel.*] Well—what did I say I would do if you did not find that bill?

MRS. MANNINGHAM. [*Choked.*] You said you would lock me up.

Angel Street (or "Gaslight"), Patrick Hamilton, 1938

CONTENTS

PREFACE: GOING WRONG

[L]aid on the grass how small, how insignificant this thought of mine looked; the sort of fish that a good fisherman puts back into the water so that it may grow fatter and be one day worth cooking and eating . . . But however small it was, it had, nevertheless, the mysterious property of its kind—put back into the mind, it became at once very exciting, and important; and as it darted and sank, and flashed hither and thither, set up such a wash and tumult of ideas that it was impossible to sit still. It was thus that I found myself walking with extreme rapidity across a grass plot. Instantly a man's figure rose to intercept me. Nor did I at first understand that the gesticulations of a curious-looking object, in a cut-away coat and evening shirt, were aimed at me. His face expressed horror and indignation. Instinct rather than reason came to my help, he was a Beadle; I was a woman. This was the turf; there was the path. Only the Fellows and Scholars are allowed here; the gravel is the place for me. Such thoughts were the work of a moment.

Virginia Woolf, *A Room of One's Own*

"When will women be human? When?" asked feminist legal theorist, Catharine A. MacKinnon, in a 1999 essay.[1] Similar questions

1. Reprinted in MacKinnon (2006)—the quote with which I opened being MacKinnon's last line therein (43).

have been posed about the sexual objectification of women—by the philosophers Martha Nussbaum (1995; 2001) and Rae Langton (2009)—and misogynist threats and violence—by the popular writers Arthur Chu (2014) and Lindy West (2015), among others. The question echoes in relation to sexual assault, stalking, intimate partner violence, and certain forms of homicide. These are all crimes whose victims are generally (though by no means always) women rather than men, and the perpetrators are generally, and sometimes almost exclusively, men rather than women.[2]

Why do these patterns persist, even in allegedly post-patriarchal parts of the world, such as the contemporary United States, the United Kingdom, and Australia?[3] The same can be asked about the many other kinds of misogyny this book will consider—from the subtle to the brazen; the chronic and cumulative along with the acute and explosive; and those due to collective (or "mob") activity and purely structural mechanisms, along with individual agents' actions. Why is misogyny still a thing?—to borrow a phrase from John Oliver.

There's no doubt that, in these milieux, much progress has been made with regard to gender equality, following feminist activism, cultural shifts, legal reforms (e.g., laws against sex discrimination) and changes in institutional policy (e.g., affirmative action, whose chief beneficiaries in the United States have tended to be white women). Gains for girls and women in education have been especially impressive. And yet, as will emerge in these pages, misogyny is still with us.

The problems that persist, with some arguably on the rise, raise questions that are thorny, puzzling, and urgent. I believe that moral

2. I bracket children generally, as well as adults who are non-binary, for the moment—not because there aren't extremely important issues concerning their (mis)treatment here, but because they raise complications that are orthogonal to my present purposes. The above is what is needed to raise the question I initially want to consider.

3. These will be my primary focus in this book partly because these are the contexts in which these phenomena are often denied or, else, found puzzling. They are also contexts in which I have the relevant insider knowledge, since I will be interested in prevalent cultural narratives and pattern recognition. I say more about this in the introduction.

philosophy has a valuable role to play here—although, ultimately, it will take a village of theorists to gain a full understanding of the phenomenon. My hope in this book is to make a contribution to understanding the *nature* of misogyny, both in terms of its general logic, and one (though only one) of its key dynamics in practice. This involves men drawing on women in *asymmetrical moral support roles*. (I restrict myself to the cultural contexts mentioned above, although welcome others to generalize, or amend and adapt, beyond this.)

What do these moral support relations amount to? It's helpful to think initially about the men who are the most privileged—in being, for example, white, het (i.e., "straight"), cisgender rather than transgender, middle class, and nondisabled. They hence tend to be subject to fewer social, moral, and legal constraints on their actions than their less privileged counterparts. We can then think of a more or less diverse set of women on whom such a man is tacitly deemed entitled to rely for nurturing, comfort, care, and sexual, emotional, and reproductive labor. Alternatively, she may represent the "type" of woman who might have served, or may be recruited, for such purposes.

Of course, just because someone has tacit social permission to lean on women in these and similar ways does not mean either that he would actually want to do so, or that he will succeed in so doing (thereby taking advantage of this possibility), even if he does. Similarly, even if the external constraints on his behaviour are less stringent for him than his less privileged counterparts, he may nevertheless observe these or similar norms, regarding himself as constrained as a matter of moral principle or conscience. But, in other cases, the paucity of such constraints and the presence of such entitlements will have an effect on the way he views and treats certain women within his social orbit: specifically, as *owing* him or his brethren her distinctively human services and capacities, much more so than vice versa.

These asymmetrical moral support relations may be instantiated in many different ways, including in intimate and relatively stable social roles—as his mother, girlfriend, wife, daughter, and so on. Alternatively, these relations may be instantiated in the workplace, position him as a consumer, or involve ad hoc encounters with the girls and women whose attention he may solicit by many different means—from catcalling to trolling on social media to mansplaining.

My view is that a significant amount of (though far from all) misogyny in my milieu serves to police and enforce these social roles, and extract moral goods and resources from such women—as well as protesting her nonappearance or supposed negligence or betrayal. And some (although, again, far from all) remaining forms of misogyny— for example, that which is directed at female public figures—is plausibly derivative from this one. It reflects a kind of deprivation mindset regarding women being giving, caring, loving, and attentive, as opposed to power-hungry, uncaring, and domineering. And it involves a jealous hoarding of certain positions of presumptive collective moral approval and admiration for the men who have been its historical beneficiaries. Women who compete for these roles will tend to be perceived as morally suspect in at least three main ways: insufficiently caring and attentive with respect to those in her orbit deemed vulnerable; illicitly trying to gain power that she is not entitled to; and morally untrustworthy, given the other two kinds of role violations.

Such perceptions are erroneous and pernicious but in many ways understandable, since they are accurate by the lights of history's bad gendered bargains. She *is* morally in the wrong, as measured by the wrong moral standards—namely, his: the moral standards that work to protect historically privileged and powerful men from moral downfall. They also protect him from the ignominy of shame and the corrosive effects of guilt, as well as the social and legal costs of moral condemnation. They enable him to form views and make claims with the default presumption that he is good, right, or correct. And the women morally bound to him may not beg to differ.

As a result, such women may be less than morally reliable when it comes to many of the (often less privileged) people to whom she may owe more, or whose word she ought to believe over his. Not least of these being other, less privileged girls and women.

To the best of my knowledge, this is the first book-length treatment of misogyny (at least under that description) by someone working in the tradition of analytic feminist philosophy. However, I stress that other philosophers, feminist and otherwise, have illuminated many of misogyny's central manifestations—as well as related concepts and phenomena, such as sexual objectification, sexual assault, gendered slurs, sexism, and oppression.[4] The picture I develop will hence often involve joining dots well-drawn by other theorists. In other cases, I will embroider on background pictures or adapt them for my own (I hope not too nefarious) purposes. And some of what follows will pick up on previous work of mine on the nature of moral thinking and the social foundations of morality in the area of philosophy known as metaethics.

My argument in this book is that, in milieu like mine, for comparatively privileged women like me, e.g., me, our humanity is perfectly well-recognized in general. I think it likely has been for quite some time.[5] This is reflected in the fact that misogyny often

4. For just a few examples from the rich feminist literature on these topics, in no way intended to be exhaustive, see, for example: Anne E. Cudd (1990) and Susan J. Brison (2002; 2006; 2008; 2014) on sexual assault; Kimberlé W. Crenshaw (1991; 1993; 1997; 2012) on violence against women of color and the concept of intersectionality; Rae Langton (2009), Ishani Maitra (2009), Maitra together with Mary Kate McGowan (2010), and Nancy Bauer (2015) on sexual objectification and pornography, as well as silencing and subordinating discourse; Kristie Dotson (2011; 2012; 2014) and Miranda Fricker (2007) on epistemic oppression and injustice; Lynne Tirrell (2012) and Rebecca Kukla (2014) on discursive practices that enable violence and oppression; Lauren Ashwell (2016) on gendered slurs; and Marilyn Frye (1983), Peggy McIntosh (1998), and Patricia Hill Collins ([1990] 2000) for some of the classic texts on oppression, sexism, privilege, and Hill Collins's notion of "controlling images." Again, I emphasize that this is but a small smattering of the works that illuminate some of the concepts and phenomena closely—and most clearly—connected with misogyny. More will of course be flagged when other connections become salient; and see also my bibliography for some of the many works by feminist scholars and critical race theorists that have informed and inspired me in this undertaking.

5. I want to leave open the possibility that girls and women who occupy different social positions, for example, involving multiple intersecting systems of oppression that compound one another, together with material conditions such as poverty and homelessness, may face injustice that *is* best understood as dehumanization. This is one of the many questions in relation to misogyny that I don't feel qualified to speak

involves what P. F. Strawson ([1962] 2008) calls "the reactive attitudes," such as resentment, blame, indignation, condemnation, and (for the first-personal analogues) guilt, shame, a sense of responsibility, as well as a willingness to accept punishment when one is held to deserve it. The second-personal and third-personal reactions are supposed to be restricted, at least in the first instance, to our dealings with others who are recognized as "fellow human beings."[6] Moreover, we only tend to have these morally laden and broadly juridical or legalistic reactions to other presumptively reasonable and reasonably mature persons, who we are willing and able to remonstrate with regarding their behavior. Strawson says we take the *objective* stance, in contrast, to young children, the severely intoxicated, people having a psychotic break, and those who are "not themselves," more or less temporarily. We may instead try to manage, treat, educate, or simply avoid, someone to whom we take the objective stance. And we may also take the objective stance as a "refuge" from the "strains of involvement" with those we *could* but choose not to relate to interpersonally ([1962] 2008, 10, 13, 18). We may be too exhausted—or lazy, or overwhelmed, among other possibilities—to engage with them on this occasion.

Strawson's treatment of the reactive attitudes was brilliant, novel, and has been enormously fruitful in subsequent moral philosophy. But it is typical of the narrowness of the range of Strawson's concerns—which typify that of an Oxford don of the mid-twentieth century, nonaccidentally, since he was one—that he only considers

---

to. But I hope that the general framework for theorizing misogyny I develop (and call its "logic," as opposed to its substantive nature) makes room for other voices and other scholars who can do so. Certainly, I don't think that these questions are any less urgent than the ones I hope to shed some light on—often, quite the contrary. But they are also, I think, entangled—as I will go on to argue in the introduction.

6. Whether or not they *ought* to be so restricted, absent anthropomorphism, is another matter, but I take this to be plausible—though it is interesting to think about what exactly one feels when one's beloved corgi (for example) darts after a squirrel and refuses to come back when called, making you worry for her safety. "Moral disappointment" seems a slightly odd label, but it is probably the closest I have come to finding this sort of entirely nonpunitive but nonetheless normatively valenced dismay theorized in the literature; see Fricker (2007, chap. 4, sect. 2) for discussion.

the salutary aspects of our practices of resentment and blame and expressions of disapproval or consternation, and (for their positively valenced counterparts) forgiveness, praise, and expressions of approval or gratitude.

Strawson also considers but one person's side of the story—and hence, by default, the protagonist in a miniature drama. He is the one who *wants* to express resentment, and is expectant or hopeful of receiving an explanation, or else apology. Strawson's opening case of someone stepping on his hand, such that he will resent her unless he is assured she didn't mean it, that she bears good will toward him—it being just an accident—is the paradigm here. It is also inadvertently revealing in this context.

What if you are the agent on the other side of the divide? What if you stepped upon the hands, or toes, of another? Or, for an example recalling the opening scene from Virginia Woolf's *A Room of One's Own* (1929): what if you are held to have trespassed on verboten territory, or his turf? What if he erroneously *thinks* you are not allowed on the soft grass, and are instead bound to stick to the uninviting, unsteadying path lain with gravel? What if his sense of what's *his*, proprietarily, or is safeguarding as others' property, is exaggerated, unjust, and a vestige of history?

And what if he is less than reasonable in his reactions to your (non-)trespassing? What if he puts up signs promising that trespassers will be prosecuted or—as one sometimes sees to this day—shot at?

The person on the other side of Strawson's divide, who is resentful of your misstep, may experience genuine shock and distress as a result of your violating a norm, or refusing to play your assigned part. He may have long been accustomed to expect the compliance or performance of someone in your position. You yourself may have met his great expectations dutifully in the past. So when you cease to, he may well be resentful. He reacts as if you are in the wrong because, from his perspective, you *are* in the wrong. You are miss-stepping, or over-stepping, or deviating, or wronging him.

Most if not all of those of us with some form of unjust, unmerited privilege are susceptible to these sorts of errors. Privilege is prone to confer an inaccurate sense of one's own proprietary turf, epistemically and morally. White women's tacit sense of narrative dominance, or claim to the moral spotlight over black women, remains a serious problem within (white) feminism, for example.

When Virginia Woolf veered onto the grass at Oxbridge, she was waved angrily away by the Beadle. She found her way into the library, but she was not allowed to stay. She needed a letter of introduction from, or to be escorted by, a college fellow (pun intended). Today such rules are defunct, and the library open to people of any gender. But some people still react to women's treading on what was hitherto men's turf—or, similarly, breaking his now defunct or unevenly enforced rules—with resentment or indignation. These reactions may not, and typically do not, reveal their causal triggers—that is, her being a woman who is deviating, or aspiring, in ways historically verboten. They are hence ripe for post hoc rationalization: it just seems she's up to something. She appears vaguely threatening. She seems cold, distant, and arrogant—or, alternatively, pushy, knocking down everyone who stands in her way ruthlessly.

So perhaps the Beadle has not ceased to look askance at wayward women; he is still rankled by the sight of one straying from the path. He reaches for spurious grounds, or seizes on near universal missteps, to justify his resentment toward her. He may have little insight into the causal triggers for his hostility. And the Beadle's wife may wholly share his moral judgments. She may, as we will see, have little or no good alternative.

And so you move to try to reason with Mr and Mrs Beadle. You try to convince them that their reactions are morally off-base, reflective of old, deeply internalized social mores they themselves now claim to reject. But, as you develop your argument, their faces grow resentful (on his part) and disapproving, indignant, even disgusted (on hers). And then you realize the terrible trap: part of what women like you (e.g., me) are held to owe men in such positions of (in this case, rather petty) moral authority is *good will* of the kind Strawson says is so important to receive from one's fellow human beings. But where he says "fellow human beings," and "one," this conceals the extent to which both the desired good will and the desire for it depend on gender, among other systems of domination and disadvantage.

For one such: women positioned in relations of asymmetrical moral support with men have historically been required to show him moral respect, approval, admiration, deference, and gratitude, as well as moral attention, sympathy, and concern. When she breaks character, and tries to level moral criticisms or accusations in his direction, she is withholding from him the good will he may be accustomed to receiving from her. He may even be in some sense reliant on her good will to maintain his tenuous sense of self or self-worth. Her resentment or blame may then feel like a betrayal, a reversal of the proper moral relations between them, and this may make him seek payback, revenge, retribution. And to those who are on his side—Mrs Beadle for one, but extending far beyond that—moral criticisms of Mr Beadle are likely to seem like transgressions or bald-faced lies. Morally speaking, his critic is not to be trusted.

It follows that misogyny is a self-masking phenomenon: trying to draw attention to the phenomenon is liable to give rise to more of it. This makes for a catch-22 situation. But, as far as I can tell, there is no way around this.

It also emerges that the failure to recognize women as human beings need not, and often will not, underlie misogyny. For misogyny may target women in ways that presuppose a sense of her as a fellow human being. The key contrast naturally shifts to the second part of the idiom instead. Women may not be simply human *beings* but positioned as human *givers* when it comes to the dominant men who look to them for various kinds of moral support, admiration, attention, and so on. She is not allowed to *be* in the same ways as he is. She will tend to be in trouble when she does not give enough, or to the right people, in the right way, or in the right spirit. And, if she errs on this score, or asks for something of the same support or attention on her own behalf, there is a risk of misogynist resentment, punishment, and indignation.

So a woman's recognized humanity may leave much to be desired by way of moral freedom. And her sense of obligation is then likely to be excessive, on the one hand, and lacking, in many others.

I wrote this book largely as a prolonged attempt, as I can now see, to free myself of a sense of various spurious obligations, so that I might glean and better meet other, real ones. I also wanted to get past some of the spurious guilt and shame that I am prone to feel when I am at cross-purposes with felt (and, again, sometimes trumped-up) moral authority figures. More than anything, I was prone to feel certain forms of moral embarrassment vaguely reminiscent of that of participants in the Milgram (1974) experiments when I had to resist authoritative-seeming claims that seemed unwarranted on reflection—and, possibly, pernicious.

I felt morally embarrassed to look at the events with which I begin—the Isla Vista killings—from the perspective of the women who were targeted and killed. And I felt embarrassed, in a similar way, to dwell on them at all—as if I should be detached and cool where the female victims were concerned, rather than animated, as I in fact was, by moral horror and grief for them, and all of the other women killed in a similar spirit on a daily basis in America. I felt some pressure to turn instead to purely structural cases of misogyny, or else misogyny of the subtle or chronic and cumulative variety.

But, although these are all important phenomena to investigate, and I go on to do so in what follows, I came to doubt my initial reflexive instinct to *turn away*, as opposed to subsequently varying my lens and widening my focus. And I came to worry that such instincts were having a bad effect on my thinking, or reflected a kind of intellectual cowardice. Feminist philosophy shouldn't only focus on male dominance, patriarchy, toxic masculinity, and misogyny, of course. Still, to the extent that doing so was represented as positively passé by some disciplinary stalwarts, this seemed obviated by the fact that there wasn't a single book, or even an article-length treatment, of misogyny as such when I began this project in May 2014. But I think there is value in work of this rather old-fashioned, unfashionable nature, and arguably a need for more of it, plainly written. This thought received some support during the 2016 US presidential election campaign, and was further reinforced by the subsequent outcome, when Donald Trump was elected president. Toxic masculinity and misogyny are far from recherché now (if only).

And the more clarity we can get here, the better, I believe. We talk about waves of feminism in a way that strikes me as quite different from other areas of political discourse: why? There is, then, an inbuilt or assumed obsolescence for feminist thinking, rather than a model of amendment, addition, and new centers for new discussions.

I belabor the point because I believe that, in much of our thinking and acting, we channel and enact social forces far beyond our threshold of conscious awareness or even ability to recover—and sometimes, markedly contrary to our explicit moral beliefs and political commitments. There is hence a risk of convincing ourselves on the basis of post hoc reasoning not to look too hard at the residual patriarchal forces operating in our culture, as the patriarchal forces themselves gather in the backroom to laugh at our expense and grow stronger in our absence. In my grimmer moods, I picture party hats and hooters.

There is also a risk of exempting individual agents from blame or responsibility for misogynistic behavior. I believe blame has its limits here, as you'll see in the introduction. But if the thought is that we positively ought *not* to consider an individual's actions in an unflattering light, then the result will be predictably politic, even polite, with respect to these agents. In some ways, this would make things easier and less anxiety provoking. And this troubles me. So I spend a fair amount of time here thinking about agents channeling and purveying misogynistic social forces, against the backdrop of and enabled by social institutions.

All in all, I have tried in writing this book to let myself look long, hard, and awkwardly, sometimes from uncomfortable angles, and quite often painfully, in what felt like all the wrong places, in the wrong ways, at the wrong times, in the wrong order. The thought being that I might be missing something worth considering that was hiding in plain sight, or obscured by our usual moral and emotional fulcrums. Sometimes, I found there was not—or, if there was, I failed to glean it; these being parts of the book that never made it in here. But sometimes, I found there was more to be learned from an example than I had initially anticipated. Motifs, themes, and patterns would emerge, surprising me with their unity. Novel and fruitful lines of inquiry would suggest themselves. So I was glad, in the end, to have trusted my decision not to trust my instincts. Instead, when it came to misogyny, I attempted to deviate.

I couldn't have stayed the (crooked) course and persisted in this project without the intellectual and moral support of very many people: First of all, my parents, Robert and Anne, and my sister, Lucy, each of whom I miss every day, living as I do halfway around the world from them. I am grateful to have grown up in a family where morally serious conversation was punctuated by hysterical laughter at social and political absurdity. I'm also grateful to my former advisers and current mentors, along with many other friends and colleagues. I want in particular (and in no particular order) to thank Sally Haslanger, Rae Langton, Richard Holton, Julia Markovits, Matt Desmond, Maura Smyth, Jason Stanley, Amartya Sen, Susanna Siegel, Nancy Bauer, Susan Brison, Michelle Kosch, Hannah Tierney, Will Starr, Sarah Murray, Tad Brennan, Derk Pereboom, and Joshua Cohen, who have all helped me to think through and improve ideas that follow. For great comments, I thank Kathryn Pogin (presented at the Yale ideology conference in January 2016), and David Schraub (presented at the University of California, Berkeley, in February 2017). I also thank the commentators who generously engaged with my piece, "The Logic of Misogyny" (Manne, 2016d) which was the lead essay in a forum in *The Boston Review* (July 2016): Imani Perry, Amber A'Lee Frost, Susan J. Brison, Christina Hoff Sommers, Doug Henwood, Tali Mendelberg, and Vivian Gornick.

I'm immensely grateful for the valuable help of my students, especially those who worked through this material and gave me the benefit of their terrific insights during my graduate seminar in the spring of 2017: Bianka Takaoka, En Ting Lee, Adnan Muttalib, Amy Ramirez, Benjamin Sales, Erin Gerber, Elizabeth Southgate, Quitterie Gounot, Alexander Boeglin, and Emma Logevall. Thanks, too, to the audience members at talks I've given on this material—at Harvard University, Princeton University, the University of California, Berkeley, the University of Wisconsin–Madison, Pittsburgh University, Cornell

University, the University of North Carolina at Chapel Hill, Duke University, Queens University, King's College London, the University of Connecticut (at a conference on "Dominating Speech" run by the Philosophy Department's Injustice League), and at a *Boston Review* event hosted by Kim Malone Scott in Silicon Valley. I've had my thinking changed and improved by the astute questions and interesting examples of many people during these rewarding visits. The same goes for generous e-mail correspondents (despite my terrible habit of letting the good reply be the enemy of the prompt one), and editors I've worked with on related material since I began to write for a wider audience in October 2014.[7] I started to make a list, but it quickly became embarrassingly long while still risking being underinclusive due to gaps in my memory. Then there are my Facebook friends, whom I cherish. I feel lucky to have a community of kind as well as brilliant people from all over the world there as a presence on my laptop, many of whom have helped me immensely to work out ideas only just hatching. All in all, I feel grateful for many people's support and help in this endeavor, whatever the inadequacies of the way that I've incorporated their insights. I've also been extremely impressed with and thankful for the meticulous and astute copy-editing provided by Ginny Faber and Julia Turner, the latter of whom managed the book production side of the project beautifully.

In closing, I want in particular to thank two people without whom this book, such as it is, and for all its flaws and shortcomings, wouldn't have come to be. They each read multiple drafts of every part closely—sometimes more than once—not to mention all the dross that didn't make it in here. The first is my book editor, Peter Ohlin, who encouraged me at every step in the process. I can't imagine an editor more supportive, patient, or better at offering editorial

---

7. Some of this material first appeared in the *New York Times* (parts of chapter 5); the *Boston Review* (parts of chapter 3); *Huffington Post* (parts of chapters 4, 6, and 8); and *Social Theory and Practice* (chapter 5 being a revised version of my "Humanism: A Critique," 2016). The rest of the material is being published here for the first time, although some version of the paper that became the first two chapters has been floating around on my website and www.academia.edu page for years now.

suggestions with nary the slightest hint of mansplaining. This book is immeasurably better for his level-headed oversight and good judgment.

Most of all, I'm grateful to my husband, Daniel Manne, my partner of over a decade and co-parent to our three fur-kids—our corgi, Panko, and our sibling cats, Amelia and Freddy (RIP). I could not have continued to work through such dark and dispiriting material without the light and laughter and love of my home life, and Daniel's constant moral support, in matters practical, emotional, and intellectual. So many of my thoughts here (again, such as they are, and notwithstanding their limitations, for which I'm of course solely responsible) wouldn't have gone anywhere without our having riffed about them together. Daniel was also the one to draw my attention to several of the case studies that follow, and inspired me by example—having defended victims of domestic violence pro bono as an attorney, and studied intimate partner violence at Harvard Law with Professor Diane L. Rosenfeld. Finally, he came up with the term "himpathy," in a characteristic stroke of brilliance.

This book is dedicated to Daniel, with deepest love and thanks—not least for helping me to find the words, and wanting me to use them.

Introduction

Eating Her Words

I felt very strongly that there's been a backlash [to feminism] going on for some time. Why are we shocked? I wasn't shocked. Patriarchy has not been deeply challenged enough and changed. It was just about patriarchy getting a publicly sanctioned voice and silencing a feminist voice, as if there was this war that was going on. And then patriarchy could feel like, "We are going to win this war."

bell hooks, interview on the November 2016 election[1]

SMOTHERING

Women who are strangled rarely cooperate with the police (Resnick 2015). Often incorrectly called "choking," non-fatal manual strangulation is inherently dangerous. It can lead to death hours, days, even weeks afterward due to complications from the brain being deprived of oxygen.[2] It also causes injuries to the throat that may not leave a mark (Snyder 2015). If you don't know how to examine

---

1. Lux Alptraum, "bell hooks on the State of Feminism and How to Move Forward under Trump: BUST Interview," *Bust*, February 21, 2017, https://bust.com/feminism/19119-the-road-ahead-bell-hooks.html.

2. Whereas choking involves an internally obstructed airway—people may choke on a foreign object, such as a piece of food—strangulation is caused by external pressure exerted on the throat or neck, resulting in "one or all of the following: blocking of the carotid arteries (depriving the brain of oxygen), blocking of the jugular veins (preventing deoxygenated blood from exiting the brain), and closing off the airway, causing the victim to be unable to breathe" (Turkel 2008). It requires very

a victim's throat, what to look for in her eyes (red spots, called "pete-chiae"), and the right questions to ask, it may seem no harm has come of it (Turkel 2008). The matter will often go no further. She may not seek medical treatment. The incident will be "shrouded in silence" (Dotson 2011, 244). Sometimes, she won't wake up the next morning, or some morning hence. Moreover, victims of a non-fatal attack of this kind have also been found to be some seven times more likely to become the victim of an attempted homicide by the same perpetrator (Strack, McClane, and Hawley 2001). Yet many states in America do not have a specific statute making strangulation a crime (relegating it to a simple assault; typically a misdemeanor) (Turkel 2008).

Strangulation is a prevalent form of intimate partner violence, in addition to sometimes taking place within other family relationships. It doesn't appear to be limited to certain geographical areas; its existence tends to be confirmed wherever data are available. But for many countries, especially poorer ones, they have not been collected (Sorenson, Joshi, and Sivitz 2014).

Strangulation may be performed either manually, i.e., using bare hands, or with a ligature, e.g., rope, belt, string, electric power cord, or similar (Sorenson, Joshi, and Sivitz 2014). In a recent case reported in local news outlets in Florida, a metal leash was used to strangle a seventy-five-year-old woman who was out walking her dog. The man who attacked her appears to have been a stranger, which is atypical.[3]

In a large majority of cases of strangulation, the victims are female intimate partners—although children and infants are also disproportionately vulnerable. And in the vast majority of cases,

---

little pressure (around eleven pounds) to block the carotid arteries, and unconsciousness may occur within seconds; brain death within minutes. As a basis for comparison, almost twice as much pressure (around twenty pounds) needs to be exerted to open a soda can. "Strangulation: The Hidden Risk of Lethality," The International Association of Chiefs of Police, http://www.theiacp.org/Portals/0/documents/pdfs/VAW_IACPStrangulation.pdf.

3. "Deputies: Palm Harbor Man Used Metal Leash to Choke Elderly Woman Walking Her Dog," WFLA News Channel, April 14, 2017, http://wfla.com/2017/04/14/deputies-palm-harbor-man-chokes-elderly-woman-walking-her-dog-with-metal-leash/.

the perpetrators are men, according to meta-analyses (Archer 2002, 327). It of course doesn't follow that more than a small, perhaps tiny, percentage of men strangle.[4] The distinction between "(almost) only" and "(nearly) all" is obvious but can be obscured by generic claims such as "men strangle."[5]

Another point to note: strangulation is torture. Researchers draw a comparison between strangulation and waterboarding, both in how it feels—painful, terrifying—and its subsequent social meaning. It is characterized as a demonstration of authority and domination (Sorenson, Joshi, and Sivitz 2014). As such, together with its gendered nature, it is a type of action paradigmatic of misogyny, according to the account of it I develop in these pages. Also characteristic is the indifference or ignorance surrounding the practice, as well as the fact that many of its victims will minimize—or may, as I'll go on to discuss shortly, be gaslit (Abramson 2014; McKinnon 2017).

Because the victims of strangulation are so reluctant to testify against their abusers, some investigators are now lobbying for evidence-based cases to prosecute the offenders (Resnick 2015); the witness to the crime having been pre-intimidated or, so to speak, smothered. This last recalls Kristie Dotson's (2011) term "testimonial

---

4. Boys sometimes engage in strangulation behavior too, although data about how common this is (both in absolute terms, and in comparison with other children) seem lacking. A fictional case was pivotal in the recent HBO television series *Big Little Lies* (2017), in which a boy was accused by a girl in his class of having strangled her, using his hands, leaving visible bruises. The boy denied it, and part of the mystery as the series unfolds is whether or not he did it—and, if so, why so? And if not, then who is the real culprit? And why did the girl falsely accuse the boy she pointed to when asked to identify her attacker?

There was some debate in my social circle about whether a young child would really do this to another, their both being in the first grade. I can attest that it is possible; it happened to me at age five too. The main difference is that my classmate used a piece of yarn—technically, a ligature. After I came to, I was told he'd had some trouble processing being runner-up to me in the spelling bee.

5. These claims, in being "generics" capable of being read in either way, may be a source of confusion, to be scrupulously fair to the #NotAllMen crowd. So, unless context serves to make the intended meaning of such claims transparent, I'll try to avoid them.

smothering," which denotes a kind of self-silencing on the part of a speaker. This is due to it being unsafe or risky to make certain claims, likely futile anyway, due to the audience's lack of "testimonial competence" that results (or appears to result) from "pernicious ignorance."[6] It seems clear that strangulation within an intimate partner relationship will tend to give rise to testimonial smothering in Dotson's sense, according to these criteria. If she speaks out, his demonstrated willingness to do what it takes to regain the upper hand makes the situation dangerous. And, as will shortly emerge, the lack of competence regarding the concept of strangulation is extremely widespread. This book as a whole will demonstrate that such incompetence is the result of the sort of pernicious ignorance misogyny feeds, and thrives, on.

SILENCE

As Dotson's (2011, 2012, 2014) work on epistemic oppression has shown, one can silence and be silenced in numerous different ways.[7] For a metaphorical gloss on some of the possibilities for which she offers precise analyses: You can put words into her mouth. You can stuff her mouth and cheeks full of deferential platitudes. You can threaten to make her eat certain words that she might say as a prophylactic against her testifying or so much as recognizing what is

---

6. More precisely, Dotson defines "testimonial smothering" as "the truncating of one's own testimony in order to insure that the testimony contains only content for which one's audience demonstrates testimonial competence. Three circumstances identify testimonial smothering in a testimonial exchange: 1) the content of the testimony must be unsafe and risky; 2) the audience must demonstrate testimonial incompetence with respect to the content of the testimony to the speaker; and 3) that testimonial incompetence must follow from, or appear to follow from, pernicious ignorance" (2011, 249).

7. See also Miranda Fricker (2007) on the form of epistemic injustice she dubs "testimonial injustice," and Rachel V. McKinnon (2016) for a helpful overview of the literature on epistemic injustice in general. Later, in chapter 6, I will also draw on the work of José Medina (2011, 2012), Gaile Pohlhaus Jr. (2012), and Marita Gilbert's joint work with Dotson (2014) in this connection.

happening to her and others. You can stonewall, and make her utterance doomed to fail, less than hollow.

You can train her not to say "strangle" but rather "choke," or better yet "grab," or best of all, nothing. It was nothing; nothing happened. When he boasts of grabbing women's genitals, it becomes "locker room talk," as if that was sufficient to silence comment.[8] In consequence, for many people, it effectively became so. His ex-wife had testified to his raping her. This was "old news and it never happened," according to his spokesperson. And it was, according to his lawyer, Michael Cohen, "not the word you're trying to make it into." Ivana Trump had "felt raped emotionally. . . . She was not referring to it [as] a criminal matter, and not in [the] literal sense, though there's many literal senses to the word." This was after Cohen had vehemently maintained (to a *Daily Beast* reporter, in 2015) that it *couldn't* have been rape, because one cannot rape one's own wife, according to well-established legal precedent. As it was soon pointed out, marital rape had in fact become illegal in New York State some years prior to the incident—shamefully late, but not late enough to exonerate Donald Trump automatically (Darcy 2015). So, other semantic evasions were needed. The upset took place on an "emotional" level, the problem being all in Ivana's head, essentially. It was not a violation in a "legal or criminal sense," as she herself was pressured (again, by Trump's lawyers) to add as a disclaimer when Harry Hurt III's *The Lost Tycoon* (1993) was published, in which the incident is narrated based on her testimony. Trump has denied the allegations in a general way, but only one detail of her story—which I'll get to.

There are many forms such denials may take. "Not rape, not quite that, but undesired nevertheless, undesired to the core"—is how the character of David Lurie, a fifty-two-year-old professor, describes the sex he takes from his student, Melanie, in J.M. Coetzee's novel *Disgrace*. "As though she had decided to go slack, die within herself for

---

8. David A. Fahrenthold, "Trump Recorded Having Extremely Lewd Conversation about Women in 2005," *Washington Post*, October 8, 2016, https://www.washingtonpost.com/politics/trump-recorded-having-extremely-lewd-conversation-about-women-in-2005/2016/10/07/3b9ce776-8cb4-11e6-bf8a-3d26847eeed4_story.html.

the duration, like a rabbit when the jaws of the fox close on its neck" (1999, 23). What does one call that? If not quite rape, then what?[9]

Trump's lawyer, Michael Cohen, discouraged the *Daily Beast* reporter who approached him with the above story from making mention of it at all. Otherwise, he vowed:

> I will make sure that you and I meet one day while we're in the courthouse. And I will take you for every penny you still don't have. And I will come after your *Daily Beast* and everybody else that you possibly know. . . . So I'm warning you, tread very f*cking lightly, because what I'm going to do to you is going to be f*cking disgusting. You understand me?

Cohen continued:

> There is nothing reasonable about you wanting to write a story about somebody's usage of the word "rape," when she's talking [about] she didn't feel emotionally satisfied.

He reiterated:

> Though there's many literal senses to the word, if you distort it, and you put Mr. Trump's name there onto it, rest assured, you will suffer the consequences. So you do whatever you want. You want to ruin your life at the age of 20? You do that, and I'll be happy to serve it right up to you. (Darcy 2015)

Trump's campaign moved to distance Trump from these threats. "Mr Trump didn't know of [Cohen's] comments, but disagrees with

---

9. I make some suggestions (Manne 2017) in cases where, as here, she helps him, even, by lifting up her hips to allow him to undress her more easily: with so little resistance, "everything done to her might be done, as it were, far away" (1999, 23). Is the distance sought space, time, or both, I now wonder. It is as if she fast-forwards, projecting herself into a future in which she was not pawed at and preyed upon. Rather, she let him do it; she consented.

them. . . . Nobody speaks for Mr Trump but Mr Trump," said his spokesperson (Santucci 2015).

Ivana now denies her previous account (and sworn testimony during divorce proceedings) vehemently enough for both of them, on the face of it. She maintains her own story was "totally without merit." Upon the publication of the *Daily Beast* article above, she issued a press release:

> I have recently read some comments attributed to me from nearly 30 years ago at a time of very high tension during my divorce from Donald. The story is totally without merit. Donald and I are the best of friends and together have raised three children that we love and are very proud of. (Santucci 2015)

This is the man she had once described as tearing out fistfuls of her hair in a rage for recommending the surgeon who botched his scalp operation—which was apparently unsuccessful, in addition to being painful. Thereafter, Ivana wrote that her husband "jammed his penis" inside her without warning (and ipso facto nonconsensually). She wrote of him smirking the next morning and asking, "with a menacing casualness," "Does it hurt?" The implication being, he had wanted it to. It was payback for making his head hurt. Trump denies just one thing: having had the procedure to address a nonexistent problem—his bald spot (Zadrozny and Mak 2015).

Ivana's press release concluded:

> I have nothing but fondness for Donald and wish him the best of luck on his campaign. Incidentally, I think he would make an incredible president.

At the time of writing (May 2017), the first hundred days of Trump's presidency have indeed strained credulity.

VOCAL CHANGES

In some cases, it is difficult to recognize the same voice in women who once spoke about the men who abuse them forthrightly and publicly. Lisa Henning was determined to keep her focus on herself and recommended other women do the same, rather than on changing her abusive husband's ways. She realized she couldn't change him, she said. So she left him, losing everything:

> The focus for me, and I think for most women, we need to stop focusing on the men and what they're doing and how we can change them. We have to begin to focus on ourselves. We can't control them. It has to go back to ourselves.

This quote was from Lisa Henning's appearance on *The Oprah Winfrey Show* in 1990, using a pseudonym, "Ann," wearing huge glasses and a wig. The episode was called "High-Class Battered Women." Henning spoke eloquently about the patriarchal forces she realized had left her without the prospect of legal help or the anticipated protections. She spoke of the problem of society not being on her side, especially with her husband a well-to-do and very successful lawyer. This was evident:

> Particularly when you're fighting the judicial system. . . It's a very patriarchal system. These are good old boys. And they hang in there together and we are up against a major, major problem.

The major problem was partly her husband having legal impunity and knowing this too well. He could do what he liked without fear of legal consequences. And what he liked, Lisa Henning testified, was brutal. She testified during a deposition for their divorce proceedings in 1986 that he had beaten her badly, and, notably, choked her:

> He attacked me, choked me, threw me to the floor, hit me in the head pushed his knee into my chest twisted my arm and dragged me on the floor, threw me against a wall, tried to stop my call to 911 and kicked me in the back.

Henning also testified to his having punched her in the car, and the police having been called to their joint home twice. Still, on *The Oprah Winfrey Show*, she said:

The most frightening thing was leaving because once I made that break and once I made it public, and remember my ex-husband was a public figure—everyone knew him and knew what he was doing—and once I made that public, he vowed revenge. He said, "I will see you in the gutter. This will never be over. You will pay for this."

And did she?

Lisa Henning has since remarried, and changed her name. So it was Lisa Fierstein who received the news in 2016 that her ex-husband, Andrew Puzder, had been tapped as President Donald Trump's pick for labor secretary. Everybody knew about the allegations. However, after the *Oprah* footage was released to members of the Senate for a private screening and subsequently made available to the media, it was essentially over. Puzder withdrew his name from consideration.

Why, though? Lisa Henning had recanted her account. Lisa Fierstein maintains that she made it all up—or rather, that Lisa Henning, her former self, did. The lawyer who represented Henning at the time says he believed her then, and doesn't believe her now—partly on the basis of her medical records, as well as their discussions. He thinks she is now dissembling about the abuse (not) having happened. Or, perhaps better, he still believes the testimony of the former Lisa. "I thought her story was not only credible but true," he stated (Fenske 2016).

Puzder denied the abuse both in a deposition for his divorce and in the *Riverfront Times* story, calling his ex-wife Lisa Henning's allegations "baseless."

"There was no physical abuse at any point in time," Puzder asserted.

Lisa Fierstein now agrees with her ex-husband completely.

From an email she wrote, dated November 30, 2016, she states—point blank and, as the above story aptly put it, flatly: "You were not abusive." She writes:

You know how deeply I regret many of the rash decisions I made at that time and I sincerely hope that none of those decisions will become an issue for you at this time. I impulsively filed for a divorce without your knowledge and was counselled then to file an allegation of abuse. I regretted and still regret that decision and I withdrew those allegations over thirty years ago. You were not abusive.

I will most definitely confirm to anyone who may ask that in no way was there abuse. We had a heated argument. We both said things to one another that we regret to this day. I have always been grateful that we have been able to forgive one another for the hurt we caused each other.

So many "regrets"—four (including cognates) in two paragraphs. The email continues, with mounting conviction:

You and I resolved this long ago. We put it behind us and now enjoy what I consider to be a loving and respectful relationship. That is a testament to your integrity and grace. This would not have been possible if you had been a violent or abusive husband. You were not. I wish you always the best of luck in any and all of your endeavors. I know you would be an excellent addition to the Trump team. (Fenske 2016)

You can see now why the Senators who watched that Oprah footage and read the letter might have drawn a line.[10] The turnaround, back toward her ex-husband, is startling. It's not an explanation, but what logicians call a possibility proof: the possibility that a woman could write such an email having appeared on Oprah in disguise—as "Ann"—to speak the words in the passages just cited. In addition to this, Lisa Henning (as "Ann") had elaborated: "Most men who are in positions like that don't leave marks. The damage that I've sustained, you can't see. It's permanent, permanent damage. But there's no mark. And there never was."

---

10. And lest Fierstein's email be interpreted as mere boilerplate, it should also be noted that she offered to speak with the Senators not only personally, but repeatedly, seemingly genuinely dismayed by the tape's resurfacing.

And there still isn't. But the woman who said those words is gone, on the face of it. Read the earlier passages again. She tried so hard to hang onto a different focus and perspective: that of herself over her ex-husband. She found the words. She spoke the words. And, somehow, somewhere, she lost them—or was made to eat them.

This assertion and recanting: any given instance could have any number of explanations, including the original testimony having in fact been false. But put these and other such cases together and one begins to suspect a pattern. Part of male dominance, especially on the part of the most privileged and powerful, seems to be seizing control of the narrative—and with it, controlling her, enforcing her concurrence. It is not exactly deference: rather, it closely resembles the moral aim of gaslighting, according to Kate Abramson's (2014) illuminating account of it.[11] The capacity for the victim's independent perspective has been destroyed, at least when it comes to certain subjects. She is bound to agree with him; she may not only believe, but take up and tell, his story.

In some ways, this is an extension of a general modus operandi of such powerful and domineering agents: issuing pronouncements that simply stipulate what *will* be believed, and then treated as the official version of events going forward. His world-directing claims (beliefs on the surface, commands underneath) target *minds*, and tell people to change theirs: to adopt the world-guided states (i.e., beliefs, at least ostensibly), which we are not ordinarily thought to be able to adopt voluntarily. To form beliefs, we usually need arguments or evidence or some such: something that bears on the truth of what is to be believed, and not just the practical benefits of so doing. Whether we can truly change our minds on demand in this way or not (and I suspect this is, sadly and puzzlingly, possible), not only is his will law, but his word will be gospel.

11. See also McKinnon (2017) for an important discussion of the ways the concept of a political "ally" can be a smokescreen for gaslighting and then testimonial injustice.

AIMS

It's a familiar point, indeed arguably a cliché: morally loaded words matter in politics: "rape" and "strangulation" being among them. It is not, however, as simple as having a name for a problem (cf. Friedan 1963). When words have a serious moral or legal meaning, this can become a motive or pretext for those who refuse to apply them. It can't be *that*. He's not *like* that. Different senses of the term are posited; more than men dreamed of prior to being subject to such accusations. So there is a need to assert our entitlement to use them to name morally serious problems, given the risk of having this potentially genuine entitlement eroded.

The term "misogyny" is, I believe, a prime example; it is both a word we need as feminists, and one we are in danger of losing. This book is hence intended as a bulwark against gaslighting in this arena: the siphoning off of heat and light from the problem of misogyny, in both private life and public discourse, and the concomitant denialism.

There's a question about the appropriate aims and ambitions to have in writing a book about as big and fraught a topic as misogyny—especially since this is the first book-length treatment by someone with my training, as discussed in the preface. A limiting factor for my authority is my own (highly privileged) social position and the associated epistemic standpoint or vantage point. I am also constrained by the kind of lens I can bring to bear on the subject matter, as someone trained in moral and feminist philosophy, rather than psychology, sociology, gender studies, anthropology, or history, for instance.[12] I'll often be expressing my own views about whether certain controversial cases count as misogyny, according to my conception. But bear in mind that there's often room for reasonable disagreements here, and you don't have to agree with any particular verdict I reach for my primary

---

12. So, to avoid disappointment, I should warn you: I won't be able to speak to the interesting anthropological question of why misogyny arose in the first place, and why it has persisted in so many times, places, and cultures.

goal to be met. I want to offer a useful toolkit for asking, answering, and debating such issues, as well as to provide room for detailed, substantive accounts of misogyny as they affect particular groups of girls and women.

What I've aimed to do in the first part of the book is to construct what you can envisage as a sort of conceptual skeleton: a general framework which understands misogyny in terms of what it *does* to women. Namely, I argue that we should think of misogyny as serving to uphold patriarchal order, understood as one strand among various similar systems of domination (including racisms, xenophobia, classism, ageism, ableism, homophobia, transphobia, and so on). Misogyny does this by visiting hostile or adverse social consequences on a certain (more or less circumscribed) class of girls or women to enforce and police social norms that are gendered either in theory (i.e., content) or in practice (i.e., norm enforcement mechanisms).

Notice what this claim says and what it doesn't: both the content of the norms themselves and the mechanisms of enforcement may vary widely, depending on the overall social position of differently situated girls and women. This may also have an important effect on either the experience or impact of misogyny, given forms of disadvantage or vulnerability that may be mutually compounding. I take this to be one of the key lessons of the method and approach to political thought known as intersectionality, pioneered by Kimberlé W. Crenshaw (1991; 1993; 1997; 2012). In chapter 2, I'll say more about how my ameliorative analysis explicitly builds in space for these insights.

Hence you might think of this account as the bare outlines, which invite filling in by theorists with the relevant epistemic and moral authority to do so, should they so choose. This process would involve taking a given set of the social norms to which a particular class of girls and women are subject, and considering not only their content and how they are enforced (or over-enforced), but their specific subsequent impact and interaction with other socially mediated systems of privilege and vulnerability.

The implication for me, when I shift gears from the logic of misogyny to its concrete substance or nature, would seem to be that I should be particularly (though not exclusively) interested in the misogyny familiar to me in my particular social position. But in my case, as someone who is highly privileged, white, middle class, het, cis, non-disabled, and living in contemporary Anglo-American society (Australia included, originally), this focus might initially sound less than promising. Indeed, it might sound absurd or obscene to some readers. Middle-class het white women (in particular) have rightly been criticized for doing feminism in ways that illicitly over-general-ize, even universalize, on the basis of our own experiences. (Audre Lorde's [1979, repr. 2007] "The Master's Tools Will Never Dismantle the Master's House," is a justly famous call to action in this connec-tion.) But, although my limitations will have me daubing at the small corner of the overall canvas I can reach without overextending myself and inevitably (as opposed to potentially) making a mess of it, I do so partly because of what lies beyond my paintbrush.

I am interested in the misogyny dominant social actors visit on girls and women—which encompasses most if not all of us, albeit in potentially radically different ways—given other facets of social posi-tion (as I go on to discuss shortly). But in a way, I *do* want in particular to understand what white women face at the hands of white men not only because it is a moral problem in its own right, though that is part of it, but because I believe it feeds directly into moral problems still more serious: the misogyny faced by more vulnerable women, in being, for example, nonwhite, trans, and otherwise less privileged. To put it simply and crudely at the outset, the misogyny of the most powerful white men—who are the least subject to moral and legal sanctions and, indeed, may inflict harm with impunity—clearly harms the most vulnerable women disproportionately. But it is we, as white women, who tend to enable it, in ways that may be more or less connected with the aim of self-preservation. The misogyny white women face argu-ably does disproportionate damage of one kind: *moral* damage (cf. Tessman 2005). I hence believe we need to get clear on this form of misogyny partly to understand how we err—and how to do better.

The magnitude of the problem in the US context became clear following the general election, when just over half of the white women who voted cast their ballot for Trump over Hillary Clinton. This was despite Trump's long history of misogyny, sexual assault, and harassment, which I'll be considering in some detail later on. But for now, the question as concerns white women is this: What were we thinking? Why were so many of us prepared to forgive and forget the misogyny of someone like Trump? Are we pre-gaslit? Are we self-gaslighting?[13]

NONAPPEARANCE

Andrew Puzder was not the only person with a history of violence toward women who was destined for Trump's White House. Along with Trump himself, Steve Bannon was charged with domestic violence in 1996, a decade more recently than Puzder. Yet Bannon was tapped as Donald Trump's chief strategist a few days after the November 2016 presidential election, having been his campaign manager in the lead-up to Trump's upset victory over Clinton. He is still serving in that role, at the time of writing (May 2017).

The incident began with Bannon getting angry with his then wife, Mary Louise Piccard, for being too noisy. She had gotten up to feed their seven-month-old twin daughters. She made some noise in the process and woke up Bannon, who had fallen asleep on the sofa. It was New Year's Day, 1996 (Gold and Bresnahan 2016). They had been married seven months earlier, three days before the twins were born, after amniocentesis confirmed that they were "normal" (the condition for Bannon's going through with the marriage) (Irwin 2016).

Piccard then asked Bannon for the credit card to buy some groceries. It was *his* money, he maintained, telling her to use the checkbook. As

13. See Crenshaw et al. (2016) for excerpts from her discussions with sixteen social justice leaders in the wake of the election, who offered a range of interesting perspectives on this question among others.

he made to leave the house, Piccard followed him out to the car, where they argued through the driver's side window. She threatened him with divorce and he laughed at her, saying he would never move out. She spat at or on him (the police report doesn't specify), whereupon he reached up to her from the driver's seat, grabbing her by one wrist, and then by her neck. He tried to pull her down into the car, toward him. She fought back, and struck at his face, so as to get free. After a short time, she got away and ran into the house to call 911. He followed.[14]

She ran with the portable phone into the living room. She dialled 911, as he jumped over the twins to his wife and snatched the phone out of her hand. He threw it across the room, screaming: "You crazy fucking cunt!" she subsequently testified. After he left the house and drove off, she found the phone smashed into several pieces, useless.

The police came anyway, following a 911 hang-up call, as is standard practice. The officer saw red marks on Piccard's wrist and neck, and the police photographer took pictures to file with the report. Piccard later described Bannon as "choking" her, as did the media after the story came out in 2016 on *Politico* (Gold and Bresnahan 2016; Irwin 2016). The word is not in the police report, but they may not have known what questions to ask; many officers still don't.

For anyone with some familiarity with the research on intimate partner strangulation, however, the fact that Piccard complained of soreness in her neck, that he pulled her down toward the car by her neck, which he had grabbed along with her wrist in such a way that she moved to struggle and scratch at his face (with her free hand, presumably) would seem consistent with what one would expect during the ten- to fifteen-second window when an adult being strangled will usually instinctually fight hard before losing consciousness.

14. A copy of the police report, linked to from Gold and Bresnahan's *Politico* story (2016), can be found at the URL below. Unless otherwise stated, the details above are all taken from the report itself as written (i.e., close to verbatim, making only small syntactic and non-materially relevant stylistic changes, based on my own transcription of the officer's handwritten description). http://www.politico.com/f/?id=00000156-c3f8-dd14-abfe-fbfbbe310001 (last accessed May 22, 2017)

That the officer saw red marks on her neck that were visible so quickly and pronounced enough to be photographed for the file, is significant, too—again, if it was indeed a strangulation. Only 15 percent of strangulations result in visible marks that show up in photographs to file with a police report; most of the damage is internal (Snyder 2015). Research has shown that the more intense the attack, the more pronounced the marks tend to be, among other physical symptoms (Plattner, Bolliger, and Zollinger 2005). Another such are petechiae, red spots in the whites of someone's eyes. The police report opens by noting Piccard's eyes were "red and watery," and that she "seemed very upset and had been crying." When she met the officer at the front door, she said, "Oh, thank you, you're here. How did you know to come?" He explained he had come because of a 911 hang-up from that address. For three or four minutes, Piccard could not speak to explain what happened—because she was crying, wrote the officer.

Based on conversations with Gael Strack, the CEO of the Training Institute on Strangulation Prevention, the journalist Rachel Louise Snyder explains that, in cases of strangulation:

> [Police] officers often downplayed the incidents, listing injuries like "redness, cuts, scratches, or abrasions to the neck." And emergency rooms tended to discharge victims without CT scans and MRIs. What Strack and the domestic-violence community understand today is that most strangulation injuries are internal, and that the very act of strangulation turns out to be the penultimate abuse by a perpetrator before a homicide. "Statistically, we know now that once the hands are on the neck the very next step is homicide," Sylvia Vella, a clinician and a detective in the domestic-violence unit at the San Diego Police Department, says. "They don't go backwards." (Snyder 2015)

So, when people wanted to raise objections to Steve Bannon's position as chief strategist to the White House, why didn't they take the above incident more seriously? Why is there so much ignorance about strangulation in general, despite excellent pieces like Snyder's appearing in prominent venues (in this case, *The New Yorker*) in recent memory? Even among medical professionals, ignorance—and sometimes sheer hostility—remains a problem. "Maybe you should stop screaming at your husband," one ER doctor in San Diego opined to a woman who had been strangled not long ago (Jetter, Braunschweiger, Lunn, and Fullerton-Batten 2014).

Mary Louise Piccard was taken more seriously than most victims. Steve Bannon was charged with domestic violence with traumatic injury and battery, and misdemeanor witness intimidation. Bannon pled "not guilty," and the case was eventually dismissed when Mary Louise Piccard did not appear in court to testify against him. This was because she had been threatened by Bannon, she later explained, and was told by his lawyer to leave town until the case went away. Otherwise, Bannon had threatened, she would have no place to live and no money to care for their daughters. Piccard added, "He told me that if I went to court, he and his attorney would make sure that I would be the one who was guilty." She didn't, and he didn't make good on his threat. And now, "The bottom line is he has a great relationship with the twins, he has a great relationship with the ex-wife, he still supports them," according to his spokeswoman.

Silence is golden for the men who smother and intimidate women into not talking, or have them change their tune to maintain harmony. Silence isolates his victims; and it enables misogyny. So, let us break it.

OVERVIEW

This book begins by canvassing a common, dictionary-definition-style understanding of the notion of misogyny. On this "naïve conception," as I call it, misogyny is primarily a property of individual misogynists who are prone to hate women qua women, that is, because of their gender, either universally or at least very generally. On this view, agents may also be required to harbor this hatred in their hearts as a matter of "deep" or ultimate psychological explanation if they are to count as bona fide misogynists. Misogyny is as misogynists are, then. And misogynists are agents who fit a certain psychological profile.

In the remainder of chapter 1, I go on to argue that the naïve conception of misogyny is not helping its victims, targets, or those accused of misogyny who are genuinely innocent. It makes misogyny a virtually nonexistent and politically marginal phenomenon, as well as an inscrutable one. On the victim side, the naïve conception makes it very difficult to justify the claim that some practice or action is misogynistic. And on the agent side, a successful defense against charges of misogyny ceases to have much meaning. It places one in some very dubious company with agents who appear to target women specifically, though not necessarily exclusively. But, as I go on to argue, it's not at all clear why it *would* be exclusive. Different forms of bigotry often have a high comorbidity.

According to the positive proposal about misogyny I go on to develop in chapter 2, we should instead understand misogyny as primarily a property of social environments in which women are liable to encounter hostility due to the enforcement and policing of patriarchal norms and expectations—often, though not exclusively, insofar as they violate patriarchal law and order. Misogyny hence functions to enforce and police women's subordination and to uphold male dominance, against the backdrop of other intersecting systems of oppression and vulnerability, dominance and disadvantage, as well as disparate material resources, enabling and constraining social structures, institutions, bureaucratic mechanisms, and so on.

There is hence no supposition of some notional universal experience of misogyny on my view. It is rather meant to be a name for whatever hostile force field forms part of the backdrop to her actions, in ways that differentiate her from a male counterpart (with all else being held equal). She may or may not actually *face* these hostile potential consequences, depending on how she acts. That is how social control generally works: via incentives and disincentives, positive and negative reinforcement mechanisms. She can escape aversive consequences by being "good" by the relevant ideals or standards, if indeed any such way is open to her. Sometimes, there will not be. Double binds—and worse—are common.

Notice then that on my proposed analysis misogyny's essence lies in its social function, not its psychological nature. To its agents, misogyny need not have any distinctive "feel" or phenomenology from the inside. If it feels like anything at all, it will tend to be *righteous*: like standing up for oneself or for morality, or—often combining the two—for the "little guy." It often feels to those in its grip like a moral crusade, not a witch hunt. And it may pursue its targets not in the spirit of hating women but, rather, of loving justice. It can also be a purely *structural* phenomenon, instantiated via norms, practices, institutions, and other social structures.

All told, on my way of thinking, misogyny should be understood from the perspective of its potential targets and victims—girls and women. Misogyny *is* then what misogyny *does* to some such, often so as to preempt or control the behavior of others. Misogyny takes a girl or a woman belonging to a specific social class (of a more or less fully specified kind, based on race, class, age, body type, disability, sexuality, being cis/trans, etc.). It then threatens hostile consequences if she violates or challenges the relevant norms or expectations as a member of this gendered class of persons. These norms include (supposed) entitlements on his part and obligations on hers. She may also be positioned as the *type* of woman who is representative of those who are not playing their assigned parts properly or are trespassing on his territory.

In chapter 3, I argue that, given that the terms "sexism" and "misogyny" can be usefully employed to mark an important contrast, we should do so. I propose taking sexism to be the branch of patriarchal ideology that *justifies* and *rationalizes* a patriarchal social order, and misogyny as the system that *polices* and *enforces* its governing norms and expectations. So sexism is scientific; misogyny is moralistic. And a patriarchal order has a hegemonic quality.

Over the course of these three chapters, which theorize the 'logic' of misogyny, I argue that my analysis has several important theoretical and practical advantages. Here are the main benefits I argue accrue to my analysis, in the order in which I tout them:

- It enables us to understand misogyny as a relatively unmysterious, and epistemologically accessible, phenomenon, as compared with the naïve conception, which threatens to make a mystery of misogyny—epistemologically, psychologically, and metaphysically speaking.

- It enables us to understand misogyny as a natural and central manifestation of patriarchal ideology, as opposed to being a relatively marginal, and not inherently political, phenomenon.

- It leaves room for the diverse range of ways misogyny works on girls and women given their intersectional identities, in terms of the quality, quantity, intensity, experience, and impact of the hostility, as well as the agents and social mechanisms by means of which it is delivered. Misogyny may also involve *multiple* compounding forms of misogyny if she is (say) subject to different parallel systems of male dominance (depending, again, on other intersecting social factors), or required to play incompatible roles in virtue of multiple social positions which she occupies simultaneously.

- It enables us to understand misogyny as a *systematic* social phenomenon, by focusing on the hostile reactions women face in navigating the social world, rather than the ultimate psychological bases for these reactions. Such hostility need not have an immediate basis in individual agents' psychologies whatsoever. Institutions and other social environments can also be differentially forbidding, "chilly," or hostile toward women.

- It yields an extension for the term "misogyny" broadly in keeping with recent "grass-roots" semantic activism, which has already pushed the term's usage, and to some extent its dictionary definition, in this more promising direction. It also helps to explain what various apparently disparate cases have distinctively in common.

- It delivers plausible answers to many of the questions about misogyny that have been controversial recently, in the wake of some such cases.
- It enables us to draw a clean contrast between misogyny and sexism.

In chapter 4, I go on to consider one central substantive dynamic of misogyny under a white heteropatriarchal order in the milieux on which I focus. In this economy of moral goods, women are obligated to *give* to him, not to ask, and expected to feel indebted and grateful, rather than entitled. This is especially the case with respect to characteristically *moral* goods: attention, care, sympathy, respect, admiration, and nurturing. The flipside of this is his being entitled to take much in the way of these moral goods, including—it would seem—the lives of those who can no longer give him what he wanted in terms of moral succor. He may love and value her intrinsically—that is, for her own sake—but far too conditionally, that is, not on her identity as a person (whatever that amounts to) but her second-personal attitude of good will toward him.

I then pause in chapter 5 to consider and argue against a popular rival approach to "man's inhumanity to man"—or, rather, in this case, to women—which one might take to understanding misogyny. On this view, which I call "humanism," misogyny has its psychological source in a failure to recognize women's full humanity. I argue that, often, it's not a sense of women's humanity that is lacking. Her humanity is precisely the problem, when it's directed to the wrong people, in the wrong way, or in the wrong spirit, by his lights. So, rather than thinking of recognized human beings versus subhuman creatures or mindless objects, we should explore the possibility of locating the key contrast in the second part of the idiom. Women embroiled in the giver/taker dynamic of chapter 4 are human *givers* as well as human beings. Her humanity may hence be held to be owed to other human beings, and her value contingent on her giving moral goods to them: life, love, pleasure, nurture, sustenance, and comfort, being some such. This helps to explain why she is often understood perfectly well to have a mind of her own, yet punished in brutal and inhumane ways when that mind appears to be oriented to the wrong things, in the wrong ways, to the wrong people—including herself and other women.

Much of the remainder of the book concerns misogyny's (in my view) undernoticed attendant biases, resources, methods, and enabling/self-masking mechanisms. I believe these are reflected in the form of dominant cultural products ranging from moral narratives, social scripts, artworks, and patterns of group activity, and are influenced by the giver/taker dynamic at work in the background.

Chapter 6 considers the exonerating narratives that hyperprivileged men tend to be the beneficiaries of. I also discuss the flow of sympathy away from female victims toward their male victimizers—which I call "himpathy." And, by way of a contrast to the much-discussed Isla Vista killings, I consider the far less publicized recent case of the serial rapist in Oklahoma who preyed on black women. He was betting on the fact that his victims wouldn't report him and that, even if they did, they wouldn't be able to bring him to justice—his being a police officer. His bet didn't come off in the end; but it was a canny move, considered purely from the perspective of getting away with it. And that seems telling with regard to misogynoir, Moya Bailey's apt term (2014) for the distinctive intersection of misogyny and anti-black racism, in America.

In chapter 7, I turn to another predictable result of privileged women's social position as moral "givers": the hostility and suspicion shown toward the victims of misogyny and male aggression when it comes from her no less privileged male counterparts. Whereas, if it emanates from male threats to white supremacy, that is, locally dominant nonwhite agents, the opposite sympathies predominate. This is because such narratives involve casting its subjects in the role of *victims*, and hence putting her in the moral spotlight, as the designated locus of care, concern, sympathy, and attention. But this is contraindicated by misogynistic mechanisms, and modulated by racist ones, both of which uphold the norm that women, especially women of color, should bestow such attentions on others, not ask for them.

Finally, in chapter 8, I apply my theory to explaining Hillary Clinton's loss of the 2016 presidential election. This case illuminates the way misogyny often targets women who trespass on men's historical turf and threaten to *take something from him*, by targeting her in a moral "giver" capacity. This may involve transforming a collective problem of which she is part into *her* problem, in particular; and, as well as getting personal, there are re-descriptions of her intentions or behavior so as to assume the perspective of one who is her rival in all things, and who deserves all the spoils which are in finite supply. So possession becomes greed; aspiration becomes grasping; winning equals theft; and omissions are erasing.

These kinds of conceptual transformations are common. But they may not be good inferences; indeed they are, on the face of it, non sequiturs. Omissions *may* be negligent and insulting. Or they may be due to a morally and epistemically healthy humility, and involve the recognition that one is just one member of a community of moral agents or inquirers. And even when this community is lacking in diversity, as is sadly the case in philosophy all too often, there are limits of the extent to which one can single-handedly correct for this. There may still be value in what one can contribute.

With that in mind, let me explain some of the many important subjects this book will not cover, or will cover only within limits, and the thinking behind this.

REGRETS

Perhaps the biggest omission (although there are many) in this book is a discussion of transmisogyny. This is a deeply important, indeed urgent, issue, given that trans women—trans women of color in particular—are an extremely vulnerable population in the United States, among many other parts of the world, today. Welcome increases in visibility have sadly, yet all too predictably, led to backlash. And trans men are also highly vulnerable.[15] Given the prevalence of transphobic and transmisogynistic violence, harassment, and both individual and structural forms of discrimination, I regret not being able to speak to its nature. That being said, it seemed evident to me I didn't have the requisite authority to do so. Recent controversies in philosophy at the time of writing (May 2017) have highlighted the need for lived experience to speak on these matters.[16] For readers who wish to learn more about trans feminism, my bibliography contains some of the works that I have found most helpful and illuminating on the subject: work by Talia Mae Bettcher (2007; 2012; 2013; 2014), Rachel V. McKinnon (2014; 2015; 2017), and Emi Koyama (2003; 2006), as well as Julia Serano ([2007], 2016), being among them.

I've also tried to frame what I say about misogynoir (as indicated above) with even more epistemic caution—and humility—than usual. I have moral qualms about writing as a white woman in ways that graphically position black women's bodies as the subjects of degradation and violence; this can have a problematically prurient quality that adds insult to the injury of historical and ongoing indifference and exploitation on our part. But I do spend some time on the case of Daniel Holtzclaw, in order to shed light on the way an authority figure preyed on black women who were highly vulnerable, in being poor, legally compromised (in having, e.g., outstanding warrants for their arrest), being sex workers, or having drug addictions. I couldn't help but be struck by the way the white women on the jury

15. Note that whether or not the transphobia to which trans men are subject counts as transmisogyny will depend on whose definition of transmisogyny one is working with; see Julia Serano ([2007], 2016) for discussion of the continuities she intended as the theorist who first coined the term; and see Talia Mae Bettcher (2007) for a discussion, compatible with Serano's as far as I can tell, of some of the ways transphobia may differ for trans men versus trans women.

16. Jennifer Schuessler, "A Defense of 'Transracial' Identity Roils Philosophy World," *New York Times*, May 19, 2017, https://www.nytimes.com/2017/05/19/arts/a-defense-of-transracial-identity-roils-philosophy-world.html.

cried sympathetic tears for the perpetrator, despite convicting him of egregious sexual crimes against black women. And white women in the mainstream feminist media were also largely silent. Together, this illustrates one form of the misogynoir of complicity and ignorance white women are guilty of all too often. I include myself in the class of those who can, must do better.

These are just a few of the decisions on which I came to the conclusion there was no morally perfect way to proceed. Even "moving over" is something that is done from a position of privilege, as Linda Martín Alcoff (1991–92) has pointed out. Yet, as she then goes on to say, it is still sometimes called for (24–25). That does not mean there aren't things to be regretted about one's subsequent silences.

I have tried to strike a balance here between making each of the eight chapters and the conclusion self-contained enough to read as an essay in its own right (knowing that readers will find different ways into, and out, of the material) and trying to show how each contributes to a systematic if far from comprehensive approach to the subject matter. Again, I say the former rather than the latter because, while the framework I develop for thinking about misogyny is intended to be general, the work of filling it in will require a village of different theorists. And the detail work that I do here myself, in the later chapters, is focused deliberately on cultures in which I've been a political participant—the contemporary United States and Australia. This is not owing to a misplaced ethnocentrism (I think; I hope), but because my methodology combines elements of cultural criticism, ideology critique, and philosophical analysis. So I need insider knowledge. And it's also important to diagnose misogyny in a context in which it's often denied, instead of pointing the finger—sometimes in racist and xenophobic ways—to other, othered cultures. This is typically not my place, as a white Australian ex-pat. I welcome others to amend and to generalize.

Another caveat I want to make explicit at the outset, and another reason why this book carries the subtitle it does, is that I regard the gender binary system—where people are divided into two mutually exclusive and exhaustive categories, of boys and men, on the one hand, and girls and women, on the other—as inaccurate and pernicious. Some people are intersex; some people are agender; and some people are genderqueer, moving back and forth between different gendered identities, among other non-binary possibilities. So I certainly do not mean to endorse the gender binary, and indeed I emphatically reject it. But I intermittently proceed as if such falsehoods are true, in order to see what follows. For the logic of patriarchy, hence misogyny, very much includes a commitment to gender binarism (see Digby [2014]), as well as an anti-trans metaphysics of gender (see Bettcher [2007, 2012]), a heteronormative view of human sexuality (see Dembroff [2016], for an alternative conceptual framework to the usual distinctions between homo-, hetero-, and bisexuality), as well as ideals of love which make monogamy compulsory. (See Jenkins [2017] for a feminist defense of polyamory.)

Investigating the logic of misogyny often involves exploring what is entailed by such problematic or indeed flatly false assumptions, which exclude many people, and assume away legitimate and salutary ways of being embodied, living, and loving—and even some people's very humanity or existence. But it can be useful to understand the inner workings of a system that upholds the status quo in intricate, and sometimes even morally gory detail, in order to see how best to combat it. This is my intention when I intermittently grant certain objectionable assumptions, for the sake of argument— and, ultimately, trying to expose and disrupt misogyny's operation (Haslanger 2012).

That brings me to the final reason I'll mention here for the book's "logic" subtitle. I try to understand misogyny throughout from the inside, not primarily as a psychological matter—but rather, as a social-political phenomenon with psychological, structural, and institutional manifestations. I present misogyny as a system of hostile forces that by and large *makes sense* from the perspective of patriarchal ideology, inasmuch as it works to police and enforce patriarchal order. Since I believe that patriarchal order is oppressive and irrational, and that it casts a long historical shadow, I also believe that misogyny ought to be opposed, and that individual agents often have reasons, and sometimes obligations, to try to resist it. (See, e.g., Hay [2013] and Silvermint [2013] for discussion.)

However, following the lead of the critical race theorist Charles Lawrence III (1987; 2008), this book primarily takes what he calls an "epidemiological" approach to matters of social justice. That is, I concentrate largely on moral *diagnosis*, or getting clear on the *nature* of misogyny, construed as a moral-cum-social phenomenon with political underpinnings. This is as opposed to making explicit moral prescriptions and characterological judgments, and effectively putting people on trial—and hence on the defensive. I think that such an approach to misogyny tends to be unhelpful by encouraging moral narcissism, among other things: an obsessive focus with individual guilt and innocence. Moreover, as we will see time and again over the course of these pages, misogyny frequently involves moralistic take-downs or the unforgiving shaming of women for their (real or supposed) moral errors. Misogyny also subjects women to what I have come to think of as a kind of tyranny of vulnerability—by pointing to any and every (supposedly) more vulnerable (supposed) person or creature in her vicinity to whom she might (again, supposedly) do better, and requiring her to care for them, or else risk being judged callous, even monstrous. Meanwhile, her male counterpart may proceed to pursue his own "personal projects," as the English moral philosopher Bernard Williams called them (1981), with relative impunity. She is, in view of this, subject to undue moral burdens.

So trying to fight misogyny primarily using juridical moral notions is a bit like trying to fight fire with oxygen. It might work on a small scale—we do manage to blow out matches and candles, after all. But, when we try to scale up the strategy, it is liable to backfire. We would be trying to put out a fire while feeding right into it.

What are the alternatives? Following Williams, I like to draw a distinction between moral and political claims we may call "evaluative" versus those that are "prescriptive." The former are claims about the *goodness* or *badness* of certain states of affairs in the world (or, alternatively, ascribing to them more elaborate, or "thick," moral-cum-political qualities). Evaluative claims are hence claims about what *ought (or ought not) to be the case*. And they are often, in Williams's view, the form answers should take when it comes to questions of social justice. Whereas claims that advance *prescriptions* (or, on the negative side of the same coin, issue *prohibitions*) are the bases for giving commands or instructions to an individual agent about what *she ought (or ought not) to do*. Williams also glossed the idea of these prescriptions as the basis for advice offered in the "If I were you. . ." mode, to a second party.

I am sympathetic to Williams's "internalist" view that prescriptive claims, indexed to particular agents, depend for their very truth on that agent's "personal projects" and values (Manne 2014a). But even if one rejects this controversial claim, the existence of the evaluative mode above shows that we do not have to choose between a morally accusatory or even inevitably prescriptive stance, which will often garner resentment, for reasons canvassed in the preface, versus a pointed moral neutrality that would be craven, sometimes offensive, in this context. Most of my work in the book will hence lie in describing states of affairs that it will be evident I regard as morally bad—for example, unjust and oppressive—and in need of reform. I invite you as a reader to draw the same conclusions—or, by the same token, to find reasons on which to base a potentially fruitful disagreement. There is nothing morally neutral about any of this. Still, I *do* leave it largely open how (much) to apportion blame, to whom, and how we might go about improving the situation. Sometimes, the question of how to combat misogyny is all too obvious: don't participate in or encourage it, try to stop it, and so on. Sometimes, there are various possibilities, with risks and costs to be weighed against potential rewards and benefits. And sometimes it is not in the least clear what to do, and we will have to strategize, experiment, feel our way, and so on. Whatever the case, I suspect that combating misogyny is likely to be a messy, retail business that permits few wholesale answers, as in most long-term projects of moral and social overhaul.

Another reason to think that combating misogyny in particular will be a piecemeal process is that its mechanisms and methods are so opportunistic—or enterprising, depending on how you look at it—and so various. Girls and women may be down-ranked or deprived relative to more or less anything that people typically value—material goods, social status, moral reputation, and intellectual credentials, among other realms of human achievement, esteem, pride, and so on. This may happen in numerous ways: condescending, mansplaining, moralizing, blaming, punishing, silencing, lampooning, satirizing, sexualizing, belittling, caricaturizing, exploiting, erasing, and evincing pointed indifference.

This is another reason why I chose my title: that and the fact that it is a command and need not sound authoritarian—it can be said gently and obeyed with a sense of pleasure, purpose. My dog Panko proves it. But what for her constitutes a "liberating duty," to use Joseph Raz's notion (1989), would hardly be so for me. As human beings, our freedom lies in other kinds of rule-following, as well as revision, creation, breakage, and reformation.

Chapter 1

Threatening Women

> Well, of course, though darkling, one has some inkling—some
> notion of what sort of thing is being talked about.
>
> P. F. Strawson, "Freedom and Resentment"

"Misogyny" is a loaded word. And its prevalence in news headlines
has been increasing recently.[1] But so has disagreement about its
meaning and its reference. "I can't be the only man confused about
misogyny," wrote Tom Fordy in *The Telegraph* (London), on July 2,
2014.[2] Fordy is clearly right. But men are not the only ones who are
grappling with the notion. At stake is how many girls and women are
grappling, in various ways, with the actual phenomenon. "Is there a
misogynist inside every man?" Fordy wondered, bleakly. And are all
women really subject to misogyny in some form, as was seemingly
the premise of the #YesAllWomen campaign on Twitter?

This chapter is devoted to the meaning, use, and point of
the notion of misogyny. These are issues about which analytic
philosophers—feminist and otherwise—have said little to date.[3] But

---

1. For some evidence of its increasing prevalence in news headlines since 2012,
particularly in the United States, Canada, and Australia, see the graph on Google
Trends, https://www.google.com/trends/explore#q=misogyny (accessed March 31,
2015 and again on May 11, 2017, confirming that this trend has since continued).

2. Tom Fordy, "Is There a Misogynist Inside Every Man?" *The Telegraph*, July 2, 2014,
http://www.telegraph.co.uk/men/thinking-man/10924854/Is-there-a-misogynist-
inside-every-man.html.

3. To briefly give some sense of this—entering the search terms *misogyny* and
misogynist on philpapers.org returns sixty-seven and thirty-one results, respectively,
at the time of writing (May 11, 2017). But the vast majority of these works primarily

they turn out to be philosophically rich, psychologically complex, and politically important. For all of these reasons and more, I believe it is high time we started paying misogyny more attention. By the end of chapter 2, I'll have proposed a constitutive account of it.

You might wonder why such an account is needed, however. For you might think that the question "What is misogyny?" has a simple answer. According to a common, dictionary definition–style understanding of the notion, which I call the *naïve conception*, misogyny is primarily a property of individual agents (typically, although not necessarily, men) who are prone to feel hatred, hostility, or other similar emotions toward any and every woman, or at least women generally, *simply because they are women*. That is, a misogynist's attitudes are held to be caused or triggered merely by his representing people as women (either individually or collectively), and on no further

address the question of whether some figure in the canon counts as a misogynist. (This question is asked of Nietzsche, unsurprisingly, but also of Iris Murdoch and Julia Kristeva, rather more so.) Nor do these concepts figure prominently as a rule in the current literature in analytic feminist philosophy. To take three leading analytic feminist philosophers whose work will play an important role in developing my analysis: in Sally Haslanger's (2012) *Resisting Reality*, the term "misogyny" and its variants only appear in the text in connection with a particular example about misogynistic song lyrics (387–389). They appear a half dozen times by my count in Rae Langton's (2009) *Sexual Solipsism*, but for the most part only in passing. Langton's single substantive remark about the aetiology of misogyny will be considered later on, in chapter 3, though.

One might naturally have thought that Martha C. Nussbaum's (2011) "Objectification and Internet Misogyny" would have more to say about the concept. But strikingly, although the essay has much to say about objectification that I find congenial and will draw on in what follows, the term "misogyny" and its variants only appear once following the title (if I am not mistaken). All told, within the existing literature in analytic feminist philosophy, there is not a great deal of work that directly addresses my opening question, What is misogyny? Fortunately, there is a good deal (in the aforementioned texts, among others) that sheds light on it from different angles. Some of the classic feminist texts that I've found particularly illuminating in this connection include: Andrea Dworkin's (1976) *Woman Hating: A Radical Look at Sexuality*, Catharine MacKinnon's (1987) *Feminism Unmodified*, Patricia Hill Collins's (2000) *Black Feminist Thought*, and Susan Faludi's (2006) *Backlash: The Undeclared War against American Women*. See also the preface, note 4, for some recommended jumping off points into the rich literatures on some of misogyny's many manifestations, as well as various associated and intersecting systems of oppression and domination.

basis specific to his targets. Such a representation, together with the agent's background attitudes toward women as, for example, disgusting, loathsome, fearsome, or mindless sexual objects is supposed to be enough to trigger his hostility in most, if not all, cases (i.e., admitting of only limited exceptions, such as for those few women who somehow manage to dispel his hostility). Misogynistic attitudes are thus unified by their psychological nature and basis— that is, their "deep" or ultimate psychological explanation. And a culture will be misogynistic to the extent that it contains, fosters, and is dominated by misogynists.

I believe that the naïve conception of misogyny is too narrow in some respects and not focused enough in others. Although I think it is right to keep the emphasis on attitudes in the family of hostility, I argue that the targets of this hostility should be allowed to encompass *particular* women and particular *kinds* of women. Otherwise, misogyny will be effectively defined so as to be rare in patriarchal settings—which I take to be its native habitat—given certain truisms about the moral psychology of hostility and hatred. The naïve conception also fails to home in on the subclass of these reactions that I think deserve to be our focus here: those that are an outgrowth of *patriarchal ideology*. For misogyny, though often personal in tone, is most productively understood as a *political* phenomenon. Specifically, I argue that misogyny ought to be understood as the system that operates within a patriarchal social order to police and enforce women's subordination and to uphold male dominance.

My goal in the first part of the book is hence to undertake what Sally Haslanger (2012) has called an "analytical" or "ameliorative" project (223–225, 366–368), or what has also been called "conceptual ethics" (Burgess and Plunkett 2013) and "conceptual engineering" (Floridi 2011). According to the ameliorative feminist conception of misogyny that I motivate in this chapter, and develop properly in the next, misogyny is primarily a property of social systems or environments as a whole, in which women will tend to face hostility of various kinds *because they are women in a man's world* (i.e., a patriarchy), who are held to be failing to live up to patriarchal standards (i.e., tenets of patriarchal ideology that have some purchase in this environment). Because of this, misogynist hostilities will often target women quite selectively, rather than targeting women across the board. And individual agents may harbor these hostilities for numerous different reasons. The full psychological explanation of their attitudes and actions may also vary widely. Such hostilities may alternatively have their source in the actions, practices, and policies of broader social institutions. What these hostilities are required to have in common is their social-cum-structural explanation: roughly, they must be part of a system that polices, punishes, dominates, and condemns those women who are perceived as an enemy or threat to the patriarchy.

My proposed feminist analysis of misogyny hence aims to ameliorate the concept by highlighting misogyny's political dimensions, rendering it psychologically more explicable, and supporting a clean contrast between *misogyny* and *sexism*. The analysis also yields an extension for the term "misogyny" that dovetails nicely with usage patterns among feminists. This limits the extent of my ameliorative proposal's revisionism, and also suggests that this pattern of usage has a theoretical unification, rather than being ad hoc. Or so I'll argue in chapter 3, on the strength of the analysis.

With that being said, let us turn to an example. What follows in the first section is a précis of the events and subsequent media controversy that prompted Fordy's article and set the #YesAllWomen campaign in motion during May 2014. It was one of three recent incidents to cause the number of dictionary and Google searches for the term "misogyny" to spike the most dramatically—each of which I'll discuss over the course of the next three chapters.

THE ISLA VISTA KILLINGS

"Hi, Elliot Rodger here. Well, this is my last video. It all has to come to this. Tomorrow is the Day of Retribution," said Rodger, aged twenty-two, from behind the wheel of his BMW. He described himself as having been "forced to endure an existence of loneliness, rejection, and unfulfilled desires, all because girls have never been attracted to me. Girls gave their affection and sex and love to other men but never to me. . . . It has been very torturous," he went on to complain.[4] He described these "girls" as "throwing themselves" at the "obnoxious brutes" they preferred to him, "the supreme gentleman." "What don't they see in me?" he wondered, rather plaintively.

Rodger then shifted from speaking about these women in the third person and started speaking *to* them—using the second-person plural, as in, "you all." As in, specifically, "I will punish you all for it." Then he laid out his plan for exacting vengeance as follows: "On the Day of Retribution, I am going to enter the hottest sorority house of UCSB; and I will slaughter every single spoiled, stuck-up, blonde slut I see inside there." He then resumed using the second-person plural form of address once again: "I'll take great pleasure in slaughtering all of you. You will finally see that I am, in truth, the superior one—the true alpha male. Yes. After I've annihilated every single girl in the sorority house, I'll take to the streets of Isla Vista and slay every single person I see there."

Rodger's long-anticipated "Day of Retribution" started off at home. He stabbed to death the three young men in his apartment (his two roommates, and a guest of theirs), before uploading his video to YouTube, and then driving to the Alpha Phi sorority house at the University of California, Santa Barbara (UCSB). But the central element in Rodger's plan was foiled when he announced his arrival at the sorority house too boldly. His knocking sounded unusually loud and aggressive, according to one of the women inside.[5] When he was

4. The video was subsequently removed from YouTube, but a transcript of it can be found on the website democraticunderground.com, http://www.democraticunderground.com/10024994525 (accessed April 4, 2015). Rodger had previously recorded and uploaded other similar videos to YouTube as well. Further evidence regarding his thinking and intentions was sought by many commentators in Rodger's so-called manifesto, "My Twisted World," which was released publicly following the incident. I draw on it myself in chapter 5. A copy of it is available at http://s3.documentcloud.org/documents/1173619/rodger-manifesto.pdf (accessed April 5, 2015).

5. "Timeline of Murder Spree in Isla Vista," *CBS News*, May 26, 2014, http://www.cbsnews.com/news/timeline-of-murder-spree-in-isla-vista/.

not let in the door, he exploded in rage and frustration and shot at a group of three young women whom he encountered around the corner.[6] They were members of the Tri Delta sorority house at UCSB. Rodger fired several rounds, killing two and wounding one of them. Afterward, he drove off, and went on a chaotic and seemingly random drive-by shooting spree, in which he killed another young man, and injured thirteen other men and women. As law enforcement officers closed in on him, Rodger turned the gun on himself, crashing into a parked car. He was found dead at the wheel, his BMW on fire.

To many feminist commentators, the Isla Vista killings seemed a very clear instance of misogyny in action—along with whatever else it might have been, additionally. And many saw it as a dramatic manifestation of a wider cultural pattern—namely, misogyny of a kind that often festers beneath the surface in America today, among other parts of the world sometimes alleged to be post-patriarchal.

Many women who watched Rodger's video in light of his violent eruption had a similar reaction. The #YesAllWomen campaign on Twitter began shortly thereafter, its name a counter to further defensive "not all men are like that"–style reactions already playing out on social media. The hashtag began to trend dramatically by the standards of the day: it was tweeted over a million times in the first four days following its coinage. Many of the tweets were from women testifying to their experiences of male aggression, hostility, violence, and sexual harassment. Others documented offenses that were less serious on the face of it, but that were held to be connected—for example, disparaging and domineering behavior of subtler varieties, including mansplaining. For although Rodger's actions were clearly at the most violent end of the spectrum, something about his rhetoric struck a nerve with many women. Specifically, it sounded a bit too familiar.

Numerous right-wing and mainstream commentators immediately resisted the feminist diagnosis of misogyny, and many

---

6. "Thwarted in His Plan, California Gunman Improvised," *CBS News*, May 25, 2014, http://www.cbsnews.com/news/thwarted-in-his-plan-california-gunman-improvised/.

dismissed the associated #YesAllWomen campaign as well. The back-and-forth had a rhythmic yes–no ping-pong quality. "Misogyny kills," wrote Jessica Valenti (2014), in a piece in *The Guardian* (London) the day after the shootings. "Misogyny didn't turn Elliot Rodger into a killer," countered Chris Ferguson (2014), a professor of psychology, in *Time* a day later. Rodger's misogyny was instead a product of mental illness, social isolation, sexual frustration, and frustration simpliciter "rather than anything 'taught' to him by society. Had he not been so focused on his own sexual inadequacies, his focus might simply have moved to mall-goers rather than sorority sisters."[7] Laurie Penny (2014) demurred that same day in the *New Statesman*, "For some time now, misogynist extremism has been excused, as all acts of terrorism committed by white men are excused, as an aberration, as the work of random loons, not real men at all. Why are we denying the existence of a pattern?"

Steven Pinker appeared to be addressing Penny's question—in a manner of speaking, anyway—in an offhand remark he tweeted shortly afterward. "The idea that the UCSB murders are part of a pattern of hatred against women is statistically obtuse," it read. The tweet linked to an article in the *National Review*, written by Heather Mac Donald. Pinker's tweet was rather cryptic; notice all the words he managed *not* to use in it. He didn't use the words "feminist," "irrational," "hysterical," or "stupid." Strikingly, he didn't even use the word "misogyny." Instead, he just linked to Mac Donald's article, which said everything he didn't—and, one might have hoped, more.

Mac Donald's article, curiously entitled "The UCSB Solipsists," was neatly summarized by its tagline: "A sociopath runs amok—and kills more men than women—and feminists ride their hobbyhorse." Mac Donald (2014) wrote off Rodger's actions as "clearly the actions of a madman . . . whose every word and gesture bespoke

---

7. Presumably, according to this line of reasoning, Rodger might have gone knocking at the door of a fraternity house instead, had he been gay. And what if Rodger had been a woman? Could *his* gender have made any difference here? It's not clear whether there is room for this, on Ferguson's analysis.

monomaniacal, self-pitying delusion, amplified in the hermetic echo chamber of his own deranged narcissism." Moreover, "there is no pattern of gender-based rampages in this country; there *is* an emerging pattern of rampages by the untreated mentally ill. But," Mac Donald continued (and we should pay attention to the "but" here), "the fundamental premise of the feminist analysis of Rodger's massacre—that the U.S. is 'misogynist'—is patently absurd." Indeed, "to the contrary,"

> ours is a culture obsessed with promoting and celebrating female success. There is not a science faculty or lab in the country that is not under relentless pressure from university administrators and the federal government to hire female professors and researchers, regardless of the lack of competitive candidates and the cost to meritocratic standards. Wealthy foundations and individual philanthropists churn out one girls' self-esteem and academic success initiative after another; boys are a distant runner-up for philanthropic ministrations, even though it is boys, not girls, who are falling further and further behind academically and socially. . . . Girls hear a constant message that "strong women can do it all," including raise children on their own. Any female even remotely in the public realm who is not deeply conscious that she has been the "beneficiary" of the pressure to stock conference panels, media slots, and op-ed pages with females is fooling herself. Corporate boards and management seek women with hungry desperation. And even were this preferential treatment to end tomorrow, females, especially the privileged, highly educated ones who make up the feminist ranks, would still face a world of unprecedented, boundless opportunity. (2014)

Was Mac Donald right? What about the women complaining of male aggression (sexual and otherwise) serving to hold them back? "These females are apparently living in a different world than mine"—along with all the feminists she deemed "solipsists," presumably.

In rejecting the feminist analyses of the Isla Vista shootings, Mac Donald was in some plentiful and mixed company. Here are some of the many reasons commentators gave for denying that misogyny had an important explanatory role to play in this particular incident:

- Rodger didn't *hate* women deep down; he desired women *too much*, as opposed to too little (by being disgusted and repelled by them, or similar). He put "pussy on a pedestal," hence making him "the first feminist mass murderer," according to one well-known men's rights activist (Valizadeh 2014).[8]
- Rodger didn't hate *women* deep down; he wasn't even *interested* in women, at some level of analysis. He ultimately hated the men who were more successful than he in wooing them. Women weren't really *real* to him, as one cultural studies scholar argued.[9]
- Women were *too* real to Rodger; he didn't view them as objects—sexually or otherwise. He attributed to women too

8. Rodger was also active on men's rights forums on the Internet, for example, "Pick-Up Artist Hate" sites, although these communities are very different from Rooj Valizadeh's own blog, *Return of Kings*, http://www.returnofkings.com, where he espoused the above ideas. The former communities are primarily frequented by those who are resentfully opposed to the "pick-up artistry" (i.e., the "game" practiced by male "players" who use highly manipulative techniques for "picking up" women) championed by the latter.

9. Dexter Thomas Jr. wrote,

> Recently, we've been hearing a lot about Elliot Rodger's supposed misogyny. Some say the killings were a hate crime. Other people prefer to steer the conversation away from the topic of women. This is fair, because really, Elliot wasn't talking about women at all. He was talking about men. . . [W]omen were generally irrelevant to Elliot. With the exception of those in his immediate family, Elliot writes about women as flat, faceless characters. They rarely have names, and never have personalities. Actually, Elliot spends about as much time describing women as he does his new BMW 3 Series. (2014)

Note that Thomas eventually does seem to acknowledge the misogyny evident in Rodger's writings. On the other hand, he never withdraws his opening contention that women shouldn't have been the main subject of discussion in the wake of the shootings, since it wasn't really *about* them, at a certain level. I return to this thought in chapter 2.

much agency, subjectivity, and autonomous sexuality to count as a misogynist. Nor did he feel sufficiently *entitled* to sexual access to women to qualify. When he was unsuccessful in attracting them, he didn't just take what he wanted.[10]

- Rodger didn't hate women *deep down*, that is, at the level of ultimate psychological explanation. He only hated women because he was narcissistic, delusional, and mentally unstable— or a "madman," as Mac Donald described him (2014).

- Rodger didn't hate women *specifically*, or at least not *exclusively*. He was also brimming with racial hatred toward black and Asian men (notwithstanding his own Chinese ancestry, on his mother's side), as his "manifesto" (really more of a memoir) made apparent. Alternatively, he hated *everyone*, thus making him a misanthrope.[11]

- Rodger didn't hate *all* women, or even women generally. His vitriol was exclusively directed at "hot" women, that is, the young women he found sexually attractive, but whom he

---

10. In an article criticizing the feminist diagnosis of misogyny as simplistic, Meghan Daum (2014) wrote, "Not only was Rodger not a rapist, his desperation to be loved by women suggests that he didn't even objectify them as much as idealize them to an intolerably painful degree." Moreover, "his problem wasn't rejection as much as it was separation . . . [he] belonged to no group. For all his privilege, he was the opposite of entitled. He was someone with nothing left to lose." As I go on to argue, Rodger evinced an *aggrieved* form of entitlement, to use a notion of Michael Kimmel's (2013).

11. Cathy Young argued in *Reason*:

> "Misogyny" is a very incomplete explanation of Rodger's mind-set, perhaps best described as malignant narcissism with a psychopathic dimension. His "manifesto" makes it clear that his hatred of women . . . was only a subset of a general hatred of humanity, and was matched by hatred of men who had better romantic and sexual success . . . . Some have argued that hating other men because they get to have sex with women and you don't is still a form of misogyny; but that seems like a good example of stretching the concept into meaninglessness—or turning it into unfalsifiable quasi-religious dogma. (2014)

An alternative that Young does not consider is that these two vices are analytically distinct but often go together.

perceived as ignoring and therefore thwarting him. He loved his mother, however, and remained emotionally dependent on her up until the incident.[12]

- Rodger's ratio was off; he killed more men than women, including himself, in the end. So how could he possibly count as a misogynist? (Mac Donald 2014)

It would be possible to respond to the above claims point by point—possible, but not that illuminating at this juncture. For those of us inclined to think that something has gone wrong in the dialectic, we might hope for a more comprehensive diagnosis of why there was so much (more or less implausible) denialism. We might also hope for a way of *reconceptualizing* misogyny that would forestall most of these (in my view) mistakes simultaneously. How might we go about this? What are the guidelines, or ground rules?

WHAT KIND OF QUESTION IS "WHAT IS MISOGYNY?"

When a term like "misogyny" is being contested, how can we settle questions about its meaning, use, and reference? Social philosopher

---

12. For an economical overview of some of the most common arguments leveled against the feminist line on Isla Vista on social media, see the following excerpt from the comments on a *Newsweek* article by Zach Schonfeld, who argued that this was indeed misogyny:

PT: Wrong, he hated pretty women for ignoring him, but he ignored all women who were average or below, he didn't hate all women, he didn't hate his mom, his female teachers, etc. He also hated his Chinese roommates, but did he hate all Asians? Be precise in your anger against him.

SA: He hated everyone.

GB: Four of the six killed were male.

AJ: If he hated women so much—why he knifed and shot mostly men?

"Misogyny and Mass Murder, Paired Yet Again," *Newsweek.com* Facebook page, May 28, 2014, https://www.facebook.com/Newsweek/posts/10152443727756101 (the names have been redacted and replaced with initials).

Sally Haslanger (2012) draws a helpful distinction between three different approaches to "what is X?"–style questions generally:

(1) "Conceptual" projects involve investigating our (or "our," or perhaps *their*) ordinary *concept* of X, often using traditional a priori methods—for example, reflective equilibrium and conceptual analysis.

(2) "Descriptive" projects involve investigating the *extension* of the term, that is, what in the world the term "X" gets used to refer or apply to. And we will ask: what, if anything, do the paradigm cases of this property, or the relatively uncontroversial cases, have distinctively in common? What are the most natural and important properties in the vicinity, if any? So we will effectively be asking what people seem to be *getting* at, when they use the term in question. For this reason among others, this kind of project will have to involve empirical investigation, i.e., be a posteriori.

(3) "Analytical" or "ameliorative" projects involve trying to formulate a concept that best suits the *point* of having such a term.[13] We will ask, what is the purpose of talking about X at all? Are these purposes legitimate or valid? If there is more than one such purpose, which is the most important? Should we prise one existing term apart, or lump several distinct terms together, in view of this? How can we work toward an overall conceptual scheme that best supports liberatory political goals, and other worthwhile projects? (2012, 222–225)

Ameliorative (or "analytical") projects hence require actively making decisions about what to mean with our words. Familiarly, if we want to change the world, we may need to conceptualize it differently. This is particularly the case when it comes to social activities and practices: as social and self-conscious creatures, we are liable to conform

---

13. The two labels are meant to be synonymous, although I'll stick with the latter here, for clarity.

to norms enshrined by our basic concepts, categories, and schemas. And when it comes to other people, we are prone to enforcing norms and expectations of which we are uncritical. For all of these reasons and more, ameliorative projects can be important for social progress.

I find Haslanger's distinction between these three approaches useful—indeed, crucial—in this context. It's hard to see how else to get a methodological foothold here other than by consciously pursuing at least one of these different avenues. But it's also useful to recognize (as Haslanger herself goes on to acknowledge) that these projects are also potentially complementary, at least in certain instances (2012, 351–354, esp. 353n23, and 376). For example, one might initially pursue a conceptual line of inquiry not out of an allegiance to traditional a priori methods but instead in order to shed light on a term's natural purposes—that is, the uses to which it might best be put, or its job description, metaphorically. These purposes may subsequently be questioned, and the meaning of the term negotiated, on this basis.

The descriptive project may similarly reveal the need to make semantic choices. For one thing, different groups may be using the term in question differently, for example, to cover different kinds of cases, or to have a narrower or broader range of application. Given this, we may have to make a judgment about which linguistic and social communities to treat as authoritative. This will plausibly often involve some consideration of our values—including political values, which there at least seems no obvious basis for excluding at the outset.

One can hence see how the first two projects might naturally segue into the third, at least if one pursues them in a certain spirit. In that vein, I will first pursue conceptual and later descriptive lines of inquiry, with a view to eventually offering an ameliorative proposal about how we *ought* to understand misogyny.

As the foregoing list of counterpoints to the feminist diagnosis of misogyny in the Isla Vista case makes apparent, some people ostensibly accept the naïve conception of misogyny. Recall that, on this view, misogyny is primarily a property of individual misogynists, who are prone to hate women qua women—that is, because they are women—either universally or at least very generally. Moreover, agents may be required to harbor this hatred in their hearts as a matter of deep or ultimate psychological explanation, in order to count as bona fide misogynists.

But the naïve conception of misogyny has serious limitations. Some of these turn on epistemological concerns. For what lies behind an individual agent's attitudes, as a matter of deep or ultimate psychological explanation, is frequently inscrutable. So the naïve conception would threaten to make misogyny very difficult to diagnose, short of being the agent's therapist (and sometimes not even that would be sufficient). This would threaten to make misogyny epistemically inaccessible to women, in particular. That is, it would threaten to deprive women of the wherewithal to acquire knowledge and justified beliefs about the manifestations of misogyny that they may encounter, and to go on to make warranted assertions on that basis. So in effect, this notion of misogyny would be *silencing* for its victims.

Given that the notion of misogyny plausibly has a certain conceptual role to play of picking out the most hostile and noxious facets of gender-based oppression, this would threaten to deprive women of a suitable name for a potentially potent problem facing them. This is all the more so in view of the apparent paucity of relevant alternatives. What other English words express similar, and similarly morally weighty, concepts that are particular to gender? As far as I can tell, there are none. The term "sexism" may initially spring to mind; but to my ear, it lacks "misogyny's" hostile flavor. (I consider the sexism/misogyny contrast at length in chapter 3.) So we allow the word "misogyny" to get away from us at our peril.[14]

---

14. Compare Miranda Fricker's (2007) notion of a *hermeneutical injustice*, when people lack the conceptual resources to understand and articulate their social experiences (chap. 7). Here, the issue is not so much a deficiency, as an active attempt to *deprive* women of a term they have been using quite successfully, as we'll see shortly. (And recalling my introduction.)

Making charges of misogyny very difficult to prosecute would have another important, albeit less obvious, cost. It would make it very difficult to do justice to those accused of being misogynists who are genuinely innocent. If even an Elliot Rodger is off the hook, then a "not guilty" verdict (so to speak) would cease to be very meaningful. The defense would almost always be successful, since the relevant offense is so inscrutable—and peculiar.

The problems with the naïve conception of misogyny do not end there, however; they extend well beyond these epistemological considerations. This conception also fails to encompass more than a psychologically and hence metaphysically obscure phenomenon.

Why so? One might have thought that misogyny would at least have the potential to be rife in a typical patriarchal setting. But it is hard to see how or why this would be so now, that is, if the naïve conception is adopted. To see this, it will help to say something about the nature of patriarchal social orders, relations, and roles as I conceive them. (Hopefully needless to say, this is not a full discussion of their complex sociology, but rather a canvassing of some useful—and not very controversial—basics.) I will then be in a position to argue that the naïve conception of misogyny would effectively define misogyny out of prevalence within a patriarchal order, which I take to be the setting in which it should be (most) naturally occurring.

I take it that a social milieu counts as patriarchal insofar as certain kinds of institutions or social structures both proliferate and enjoy widespread support within it—from, for example, the state, as well as broader cultural sources, such as material resources, communal values, cultural narratives, media and artistic depictions, and so on. These patriarchal institutions will vary widely in their material and structural, as well as their social, features. But they will be such that all or most women are positioned as subordinate in relation to some man or men therein, the latter of whom are thereby (by the same token) dominant over the former, on the basis of their genders (among other relevant intersecting factors).

Three somewhat subtler points are worth noting before proceeding. First, I do not take subordination to be a success term in this context. As I intend the notion of subordination to be understood, it can be a matter of social pressures that *tend* to relegate women to this position but may not "succeed" in so doing, having been defeated or even canceled on occasion (as well as counteracted, of course, by opposing social pressures, in virtue of other systems of class-based oppression that intersect with gender, among other things). Second, some patriarchal structures are not only bastions of male privilege but will be exclusively male or heavily male dominated. However, I take it that these structures will generally require the social support of other patriarchal structures in which women *are* positioned as subordinate, given the characteristic forms of service work women are tasked with (of which more in a moment). Third, these relations of domination and subordination are often *local* to a particular patriarchal structure and the individuals therein. Given, again, the intersection of power relations—along the lines of race, ethnicity, class, sexuality, and disability—this is important to recognize. For a man may be the master of his domain but subordinated, exploited, or marginalized in other contexts. A man hence need not, and typically will not, be positioned as dominant over any and every woman, or even women generally, to count as a fully functioning patriarch. He need only be dominant over *some* woman or women, often in the context of familial or intimate relationships. Patriarchal ideology—which governs these social relations, structures, and the substantive roles I now turn to—may also require all or most men to be patriarchs in this sense, i.e., dominant over some woman or women, in order to conform to its overall normative vision.

But the hierarchical nature of gendered social relations within a patriarchal culture can be in a kind of tension with the substantive content of women's subordination therein. Take some feminine-coded forms of care work in particular. When women are tasked not only with performing certain forms of emotional, social, domestic, sexual, and reproductive labor but are *also* supposed to do so in a loving and caring manner or enthusiastic spirit, patriarchal norms and expectations have to operate on the down-low. Their coercive quality is better left implicit. Patriarchal ideology enlists a long list of mechanisms in service of this goal—including women's internalization of the relevant social norms, narratives about women's distinctive proclivities and preferences, and valorizing depictions of the relevant forms of care work as personally rewarding, socially necessary, morally valuable, "cool," "natural," or healthy (as long as women perform them). Women's adherence to the relevant social roles—as, for example, loving wives, devoted moms, "cool" girlfriends, loyal secretaries, or good waitresses, to name just a few of the most obvious examples—is supposed to look as natural or freely chosen as possible. The same goes for unofficial feminine-coded roles, for example, the work women often do as emotional under-laborers within the family or in the workplace, as well as in public settings. On the whole, however, this seamless appearance is almost inevitably deceptive, since more or less subtly hostile, threatening, and punitive norm-enforcement mechanisms will be standing at the ready, or operating in the background, should these "soft" forms of social power prove insufficient for upholding them. These mechanisms will range widely in the consequences they visit on women, from life-threatening violence to subtle social signals of disapproval (e.g., when people are unconsciously slightly "taken aback" when women are as interpersonally direct or unapologetic as their male counterparts). These coercive enforcement mechanisms vis-à-vis patriarchal norms and expectations, and the social roles they govern, are the functional essence of misogyny. Or so I will be arguing from the next section onward.

But first, to see why misogyny would be rare within a patriarchal setting if the naïve conception of misogyny and misogynists is accepted, consider: Why would any given man in a typical patriarchal setting have a problem with women universally, or even very generally, regardless of their relations? On the contrary, we would expect even the last enlightened man to be well-pleased with some women, that is, those who amicably serve his interests. It is not just that being hostile toward these women would be doubly problematic, in being both interpersonally churlish and morally objectionable. It is that it would be highly *peculiar*, as a matter of basic moral psychology. To put the problem bluntly: when it comes to the women who are not only dutifully but lovingly catering to his desires, what's to hate, exactly?

Granted, in a typical patriarchal setting, some men might be hostile toward most or even all of the women whom they *in fact* come into contact with, insofar as these women happen to wind up disappointing them. But that does not make for a true universally quantified claim, or even a true, somewhat less stringent generalization. These quantifiers are supposed to range over *any* or *most* of the women the agent might encounter (respectively), at least in a psychologically and socially realistic scenario. And this remains unlikely. An analogy: someone who has been disappointed by all or most of the restaurants he has been to in his life does not thereby hate restaurants universally or even very generally. Maybe he has just been unlucky, or limited, or thwarted in his choices. Were there a restaurant designed specially to please him, that is, to cater to his particular interests and appetites, his hating that restaurant too would be at least somewhat surprising.

Consider an Elliot Rodger, then. It might have been the case, and it is certainly intelligible, that he would *not* have been hostile toward women who gave him the attention and the affection he was craving. Indeed, it would be quite natural for a man in this general social position to *valorize* such women or to "put them on a pedestal." Such a man would hence fail to satisfy the relevant universally quantified claim or even the somewhat less stringent generalization. For how many women he could be expected to be hostile toward would tend to vary widely with contingent social factors. Given the mere possibility of his being satisfied with his lot and hostile toward relatively few women in consequence, he would not qualify as a misogynist by the lights of the naïve conception. But how many men (let alone women) *would* then? One suspects that this property will be instantiated very rarely, if the only agents who would qualify would have to keep (relentlessly, perversely) biting the hands that soothe and serve them. The naïve conception of misogyny is hence subject to a classic "no true Scotsman" problem (or, rather, objection). The defense "no *true* misogynist . . . " will almost always be available.

All told, this makes me think that the naïve conception of misogyny is hopelessly inadequate. It is a waste of the only word in English that, as we'll soon see, is increasingly being used to refer to a problem that women need a name for. And the fact that the term was originally coined for this very purpose—by seventeenth-century English feminists pushing back against the moral "defamation" of women on the part of Renaissance bro Joseph Swetnam—only adds to the irony that the word has been unwittingly appropriated by antifeminists and leached of its politics.[15] By the lights of the naïve conception, misogyny essentially becomes too psychologistic a notion, on the model of a phobia or a deep-seated aversion. It becomes a matter of psychological ill health, or perhaps irrationality, rather than a systematic facet of social power relations and a predictable manifestation of the ideology that governs them: patriarchy.

WHAT MISOGYNY MIGHT BE

We can make a fresh start here by asking what we might naturally *expect* misogyny to be, in light of the foregoing. That is, what would be a natural basis for hostility and aggression directed toward women at least partly, although not necessarily purely, because of their gender, and which makes sense of misogyny as a facet or manifestation of patriarchal ideology? In view of some women's social roles in a patriarchal culture as men's attentive, loving subordinates, this suggests one obvious possibility to consider. A woman's perceived resistance to or violation of the norms and expectations that govern these social roles would naturally tend to provoke just these kinds of reactions. What could be a more natural basis for hostility and aggression than defection from the role of an attentive, loving subordinate? This could be expected to leave some of the characteristic beneficiaries of

15. The term "misogyny" is probably best viewed as a neologism (or, at a stretch, it was reintroduced to English from a few textual fragments in ancient Greek) by anonymous feminists in response to a popular antiwoman pamphlet penned by Swetnam; see the book's opening epigraphs as well as the final chapter's.

gender (viz., men) feeling both usurped and neglected. And, emotionally speaking, this combination could be disastrous.

It may be helpful to consider a schematic illustration. Imagine a person in a restaurant who expects not only to be treated deferentially—the customer always being right—but also to be served the food he ordered attentively, and with a smile. He expects to be made to feel cared for and special, as well as to have his meal brought to him (a somewhat vulnerable position, as well as a powerful one, for him to be in). Imagine now that this customer comes to be disappointed—his server is not serving *him*, though she is waiting on other tables. Or perhaps she appears to be lounging around lazily or just doing her own thing, inexplicably ignoring him. Worse, she might appear to be expecting service *from* him, in a baffling role reversal. Either way, she is not behaving in the manner to which he is accustomed in such settings. It is easy to imagine this person becoming confused, then resentful. It is easy to imagine him banging his spoon on the table. It is easy to imagine him exploding in frustration.

Obviously, this is just one schematic illustration. But I think it does make a promising basis for elaboration and expansion. It is the first we have seen of something readily intelligible when it comes to attitudes in the vicinity of hatred and hostility that could plausibly be triggered in part by a woman's gender—together, in this case, with her perceived violation of patriarchal norms and expectations. And, if it is admitted as a valid illustration, it also tells us something about what misogyny need *not* be. For one thing, it need not target women across the board; it may instead target women selectively—for example, those who are perceived as insubordinate, negligent, or out of order. For another thing, the model puts paid to the idea (bizarre but, as we've seen, not without its adherents) that misogyny and sexual desire are somehow incompatible. Rodger's sexual desire for the women of Alpha Phi—and his desire that they desire him in turn—played a crucial role in spawning his resentment. It meant that he felt powerless with respect to them. From his point of view, they had a "hold over" him. And he deeply resented the impending humiliation—just as the vulnerability of a diner, in his hunger, is likely to feed into his rage at a server who has gone AWOL.

The model also yields some preliminary predictions regarding some of misogyny's typical targets and victims. The former will include those perceived as *unbecoming* women—traitors to the cause of gender—bad women, and "wayward" ones.[16] And the victims of misogyny hence tend to include women entering positions of power and authority over men, and women eschewing or opting out of male-oriented service roles. Among others, its natural targets will be (surprise) feminists.

Consider in this vein the experience of feminist writer Lindy West, who was harassed by an Internet troll who subsequently repented.[17] Here is an excerpt from West's interview with the man a few years later, in which he explains his thinking at the time with unusual candor and insight:

MAN: When you talked about being proud of who you are and where you are and where you're going, that kind of stoked that anger that I had.

LINDY WEST: OK, so you found my writing. You found my writing, and you did not like it.

MAN: Certain aspects of it. You used a lot of all caps. You're just a very—you almost have no fear when you write. You know, it's like you stand on the desk and you say, "I'm Lindy West, and this is what I believe in. Fuck you if you don't agree with me." And even though you don't say those words exactly, I'm like, "Who is this bitch who thinks she knows everything?"

LINDY WEST: I asked him if he felt that way because I'm a woman.

16. The idea of "unbecoming" a woman by resisting patriarchal oppression can be interpreted semi-literally on some accounts of what it *is* to be a woman, including Haslanger's (2012, chap. 7). According to her analytical or ameliorative account of gender, to be a woman *just is* to be socially subordinate to men, on the basis of one's perceived or actual biological sex. However, as Haslanger herself has subsequently acknowledged, her account at least requires amendments to do justice to trans women's experiences: see Kathryn Jenkins (2016) for discussion and Talia Mae Bettcher (2013) for an alternative approach here.

17. Among other things, this man impersonated Lindy West's recently deceased father on Twitter. His satirical biographical description there read: "Embarrassed father of an idiot—other two kids are fine, though"—the "idiot" being Lindy. "If You Don't Have Anything Nice to Say, Say It in All Caps," *This American Life*, episode 545,

MAN: Oh, definitely. Definitely. Women are being more forthright in their writing. There isn't a sense of timidity to when they speak or when they write. They're saying it loud. And I think that—and I think, for me, as well, it's threatening at first.

LINDY WEST: Right. You must know that I—that's why I do that, because people don't expect to hear from women like that. And I want other women to see me do that and I want women's voices to get louder.

MAN: I understand. I understand. Here's the thing. I work with women all day, and I don't have an issue with anyone. I could've told you back then if someone had said to me, "Oh, you're a misogynist. You hate women." And I could say, "Nuh-uh, I love my mom. I love my sisters. I've loved my—the girlfriends that I've had in my life." But you can't claim to be OK with women and then go online and insult them—seek them out to harm them emotionally.

I think this is right. Misogynists can love their mothers—not to mention their sisters, daughters, wives, girlfriends, and secretaries. They need not hate women universally, or even very generally. They tend to hate women who are outspoken, among other things.

No doubt the idea that I've just mooted will be resisted by some people. Misogyny must involve hating women as such, and for no further reason. So misogyny cannot just target *some* women, it might be insisted. But I see little motivation for this blanket insistence. And I suspect it draws strength from the unwarranted assumption that misogyny must resemble the most commonly—though often historically inaccurately—envisaged form of anti-Semitism, which is supposed to be leveled at the entire Jewish people in our entirety.[18] But

original air date January 23, 2015, https://www.thisamericanlife.org/radio-archives/episode/545/transcript.

18. Cf. Hannah Arendt's remarks about Adolf Eichmann in her famous account, in *Eichmann in Jerusalem*: "The Jews in his family were among his 'private reasons' for not hating Jews . . . 'I myself had no hatred against Jews, for my whole education through my mother and my father had been strictly Christian, and my mother,

why should this one type of oppression be treated as the paradigm? Why should we accept the "Paradigm Paradigm," as we might call it, whatsoever? Gender-based oppression may be partly sui generis. Or, it may be a useful paradigm for other forms of oppression—a possibility chapter 5 briefly expands on.

Whatever the case, it would make little sense in view of the aims of patriarchal ideology to try to rid the world of women—or even, in any straightforward sense, to relegate women to the ghetto. Women are thoroughly integrated into prototypical patriarchal households, where they are tasked with a wide range of critical domestic, social, emotional, as well as (hetero)sexual, services. Such women are too useful to the dominant for all women to be dispensable—or even for spatial segregation to be capable of serving dominant needs and interests.

But although misogyny's targets hence tend not to be women across the board, it doesn't mean that the #YesAllWomen campaign was wrong to hold that virtually every woman is potentially vulnerable to misogynist threats and punishment. For it may be that, as well as *perceived* and *actual* violations of patriarchal norms and

---

because of her Jewish relatives, had different opinions from those current in S.S. circles.' He went to considerable lengths to prove that he had never harbored any ill feelings against his victims." Moreover,

> had Eichmann been a bit less prim or the police examination less discreet (it did not extend to cross-examination, presumably so that the examiner would be assured of his coöperation), his "lack of prejudice" might have shown itself in another aspect as well. It seems that in Vienna, where he was extraordinarily successful in forcing Jews to leave the country, he had a Jewish mistress, an "old flame" from Linz. *Rassenschande*—a word that literally means "race-defilement" but that in the Nazi vocabulary simply meant sexual intercourse with Jews—was probably the greatest crime a member of the S.S. could commit; though during the war the raping of Jewish girls became a favorite pastime at the front, it was by no means common for a higher S.S. officer to have an affair with a Jewish woman. (Arendt 1963, 30)

Consider too the fact that the Jews were particularly successful in and assimilated into German society prior to 1933, compared with their position in many other European nations of greater precarity and marginalization. Historians such as Amos Elon and Götz Aly have recently (independently) argued that the sense of Jews therefore not "knowing their place" in Germany played an important role in provoking anti-Semitic backlash; see chapter 5, note 40.

expectations, there may be purely *symbolic* or *representative* ones, where one woman is made to pay for the supposed sins of others.

More broadly, I believe that misogyny's grasp may also exceed its reach because of its tendency to try to restore patriarchal order by treating some women as stand-ins or representatives for others, as well as engaging in "punching down" behavior—that is, taking other frustrations out on her, since she's available and may lack recourse (in the context of intimate partner violence, say).

Most importantly, for my ensuing purposes, small violations may be blown out of all proportion, and taken to indicate something damning about a woman's *character*. She may be represented as breaking promises, telling lies, or reneging on *her* side of the bargain—and hence as deeply untrustworthy, duplicitous, irresponsible, and so on. If we look hard enough, we can often find some (more or less) nominal basis for such complaints in a woman's behavior. But the broken promises and undone deals were illicitly made on her behalf by the patriarchy.

This sheds light on one of the objections to the feminist diagnosis of the Isla Vista shootings that was made in the aftermath—namely, Elliot Rodger's targets and victims (respectively) didn't *really* violate patriarchal norms and expectations with regard to him. They were merely representative of the kind of women he felt neglected and humiliated by. The women he targeted at the Alpha Phi sorority house at UCSB never in fact had an opportunity to pay him any attention—because, despite having stalked them, he never introduced himself.

Does this mean, though, that Rodger was delusional in a sense that speaks against the feminist diagnosis in his case? No. As I'll show in the next chapter, misogyny frequently involves delusions of this nature—even among agents whose undoubted susceptibility to moral criticism hinges on their knowing exactly what they're doing.

For the sake of illustration, enter Rush Limbaugh.

Chapter 2

Ameliorating Misogyny

Philosophers have hitherto only interpreted the world in various ways; the point is to change it.

Karl Marx, *Theses on Feuerbach*

RUSH LIMBAUGH ON SANDRA FLUKE

Right-wing pundit Rush Limbaugh is not exactly known for his feminist-friendly attitudes. But in February 2012, charges of misogyny nevertheless landed him in hot water, when he made the following remarks about Sandra Fluke on his daily radio show:

> What does it say about the college co-ed Susan Fluke [*sic*], who goes before a congressional committee and essentially says that she must be paid to have sex, what does that make her? It makes her a slut, right? It makes her a prostitute.[1]

Fluke—who was actually a law student at Georgetown at the time— had argued before House Democrats that birth control ought to be covered by health insurance at religious institutions. Limbaugh naturally concluded that Fluke was asking to be *paid* by him and the American taxpayer for all the sex she must be having, if she couldn't

---

1. This excerpt, and the one immediately below it in the main text are both taken from the archived transcript of Limbaugh's show on February 29, 2012, available on the *Rush Limbaugh Show* website. "X—Butt Sisters Are Safe from Newt and Rick," *Rush Limbaugh Show*, February 29, 2012, https://www.rushlimbaugh.com/daily/2012/02/29/x_butt_sisters_are_safe_from_newt_and_rick/.

afford to foot the bill herself for a sufficient supply of contraceptives. Hence his calling Fluke a "slut" and a "prostitute"—"insulting word choices," as he later admitted, adding they were intended to be "humorous."[2] But more than anything, Limbaugh appears to have struggled at the time to settle on his metaphor:

> What does that make us? We're the pimps. (*Interruption*). The johns? We would be the johns? No! We're not the johns. (*Interruption*). Yeah, that's right. Pimp's not the right word. Okay so she's not a slut. She's "round heeled." I take it back.

Limbaugh did not take it back for very long, however. He called Fluke a "slut" again on his show just one day later. Ultimately, he recanted, saying by way of apology: "I chose the wrong words in my analogy of the situation. I did not mean a personal attack on Ms. Fluke."[3]

This brings us to an important puzzle about misogyny's aetiology and targets. How, and why, is it often so delusional? How do people manage to harbor or inspire others to form such personal-seeming grudges against women who remain personally unknown to them, on such manifestly thin bases? And, clearly, Limbaugh was counting on his diatribe being not only intelligible but also appealing to his listeners.

Limbaugh's remarks about Fluke expose this puzzle starkly.[4] But they also help us to solve it. A revealing aspect of the images Limbaugh chose was the way that they allowed him to project himself and his listeners into them. He depicted a woman articulating a need, or

2. Rush Limbaugh, "A Statement from Rush," *Rush Limbaugh Show*, March 3, 2012, http://www.rushlimbaugh.com/daily/2012/03/03/a_statement_from_rush.

3. From the March 3 statement released by Limbaugh (see note 2, above).

4. Consider too the inappropriately personal tone often taken in remarks about female politicians (not only the negative ones but also those that are neutral, or even positive, in tenor). One symptom of this is the use of female politicians' first names, as in "Hillary" and "Julia," for Julia Gillard, the first female prime minister of Australia, whose political rise and fall I'll discuss in later chapters. For one more example, German chancellor Angela Merkel's nickname is "Mutti" ("mother").

claiming her due, as entitled and demanding. And he depicted Fluke as demanding something from *them*, qua taxpayers, specifically—nay, demanding to be *paid* by them, for indulging in sexual congress. This is a stretch, to put it mildly. But it enabled Limbaugh to depict Fluke as *owing* something to them. Consider Limbaugh's subsequent vacillation between the image of being serviced by Fluke, sexually (i.e., of being "the john") and the idea of Fluke being his underling (i.e., making him "the pimp"). At one point, Limbaugh proposed the following little arrangement. Fluke could have his money—if she posted the sex in an online video:

> We are getting screwed even though we don't meet her person-ally! Ms. Fluke, have you ever heard of not having sex? So, if we're gonna sit here, and if we're gonna have a part in this, then we want something in return, Ms. Fluke: And that would be the vid-eos of all this sex posted online so we can see what we are getting for our money.[5]

This passage is striking partly because, as with Elliot Rodger's con-fessional video, it involves a transition from the third-person to a second-personal mode of address—or, rather, accusation. But who is Limbaugh talking *to*? Even he seemed to recognize the oddity of feel-ing so "screwed over" by someone who remained a perfect stranger.

Part of the solution to this puzzle, I believe, involves recognizing that women's subordination casts them in terms that are *functional* and *relational* (Haslanger 2012, 57–63). Recall from the previous chapter that, by the lights of patriarchal ideology, a woman is often expected to play the role of a man's attentive, loving subordinate—to maintain a loving gaze toward the dominant, metaphorically. It hence plausibly goes deep in the nature of patriarchal gender rela-tions that women's conduct vis-à-vis men is taken unduly personally

---

5. Rush Limbaugh, "The Dumb Don't Know They're Dumb," *Rush Limbaugh Show*, March 1, 2012, https://www.rushlimbaugh.com/daily/2012/03/01/the_dumb_don_t_know_they_re_dumb.

(by them and on their behalf, moreover). So women's indifference becomes aversion; ignorance becomes ignoring; testimony becomes tattling; and asking becomes extortion.

The other element of the solution to this puzzle, I suggest, involves noticing the way in which women are often treated as interchangeable and representative of a certain *type* of woman. Because of this, women can be singled out and treated as representative targets, then standing in imaginatively for a large swathe of others.[6] Elliot Rodger declared his intentions in his so-called manifesto thus: "I will attack the very girls who represent everything I hate in the female gender: The hottest sorority of UCSB." And Limbaugh called Fluke "a representative liberal." But these representative women need not exemplify the qualities of the kind of women they are held to epitomize: for example, selfish, childish, domineering "Feminazis" who want to maximize the number of abortions that take place in human history. Sometimes, it is in fact crucial that they do not, since the class of women of this kind may be empty.

In each of these examples, attitudes in the family of hostility have played a prominent role. These have included resentment, spite, ill will, and various threatening and punitive tendencies. If these cases are any guide—as a descriptive approach to the subject in Haslanger's (2012) sense treats as presumptively the case—misogyny frequently involves what P. F. Strawson called the "interpersonal" reactive attitudes. As discussed in the preface, these are the attitudes that are more or less distinctive to our dealings with other mature, autonomous, compos mentis human beings, and are supposed to include "all the essentially *personal* antagonisms" (Strawson [1962] 2008, 11). They hence have the potential to be leveled second-personally. But

---

6. Compare Nussbaum (1995, 257) and Langton (2009, 226) on objectification and fungibility. More on each of their views will follow in chapter 3 here.

oftentimes, it seems to be the second-person *plural*. Recall Rodger's words: "I will punish you all for it." In many ways, this seems to be misogyny's characteristic sentiment. It is punitive, resentful, and personal, but not particular. And the psychological targets of such attitudes may little resemble the actual victims. They are often instead directed toward a crude composite image of a woman pasted over the face of a real one.

Some people have suggested to me that this might provide the basis for some optimism. The idea being that misogyny isn't *really* about the women who are its victims, at some level of analysis. (See, for example, Thomas 2014.) But why think that this would be the case in the first place? Anti-Semitism and other forms of racial and ethnic hatred are not generally held to be a matter of deep or ultimate psychological explanation, in contrast. Imagine someone arguing that Hitler wasn't really anti-Semitic, deep down; he was just insecure about his lack of artistic talent, as well as taking vast quantities of opiates and methamphetamines. Although this seems to have been the case, and might conceivably have played a causal role in ratcheting up the vitriol at key moments, the subsequent suggestion about Hitler's not being anti-Semitic wouldn't be worth dignifying, clearly. And yet the analogous suggestion about misogyny is common. The fact that the people who are liable to channel misogynist social forces have various anxieties and other psychological and social adjustment problems is hardly surprising. How is this supposed to mitigate the problem facing *women* though? When one's effigy is one's body, one burns right along with it.

This suggests a shift in focus may be salutary. Rather than conceptualizing misogyny from the point of view of the accused, at least implicitly, we might move to think of it instead from the point of view of its *targets* or *victims*. In other words, when it comes to misogyny, we can focus on the hostility women *face* in navigating the social world, rather than the hostility men (in the first instance) may or may not *feel* in their encounters with certain women—as a matter of deep psychological explanation, or indeed whatsoever. (More on this last possibility in a moment.)

Advantages of this approach would include that it

1. avoids psychologism, without denying the hostile "flavor" of misogyny, or the fact that it *may* involve hostile attitudes on the part of individual agents; but it need not. It would also help to unify the many ways misogyny can be instantiated (e.g., via domineering vs. disappointed misogynists, and via individual agents or purely structural mechanisms);

2. avoids individualism, by allowing that social practices, institutions, policies, etc., can manifest hostility toward women, as with, for example, a "hostile work environment" or a differentially "chilly" social climate; and

3. makes misogyny more epistemologically tractable in the ways that matter here, by enabling us to invoke a "reasonable woman" standard: or, more precisely, and better (since less ableist), we can ask whether a girl or woman who the environment is meant to accommodate might reasonably *interpret* some encounter, aspect, or practice therein as hostile.[7] This is as opposed to doing psychology to glean an agent's intentions, or having to take their word for it.

This shows how to forestall a natural objection to my developing account here, given the foregoing idea that misogyny in individuals characteristically involves negative interpersonal reactive attitudes. For, it's now natural to wonder how my account of misogyny could avoid the psychologism and subsequent epistemological problems that were part of my argument against the naïve conception. How would we know if someone who behaves in a resentful, spiteful fashion is *really* resentful, deep down, or rather ultimately anxious (say)?

---

7. I take as a model here the legal concept of sexual harassment developed by Catharine MacKinnon among others. And see Miranda Fricker (2007, chap. 7) for a discussion of the importance of this concept in gender-egalitarian workplace reform, as an example of a hermeneutical injustice that existed prior to its advent.

The answer is that what matters is *not* deep down, but right there on the surface, in view of the proposed shift in focus from misogyny's agents to its subjects. For while I do want to defend the importance of reactions like resentment and disapproval to the nature of misogyny, I am also construing these attitudes less *psychologistically* than is common, by placing the emphasis more on the "reactive" part and less on the "attitude." These are the responses women *face* in navigating their social environments, as subject to whatever constraints may emerge from how they may reasonably be interpreted (as spelled out more precisely directly above, in (3)). Hostility that is expressed but not consciously experienced as such can therefore count as real hostility, on this way of thinking about it. Agents do not have a monopoly on the social meaning of their actions. And their intentions will rarely settle, although they may bear on, this.

So, on the analysis of misogyny that follows, a misogynist social environment may but need not be the product of individual agents' bigotry. It may rather be the result of some people's inchoate discomfort and hostility when more or less *any* well-entrenched system of social norms is being dismantled. Women who resist or flout gendered norms and expectations may subsequently garner suspicion and consternation, which has less to do with their challenging gendered norms per se, and more to do with their challenging entrenched norms simpliciter. And for some people, feminism in particular has profoundly disrupted their sense of the social order. The hostility they display to women who disrupt or pose a threat to gendered social hierarchies, say, is compatible with their being egalitarians in the abstract. They may nevertheless perceive powerful women who do not wield their power in service of men's interests as abrasive and threatening. For that reason among others, a misogynist social environment may be partly the result of more or less well-intentioned people acting out of disavowed emotions, or exhibiting flashes of aggression that are not consciously experienced. And indeed, such aggression may be acted out partly as a *substitute* for feeling it: the expression "acting *out*" is suggestive in this context.

Misogyny may alternatively be the product of collective (or "mob") activity.[8] Such hostility helps to drum up more of the reactions it channels. But such activity is often diffuse and disorganized, and not sufficiently coordinated to count as the actions of a plausible group agent. Misogyny may also be the product of institutions and social practices that have an expressive value and *say* something to women who fail or refuse to toe the line in some way. Sometimes, the misogynistic elements of these institutions and social practices (including the law and public policies) will be largely vestigial at this point in time. And sometimes they will be pioneered or revived by the more powerful, who are playing on the insecurities and sense of disenfranchisement common among the less powerful in the wake of the achievements of progressive social movements. Whether or not these powerful people are merely exploitative and cynical (e.g., trying to gain votes or drive up the ratings), or actually subscribe to the poison they peddle, is irrelevant from the perspective of my ensuing analysis of misogyny. What matters is the contributions they make to a misogynist social environment—that is, the extent to which they tend to police and punish women, in accordance with patriarchal law and order. Elliot Rodger and Rush Limbaugh are, in this respect, overachievers—and hence count as misogynists on the analysis that follows.

AN AMELIORATIVE, INTERSECTIONAL PROPOSAL

Ameliorative projects are partly stipulative in nature. This does not (or at least ought not) make them arbitrary, however. As Haslanger

---

8. But it should be noted that not everyone who buys into such a misogynist "mob" mentality must be channeling misogynistic social forces *directly*. Some people will rather be picking up on, and emulating, the (moral) disgust reactions of others— i.e., *vicariously*, or second hand, so to speak. More on this mechanism for the takedown of women in public life will follow in chapter 8 here.

(2012) puts it, their characteristic animating thought is, "*This* is the phenomenon we need to be thinking about" (224). So, at this point, having pursued both conceptual and descriptive lines of inquiry in the spirit of seeing where they lead, I want to offer an ameliorative proposal about how we *ought* to understand misogyny, at least for many purposes.

I propose that, at the most general level of description, misogyny should be understood as the "law enforcement" branch of a patriarchal order, which has the overall function of *policing* and *enforcing* its governing ideology. We can make this more precise as follows:

Constitutively speaking, misogyny in a social environment comprises the hostile social forces that

(a) will tend to be faced by a (wider or narrower) class of girls and women because they are girls and women in that (more or less fully specified) social position; and

(b) serve to police and enforce a patriarchal order, instantiated in relation to other intersecting systems of domination and disadvantage that apply to the relevant class of girls and women (e.g., various forms of racism, xenophobia, classism, ageism, transphobia, homophobia, ableism, and so on).

And, as a *substantive matter of fact*, these misogynistic social forces will:

Often target girls and women (in the relevant class) for actual, perceived, or representative challenges to or violations of applicable patriarchal norms and expectations (again, operating in conjunction with applicable intersecting oppressive forces).

Where patriarchal norms and expectations may involve, for example,

(a) distinctively gendered *contents*, which reflect and help to regulate or restore patriarchal order; or

(b) particularly harsh *enforcement mechanisms* for girls and women (in the relevant class), as compared with boys and men (in this class, i.e., male counterparts);[9] or

(c) particularly intense and/or invasive forms of policing (for example, surveillance, scrutiny, and suspicion) for girls and women (in the relevant class), as compared with male counterparts.

So, as compared with the naïve conception, my account holds that

misogyny primarily targets women because they are women in a *man's world* (i.e., a historically patriarchal one, among other things), rather than because they are women in a *man's mind*, where that man is a misogynist.

Recall too, that on my analysis as I intend it to be understood, the relevant hostilities may be manifested by individual agents, collective (or "mob") activity, or purely structural mechanisms. Some further points to notice before we continue are as follows.

On this definition, misogynist forces can be distinctive for girls and women located in different positions in social space, or they can operate on girls and women in a way that is more general.

For example, there are forms of erasure and subsequent invisibility that are arguably distinctive to, and certainly endemic of, "misogynoir," Moira Bailey's term (2014) for the kind of misogyny faced by black women in America given their particular social location, and the operation of anti-black racism in conjunction with heteronormative and patriarchal forces. Or so I will have suggested by the end of chapter 6, drawing on work by Kristie Dotson and Marita Gilbert, among others.

Even so, *general* does not mean *uniform* in the way it is experienced, nor in its subsequent *impact* on girls and women. That doesn't follow, and would be false in many cases, in ways that would obscure

9. Here, I deliberately leave open the possibility that people who are non-binary may be subject to still worse in this connection than *either* girls/women or boys/men in the relevant comparison class.

important ways in which vulnerabilities can augment one another, or alternatively be mitigated by privilege (among other possibilities) (Crenshaw 1991; 2012).

For an example of this, consider the recent case of Rosetta Watson, a black disabled woman living in Maplewood, Missouri. She called the police four times over a short period, due to incidents of domestic violence—including "choking" or, as it is better termed, nonfatal manual strangulation (as discussed in the introduction) by her boyfriend. As someone who was renting an apartment, she was declared a "nuisance" after calling more than twice within a 180-day time frame. This is a common kind of local ordinance in many towns and cities throughout the United States. Watson hence lost the occupancy permit required to live in the city, and was essentially exiled for six months—all because she sought protection from a potentially lethal, and terrifying, form of violence.[10]

Eviction is a ubiquitous problem for black women, one that sociologist Matthew Desmond takes to be the undernoticed analogue of mass incarceration for black men, which constitutes a deep source of systemic injustice and disadvantage. "Poor Black men are locked up while poor Black women are locked out," Desmond argues (2016). This suggests misogynoir is tied to, and makes poor black women especially vulnerable to, housing insecurity, homelessness, legal trouble, and incarceration too, among other adverse outcomes.[11] Women in such positions may become yet more vulnerable to domestic violence and sexual assault due to the combination of these factors (being disproportionately vulnerable already). Misogynoir begets itself, and the cycle may continue.

10. Melissa Jeltsen, "A Missouri Town Exiled a Woman for Calling the Police on Her Abusive Ex," *Huffington Post*, April 11, 2017, http://www.huffingtonpost.com/entry/rosetta-watson-maplewood-missouri-abuse_us_58ebece5e4b0ca64d91864f0.

11. As Kimberlé W. Crenshaw (2012) shows, the rates of incarceration were elevated by a similar factor for black women as compared with white women, as for black men compared with white men, in recent memory (1437). Although the former disparity seems to have decreased significantly since then, the point remains that it has never attracted the attention the latter has, in ways that are plausibly symptomatic of black women's erasure from public discourse in general.

Having defined misogyny as a property of social environments first and foremost, we can now say that

> *derivatively*, an individual agent's attitudes or behavior counts as misogynistic within a social context insofar as it reflects, or perpetuates, misogyny therein.

We can give analogous definitions of misogyny as a property of practices, institutions, artworks, other artifacts, and so on.

But, when it comes to calling an *agent* a misogynist on the whole, there are reasons to be cautious about the risk of overplaying our hand and engaging in some of the very moralism that attending to misogyny teaches us to be wary of. And, of course, there are also relevant considerations of fairness. One generally does not want to attach a shaming label to someone in virtue of a near-universal trait of character, attitude, or behavioral disposition.

I hence suggest that the term "misogynist" is best treated as a *threshold* concept, and also a *comparative* one, functioning as a kind of "warning label," which should be sparingly applied to people whose attitudes and actions are *particularly* and *consistently* misogynistic across myriad social contexts. On this view

> individual agents count as misogynists if and only if their misogynistic attitudes and/or actions are significantly (a) more extreme, and (b) more consistent than most other people in the relevant comparison class (e.g., other people of the same gender, and perhaps race, class, age, etc., in similar social environments).

"Significantly" and "relevant" are, in a sense, weasel words, but deliberately so, since for my purposes in this context I don't have to take a stand on how to fill out the definition. So it's best to leave room for people to go their different ways here, based on different commitments in normative and moral theory.

Having laid out my ameliorative analysis of misogyny, I now pause to highlight some of its key features and, to my way of thinking, attractions or benefits. These include both further conceptual and substantive implications of the account and hence when misogyny is likely to arise: how it works, on whom, and by (or, sometimes better, *through*) which agents and social practices, institutions, artworks, artifacts, and so on. I'll also say something preliminary about the *epistemology* of misogyny: that is, how we can recognize misogyny and misogynists in the world, and what counts as defeasible evidence of its, or their, existence.

The Metaphysical Dependence of Misogyny on Patriarchy

The analysis I've proposed makes misogyny out to be an inherently *political* phenomenon. Specifically, it makes misogyny in a social environment metaphysically dependent on there being norms and expectations of a patriarchal nature. This does not mean that misogyny can only obtain within a fully functioning patriarchy. But it does mean that there must be some historical connection with one—with "connection" construed liberally enough to include *borrowing* from another culture, *incipient* norms and expectations, as well as direct inheritance.[12] Given these important caveats, I fully intend this consequence. Hostility toward women would simply be an individual quirk or something like a phobia absent a system of patriarchal oppression in the background.[13] I am not saying that such (as it were) "gynophobia" is never a genuine problem—due to, for example, the

12. It is worth noting a corollary of this: if *misandry* is understood on analogy with misogyny (as presumably it ought to be), then there will be no instances of genuine misandry absent the operation of *matriarchal* norms and expectations deriving from matriarchal ideology, such that men's violation of them tends to rankle people. I believe that this is entirely as it should be. How common such norms have been, historically, is a question beyond my pay grade as a philosopher; it is a question for the historian or anthropologist, as I noted in the introduction. But see Gerda Lerner (1986) for a classic text on the historical prevalence and hegemonic nature of patriarchy.

13. I opened in chapter 1 with the observation that, metaphorically speaking, misogyny is a "loaded" word. But note that, according to my analysis, misogyny is not a moralized notion in the strictest sense of the term. However, given the claim

sorts of pathological "mother issues" that people sometimes refer to in this connection, as we'll see in the next chapter.[14] But I don't think that this is a problem to which we ought to pay much attention in the current political climate, when women face so many problems of a more systematic nature.

The Varieties of Misogynist Hostility

According to my account, misogynist hostility can be anything that is suitable to serve a punitive, deterrent, or warning function, which (depending on your theory of punishment) may be anything aversive to human beings in general, or the women being targeted in particular. Misogynist hostility encompasses myriad "down girl" moves—so many as to make the list seem likely to be indefinitely extensible. But, to generalize: adults are insultingly likened to children, people to animals or even to objects. As well as infantilizing and belittling, there's ridiculing, humiliating, mocking, slurring, vilifying, demonizing, as well as sexualizing or, alternatively, *desexualizing*, silencing, shunning, shaming, blaming, patronizing, condescending, and other forms of treatment that are dismissive and disparaging in specific social contexts. Then there is violence and threatening behavior: including "punching down"—that is, deferred or displaced aggression. And since, on my account, one woman can often serve as a stand-in or representative for a whole host of others in the misogynist imagination, almost any woman will be vulnerable to some form of misogynist hostility from some source or other.

In what follows, I will be especially interested in the ways misogyny works via regular social-norm enforcement mechanisms,

that systems of patriarchal oppression are morally objectionable, and the standard view of such moral facts as being metaphysically necessitated by the descriptive facts they supervene upon, it is nevertheless true that claims regarding misogyny will have significant moral implications as a matter of metaphysical, if not conceptual, necessity.

14. I allude here to the remarks made by lexicographer Sue Butler, to be discussed in the following chapter. "Misogyny Definition to Change after Gillard's Speech,"

moralism, and other negative character-level generalizations, hierarchical social moves, and similar. On my view, misogyny need not and usually will not arise from specialized and, to my mind, fairly puzzling putative psychological attitudes, like the idea that women are seen as sexual objects, viewed as subhuman, or as having a hateful, detestable "essence." Rather, it's generally about the enforcement and re-establishment of patriarchal order and the protests when it gets challenged. Disgust flows from, and augments, these social processes. These will be the upshots of chapters 5 and 8, respectively.

In other words, these various "down girl" moves may not reflect how women are literally *viewed* much of the time, except perhaps as the result of wishful thinking and willful denial. They're dynamic, active, and forceful *maneuverings*. They put women in their place when they seem to have "ideas beyond their station." So I think of the misogyny of individual agents as less a matter of beliefs than desires—desires and other similar states of mind that ask the world be kept or brought in line with a patriarchal order, at least in the first instance.[15] I come back to this point in chapter 3, in connection with the distinction between misogyny and sexism.

The Epistemology of Misogyny

When it comes to the epistemology of misogyny, two different contrasts will be particularly relevant at the outset. (Although indirect evidence of these contrasts may then be sought by various methods.) The claim that a certain woman is subject to misogyny can be demonstrated by showing that her male counterpart in an otherwise comparable social position (so holding fixed, e.g., race, class, sexuality,

---

Sydney Morning Herald, October 17, 2012, http://www.smh.com.au/national/misogyny-definition-to-change-after-gillard-speech-20121016-27q22.html.

15. Whereas beliefs purport to *represent* the world and hold that it is a certain way already (or, in the case of predictions, hold that it *will* be so in the future). So beliefs are called "world-guided" or "world-directed" mental states; desires are "world-directing" mental states, as per the above (rough) characterization of their "direction of fit." See G. E. M. Anscombe (1957) for the locus classicus of this contrast.

cis/trans status, disability, age, and so on) wouldn't plausibly be subject to such hostility, in terms of its intensity, prevalence, quality, quantity, or duration. This finesses a common "folk" criterion for misogyny, I take it.

Note that such hostility need not be leveled at women *disproportionately* (i.e., as compared with a male counterpart), in order to count as symptoms or expressions of misogyny. It is enough that the treatment be *distinctive* along some gendered dimension. So we can allow that some men in a comparable position would be subject to just as *much*, if not more, by way of hostility. If the hostility directed toward a woman nonetheless has a distinctively gendered *basis* or *quality*, it may still count as being misogynistic, according to my analysis.

A diagnosis of misogyny can also be substantiated, on my view, by the fact that a similarly embodied person in a world that lacked norms and expectations of a patriarchal nature wouldn't plausibly be subject to such hostility either—for example, such that those who get pregnant (typically cis women, as well as some trans men and non-binary people) are routinely denied medically necessary and financially feasible accommodations by their employers and are instead laid off. I take this to be an important benefit of my analysis, since it hence allows us to handle cases involving pregnancy appropriately, for one thing. If cis men got pregnant, would they be subject to similar employment penalties? Or would they simply join the ranks of reproductive underlaborers? It is difficult to know, and it does not seem a fruitful question; one suspects it may lack a determinate answer. Such a socially (if not scientifically) distant possible world is not a good basis for comparison in cases involving pregnancy, lactation, menopause, and so on. Better to think about what *would* be the case if pregnant bodies navigated not a "man's world"—that is, the actual world, with its heteropatriarchal and transphobic structures—but rather a world that recognized everybody's claims to have equal moral purchase. And in this world, significantly more effort would be made to accommodate those tasked with bearing the next generation of human beings, I would argue.

(Latent) Misogyny as a Disposition

Another aspect of my account of misogyny worth flagging at this juncture is that it deliberately invokes *dispositions*, or tendencies. Because of this, a social environment need not actively manifest negative attitudes or actions toward *anyone* at the time to qualify as genuinely misogynistic. It is enough that certain counterfactuals hold with respect to it. And this, I believe, is exactly as it should be. Misogyny, on this view, can be latent and lie dormant.

In view of this point and the previous one, it's natural to wonder: will there be any way of knowing that a social environment is misogynistic, if the relevant social mechanisms have done their job too well? That is, if women are subject to very little by way of misogynist hostility or aggression at the moment, but only because they have been relegated to certain subordinate social roles so successfully, how could we determine this?

This brings me to a point that I think represents an important rider to this chapter in its entirety and will animate subsequent discussions.

Misogyny as Systemic, and as Itself Part of a (Much) Larger System

Although I believe it makes sense to focus initially on hostile attitudes directed toward women, as well as their characteristic manifestations (given both their salience and their capacity to do irrevocable damage), it is also important to remember the flipside of the coin. Actually, my analysis suggests two coins will need to be flipped over—that of negativity, and also that of gender.

For, while misogyny's primary manifestations may be in punishing bad women, and policing women's behavior, a system of punishment and reward—and conviction and exoneration—almost invariably works holistically. So, by reflecting just on the structural features of the account, we would predict that misogyny as I've defined it is likely to be continuous with a whole host of ways of enforcing gender conformity. And a cursory look at the social world around us serves as preliminary confirmation of this: hostility toward women is really only the tip of a large and troubling iceberg. We should also be concerned with the rewarding and valorizing of women who *conform* to gendered norms and expectations, in being (e.g.) loving mothers, attentive wives, loyal secretaries, "cool" girlfriends, or good waitresses. Another locus of concern should be the punishment and policing of men who flout the norms of masculinity—a point that is fairly well-recognized and, up to a point, well-taken. (And though it is not my topic in this book, this is certainly not to deny that it matters; see Digby [2014] for discussion.) Perhaps less well-recognized, however, are the *positive* and *exonerating* attitudes and manifestations thereof of which men who dominate women tend to be the beneficiaries. But I anticipate: these are some of the possibilities that chapter 6 canvasses.

The Analysis Exposes Underlying Moral Characteristics of Misogyny

Another feature of my account is that it is capable of accommodating plausible instances of misogyny that might initially look quite different: misogyny that arises in the wake of progressive social movements, and misogyny that arises under more repressive social conditions. And it exposes their shared underlying *moral* characteristics. Take, for example, the practice of acid attacks, or "vitriolage," in Bangladesh, where almost 80 percent of attacks are directed against girls and women. These attacks cause severe injuries, scarring, and tissue and bone damage to the faces, breasts, and genitals of the victims; sometimes, these prove fatal. According to a recent report, "[T]he most common reasons for attack [are] the refusal of marriage, the denial of sex, and the rejection of romance" (Pawan and Dhattarwal 2014). Moreover, according to one scholar, such crimes are characteristically motivated by "the intention of injuring or disfiguring her out of jealousy or revenge" (Swanson 2002). Mridula Bandyopadhyay and M. R. Khan (2013) further explain that these "attacks provoked by rejection both punish the woman for her rejection and strip her of her social/sexual capital" (72). And their overall conclusion about the relationship between repressive social norms and violence against women in Bangladesh is that

> [t]he conditions, forms and risks of violence are shaped by local ideologies of sex and gender. The sexual division of work constructs a 'gender hierarchy,' which relegates women to the private realm, maintains their dependence on men for survival, and places them in a vulnerable position. Violence is thus linked to and is an index of gender differences in economic power and participation. Acid attacks emphasize women's extreme dependency on men, and serve as a warning to many women who might resist male authority. (Bandyopadhyay and Khan 2013, 73)

Given this characterization of the practice of acid attacks in Bangladesh, it is clearly deeply misogynistic, according to my analysis. And it's instructive to reflect on the similarities between this practice and the actions of an Elliot Rodger, which the analysis brings out. Contra Heather Mac Donald (2014), the racist stereotype that misogyny is primarily committed by racialized others obscures deep structural similarities that deserve close attention by people suitably positioned to explore them.[16]

Misogyny Can Exist with or without Misogynists

I have already listed off some of the many ways in which misogynistic social mechanisms can operate without the dedicated efforts of individual bigots. But given the addendum, which encompasses individual agents, my account explicitly affirms the possibility of individual agents who deserve to be called misogynists. And it is important to me on reflection to preserve this possibility. I think the "bad apple" picture of misogyny is clearly false and unhelpful,

16. Even if they take different forms and demand very different solutions, which show the proper sensitivity—which is not to say uncritical deference—to cultural differences, variable social meanings, and the risks of adopting a practical and epistemic posture reflective of colonialist moralism.

and have been keen to move beyond it. But we shouldn't be in too much of a hurry to exonerate everyone, either. And, by the lights of my account, misogynists are just as misogyny does, roughly speaking. That is, misogynists may simply be people who are consistent overachievers in contributing to misogynist social environments (whether or not the system counts as misogynistic, all things considered. The point is that their efforts are pushing strongly in this direction). Alternatively, misogynists may be people who have been heavily *influenced* in their beliefs, desires, actions, values, allegiances, expectations, rhetoric, and so on, by a misogynist social atmosphere. Thus, according to my account, Rodger and Limbaugh have all done quite enough to have earned themselves the moniker. We'll see some more agents who fit the bill during the chapter that follows.

· My approach to misogyny hence tries to avoid two extremes that I take to be mistaken here: the first being to think about misogyny as a blight spread by individual "bad apples," and the second being to think about it in terms that are *purely* structural and social, to the exclusion of the distinctively agentic and interpersonal. As Haslanger (2012) has argued, we need to try to do justice in our theorizing to both agents and social structures, and also to the complex ways in which they are intimately related, within material reality (11, 411–418, esp. 414n8). And one of the subsequent possibilities that I am trying to highlight here is that of a social system or environment that has a particular atmosphere or "climate" for certain people within it, which needs to be described in broadly attitudinal terms, in order to do justice to people's experiences therein. Such climates may be described as differentially hostile, forbidding, or "chilly" to certain women.

That completes a brief overview of misogyny's logic, that is, its *constitutive* nature, on my analysis, as compared with the naïve conception. But when it comes to the *substance* of misogyny, much of the work still lies ahead of us; and some of it will be particular to specific local contexts. I will make this transition over the course of the next chapter by considering how misogyny contrasts with sexism, as well as how the two often work together, in contemporary US politics. I also consider some different kinds of misogynists, and the way misogyny can be instantiated via purely structural mechanisms, political movements, and the operation of social practices.

But first, let me return to the Isla Vista killings to tie up some of the remaining loose ends from the opening discussion.

NO MAN'S ISLAND

How many of the objections to the feminist diagnosis of misogyny from chapter 1 now remain? Most are rendered moot by my analysis, according to which they rest on the following series of false contrasts:

- There is no conflict between a man being a narcissist or delusional and his being a misogynist, that is, someone who powerfully and consistently channels misogynist social forces. For misogyny is narcissistic and delusional *by its very nature*. It transforms impersonal disappointments into embittered resentment—or a sense of "aggrieved entitlement," to use sociologist Michael Kimmel's term for it (2013, 18–25; chap. 1). And misogyny can also transform an agent's relationships with women entirely unknown to him into intimate ones, imaginatively.
- There is no conflict between a man being vulnerable and insecure and his being a misogynist. Indeed, this kind of vulnerability would be predicted on my analysis to be a common trigger. Similarly, there is no conflict between someone being a racist (say) and his being a misogynist. On the contrary, it makes sense that a person would be fixated on his position in multiple salient social hierarchies.
- There is no conflict between a man aggressing against other men and his being a misogynist as well. The desire of an Elliot Rodger to achieve dominance over both higher-status men and the women who are drawn to them is a perfectly natural combination. Such domination may indeed be the only viable way for someone like Rodger to achieve the status of an "alpha male," as per his express desire, at least if his own sense of his

position in the social hierarchy was accurate. He would have needed to rise in the social world in relation to other men, and in order to do so, his rising in the sights of "hot," that is, high-status, women would have been useful, perhaps vital. The converse plausibly holds as well; intra- and intergender hierarchies are naturally deeply entangled.

- There is no reason to expect that misogyny will typically manifest itself in violence or even violent tendencies, contra Steven Pinker. From the perspective of enforcing patriarchal social relations, this is not necessary. It is not even desirable. Patriarchal social relations are supposed to be amicable and seamless, when all is going to plan. It is largely when things go awry that violence tends to bubble to the surface. There are numerous nonviolent and low-cost means of defusing the psychic threat posed by powerful women who are perceived as insufficiently oriented to serving dominant men's interests. For example, women may be taken down *imaginatively*, rather than literally, by vilifying, demonizing, belittling, humiliating, mocking, lampooning, shunning, and shaming them.

- There is no reason to think that misogyny will be transmitted culturally by being taught directly, contra Chris Ferguson (2014). Again, this is unnecessary. What gets taught to—or, better, *learned* or internalized by—individual agents are, rather, the various patriarchal norms and expectations that govern women's social roles in service of dominant men's interests, together with a potent sense of personal entitlement. Hence, when a woman is perceived as challenging, resisting, or violating these norms and expectations, she and other women are liable to be punished, among other things. So misogyny often involves run-of-the-mill reactions to an agent's feeling threatened, cornered, thwarted, put down, let down, dressed down, wounded, defeated, bested, corrected, surpassed, usurped, displaced, disappointed, humiliated, chastened, undermined, or ousted, by women.

- There is no conflict between social progress for women and misogynist aggression toward them, contra Heather Mac Donald (2014). Progress and resentment are perfectly compatible. Indeed, women may be resented precisely *because* they are achieving rapid social progress in some areas. Some women's success in hitherto male-dominated roles, as well as their abandonment of traditionally feminine forms of care work, would be predicted on my analysis to provoke misogynist hostility. Misogyny often stems from the desire to take women down, to put them in their place again. So the higher they climb, the farther they may be made to fall because of it. The glass ceiling may be broken; but then there may be smackdown. And some women get hit by the shards of glass that rain down from others' rising.

Finally, is there a misogynist inside every man, as Tom Fordy wondered? No, not as I've defined the term here, so as to be a threshold concept. And one need not be a man to be a misogynist either: women can fit the description too, as can non-binary people, for that matter. (Although how common will be the requisite consistency of misogynistic attitudes and actions for women in particular remains an open empirical question, which research canvassed in the final chapter will bear on.) But, beyond that, many if not most of us at the current historical juncture are likely to be capable of channeling misogynistic social forces on occasion, regardless of sincere egalitarian beliefs and feminist commitments. I am sure I am no exception to this. Such channeling may take the form not only of unwittingly policing and enforcing distinctively gendered norms and expectations but also, on my analysis, over-policing and over-enforcing gender-neutral and potentially valid norms, e.g., genuine moral obligations. If the result is that we evince excessively or distinctively hostile reactions to the women implicitly deemed to be wayward in some way (again, rightly or wrongly), as compared with her male counterparts, then it will still count as misogyny that she faces in my book. There will be no shortage of cases in point involving double standards in examples therein to follow.

Chapter 3

Discriminating Sexism

What would men be without women? Scarce, sir, mighty scarce.

Mark Twain

SEXISM VS. MISOGYNY

An important potential objection to my account of misogyny is that it is *still* too narrow, in continuing to affirm misogyny's hostile "flavor" or quality. Should we construe misogyny more broadly, to encompass *any* belief, claim, or narrative that portrays women as inherently or naturally *inferior* to their male counterparts? (At least, in the absence of the kind of evidence that is usually lacking, without a suitable control group of people raised in an enduringly gender-egalitarian setting.)

I think this would be the wrong move at this juncture. My ameliorative proposal about misogyny as it stands has the advantage of inviting a clean, useful contrast between misogyny and *sexism*.[1] Recall from the previous chapter the first pass definition (which I then went on to finesse): viz., constitutively speaking,

> misogyny should be understood primarily as the "law enforcement" branch of a patriarchal order, which has the overall function of *policing* and *enforcing* its governing norms and expectations.

1. When undertaking an ameliorative project, I think it's helpful to consider relatives of the term and concept and to try to make them work together in the most harmonious and effective way. And often this will involve semantic divisions of labor: in this case, between the terms "misogyny" and "sexism." To my ear, the latter term lacks the hostile connotations of the former. Indeed, it arguably lacks any affective connotations whatsoever, except insofar as calling something sexist entails or implicates that it is pro tanto wrong in a "thin" sense, in being discriminatory.

Similarly, we can say that, constitutively speaking,

> sexism should be understood primarily as the "justificatory" branch
> of a patriarchal order, which consists in ideology that has the over-
> all function of *rationalizing* and *justifying* patriarchal social relations.

As a substantive matter of fact, sexism often works by *naturalizing* sex
differences, in order to justify patriarchal social arrangements, by making them seem inevitable, or portraying people trying to resist them
as fighting a losing battle. The unstated premise here is a version of an
"ought implies can" principle—possibly weakened to something like
"can't even implies don't bother." If certain social differences between
men and women could hardly be otherwise, then is it worth the effort
to try to combat them? Alternatively, and more modestly, if men and
women tend to have quite different capacities and proclivities, it may
make the best sense (i.e., be the safest bet in general, or the most efficient
default assumption) to encourage or at least not *discourage* a patriarchal
division of labor. Perhaps most importantly, such a division of labor will
be far from compelling evidence of discrimination, structural barriers, or
so-called pipeline problems differentially leaking female talent.

So sexist ideology will often consist in assumptions, beliefs, theories, stereotypes, and broader cultural narratives that represent men and
women as importantly different in ways that, if true and known to be
true, or at least likely, would make rational people more inclined to support and participate in patriarchal social arrangements. Sexist ideology
will also encompass *valorizing* portrayals of patriarchal social arrangements as more desirable and less fraught, disappointing, or frustrating
than they may be in reality. Whereas, as I've defined misogyny, it functions to *police* and *enforce* a patriarchal social order without necessarily
going via the intermediary of people's assumptions, beliefs, theories,
values, and so on. Misogyny serves to enact or bring about patriarchal
social relations in ways that may be direct, and more or less coercive.

On this picture, sexist ideology will tend to discriminate *between*
men and women, typically by alleging sex differences beyond what is
known or could be known, and sometimes counter to our best current

scientific evidence. Misogyny will typically differentiate between good women and *bad* ones, and punishes the latter. Overall, sexism and misogyny share a common purpose—to maintain or restore a patriarchal social order. But sexism purports to merely be being reasonable; misogyny gets nasty and tries to force the issue. Sexism is hence to bad science as misogyny is to moralism. Sexism wears a lab coat; misogyny goes on witch hunts.

How do sexism and misogyny stand in relation to one another? Sexist ideology (and its bearers, i.e., sexist attitudes, actions, practices, institutions, and artworks or other artifacts, inasmuch as they reflect or perpetuate sexist ideology)[2] *may* be used in service of misogynist ends in practice. But whether it actually does so, and therefore counts as misogynistic, will be a question of how the sexist representations actually *function*. Do they constitute a *barrier* or form of *hostility* as the girls and women in that environment will tend to encounter, and would naturally interpret, them? (Assuming the girls and women in question are being reasonable, by which I don't mean anything too idealized, as per the discussion in the previous chapter.) Or will some sexist artifact (a text or an image, for instance) just be seen as ludicrously pseudo-scientific and kitsch-seeming nonsense, as many women will now react to ads from the 1930s? The answer will depend on both background information about the context and the audience. The same goes, as we will see, for the sexist attitudes espoused or harbored by individual agents.

But first, recall my argument in chapter 1 that my (at that point, incipient) ameliorative proposal about what misogyny might be, at least in one central set of cases, made better psychological sense of the hostile reactions women face as compared with the competition, that is, the naïve conception. For the naïve conception would

---

2. As with the term "misogynist" as applied to individual agents, however, we might choose to define the analogous term "sexist" as a threshold term, rather than as a gradable adjective. Because it seems to me somewhat less common to talk about "a sexist" in practice, and I haven't found the need to do so in this book, I leave this terminological question open, for theorists to go their different ways on.

seldom predict any hostility whatsoever, I argued. At this point, I am prepared to go further and suggest that the ameliorative analysis, and with it the sexism/misogyny contrast I've drawn, is broadly in keeping with recent "grass-roots" semantic activism that has already pushed the latter term's usage, and to some extent its dictionary definition, in this more promising direction. If this is so, then the significance is twofold. First, my ameliorative proposal is in line with one pattern of ordinary usage, which I'll call the "feminist" one. The naïve conception is therefore out of step with what this group of language users are getting at when *they* use the term "misogyny." This further weakens the naïve conception's claim to our allegiance. The proposal I am making will only be revisionary for some language users and not others.

Second, it suggests that the feminist usage has a theoretical unification and underlying rationale. The term is not being used in an ad hoc manner; nor does it name a ragbag phenomenon. The feminist usage is getting at an importantly unified property—and one to which we ought to be paying attention, as compared with the naïve conception. So these descriptive and ameliorative lines of inquiry turn out to converge nicely in the end, and to complement each other.

To see this, consider the now well-known "misogyny speech" made by then prime minister of Australia, Julia Gillard, in October 2012, taking to task then leader of the opposition, Tony Abbott, for his sexist and misogynistic behavior. When it came to sexism and misogyny in politics, Gillard told Abbott to take a look in the proverbial mirror. Some of Abbott's behavior Gillard only described as being sexist. "What if men are by physiology or temperament more adapted to exercise authority or to issue command?" Abbott had mused in a debate about women's underrepresentation in positions of power in Australia. "If it's true that men have more power generally speaking than women, is that a *bad* thing?" was Abbott's next semi-rhetorical question. Gillard also described as being sexist Abbott's tailored explanation of the economics of carbon pricing to the women of the household ("What the women of Australia need to understand, as they do the ironing . . ."). Finally, she described as sexist Abbott's having called abortion "the easy way out" when he was health minister.

So all the remarks Gillard described solely as sexist represented women as either inferior to men in a masculine-coded domain or else as naturally consigned to feminine-coded forms of labor. They hence all had the effect of depicting these arrangements as either natural or desirable—or the alternatives as *less* than desirable, in the case of impugning a woman's decision to have an abortion as a "cop out." Gillard only began talking about misogyny, in particular, when she turned to certain offensive remarks either made to her by Abbott himself or that he had publicly signaled support for:

> I was offended too by the sexism, by the misogyny of the Leader of the Opposition catcalling across this table at me as I sit here as Prime Minister, "If the Prime Minister wants to, politically speaking, make an honest woman of herself . . ." something that would never have been said to any man sitting in this chair. I was offended when the Leader of the Opposition went outside in the front of Parliament and stood next to a sign that said, "Ditch the witch." I was offended when the Leader of the Opposition stood next to a sign that described me as "a man's bitch." I was offended by those things. Sexism, misogyny, every day from this Leader of the Opposition.[3]

Gillard's speech resonated with many people—women, in particular—both in Australia and internationally. But there were also some snide reactions regarding Gillard's grasp of the English language. Everyone knows that the word "misogyny" means "the hatred of women," some of Abbott's cronies complained; and few people thought that this was what Gillard was accusing Abbott of, exactly. But Gillard's use of the word "misogyny" seemed apt to many people—including certain lexicographers, who went on to revise the dictionary on this basis. Sue

---

3. "Transcript of Julia Gillard's Speech," *Sydney Morning Herald*, October 10, 2012, http://www.smh.com.au/federal-politics/political-news/transcript-of-julia-gillards-speech-20121009-27c36.html.

Butler, the editor of the *Macquarie Dictionary*, a classroom standard in Australia, was the first who moved to do so. The above definition hadn't really been keeping pace with the way the word had come to be used for the past twenty or thirty years, especially in feminist circles, Butler explained in an interview.[4] It's not that Gillard thought Abbott needed some time on the "psychiatrist's couch" to deal with his pathological hatred of women, she added. The *Macquarie Dictionary* went on to update its definition of "misogyny" to encompass the "entrenched prejudice against women," as well as the hatred thereof. Other dictionaries have also moved for further inclusions, including mistrust, disdain, mere dislike, and so on.

It's not clear that adding "entrenched prejudice" quite captures Gillard's usage though. The cases that saw her reach for the term "misogyny" were all nasty put-downs directed at Gillard personally. And they all seemed designed to diminish, belittle, shame, or lower her—to put her in her place, metaphorically or otherwise. It is the sense of *place* or role that stems from entrenched prejudice (see note 4).

---

4. From a story in the *Sydney Morning Herald* at the time: "Editor Sue Butler said it's time [the definition of misogyny] changed to reflect what Ms. Gillard really meant last week when she accused Opposition Leader Tony Abbott of sexism and misogyny in Parliament. Not that he needs a session on the psychiatrist's couch, but that he merely has an 'entrenched prejudice against women.' That will be the official second definition in the next updated edition of the dictionary. 'We decided that we had the basic definition, hatred of women, but that's not how misogyny has been used for about the last 20, 30 years, particularly in feminist language,' Ms. Butler told ABC radio on Wednesday. '"Sexist" does seem to be moving toward this description of surface features and "misogynist" applies to the underlying attitude.' It was the underlying prejudice that gave rise to these instances of sexism, Ms. Butler said. Misogyny was like sexism, with a 'stronger edge to it.'"

"Misogyny Definition to Change after Gillard Speech," *Sydney Morning Herald*, October 17, 2012, http://www.smh.com.au/national/misogyny-definition-to-change-after-gillard-speech-20121016-27q22.html.

From another representative piece on this rewriting of the dictionary: "Sue Butler, the editor of the Macquarie Dictionary, which is regarded as the definitive authority on Australian meanings of words, said Wednesday that the political furor revealed to her fellow editors that their dictionary's definition was decades out of date . . . Butler said while the Oxford English Dictionary had expanded its definition of the word from a psychological term to include its contemporary meaning a decade ago, it took the

Misogyny attempts to force women back into it, or to punish them for desertion. Alternatively, it may punish women for taking men's place, or trying to. It does so via hostile treatment enacted by individual agents as well as collective or group activity, and purely structural mechanisms. It comes in a range of flavors, from sheer nastiness and aggression to pointed indifference and stony silence, among other possibilities. For the prospect of hostility of any such kind can be an effective deterrent in being aversive to human beings, in view of our social nature. People in general, and arguably women in particular (in often being social-ized to be particularly agreeable), do not want to lose others' respect or approval or to be shunned, shamed, or excluded. We may also need other people's help, cooperation, and protection in the future. So the prospect of widespread hostility can be an especially effective deterrent to women who might otherwise engage in bad (or, rather, "bad") gen-dered behavior, or alternatively fail to provide certain feminine-coded goods and services.

MISOGYNY AND SEXUAL OBJECTIFICATION

Rae Langton draws a distinction that provides a useful illustration of the sexism/misogyny contrast, between two different forms sexual objectification may take. The discussion will also clarify how misog-yny is related to and can enlist this important form of patriarchal thought, a subject of considerable interest to feminists. The idea is

debate over Gillard's speech to prompt Macquarie to review its definition. 'Perhaps as dictionary editors we should have noticed this before it was so rudely thrust in front of us as something that we'd overlooked,' Butler told Associated Press. She said the deci-sion had drawn complaints." For one such: "It would seem more logical for the prime minister to refine her vocabulary than for the Macquarie Dictionary to keep changing its definitions every time a politician mangles the English language," said Fiona Nash, one of Tony Abbott's senators. Rod McGuirk, "Misogyny Fight in Australia Sparks a Change in Dictionary Definition," *The Star*, October 17, 2012, http://www.thestar. com/news/world/2012/10/17/misogyny_fight_in_australia_sparks_a_change_in_ dictionary _definition.html.

that a central feature of personhood—namely, autonomy—can be denied in cases of sexual objectification in one of the following two distinct ways:

(1)   the *non-attribution* of autonomy to a subject; versus
(2)   the *violation* of the autonomy of a subject (Langton 2009, 233).

(1)-type cases of objectification may be the result of an agent's being *ignorant* of a subject's fully autonomous and minded nature, or perhaps just not caring about what (or, rather, who) she really is. Women may then be envisaged as vacant, naïve, inarticulate, and stupid; they may be treated with condescension, as if they are children, as well as manhandled and exploited in ways painful and demeaning. In contrast, (2)-type cases of objectification often result from an agent positively *desiring* to disrupt a subject's peace of mind, or to "get inside her head," by overriding her will, causing her to suffer, or violating her bodily integrity (Langton 2009, 234–235). The latter form of objectification hence seems to *presuppose* the very sorts of capacities that are deliberately being violated, in (e.g.) treating a person like an inanimate object of the sort that may be bought, sold, collected, used, used up, broken, fused, destroyed, and discarded with impunity (Nussbaum 1995, 257; Langton 2009, 225–229).

It is plausible to think that cases of (2)-type objectification will almost always count as misogynistic; whereas (1)-type cases may only evince an extreme form of sexism, insofar as they function to justify certain social arrangements, including congruent sexual relationships and forms of pornography.

Taking up this distinction of Langton's, Martha C. Nussbaum (whose pioneering work on objectification Langton was drawing on in turn) has recently argued that this second, "autonomy-violating" form of objectification is always punitive in its tenor. It thus plays an important role in giving vent to misogyny on the Internet (2011, 68–71). Hence Nussbaum's proposal that the kind of objectification at issue in such cases is often the result of Nietzschean *ressentiment*, in which a person's sense of their lowly or declining status in the social world prompts them to lash out at those they perceive as more powerful. (Perhaps needless to say, these perceptions need not be accurate, though they can be.)

These claims of Nussbaum's are clearly congenial for my purposes.[5] They are also very plausible, though I would suggest a few additions. Such objectifying forms of treatment can seemingly serve not only as punishment but also ways of defusing the psychic threat that certain women pose. And, along with *ressentiment*, there is also the possibility of willful denial and self-aggrandizement to consider, wherein the agent refuses to see himself as coming down in the social world in relation to women, or even to be at any risk of this happening.

This takes me neatly from the former leader of my home country, to the current President of my adopted one: Donald Trump. In the next section, I'll show that my analysis captures his pattern of behavior nicely too. This is all to the good, since this has been one of the most widely accepted cases of misogyny in the media—which makes it all the more dispiriting that Trump was nevertheless elected.

---

5. Langton also makes the following similar, suggestive, remark: "It is worth noting that resentment seems compatible with an objectifying attitude.... Someone who views women reductively, as brutish creatures whose purpose is the satisfaction of men's lusts, may also manifest resentment toward women. Misogyny may sometimes present just this combination. And perhaps the connection between the resentment and the objectifying attitude is not coincidental. Perhaps it is caused by a horror that one's desires put one in the power of such contemptible creatures" (2009, 332). This is Langton's one explicit substantive remark about misogyny mentioned in chapter 1, note 3. I am skeptical of the possibility Langton points to, wherein women are seen as "brutish creatures" but are nevertheless resented, for reasons chapter 5 will canvass. In the meantime, let me preview another possibility: that the resentment-horror combination is the result not of such extreme sexism combined with misogyny, but of misogyny on its own, or combined with a milder form of sexism. Consider the epigraph from my preface, where Virginia Woolf inspires horror as well as indignation in the Beadle for treading on men's turf at Oxbridge. That he was resentful of her *nonchalance* or *insolence*—or, in more general terms, her freedom—is a natural reading of the passage. Woolf was taking *liberties* in veering off the gravel path that women were bound to stick to, whether or not the rule was backed by some sexist theory that made the grass best reserved as men's exclusive province. The horror here may stem from a *social role reversal* or *violation*; or so I suggest in chapter 5, in the final section.

THE ART OF THE SMACKDOWN

The last chapter featured snapshots of two very different kinds of misogynists, understood as consistent overachievers in enforcing patriarchal law and order. First, there was the disappointed diner, someone like Elliot Rodger, who bangs his spoon on the table when he doesn't receive good service (relative to patriarchal norms and values). And, second, we had the exploitative storyteller, someone like Rush Limbaugh, who gives men like Rodger women to point to and blame for wrongdoing of the same general kind as they feel aggrieved about in their own case—for example, being selfish, negligent, irresponsible, ungrateful, and unfair to them. By conjuring up a sketchy and circuitous personal connection between Sandra Fluke and his listeners via the idea that their tax dollars were going toward her birth control prescription, even though they never receive the "benefit" of this (non-)relationship, Limbaugh supplies a criminal to fit the supposed crime. Fluke became representative of the kind of woman failing to make good on her end of the bargain.

There are other kinds of misogynists too, of course. Consider the diner who is seldom if ever disappointed because, when he receives poor service, he is liable to get *nasty*. His reputation begins to precede him, particularly when he enjoys other forms of power, prestige, influence, and privilege. Having mastered the art of the smackdown, he has less need to practice it. There is always a veiled threat toward women lurking—a threat comes to inhere in his very persona.

This is Donald Trump's brand of misogyny: one of his traits most consistently on display over the years, as many commentators have noted. His smackdowns have primarily taken the form of serial sexual harassment, sexual assault, and grade-school insults of the women who cross or threaten him. Rosie O'Donnell (very funnily) questioned his moral authority to pardon Miss Universe for indulging in underage drinking: Trump called O'Donnell a "pig" and a "dog," among other epithets. Carly Fiorina competed with Trump for the Republican nomination: he implied that her face was not presidential-level attractive. Megyn Kelly, then of Fox News, pressed Trump about his history of insulting women: Trump fumed that she had blood coming out of her eyes and "wherever," thus coining a new euphemism by way of word-finding problems.

These examples all clearly count as misogyny according to my analysis, showing that it applies just as much to a domineering misogynist as a disappointed one; to the powerful as much as the powerless; and to those who are reacting to (actual or perceived) threats to patriarchal law and order, as well as neglecting designated feminine-coded duties. These points all count in favor of my analysis—as does the fact that it fits Trump's behavior so neatly, given that the term "misogynist," not "sexist," was the one people tended to reach for in describing him.

The metaphor of misogyny as the law enforcement branch of a patriarchal order is particularly apt here, given (a) Trump's marketing of himself as the "law and order candidate," and (b) his being the embodiment of toxic masculinity (a theme I expand on in chapter 4, in connection with shame and humiliation).

Recall that, on my view, misogyny upholds the social norms of patriarchies by policing and patrolling them; whereas sexism serves to *justify* these norms—largely via an ideology of supposedly "natural" differences between men and women with respect to their talents, interests, proclivities, and appetites. On this view, sexism is to misogyny as civic order is to law enforcement. Sexism taken alone involves believing in men's superiority to women in masculine-coded, high-prestige domains (such as intellectual endeavors, sports, business, and politics), and the naturalness or even inevitability of men's dominance therein. Misogyny taken alone involves anxieties, fears, and desires to maintain a patriarchal order, and a commitment to restoring it when it is disrupted. So sexism can be complacent; misogyny may be anxious. Sexism is bookish; misogyny is combative. Sexism has a theory; misogyny wields a cudgel.

Notice now that sexism and misogyny so understood can come apart from each other at the level of individual agents (whereas, it is plausible to think that the two are both causally necessary, though analytically distinct, elements of patriarchy—along with himpathy, exonerating narratives, and other of the scripts and resources I'll go on to canvass later). Trump illustrates the possibility of misogyny without sexism in practice (whether or not this is so, it's a live possibility, which is sufficient for my purposes). For it's not obvious on the face of it that Trump has especially sexist beliefs about women's (in)ability to compete with him in business and politics at his own level (such as it is). For one thing, Trump employs women in high-powered positions in his companies, which suggests he doesn't underestimate (all) women—rather, he needs to control them, and head off the risk of their outshining him. ("I have many executives who are women. They make money for me," Trump has boasted.) For another thing, sexism tends to make men in Trump's position relatively complacent about such ignominious possibilities when they are competing with a woman for some sought-after prize or position. But when Trump went head to head with Hillary Clinton during the 2016 presidential election, things quickly turned ugly in terms of the hostility he displayed toward her— particularly during the three presidential debates, in which his rhetoric and demeanor was menacing, vindictive, spiteful, and childish. This suggests Trump's (characteristically strong) desire to win may not have been accompanied by a confident belief that he would do so, as would tend to arise from sexism. And this notwithstanding the literal content of some of his claims—for example, when Trump said that Clinton wouldn't have gotten even 5 percent of the vote if she hadn't played the "woman card," or attracted "wherever" voters. But this was surely merely wishful thinking on Trump's part, evincing his desire to believe Clinton a truly terrible candidate absent so-called identity politics. In which case, if he won, he wouldn't have to feel that he had won anything but *fairly*. And if he lost, the game was rigged, i.e., the result of political correctness. So this wishful thinking also served a preemptive ego protection function.[6]

6. In addition to that, these claims constituted shameless pandering to a support base who felt aggrieved about so-called victim culture, to anticipate the theme of chapter 7. For people who fit into this category, pulling the "'card' card" and automatically rejecting any complaints others make of systematic injustices leveled against them, in virtue of race or gender (in particular), is hence a common move—superficially paradoxically, and plausibly hypocritically. See Schraub (2016) for relevant discussion.

Sometimes the desire-driven nature of such low opinions expressed of women is even more transparent. Bob Sutton, a chairman of the GOP Executive Committee in Florida, recently claimed that Trump would surely best Clinton in a presidential debate. "I think when Donald Trump debates Hillary Clinton she's going to go down like Monica Lewinsky," said Sutton.[7] (She didn't; but it hardly mattered.)

But even though misogyny and sexism can and sometimes do come apart in individual agents, and in other piecemeal ways, they are of course generally deeply in cahoots in upholding a patriarchal order. This is seldom clearer than in the realm of reproductive rights—which brings me to Indiana abortion laws, under its then governor, Mike Pence, now Trump's vice president.

The discussion here will also serve to highlight several crucial points about misogyny—some of which have already been mentioned, but deserve further emphasis and drawing out by way of a detailed example:

1. Misogyny isn't just about second-personal hostility (à la Rodger and Trump, as well as Limbaugh's listeners, on the basis of the relevant circuitous relationship), but also third-personal *indignation*, outrage, condemnation, and similar. That is, people can show hostility toward women who are held to wrong *others*, including those deemed the most vulnerable and in need of defending, protection, and justice. ("Won't somebody think of the—in this case, unborn—children?")

2. Misogyny comprises social practices and institutions, as well as agents' actions and attitudes, toward women. For, social structures can support meanings and represent political bodies in such a way as to make for hostile, demeaning, and

7. Sara Jerde, "GOPer: Clinton Will 'Go Down Like Monica Lewinsky' Debating Trump," *Talking Points Memo*, April 28, 2016, http://talkingpointsmemo.com/livewire/florida-republican-clinton-down-like-lewinsky.

punitive forms of treatment (as in the notion of a "chilly" environment).

3. Misogyny and racism are inseparably connected; and the treatment of nonwhite women (especially poor ones) within a white supremacy seems particularly liable to encompass various forms of *erasure*; this is a point I canvass briefly below, and chapter 6 will return to.

In some cases of misogyny, women are blamed and punished for wronging a second party with whom they have a more or less hazy and nominal connection—for example, the taxpayer, in Sandra Fluke's case. In other cases of misogyny, the setup is different. In the realm of reproductive rights (or lack thereof), for instance, women are blamed and punished for wronging a novel, indeed in some ways ad hoc, class of persons—third parties who cannot speak for themselves, and who do not seem in any case to have anything much to say, that is, interests or claim-rights prior to sentience. Note, too, that the fetus had not been recognized as a person by Evangelicals until recently. (So even if, pace basic metaphysical assumptions I subscribe to, their position did turn out to be correct, it would be the right stance for the wrong—and, at the level of ideology, deceptive— reasons.) This changed after the advent of an "astroturf" (as opposed to grass-roots) movement explicitly designed to curb and roll back feminist social progress. I speak of the anti-abortion movement: a paradigm example of misogynistic backlash.

LOVING MOTHERS, ERASING OTHERS

In an interview with MSNBC's Chris Matthews, in March 2016, that quickly acquired some notoriety during the primary season, Trump erred by admitting (after some hesitation) something most Republicans had only whistled to date: namely, that by the lights of their own alleged views on reproductive rights (or, again, lack thereof), "there would have to be some form of punishment for the woman" who seeks or obtains an illegal abortion.[8] As one politician put it shortly afterward, with unusual and, to my mind, impressive candor:

> Trump may be the most outrageous of the Republicans, but he is saying what all of them believe. They want abortion to be illegal, and they do want to punish women and doctors. Trump just committed the sin of telling people what [Republicans] think.

The politician in question was Hillary Clinton, speaking at a campaign rally in Brooklyn, New York.[9]

Clinton was right. And though such claims may be impolitic, they are also important to make, as opposed to maintaining the pretense that this is a purely ethical and religious question—as philosophers have tended to grant, for the sake of argument. I believe it is too late in the day to keep up the charade, in the overall framing of the debate (though not for the sake of making specific arguments within it). Abortion has become a deeply feminist issue, since a powerful locus for designing and trying to enact bureaucratic forms of social control that withhold healthcare from women who need it. Even if it kills them—as when, for example, the GOP-led House of Representatives passed H.R. 358, a bill allowing doctors to let women die rather than perform emergency abortions, on the grounds of conscience. It was clear that this bill would be vetoed. It hence seemed expressive of a desire or fantasy, more than anything—and constituted a warning, as we can now see in retrospect.

That was back in 2011. But the antichoice movement's political roots, and tenuous relationship to mainstream Christianity,

---

8. "Donald Trump Advocates Punishment for Abortion," *Hardball with Chris Matthews*, MSNBC, March 30, 2016, http://www.msnbc.com/hardball/watch/trump-s-hazy-stance-on-abortion-punishment-655457859717.

9. Nick Gass, "Clinton: Trump Said What He Believes on Abortion," *Politico*, April 5, 2016, politico.com/blogs/2016-dem-primary-live-updates-and-results/2016/04/donald-trump-hillary-clinton-abortion-221594.

go back much further, as has been well-documented by Yale law professor Reva B. Siegel, partly in joint work with the Pulitzer Prize–winning *New York Times* journalist Linda Greenhouse. Greenhouse and Siegel (2010) show that a position previously held only by strict Catholics was deliberately appropriated as part of the Southern Strategy that helped Nixon win in 1972 (the year before the Roe decision). In a piece in *New York* magazine by Kevin Phillips, one of the Southern Strategy's chief engineers and proponents, "How Nixon Will Win," he laid out the rationale behind the opposition to abortion (along with "acid", or LSD, and amnesty for so-called draft dodgers). Siegel (2014) summarizes the idea thusly: "[A]bortion rights . . . validated a breakdown of traditional roles that required men to be prepared to kill and die in war and women to save themselves for marriage and . . . motherhood."

So the hope that working-class whites could be mobilized against a powerful material means and cultural symbol of women's liberation involved intentionally extracting one piece of a metaphysically and morally highly committal—and intricate—Catholic package deal. And this was for cynical political gain, according to Siegel's reconstruction of Phillips's reasoning (2014, 1371).

The appropriation of Catholic ideology did not end there, either. The idea that life begins at conception has been proclaimed only recently. But there have since been numerous attempts to enshrine this idea in law, via several states' proposed personhood amendments. Whether or not these efforts will eventually be successful, reproductive rights have been under systematic and unprecedented attack in the United States by Republicans for several years, intensifying recently. Abortion clinics have been shutting down around the country, as the result of restrictions that, as providers have protested, lack any valid medical rationale. Clinicians are required to have hospital admitting privileges, and clinics must conform to exacting surgical standards, such that, for example, corridors have to be wide enough to accommodate two gurneys side-by-side. As a result, five states in the heart of the nation are down to just one clinic apiece, at the time of writing (February 2017).[10] And defunding Planned Parenthood was the first intended move the GOP announced following the 2016 general election.[11]

Because of these and other barriers to abortion access—for example, the imposition of waiting periods, the requirement of multiple appointments prior to the procedure, the difficulty of obtaining appointments in a timely fashion, in addition to tight restrictions on abortions after twenty weeks in many states—many women have been resorting to illegal, back alley, and self-induced abortions. As the result, maternal mortality rates have been rising—doubling in Texas since 2011, when Planned Parenthood was defunded there.[12] Many women's experiences, even for those whose health is not endangered, are harrowing. One woman who began to miscarry had to deliver a fetus whose heart was still beating but who was known to have no chance of surviving ex utero, due to severe congenital abnormalities. The woman was sent home from the hospital several times, even though the fetus's feet were already protracting, and a still birth was inevitable. This lasted four days, until her water broke naturally. At various points, she was screaming for help from a doctor. But the hospital was forbidden from performing an emergency abortion at just past twenty weeks, the point past which Texas's "fetal pain" law prohibits the procedure even in circumstances of this kind. The evidence suggests that fetuses cannot feel pain until the third trimester—that is, week twenty-seven.[13]

10. Rebecca Harrington and Skye Gould, "The Number of Abortion Clinics in the US Has Plunged in the Last Decade—Here's How Many Are in Each State," *Business Insider*, February 10, 2017, http://www.businessinsider.com/how-many-abortion-clinics-are-in-america-each-state-2017-2.

11. Tara Culp-Ressler, "Paul Ryan Pledges GOP's First Legislative Action Will Defund Planned Parenthood," *Think Progress*, January 5, 2017, https://thinkprogress.org/republicans-health-care-3bbcb30f626a#.jrdu5sutu.

12. Katha Pollitt, "The Story Behind the Maternal Mortality Rate in Texas Is Even Sadder Than We Realize," *The Nation*, September 8, 2016, https://www.thenation.com/article/the-story-behind-the-maternal-mortality-rate-in-texas-is-even-sadder-than-we-realize/.

13. Brandy Zadrozny, "Texas Forced This Woman to Deliver a Stillborn Baby," *Daily Beast*, March 31, 2016, http://www.thedailybeast.com/articles/2016/03/31/texas-forced-this-woman-to-deliver-a-stillborn-baby.

At the same time as these restrictions have been imposed, there has been the introduction of laws against feticide in some states, in addition to the laws against fetal homicide that already existed in most of them. In Indiana, the first two women to be charged with feticide—Bei Bei Shuai and Pavi Patel—are Asian American in a state where Asian Americans comprise less than 2 percent of the general population. These women may hence be vulnerable to undue suspicion based on stereotypes regarding—ironically—the devaluation of girls and women, and the practice of sex-selective abortion in their countries of familial (and, in Shuai's case, personal) origin, according to some advocates.[14]

Purvi Patel's case was the one to make the headlines. She was arrested, charged, tried, and convicted of self-inducing an abortion using pills bought online and abandoning the fetus, which, Patel testified, had been stillborn at twenty-three to twenty-four weeks (an age at which abortion is still legal in some states). The facts of the case were disputed in court by the state's expert witness, who testified that the fetus was a week or two older and had drawn breath. But, according to Deepa Iyer, an activist and scholar who became involved in the case because of Indiana's repeated and potentially deliberate targeting of Asian American women under this law: "Purvi Patel's conviction amounts to punishment for having a miscarriage and then seeking medical care, something that no woman should worry would lead to jail time."[15]

Patel was sentenced in March 2015 to twenty years in prison, of which she served one year and four months—until her appeal to the Indiana Supreme Court was successful. But how many women will

14. "Asian American Women's Reproductive Rights Are Being Targeted, Says Advocate," *NYT Live New York Times*, November 11, 2015, http://nytlive.nytimes.com/womenintheworld/2015/11/05/asian-american-womens-reproductive-rights-are-being-targeted-says-advocate/.

15. Jessica Valenti, "It Isn't Justice for Purvi Patel to Spend 20 Years in Prison for an Abortion," *The Guardian*, April 2, 2015, https://www.theguardian.com/commentisfree/2015/apr/02/it-isnt-justice-for-purvi-patel-to-serve-20-years-in-prison-for-an-abortion.

avoid going to the ER now, under similar circumstances (profuse vaginal bleeding), even following a miscarriage, for fear of being arrested, charged, and imprisoned?[16] Moreover, the seemingly racist nature of the law's implementation—with brown bodies being treated as disposable in order to teach other women a lesson is a vivid example of the entanglement of sexism, misogyny, and racism. But it is merely, and shamefully, one such among many.[17]

So women are *already* being punished for having abortions under conservative lore. Of course, they don't say that. "Love them both," is the stock phrase, when it comes to both the pregnant woman and the embryo or fetus in utero. But it is a strange kind of love that would force even the victim of rape or incest to bear a pregnancy to term. It is a strange kind of love that would enforce a pregnancy at all, as the feminist philosopher Ann Cudd has argued (1990).

And it is a strange kind of love that takes a third of American women to be guilty of homicide and, collectively, genocide. This dim view of women who have abortions was explicitly propounded by Troy Newman, an Evangelical antichoice extremist who was praised for his moral leadership by another Republican presidential candidate in 2016, Ted Cruz. Newman wrote in his book, *Their Blood Cries Out* (2000):

> By comparing abortion directly to any other act of premeditated contract killing, it is easy to see that there is no difference in principle. However, in our society, a mother of an aborted baby

---

16. Consider too Vice President Pence's mandatory cremation of remains (or so-called funerals) for fetuses; the growing trend of criminal investigations for women who miscarry (Grant 2016); and the fact that, in many states, a sexual assailant will have full paternity rights (sometimes, even with a conviction). See, e.g., Eric Berkowitz, "Parental Rights for Rapists? You'd Be Surprised How Cruel the Law Can Be," *Salon*, October 4, 2015, http://www.salon.com/2015/10/04/parental_rights_for_rapists_youd_be_surprised_how_cruel_the_law_can_be/.

17. See, for example, Angela Davis (2003, chap. 4), for a powerful discussion of this issue in connection with incarceration practices.

is considered untouchable whereas any other mother, killing any other family member, would be called what she is: a murderer.[18]

In the chapter, "Moms Who Murder," Newman continues:

In our current social climate, it is acceptable to lay blame for abortion at the feet of the abortionists, the social liberals who encourage the abortions, and the law-makers who allow and even pay for them. But the mother is the one person we are not allowed to call guilty. Ironically, she is the one who needs most to see what she has done. . . .

Even in the pro-life movement, rescuers, those who take direct action to save a life, want to call abortion murder, but they are hesitant to call the mother a murderer to her face for fear of offending her and the "politically correct" crowd. By confronting the woman with her sin, our objective is to get her to see the evil that has resulted from her actions. By withholding truthful confrontation from her, we prevent her from being brought to repentance and ultimate restoration.

In light of these views, we can see that Trump's remarks about punishing women for having abortions are not in fact the most hyperbolic version of conservative thinking on this matter, pace Clinton. Trump at least readily accepted, indeed assumed, that there are women who would seek abortions even if they were banned—and this regardless of all the love in the world that Republicans proclaim, and the material support they refuse to provide, to the women who bear a pregnancy to term without adequate material, social, and financial resources. Others in the antichoice movement effectively resist the logical pressure to acknowledge that these women would

18. Quoted in Miranda Blue, "Anti-Planned Parenthood Activist Troy Newman's Terrifying, Woman-Shaming, Apocalyptic Manifesto," *Right Wing Watch*, September 14, 2015, http://www.rightwingwatch.org/post/anti-planned-parenthood-activist-troy-newmans-terrifying-woman-shaming-apocalyptic-manifesto/.

have to be punished by erasing them from the discourse. Sometimes the thought seems to be that such women would simply cease to exist in their envisaged America—that when abortion providers have been shut down, and pro-choice ideologues are no longer permitted to lead women astray, there would be no women who would still seek an abortion whatsoever. They will *want* to lend their wombs to the cause, even in cases of rape and incest. The historical record tells against this prediction strongly.

Troy Newman writes in closing in his book that those "murderesses" who have abortions and die in an "unrepentant state"

> will probably go to their grave blood-guilty, their souls corrupted with the innocent blood of murdered children. They can only look forward to the time when, at death, they will hear the innocent children howling their names in testimony against them, demanding vengeance.

By the lights of such ideology, good mothers deserve to be celebrated on earth and subject to infinite rewards in heaven. But for women who would choose to have an abortion, hell may be too good for them. Worse than immoral, such women are profoundly unnatural— a veritable abomination. This is what we find at the toxic intersection of the misogyny and sexism of Republicans. Who, in truth, is howling, and for whom, we might wonder.

WITHHOLDING (FROM) WOMEN

So it turns out that women are being not only punished but denied life-saving healthcare measures. What are they being punished *for*, however? And to what end such withholding?

There's a common assumption on the left that the right seeks to punish women for having sex outside of marriage—and that abortion is therefore largely a matter of policing women's bodies and controlling their sexuality. Doubtless those motives are part of the murky mix. But if that was all there was to it, then why prohibit access to abortion for women who were the victims of rape and incest? Yet this remains a commonly endorsed prohibition. According to a recent Gallup poll, almost one in five Americans said in 2016 that abortion should be illegal under *any* circumstances, which would rule out even "life of the mother" exceptions.[19] So it is hard to credit the idea that this is about saving lives either. Yet, if it was about preventing abortions as such (the thought being that letting one or two persons die is better than murdering a fetus or even an embryo), then why not do everything in one's power to make available those many—and often cheap—forms of contraception that demonstrably do not allow fertilization to occur? But this is manifestly not happening, as we see in the Supreme Court's decision in *Burwell v. Hobby Lobby* (2014).

So there's a puzzle: what are women held to be guilty of doing or being?

Withholding and failing to give, I think; being cold, callous, and heartless; neglecting their natural duty to provide safe haven and nurture, by evicting a vulnerable being from their rightful home, their birthright. Hence women who seek abortions, even to save their own lives, are a blank canvas on which to project a set of grievances borne of unmet felt needs in turn borne of a sense of entitlement. This is an idea which the next chapter will elaborate.

Limbaugh repeatedly called Sandra Fluke "irresponsible" and a "typical liberal." Especially striking among his rants: "Here is a woman who is happily presenting herself as an immoral, baseless, no-purpose-to-her-life woman." One might have thought that the problem was too *much* purpose and direction in her life, not too little.

Limbaugh is an expert at channeling a sense of confusion, loss, and sadness common among his target audience—primarily white male conservatives, as well as some of their white female counterparts—and transforming it into anger, partly by furnishing them with a suitable moral narrative that casts them in the role of victims.

19. "Abortion," *Gallup*, http://www.gallup.com/poll/1576/abortion.aspx (last accessed May 12, 2017).

Fluke was depicted partly as violating the social contract (by "taking the money" of Limbaugh and his listeners, without providing them with sex in return). The point of the metaphors of Fluke being a prostitute in relation to Limbaugh and his audience—with them being either her client or her pimp, recalling his oscillation—is that Fluke owed them a piece of her womanhood. The focus on sex was natural but not essential, I suspect. Moreover, as the story went, Fluke also felt illicitly *entitled*. She expected something from them, without repaying them in the coin of personal attention. And underneath it all, in the background, she was *failing to nurture, refusing to give life* or to *care for the vulnerable*.

A structurally feasible alternative to such a story would be one that pointed to another subject of such women's wrongdoing, and allowed for anger, via identification or moral crusading. Hence, I think, the power of the narrative that depicts pregnant women as suspect and feckless—but, tellingly, perhaps not irredeemable—being misled by truly evil abortion advocates and providers to cast the helpless fetus out of their rightful sanctuary. The fetus hence serves as a powerful cultural symbol or surrogate for certain men's sense of being neglected or deprived by women. And their sense of vulnerability can be projected onto the fetus, thus allowing them to feel outrage on behalf of another supposed person—who, conveniently, has no plans of their own, and no voice to deny their interest in coming into existence as a sentient creature prior to actually being one. And it is often easier to take the moral high ground than admit to feeling rejected and wounded. Wrote one author:

> The unborn, though enclosed in the womb of his mother, is already a human being, and it is an almost monstrous crime to rob it of life which it has not yet begun to enjoy. If it seems more horrible to kill a man in his own house than in a field, because a man's house is his most secure place of refuge, it ought surely to be deemed more atrocious to destroy the unborn in the womb before it has come to light. (Calvin 1999)

These were the words of John Calvin, in the sixteenth century. The analogy between a mother's womb and a dominant man's home-cum-haven—or safe space—has long been a part of patriarchal ideology. And it remains so.

That, at any rate, is my working hypothesis. It has the virtue of explaining why conservatives' views about abortion are so inconsistent, ad hoc, and never seem to quite scratch the itch, even when they get what they're ostensibly campaigning for.

MISOGYNY AS BACKLASH

There is often a sense that misogyny is a thing of the past, or that it died out in its historical form, to be replaced with a New Misogyny (Brooks 2016; cf. Manne 2016d). I doubt that this is true though, and it defies considerations of parsimony. Although a patriarchal order is something broader than misogyny, the latter is a ubiquitous and arguably causally necessary aspect of the former, insofar as it serves to enforce patriarchal norms and expectations. This helps to explain why misogyny is both prevalent in ostensibly oppressive regimes and why we have also been seeing a good deal of it coming to the surface in the United States lately. Feminist progress has been rapid and impressive in many ways. But this has led to resentment, anxiety, and misogynistic backlash. We see this coming out under the mantle of moralism, as well as under the cover of anonymity, as in Internet comments sections.

For even when people become less *sexist*—that is, less skeptical about women's intellectual acumen or leadership abilities, and less inclined to buy into pernicious gendered stereotypes about women's being overly emotional or irrational—this does not mean that feminism's work is done. On the contrary, misogyny that was latent or lay dormant within a culture may manifest itself when women's capabilities become more salient and hence demoralizing or threatening. And this may result in more or less subtle forms of lashing out, moralism, wishful thinking, and willful denial, as well as the kind of low-grade resentment that festers and alights on effigies and scapegoats.

Women are sometimes told they need to be twice as good as men, all else being equal, in order to be just as respected, successful, admired, and so on. Whether or not this is in fact necessary, given whatever kinds of sexism may or may not be in play, it is certainly not sufficient. And, sometimes, it's not even clear what would be. Such excellence in a woman may have the opposite effect on some people, resulting in her being a polarizing figure. In other words, women may be penalized for being too qualified, too competent. People may be "taken aback," and unwittingly engage in post hoc rationalization to make sense of their inchoate feelings of suspicion or consternation. I return to this theme in chapter 8 here.

After the election, I looked back at some of the notes I made during the campaign. From March 2016:

> As Trump's campaign has amply demonstrated, [contemporary America] is a world in which some formerly privileged men are reeling, taking with them women who are disoriented by their downfall. Women who reverse gendered hierarchies and aspire to masculine-coded social roles are therefore liable to provoke misogyny. One can think of few more obvious triggers than seeking political office—especially when it would come at the expense of rival male politicians. . . .
>
> If this is roughly right, then it affects and clarifies the questions we need to ask about women in politics. Even if women like Clinton aren't subject to false beliefs or defunct gendered stereotypes per se, they may be viewed and treated in a hostile way precisely because of their manifest competence. Clinton's competence in politics is likely to be threatening to some people in some contexts.
>
> On this understanding, misogynist hostility may be more or less overt, and more or less strong [vs.] low-grade—ranging from mild dislike and suspicion to outright hatred and violence. Misogyny may also be channeled and evinced by both men and women. This ought to be obvious, given the fact that the crumbling of patriarchal social structures can be confronting for anyone. And yet Glen Greenwald has argued that the charges against

so-called Bernie bros are overstated, on the grounds that some of [the] slurs that are [being] leveled come from women. . . .

People these days are often ready to admit that they may suffer from implicit biases, i.e., subtle race and gender-based biases that may affect their thinking and behavior without any conscious awareness on their part. This is not the unapologetic bigotry of a Donald Trump; it is compatible with a commitment to egalitarian values. But, when it comes to gender, the notion of implicit bias seems to be ambiguous between inchoate sexism and inchoate misogyny. And the latter will plausibly often be subject to post hoc rationalization, a well-documented phenomenon in psychology. We experience a hostile feeling toward someone without quite knowing why, for example. Our minds subsequently search for a rationale to justify our ill feelings. Her voice is shrill; she is shouting; and why isn't she smiling?

I can think of at least one reason. For, whether or not Clinton should be president, this is clearly unfair. And I fear that it is likely to affect voter turnout come November.

Whatever one thinks of Hillary Clinton, as a feminist candidate or otherwise, it is a feminist achievement of note that a woman may be the next president of the United States of America. It is not in spite of this fact, but plausibly partly because of it, that we have been seeing a lot of misogynistic backlash of late. Ironically, the fact that we might well have elected a woman president may now be the thing that prevents this from happening. And a Clinton victory would expose her, along with many other women, to resentment on the part of the white men who comprise the majority of Trump's voting base.[20]

My point here isn't that any of this was prescient. On the contrary, it's that aspects of what happened were all too predictable. Female

20. Kate Manne, "What Misogyny Means (Or, Rather, Meant) for Hillary Clinton," draft available at https://www.academia.edu/29785241/What_Misogyny_Means_or_Rather_Meant_for_Hillary_Clinton_--_Draft_of_March_21_2016.

politicians are a tempting and common outlet for misogynist aggression, in being very public figures and objects of collective attention, as well as Rorschach inkblots, morally speaking. For they are virtually sure to have been compromised in some manner, and to be subject to genuine moral criticisms. But the question is not only whether they are judged by sexist or more or less explicitly gendered standards, but how much moral criticism they face, and how much damage this does to their moral reputation, in relation to male counterparts.

Many on the left vehemently insisted they were not biased against Clinton. But they were nevertheless convinced she was corrupt, conniving, greedy, entitled, and callous. One contributor to the *Huffington Post*, who characterized himself as a Bernie Sanders supporter and small-town blogger who likes Ellie Goulding (a signal of being moderately hip, I'd hazard) wrote about losing a female friend over the election. This friend accused him of being prejudiced against Hillary. He demurs, "The exact reason she felt this way was never made clear . . . when I choose not to support a candidate, I try to have very good reasons for that decision." To wit, Clinton's "seemingly insatiable greed;" her unproven but much speculated-about corruption, such that there must be *some* truth to it, he reasons (there doesn't seem to have been; see, e.g., Abramson 2016); and her hypocrisy, as evinced by her "apparent thirst for blood, even at the risk of killing children whom she claims to care about."[21]

In other words, Clinton was held to be more entitled than Sandra Fluke, and more bloodthirsty and callous than Newman's murdering mothers. A salutary push for sweeping economic and structural reform began to sound increasingly Manichean, individualistic, and accusatory as the primary season wore on—with some Sanders supporters calling to "bern the witch," viz., Hillary, in America. They were

---

21. Jason Fuller, "Hillary Clinton May Have Experience but She Lacks Judgment," *Huffington Post*, April 14, 2016, http://www.huffingtonpost.com/jason-fuller2/it-is-not-sexist-to-say-h_b_9699060.html.

thereby unwittingly echoing the chants recently audible in Australia, which (as we saw in this chapter) dogged Julia Gillard during her brief time in office as prime minister. This was among several striking parallels in the misogynistic invective and moralistic suspicion both women encountered, as well as the sheer volume of the latter, which I'll discuss in the final chapter. Meanwhile, the rest of the story is recent history: as Clinton went down in flames, Trump ascended to the White House.

Chapter 4

Taking His (Out)

I am ashamed that women are so simple
To offer war where they should kneel for peace;

Or seek for rule, supremacy and sway,
When they are bound to serve, love, and obey.

Kate, in Shakespeare, The Taming of the Shrew, Act V, Scene II

MISOGYNY AND ENTITLEMENT

In Elliot Rodger's video confession, he emphasized his sense of the *unfairness* of it all—the lack of a "hot woman" to give him affection, attention, admiration, sex, love, and to confer on him a higher social status among his cohort. His sense of entitlement was illicit from a moral point of view, of course. But it's also hardly unheard of among men, including young men like Rodger, in contemporary America (and likely far beyond that—but I'll leave that to others to consider). This was one reason why Rodger's words (from chapter 1) were disturbing to many women: it wasn't that they were so shocking, considered on their own. Indeed, quite the opposite. It's that they sounded so familiar— which, in light of Rodger's subsequent actions, was a grim realization.

Some men, especially those with a high degree of privilege, seem to have a sense of being *owed* by women in the coin of the associated personal goods and services that I canvass in this chapter. I won't take a stand on how common this is, in some form or other, beyond claiming (on the basis of the discussion in this chapter and ensuing ones, which I summarize in the conclusion) that it (a) remains a genuine problem in many allegedly post-patriarchal contexts, partly because

(b) it is considerably more common on the part of men toward women than vice versa, all else equal. But my main aim in what follows is to explore the contours of these relations. For if patriarchy is anything here and now, that is, in cultures such as the United States, the United Kingdom, and Australia, I believe it consists largely (though by no means exclusively) in this uneven, gendered economy of *giving and taking* moral-cum-social goods and services.[1]

Consider then that the flipside of an entitlement is, in general, an obligation: something he's *owed* by someone. So, if a man does indeed have this illicit sense of entitlement vis-à-vis women, he will be prone to hold women to false or spurious obligations. And he may also be prone to regard a woman's *asking* for the sorts of goods she's supposed to provide *him* with as an outrage, or a disgrace. This would be analogous to the waitress (from chapter 1) asking for service from her customer, after having failed to take his order. Not only is it a role reversal, but it's likely to prompt a "who does she *think* she is?" kind of sentiment: at first resentful, then scandalized, if she doesn't respond to feedback by looking duly chastened and "lifting her game," so to speak. There's something especially vexing about someone who is shameless not only in shirking their duties, but who appears blithe and unapologetic when they effectively turn the tables. They're not only failing to do their job; they're demanding that others return the non-favor—or asking them to do *their* job for them. They're feckless, careless, irresponsible, and so on.

Notice that this jives neatly with Rush Limbaugh's narrative about Sandra Fluke. Ostensibly, Limbaugh held that she'd be obligated to supply him and his listeners with sexual services in return for their hard-earned money (i.e., their tax dollars), if her contraceptive pill prescription was covered under health insurance. But of course, Limbaugh didn't mean his remarks to be taken literally. What he was offering was, in effect, a kind of reductio ad absurdum argument. Fluke shouldn't have to give them sex, presumably. So they shouldn't have to give her any of "their" money.

1. Cf. Pateman (1988), esp. chap. 6.

It's a terrible argument, even as these things go: it rests on twisting the logic of property and taxation beyond all recognition. (Not to mention betraying double standards, given that Viagra—for instance—is covered, as has been widely noted; then there is the fact that liberal women pay their taxes too.) But what interests me here is the mind-set it betrays. And this not as a psychological matter (Limbaugh might, for all we know, have been acting, i.e., giving a cynical performance), but in betraying a sense of *who owns what*, socially, and who is entitled to whose person—not only their bodies but also their *minds*, in their capacity for choice, volition, and agency. Who is assumed to have first dibs on the benefits of her attention, in having her orient toward him, and making him her *priority*? As the choice of pronouns might suggest, some subset of men, especially those who enjoy a comparatively high degree of power and privilege, seem to have this proprietary sense when it comes to women much more so than vice versa, in many domains, as will have emerged clearly by the book's conclusion. And when this sense is challenged, thwarted, violated, or threatened, this is often the trigger for misogyny toward her—or, in some cases, violence against male rivals who have trespassed on his supposed property. He might also seize what he thinks he is owed by her: that is, what he is supposed to have been *given* by a woman, and what is then supposed to be his for the taking.

A crucial complication in all of this, which the cases of Rodger and Limbaugh both bring out, is that there may be no *particular* woman to claim their supposedly rightful due from, or to blame for trying to cheat them out of it (again, according to the twisted logic of their misogyny). Instead, they each fashioned a narrative that draws a hazy, circuitous connection either between themselves (in Rodger's case) or on behalf of his listeners (in Limbaugh's). The end of the connection—and the story—is a representative woman to serve as a scapegoat for the resented absence. (Or, indeed, a double absence, for Rodger: a sin of omission committed by nobody in particular.)

Hence Rodger's need to find a woman of roughly the kind he viewed as cruelly depriving him; and she'd deprived him of *herself*, on the view behind his grievances. She didn't just overlook him; she'd been deliberately ignoring him. And she wasn't just oblivious: she was too stuck-up to notice. He didn't just feel invisible to her: she'd made him feel like *nothing*, a nonentity, less than a person.

And so he would treat her in kind—or, rather, pay her back double. He would *annihilate* her and her sorority sisters: a full house worth of testaments to the world's unfairness to him, and punishment for those within it who committed the "crime" (as he put it) of frustrating him.[2]

Notice how many women will *potentially* be subject to violence of this kind, even if the risk of this actually happening is rather low— Rodger's outburst being a particularly violent reaction to a common kind of grievance. But there may be lesser aversive consequences. Moreover, if someone roughly like you will do as a scapegoat or a target, then you join the class of those subject to an atypical kind of crime: an act of retaliation taken against you by a total stranger, yet who hunted you down, specifically (recalling the way Rodger stalked his victims). It is not irrational to find this unsettling.[3]

---

2. This is how Rodger frequently expressed himself in "My Twisted World," his "manifesto."

3. Cf. Steven Pinker's patronizing remarks following the Isla Vista killings. Recall his tweet, from chapter 1: "The idea that the UCSB murders are part of a pattern of hatred against women is statistically obtuse," linking to Heather Mac Donald's (2014) *National Review* piece, on June 1. The next day, Pinker tweeted that "the uncontrollability of disasters makes the world seem like a dangerous place, regardless of objective risk," linking to a piece by T. M. Luhrmann, "Our Flinching State of Mind," *New York Times*, May 31, 2014, https://www.nytimes.com/2014/06/01/opinion/sunday/luhrmann-our-flinching-state-of-mind.html. It's true that the statistical likelihood of Elliot Rodger's violent crime against women remains low, under one description, that is, multiple homicides by a stranger who stalked them. But under another description, it constituted a form of violence women fall prey to much more frequently and which usually receives little attention in the media: violence based on sexual jealousy and an attempt to control those women who reject men—or try to. For example, on an average day in the United States, there are between two and three intimate partner homicides, which are frequently committed for this reason.

WHAT SHE HAS TO GIVE

This idea of what women owe or ought to give: why does it persist? And what does it encompass, in addition to the goods and services just mentioned?

One reason it persists, I think, is that the goods are truly *valuable*: they are *genuinely* good and the lack thereof is bad. It is natural that people want them; some are even needed. Consider that, as well as affection, adoration, indulgence, and so on, such feminine-coded goods and services include simple respect, love, acceptance, nurturing, safety, security, and safe haven. There is kindness and compassion, moral attention, care, concern, and soothing. These forms of emotional and social labor go beyond the more tangible reproductive and domestic services that may be less expected of women, or else

---

In *Better Angels of Our Nature*, Pinker (2012) is more openly dismissive of feminist views about sexual and gendered violence. "We are all feminists now," he declares, prematurely. Left to his own devices, Pinker is nominally even-handed: "Though feminist agitation deserves credit for the measures that led to American rape decline," he allows, "feminists having muscled their way into power and rebalanced the instruments of government to serve their interest," it ultimately turns out to be mostly a kind of "A for effort" thing. For "the victories came quickly, did not require boycotts or martyrs, and [the activists] did not face police dogs or angry mobs." And when it came to sexual assault reforms, in particular, "the country was clearly ready for them," Pinker holds (403). Feminists merely hastened the inevitable happy ending. Progress was also made thanks to the men in power growing wise to the nuances of female sexuality: such as women's hitherto puzzling tendency "to find the prospect of abrupt, unsolicited sex with a stranger to be repugnant rather than appealing." (406) Although "rape is not exactly a normal part of male sexuality," it is not too far off either. Pinker:

> If I may be permitted an *ad feminam* suggestion, the theory that rape has nothing to do with sex may be more plausible to a gender to whom a desire for impersonal sex with an unwilling stranger is too bizarre to contemplate. Common sense never gets in the way of a sacred custom that has accompanied a decline of violence, and today rape centers unanimously insist that "rape or sexual assault is not an act of sex or lust—it's about aggression, power, and humiliation, using sex as a weapon. The rapist's goal is domination." (To which the journalist Heather MacDonald [*sic*] replies: "The guys who push themselves on women at keggers are after one thing only, and it's not a reinstatement of the patriarchy.") (406)

Here is Mac Donald again, serving as Pinker's antifeminist mouthpiece.

have become more evenly divided (respectively) in some heterosexual partnerships. The less tangible forms of work are still *work*; but they aren't "busy work" whose "ought-to-be-doneness" (to borrow a phrase from the moral philosopher J. L. Mackie) owes to capitalist ideology that misleads about what a good and meaningful human life must look like. Feminine-coded work does need doing—which is why it is never done, as the sexist proverb goes. And this is so not only in the home but also in the workplace, and not only in private but also in public spheres, and in many civic interactions, if they are to be civil.

So it's no surprise that this work is often safeguarded by moral sanctions and internalized as "to be done" by women. Then there's the threat of the withdrawal of social approval if these duties are not performed, and the incentive of love and gratitude if they are done willingly and gladly.[4]

And if women are not only tasked with doing more than their fair share but are also subject to more serious negative consequences for shirking their putative duties, then this of course compounds the problem. She will give, and he will take, in effect; or else she may be punished, when it comes to the relevant feminine-coded forms of caregiving labor (cf. Hochschild and Machung 1989 on the "second-shift problem").

The publicity of many of these sanctions further serves to enforce this gendered economy of moral and social labor. In other words, misogyny directed toward one woman in public life may serve as a warning to others not to follow her lead, or even to publicly lend their support to her. Women's support may also be jealously guarded and hoarded for men's benefit. This, together with norms of loyalty, may make a woman's showing solidarity with misogyny's victims dangerous: more on this in the final chapter.

---

4. It's helpful to distinguish three possibilities here: men (a) actually doing less of this work than female intimate partners with whom they cohabit, (b) being subject to less stringent norms and expectations in this regard, and/or (c) being subject to less hefty social penalties for comparable negligence or irresponsibility.

What if she takes, though? And what if she asks? We need to divide in order to conquer this question. The answer will depend on whether she asks for or tries to take what's designated:

(i)   *Hers to give to him* (i.e., a "take back" operation on her part); or
(ii) *His to give to her* without her giving him (or at least offering) the reciprocal goods and services that social norms ask her to provide him with; or
(iii) *His alone for the taking* (in competition with other men), historically.

Here then, is the norm to which a woman would be subject in virtue of (i): don't ask for or take the kind of thing you're meant to be *giving*, either to him or to society. This is particularly untoward if you're already in his debt, and perhaps even if he has been short-changed by other women, or unlucky in life in general.

And here's the norm for women that would hold in virtue of (ii) above: don't ask for the kind of goods or services that *he* once might have provided—money, chivalry, or purported chivalry (which is sometimes no more than basic consideration)—when the sorts of goods women gave in return were less contested and more available. "The deal is off, sweetheart," will then often be the message. This was essentially what was at stake in Limbaugh's Sandra Fluke diatribe.[5]

---

5. From a community member's forum post on the *Return of Kings* blog, "How to Spot a Girl Who Is a Giver and Not Just a Taker."

> I have finally come to understand my primary discontent with American women: they are mostly Takers. They take your attention, they take your time, they take your validation, they take your money, and they also take your dick. And what do they give in return? (As one latin [*sic*] girl told me) The pleasure of their company.
>
> When was the last time some girl you know gave you a massage or cooked you a meal? When was the last time a girl did something for you that didn't have any benefit for her? When was the last time a girl did something for you when you hadn't done anything for her and she wasn't expecting something in return? When was the last time a girl actually gave you something without you first giving her something? . . .

Finally, the norm to which women are subject to which I'll now turn, which holds in virtue of (iii): don't ask for or try to take masculine-coded perks and privileges, at least as long as he desires them. And, even if *he* doesn't, third parties may be outraged on his behalf by her apparent attempt to usurp him.

HIS FOR THE TAKING

What are the masculine-coded perks and privileges in question? These include social positions of leadership, authority, influence, money, and other forms of power, as well as social status, prestige, rank, and the markers thereof. Then there are less tangible facets of social "face," pride, reputation, or standing, and the relevant *absences*—for example, the freedom from shame and lack of public humiliation, which are more or less universally desired but only some people feel entitled to.

Many masculine-coded goods are in more or less short supply, even if they don't necessarily have a zero-sum structure: for example, power, prestige, money, rank, and competitive advantage. But also important in this category are masculine pride, reputation, respect, and so on. Such social goods and statuses are not *inherently* limited in supply; nor are they constrained even in theory. But they may become so when testimonial *clashes* or disagreements impose limits

. . . So this is the test: do something for a girl or give her something. It could just be a few drinks, dinner, you help her review some paper etc. If she can't thank you sincerely and mean it you won't be getting much of anything from this girl: she's a taker and not a giver. It's that simple! . . .

. . . A giver is not only important for a decent relationship but they are also the girls I like best in bed. A giver in bed will be more concerned about your pleasure. A taker will be ONLY concerned about her own and that is how most American girls are in bed. I can tell you from a lot of personal experience you DO NOT want to get involved emotionally with a girl that is not a giver. You will end up regretting it.

Nomad77, *RooshVForum*, September 27, 2014, https://www.rooshvforum.com/thread-40795.html.

on how many people can be taken to be both sincere and credible simultaneously.[6]

The norm that women not compete for or deprive men of masculine-coded goods that he wants, cost him his manly pride, and so on, are further common sources of misogynist aggression when violated. Even if the goods themselves are not especially sought after, he may be ashamed or humiliated to have lost them to a woman. I will return to this theme in chapter 8, in relation to the biases that show up when a man competes with a woman for masculine-coded power positions. There is also the fact that—as we will see—third-personal preferences and sanctions have a powerful social influence, beyond second-personal reactive attitudes and the actions that express them.

Having given this rough and partial sketch of a theory of the substantive workings of misogyny, via a gendered economy of moral labor, we can make some concrete (and, importantly, falsifiable) predictions on this basis. They would doubtless need a lot more nuance and finesse to capture differences between different milieux, subcultures, particular social relations, and so on. And I don't want to suggest that there's nothing beyond these norms—there may well be, and I note some other vestiges of patriarchal social structures in subsequent chapters. But, in a way, given my present aims, the less said here the better. The more I can generate accurate predictions using the above norms (i)–(iii), the more this will help to show that the picture has the predictive and explanatory power that should sell it.

Although I'm interested in the shape of the phenomenon more than its prevalence, it may be helpful to state for the record: my own view in general is that misogyny remains prevalent in many of the contexts on which I focus, though it's true that much social progress has been made. But I also believe that social progress has been

6. I discuss this point at length in chapter 6, and show how testimonial injustice serves to protect dominant men from being deprived of such masculine-coded "face" by women, all else being equal (i.e., given the relevant intersectional considerations).

patchy and nonlinear. And the norm (again, sporadically but some-times stringently enforced for that reason), that *she gives feminine-coded goods to him*, and *refrains from taking masculine-coded goods away from him*, continues to have a significant impact. Or so I'm inclined to think, as a working hypothesis, partly on the basis of its ability to predict and explain the following:

> *Right-wing women (an anti-prediction).* The model predicts that women's power will be better tolerated when it's wielded in service of patriarchal interests, for example, conserva-tive and right-wing "family-oriented" political movements. This is plausibly borne out by the last several decades of women on the right faring comparatively well in politics in positions of leadership: consider, for example, Phyllis Schlafly, Margaret Thatcher, and, at least for a time, Sarah Palin and Pauline Hanson, in Australia.[7]
>
> *Cat-calling.* The model suggests viewing this practice as a male bid for women's attention, which she is held to owe him (falsely). And he may also evince his sense of (again, illicit) entitlement to openly rank her in terms of her attractiveness and thus social status–conferring value. In other cases, this bid for her attention is more focused on her mind not being allowed to be (a) turned inward (such that she is thinking her own thoughts), (b) withheld from him via her putting up emotional "walls" (which tends to garner an epithet in the "bitch" family—is my anecdotal impression), or (c) averse to the attention that he foists on her boisterously and sometimes aggressively or threateningly. She *must* like it really, is a common reaction on the part of the catcaller. And she may be required to look "open" or "transparent."[8] "Smile, sweetheart"

---

7. See Dworkin (1988).

8. Cf. the recent *This American Life* episode on catcalling for the evidence it pro-vided of the phenomenon of men's rewriting women's minds, notwithstanding their explicit stated feelings and preferences. Eleanor Gordon-Smith, "Hollaback Girl," *This American Life*, Episode 603: "Once More with Feeling," December 2, 2016, https://www.thisamericanlife.org/radio-archives/episode/603/once-more-with-feeling?act=1.

is an ostensibly less offensive remark, but it is expressive of the same insidious demand that a woman's face be emotionally legible. The comparative rarity of social practices where the gender tables are reversed is instructive here, for anyone doubtful about their patriarchal nature or social meaning. The issue is not just the harm they do (which is variable), but also the underlying sense of who owes what to whom, and who may demand it, which they betray and perpetuate.[9]

Shame and the Citadel. In Susan Faludi's (2000) treatment of the previously all-male Citadel, the military college in South Carolina, the male cadets were highly averse to—indeed furious about—the idea of admitting a female cadet. For, her admission robbed them of their privacy and subsequent freedom from the risk of humiliation and shame in women's eyes—given the hazing rituals and intense competition between them, among other things. They treated this student so poorly that she only lasted a week there.

Of particular significance to the male cadets was the prospect of (a) being dressed down by the higher-ranking cadets in her presence, (b) having to do feminine-coded domestic work when she was around to do it instead, and (c) their not only breaking down and crying in front of her, but also comforting each other, as was apparently common—and done tenderly, between bouts of brutal bullying.

So her presence within those walls stood to deprive the male cadets of that to which they felt entitled, in the form of a guarantee against winding up *shame faced* in her eyes.[10]

"The absence of women makes us understand them better. In

---

9. Consider the "slut" epithet—which means, roughly, someone who gives her attention away to too many men, the wrong ones, thereby cheating *him* out of it, as its supposedly rightful recipient. This may be more or less reflective of social reality, as opposed to being based on a momentary, semiscripted social flight of fancy—or, a kind of involuntary role play.

10. Cf. the "LA Pussy posse," which Faludi compares to the Citadel in the same chapter in *Stiffed* (2000, chapter 3). Here, having sex with a new girl was a point-scoring game, adding a notch in the bedpost, with fame and notoriety being the ultimate

an aesthetic kind of way, we appreciate them more because they are not here," explained Senior regimental commander, Norman Doucet, to Faludi (2000, 114).

So, despite the waning of many obviously patriarchal social structures, we can see how male dominance may persist in these sorts of interactions and practices. In view of differential norms of giving, a woman may be held to owe characteristically feminine-coded goods to some man, ideally, or at least to society; and a man may be held to be entitled to lay claim to them from some women. Moreover, if he is not given his due, he may then be permitted to *take* such goods, that is, to forcibly seize them from her with impunity, as we'll see in chapter 6. And, inasmuch as there are differential norms of *taking* as well as giving, women may be effectively prohibited from competing with him for, or otherwise robbing him of, certain masculine-coded prizes; and he may also be deemed entitled to *prevent* her from so doing. Finally, to the extent to which she tries to or successfully beats the boys "at their own game" (as it were), she may be held to have cheated, or to have stolen something from him.

And so she has, in a way. It's just that she would have "stolen" historically ill-gotten gains, not his rightful property. She may well be entitled to do precisely what she is doing. Perhaps she is even *obligated* to do it, or at least doing something valuable, by taking that to which men have unfairly had exclusive access, historically. But although many people would agree with this, at a rational level, our moral perceptions and habits of attention often lag well behind our moral principles. This is understandable and, on its own, often forgivable. But we can, and we must, make appropriate adjustments—and not give our gendered social instincts too much credit in light of their likely causal bases. I return to this point in chapter 8, after looking at what happened to America's most wanted woman in proportion to her misdeeds: Hillary Clinton.

aim of the exercise. These are, interestingly, two halves of Donald Trump's persona and history of misogyny. Whereas Faludi bills them as different kinds of masculinity, they may just be different *modes*, which come to the fore in different contexts. One is analogous to closed, private training sessions; the other is the subsequent public game, playing to fans, before an audience.

It behooves us now to ask: When such norms of (her) giving and (his) taking are operative, what if a woman doesn't have an exclusive relationship with a male intimate partner who may lay claim to her feminine-coded goods and services? What if she is in a lesbian relationship, for example, or single, or partnered but child-free, or polyamorous (Jenkins 2017)? An initial observation to make here is that there may be variably strong associated pressures governing relationships that are heteronormative and help to uphold white supremacy too, which intersect with patriarchal ones to produce distinctively anti-LGBTQ forms of misogyny. They may also intersect with norms governing virtue and character, which often encourage a woman to direct her energy and attention *outward* rather than inward toward her own "personal projects," to take a notion from Bernard Williams (1981). The same goes for social preferences that may (again, noting wide variation, and my intention of merely listing possibilities here, rather than making empirical claims beyond my pay grade) reward her for attending to men rather than women, one person rather than many, and racially privileged men who express or harbor a desire for her favor. Otherwise, she may be condemned as, for example, selfish or narcissistic, subject to homophobic and anti-poly bigotry, or a "race traitor," among other things. In addition to this, there tend to be stringent requirements to give others every reason to believe in her sincerity and honesty, on the one hand, and her loyalty or devotion, on the other. Misogyny tends to punish failures not only to demonstrate the "openness" or legibility of her mind, but also the constancy of her intentions or the strength of her resolve to keep her promises. So far from being verboten, this suggests that women's power, strength, and agency may be highly valued, when she is standing behind a great man as the "great woman" in the background.[11]

11. Reciprocal obligations of the same nature running in the other direction, from men to women, within het relationships, will be patchier by the lights of this dynamic of misogyny, considered just on its own. They may certainly be part of the ethos of particular relationships, and enshrined in more or less local mores. But there will almost invariably be general obligations that run in this direction with *other* kinds of contents in a patriarchal order—for example, the relationship of a breadwinner to a homemaker, for the most obvious example.

Norms of genuineness *and* loyalty can be seen to be important here for closely related reasons. One is that they ensure some of the goods above *actually count as such*. Kindness is not kindness, if it doesn't come from having the beneficiary's best interests at heart, as one of its main motivating factors. Love is arguably not love if it is too fickle or too variable. Moreover, such norms prevent her from having as much power as she would have otherwise, that is, if she was free(r) to leave him. Finally, and relatedly, these norms provide reassurance that she can be allowed to get close to him without undermining him or preventing him from pursuing further masculine-coded privileges. She is a source of support, then, not a rival. A certain power differential, with him having more of it, may satisfy the same purposes—and not necessarily by his design, if the law is enforced in ways reflective of such biases.

Given the aim of preventing women from depriving dominant men of masculine-coded goods, or even threatening to do so, norms of constancy and loyalty will also be important in this connection. He needs to be assured that she means what she says. And he needs to know that she won't suddenly change her mind, and form new and threatening intentions, with no warning—to leave him, for example, or to humiliate him via "cuckolding."[12]

---

12. Cf. the controversy that sparked what became known as "Gamergate": Zoë Quinn, an indie game designer, was falsely accused in a blog post written by her exboyfriend of trading sexual favors to a video game journalist in exchange for a positive review of her game, *Depression Quest*. By the lights of "the Zoë post," the case hence involved a double dose of (supposed) disloyalty, untrustworthiness, and "feminine wiles." Moreover, Quinn had outdone many male game designers in getting a moderately positive review of her game on the website (written by another journalist, independently of the aforementioned brief relationship). This "beating the boys at their own game" *and* infiltration of a highly male-dominated subculture would have been a perfect storm of factors to elicit a disproportionately strong, intense, and prolonged misogynistic reaction from members of the gaming community, according to my analysis—which it did indeed. The details surrounding Gamergate up to that point and beyond are complex and still liable to provoke debate. So I will quote from Matt Lees' recent précis in *The Guardian* of what was primarily at issue:

> Gamergate was an online movement that effectively began because a man wanted to punish his ex girlfriend. Its most notable achievement was harassing a large number of progressive figures—mostly women— to the point where they felt unsafe or considered leaving the industry.

So she *herself* may constitute a feminine-coded good, on this way of looking at things.[13] This is borne out vividly by the statistics on intimate partner violence: if she leaves, thus threatening to deprive him of her person and sometimes his children too, the risk of intimate partner homicide skyrockets.[14]

It is also borne out by the phenomenon of family annihilators, and the sense of entitled shame they manifest, as the following disturbing case study is intended to illustrate. To anticipate: what's "his

> Game developer Zoë Quinn was the original target. Anita Sarkeesian's videos applying basic feminist theory to video games had already made her a target (because so many people have difficulty differentiating cultural criticism from censorship) but this hate was powerfully amplified by Gamergate—leading to death threats, rape threats, and the public leaking of personal information.

Matt Lees, "What Gamergate Should Have Taught Us about the 'Alt-Right,'" *The Guardian*, December 1, 2016, https://www.theguardian.com/technology/2016/dec/01/gamergate-alt-right-hate-trump.

As Lee and others argue, Gamergate played an important role in the development of the alt-right movement, via none other than Steve Bannon and his news website, Breitbart. Lees continues:

> The similarities between Gamergate and the far-right online movement, the "alt-right," are huge, startling and in no way a coincidence. After all, the culture war that began in games now has a senior representative in the White House. As a founding member and former executive chair of Brietbart News, Steve Bannon had a hand in creating media monster Milo Yiannopoulos, who built his fame and Twitter following by supporting and cheerleading Gamergate. This hashtag was the canary in the coalmine, and we ignored it.

I also consider this case in relation to testimonial injustice and male dominance in chapter 6 here.

13. This also sheds further light on the moral panic over abortion and the prochoice position (as discussed in chapter 3)—the notion of a woman selfishly or wantonly withholding reproductive and caregiving labor (having been led astray), as well as evicting fetuses from their rightful home or safe haven. Meanwhile, brown bodies may be exploited to teach all women a lesson. For example, in Indiana, when it came to self-induced abortions and the laws against feticide, these appear to have been enforced in ways that targeted Asian American women, as in Purvi Patel's case.

14. The risk of being murdered by a former intimate partner is higher during the two weeks after a woman leaves the relationship than at any other point by a factor of around seventy, according to some estimates. See, for example, "Domestic Violence Statistics," http://domesticviolencehomicidehelp.com/statistics/ (accessed May 12, 2017).

for the taking" may include the lives of his female partner and their children, when the alternative is to wind up shame-faced in their eyes, and then watch them move on without looking up to him.

TAKING LIVES: SHAME AND FAMILY ANNIHILATORS

It's often said that misogyny is a manifestation of shame, most obviously when perpetrated by individual men, but perhaps even going beyond that. And that could theoretically make for a basis for empathy or solidarity between the perpetrators and the victims. Misogynistic attacks frequently instill a sense of shame in their victims, partly via disgust-based "smearing" mechanisms, as chapter 8 discusses. Nor are such reactions necessarily irrational: shaming has social meaning. It characteristically results in a desire to sever the sightlines between the self and the other. We talk about wanting to hide our faces and the characteristic look of shame—the head bowed, the eyes lowered. But that's not the only way of achieving such separation. Rather than hide, one can instead do away with the onlooker. "He who is ashamed would like to force the world not to look at him, not to notice his exposure. He would like to destroy the eyes of the world," as Erik Erikson famously put it (1963, 227). The masculine gender pronoun here may, unwittingly, be telling.

For, the shame felt by the victims of misogyny (among other forms of oppression) seems to me to differ in precisely this dimension from that of at least the most entitled perpetrators. The former is the ordinary shame of those who weren't counting on *not* being made to feel it (or at least, not via this form of humiliation). And it will tend to manifest itself in a disposition to try to hide or flee from exposure, rather than wanting to "destroy the eyes" of others. It is the latter, entitled sense of shame that results in such proclivities for destruction. And it will often be provoked by the prospect or advent of social humiliation. Entitled shame will be my focus in this section, via one of its most vivid manifestations: family annihilators. As will emerge, this phenomenon shows us something important about the proprietary relationship of certain patriarchs to their female partners and children.

Family annihilators have been distinguished from other kinds of mass murderers, and begun to be studied, only recently. One such was Chris Foster, a British man who invented a kind of safety valve to use in drilling on an oil rig. The valve was the greatest valve. He made a huge amount of money. He bought a fleet of luxury cars and a mansion in Shropshire, into which he installed his wife, Jill, and his daughter, Kirstie. He had affairs with many women—having a thing for blondes, apparently—but his wife put up with it. He wasn't a good-looking man. But his money gave him confidence, according to his sister-in-law, quoted in a story by the writer Jon Ronson.[15]

Foster had a large collection of guns and belonged to a clay-pigeon shooting club. The other men who were members knew him as a loving husband and affectionate father. He went shooting at a barbecue there one ostensibly unremarkable afternoon. That night, at home, he shot his wife and daughter in the back of their heads, killing them. He set fire to all his possessions, and his mansion, on which he'd poured oil. Then he committed suicide as blazed his last bonfire.

Does it surprise you to learn the reason? I would hazard that it doesn't. He had gone bankrupt after a series of bad business decisions. He was going to lose everything. The possessions he burned were due to be repossessed the next day by the bailiffs.

Trying to understand his crime, Ronson found it mysterious until the moment he didn't, and its logic clicked into focus. Sitting in the well-appointed kitchen of a friend of Chris's, Ian, outside the beautiful, well-manicured town of Maesbrook, which Chris and other self-made millionaires had populated, Ronson realizes not only why Chris did it, but why he did it in the way in which he did. Ronson:

> As I sit in Ian's kitchen, it suddenly makes sense to me that Chris
> Foster would choose to shoot Jill and Kirstie in the back of their

15. Jon Ronson, "I've Thought about Doing Myself in Loads of Times . . ." *The Guardian*, November 21, 2008, https://www.theguardian.com/uk/2008/nov/22/christopher-foster-news-crime.

heads. It was as if he was too ashamed to look at them. Maybe the murders were a type of honour killing, as if Foster simply couldn't bear the idea of losing their respect and the respect of his friends. (2008)

Many of Chris's friends also found his behavior—not only taking his own life, but the lives of his family members—quite intelligible. Ronson:

> It's startling to hear Foster's friends talk about how they empathise with his actions. I wouldn't have guessed how on the edge people in this Shropshire enclave can be, and how easy it is—when lives start to go wrong, when their manhood and the trappings of their wealth are threatened—for the whole thing just to unravel. (2008)

Unraveling is one word for it: and notice who it places at the center of the story.

Less than a month after Foster's crime, another family annihilator struck in Southampton: he telephoned his estranged partner to tell her that their children had "gone to sleep forever." Having smothered them, he hanged himself.[16]

According to the criminologist David Wilson, quoted in Ronson's article, family annihilators are distinctive among murderers in typically being previously unknown to the criminal justice system—or even to mental health services. Wilson explained to journalist Katie Collins:

---

16. As Ronson pointed out, family annihilators are common in the United States as well: he cites studies showing that a family killing, and husband's subsequent suicide, occurs here once a week, on average (2008). Later research by Jack Levin suggests the rates may have increased in the months following the recession—strikingly, since correlations between unemployment and increased homicide rates are not found across the board. Catharine Skipp, "Inside the Mind of Family Annihilators," *Newsweek*, February 10, 2010, http://www.newsweek.com/inside-mind-family-annihilators-75225.

For all intents and purposes these were loving husbands and good fathers, often holding down high profile jobs and seen publicly as being very, very successful.[17]

Wilson and other researchers have come to distinguish four main types of family annihilators: *self-righteous, anomic, disappointed*, and *paranoid*. The self-righteous type blames others, often their wives or estranged wives, for their downfall. The anomic type feels humiliated by external events like bankruptcy. The disappointed type feels let down by his family, as if the social order is crumbling. The paranoid type feels his kin are under threat from outsiders. So, to stave off the threat, he takes it upon himself to murder them.

One suspects that these profiles are not mutually exclusive. And each evinces a different aspect of the kind of masculinity that is aptly called toxic, in being prone to lash out violently when threatened or humiliated. Wilson told Collins:

> It's clear that it is men that usually resort to this type of violence, and these four characteristics are closely related to a man's ideas about gender roles and his place within the family. There are a variety of ways for men to be men, but what really is happening with family annihilation is that these are usually men who will reach a tipping point about various things within the particular category of family annihilator that we identify. To see it simply [as being] about women having a greater role [in modern society] might be trying to imply the woman is responsible, whereas in fact it's always about the man. (2013)

This point of caution is well taken. Still, it may be about the man's inability to *cope* with the woman's increasing social status. And, as many of these quotes from Wilson all but imply, family annihilators are almost exclusively in het ("straight") relationships, not queer

---

17. Katie Collins, "Family Killers Are Usually Men and Fit One of Four Distinct Profiles," *Wired*, August 16, 2013, http://www.wired.co.uk/article/family-killers.

ones. This, too, is suggestive regarding the nature of the existential threat to his identity.

Neil Websdale, author of *Familicidal Hearts* (2010), has reached similar conclusions about the typical profile of family annihilators in the US context. Journalist Catharine Skipp summarizes Websdale's findings as follows:

> Annihilators are overwhelmingly male (95 percent, he estimates), and mostly white and middle-aged. They feel inadequate as men and have often suffered childhood abuse. Having felt powerless as kids, many try to exert strict control over their households and seek to create an idealized version of family that they never experienced. When the economy is in decline, jobs are scarce, tensions are high, and the control these men seek becomes harder to maintain.
>
> According to Websdale, these men fall along a continuum between what he calls "livid coercive" killers and "civil reputable" ones. The former are driven by rage: they are controlling and sometimes abusive figures who derive self-worth from the authority they exert at home. But that behavior typically plunges the marriage into crisis, often prompting the wife and children to try to leave. The resulting lack of control triggers feelings of humiliation, eventually leading the father to reassert his power in a final paroxysm of violence (Skipp 2010).

The latter kind of family annihilator—the "civil reputable" type—is driven by a sense of "narcissistic chivalry," according to Richard Gelles, another leading researcher here. This is evident in the trigger for such murders, their motive, and their nature. Gelles told Skipp:

> The father is almost always considering suicide as the only escape from some sort of financial crisis. Murdering his family members, then, becomes a way of rescuing them from the hardship and shame of bankruptcy and suicide.
>
> This narcissistic sense of chivalry is evident in the way many of these perpetrators execute their victims. The professional

wrestler Chris Benoit, who murdered his wife and son and then hanged himself in 2007, is believed to have sedated the boy before strangling him. (2010)

Most family annihilators (over 80 percent of them) also attempt suicide after committing their murders (Collins 2013). But this doesn't seem likely to be the same kind of suicidality that can result from an ordinary but chronic sense of shame. The underlying motive can't be to hide from the other, because the other's eyes have already been closed—forever.

Some family annihilators may be driven to it because they now lack a sense not only of self-esteem but selfhood simpliciter; (Richard Gelles: "His entire identity is in his family"; Skipp 2010). Releasing the escape valve from shame leaves him relieved, but lonely, devoid of purpose. His murders remove the unbearable pressure but also the point of his being. He is no longer humiliated; but he has lost the others whose admiration felt like an existential necessity. It *was* an existential necessity, when it came down to it. He made it so.

How does all this bear on the contemporary US political scene? It might be argued that family annihilators are on the most extreme end of a spectrum of toxic masculinity on which Donald Trump and Steve Bannon also sit—that there is ultimately a difference in degree, rather than kind, here. I won't speculate about this possibility (cf. Hurt 1993; loc. 4236, 5631). The point I want to take from the discussion in this context is the vivid picture of entitled shame it offers us. Witness Trump's fomenting of an entitled desire for freedom from the shaming gaze of the other, for example, Mexicans and Muslims, who would be walled out and screened off, respectively, in Trump's envisaged America. (Cf. my notion of melancholy whiteness; Manne forthcoming.) One no longer has to feel ashamed of turning away from those in need—a boon for those suffering from what is somewhat euphemistically known as "sympathy fatigue." There is equally if not more so a yen to stave off the shaming gaze of the elite liberal insider, who espouses antiracism, feminism, and other forms of that most hated of credos, political correctness. (*Lock her up*. Contain her. Sever the sightlines. Prevent her ascendency.)

So-called political correctness—I was immediately inclined to say. And so, for that very reason, you can see something of what may have been incensing Trump's supporters, once ignited. Our acts are acts of political *correction*. They often commit us, whether we like it or not, to taking the moral high ground, however uncomfortably. We can talk about loving the sinner and hating the sin. But how do we love those who hate us so badly?

I found it hard to know what to say to the Trump supporter during the lead-up to his election—the people Clinton held were either to be pitied or lumped into the "basket of deplorables," their being "irredeemable." (This being an impolitic moment on her part, for which she later apologized.) The implication was that she looked down on all of them. That seemed to many, me included, to be clearly the wrong stance. But what would be the right one? I return to this question over the course of the conclusion.

Whatever the case, those whose racism and misogyny we take it on ourselves to denounce can hardly be counted on to thank us for a moral epiphany that never arrives. And they will often become defensive, resentful, and more entrenched in their attitudes than ever—and wind up caught between feeling shame-faced and silenced. Of course, as I've just shown, there are some escape valves.

I've heard the same theory now from several different journalists about the moment they think Trump decided to run for president. It was when President Obama humiliated him at the White House correspondents' dinner in 2011, by responding to Trump's laughably transparent as well as offensive demand that Obama produce his birth certificate (where are you from, *really*? The racist's perennial question). Obama magnanimously said in his speech he'd go one better: he'd release his birth *video*. He rolled a clip from the Lion King. The guests erupted in laughter.

Except one guest, apparently. He jutted out his chin, pursed his lips, and turned a deeper shade of orange—as audience members looked gleefully in Trump's direction, then away again. When I heard that description by the *New Yorker*'s David Remnick, I wondered, is that really the face of shame? I tried to conjure to mind Paul Ekman's iconic black-and-white photos of universal emotion expressions from my old psychology textbook. I wondered about Trump in comparison with the shame of an Elliot Rodger.

But then I realized that Trump's was the face of shame turned inside out—its exterior wall, as it were—shame refused, with fury substituted, since he and his ilk are accustomed to being treated with the greatest respect on all occasions. It was the face of someone who fully expects and feels entitled to the admiring gaze of others positioned beneath him, looking upward. And, in consequence of this, with the addition of narcissism, they need this. Trump's was the face Elliot Rodger might have had with more social luck, had he managed to be the true alpha male he claimed to be. But he wasn't; and so, he moved to take down other people.

LOOKING AHEAD

In chapter 2, I proposed a general constitutive account of misogyny, which tells us what it *is*, as a property of social environments. Namely, a social environment counts as misogynistic for a specific subset of girls and women therein inasmuch as they face hostility of a kind that serves to police and enforce gendered norms and expectations within a historically and to some extent currently patriarchal order. Similarly, an action is misogynistic inasmuch as it is a product of, or conducive to, a social environment's misogyny. I also argued that the Isla Vista killings were an obvious case in point—even if they have other meanings too, which isn't in dispute, and in no way cuts against this.

This discharged one of the two questions about the feminist response to Isla Vista that was controversial in the aftermath. But it left the other one unanswered: namely, is the United States in particular a *culture* of misogyny? If so, how might Elliot Rodger have come to channel the relevant social forces? (I.e., what *mechanisms* serve to perpetuate misogyny, regardless of the details of his particular psychology or life story?)

After the 2016 US presidential election, it seems clear that fewer people would deny that there's misogyny in the water here, as it emerged from the depths and rose vividly to the surface. But I think it's also fair to say it has remained a murky and puzzling phenomenon, even for those who changed their minds, having been shocked by the campaign and the outcome in November. How can we reconcile the prevalence of misogyny in the United States today with the fact that women *do* have more power and opportunity here than virtually ever before, historically? (Cf. Mac Donald 2014) My hope is that the give/take model proposed in this chapter suggests a plausible answer.

The model also sheds light on the worry that the cases feminists refer to using the term "misogyny" encompass a messy ragbag of splashy, headline-making episodes. If that was right, then it would consign my ameliorative project to either sharing the mess, or cleaning it up at the expense of capturing feminist usage patterns. For, to summarize, misogyny seems to encompass:

- Highly variable harms (from minor to murder; and comprising a wide variety of kinds of verbal and physical attacks);
- A wide variety of moods and modes in the general family of hostility. Common themes thus far and looking forward include revenge; Strawsonian "reactive attitudes" (e.g., blame, resentment, guilt); punishment; betrayal; mistrust; hierarchical jostling; and various forms of shaming, disgusted, and "ousting" behavior;
- Policing and enforcement practices in myriad domains, including sex; motherhood; men's hitherto proprietary spaces, positions, as well as historically old boys' clubs.

For all the apparent jumble, the give/take model offers a surprisingly simple way of unifying the phenomena, and produces a theory that makes good and concrete (and, importantly, falsifiable) predictions here, given the addition of the foregoing distinction between what is deemed

> *Hers to give (feminine-coded goods and services)*: attention, affection, admiration, sympathy, sex, and children (i.e., social, domestic, reproductive, and emotional labor); also mixed goods, such as safe haven, nurture, security, soothing, and comfort; versus
>
> *His for the taking (masculine-coded perks and privileges)*: power, prestige, public recognition, rank, reputation, honor, "face," respect, money and other forms of wealth, hierarchical status, upward mobility, and the status conferred by having a high-ranking woman's loyalty, love, devotion, etc.

Given this, it turns out that most of the cases of misogyny canvassed so far, and that will be canvassed in what follows, can be brought under the heading of one of the following two complementary social norms for women:

(1) She is *obligated* to give feminine-coded services to *someone* or other, preferably one man who is her social equal or better (by the lights of racist, classist, as well as heteronormative values, in many contexts), at least insofar as he *wants* such goods and services from her.

(2) She is *prohibited* from having or taking masculine-coded goods *away* from dominant men (at a minimum, and perhaps from others as well), insofar as he wants or aspires to receive or retain them.

Some natural corollaries:

- As noted in chapter 2, misogyny is what happens to police and enforce these social norms, as well as to protest their violation.

- For many of the relevant feminine-coded goods at least, a dominant man needs to be able to "read her mind" to be assured that the relevant personal services are *genuine*. Kindness is not kindness without good will toward the other as the primary motivation, for instance.
- He will also need to be assured of (a) her honesty, (b) her loyalty, and (c) her constancy to be assured of such goods as security, stability, and ongoing safe haven (again, for example). It's not a safe space for him, if she might already have one foot out the door, or loves him only conditionally on his worldly success, his good reputation, fame, or similar.
- He will often need power over her for a variety of *instrumental* purposes, as well as perhaps wanting various forms of it for its own sake—or not, as the case may be. (Again, this seems widely variable; some misogynistic agents do not want the responsibility that comes with certain social powers and privileges; as in the notion of a "man child.")[18]

And now, with the conceptual distinctions from this chapter in hand, we can distinguish the following further questions:

- What if *he* unceremoniously seizes what's meant to be *hers to give to him*? I will argue that we tend to forgive, forget, and exonerate the crimes of dominant men that take this form, and to extend sympathy to them rather than the women they victimize. (Chapter 6, "Exonerating Men," hence canvasses rape culture, as well as what I call "himpathy.")
- What if *she* asks for or tries to take what's meant to be *hers to give to him*? When she seeks feminine-coded goods, such as

18. Moreover, some practices seem to be more about taking the high ground over her (e.g., epistemically, as in mansplaining), or his sense of entitlement to occupy more physical space than her (as in "manspreading" on public transportation).

moral attention, or draws attention to her own moral injuries, I argue that we tend to suspect her of dishonesty and being self-dramatizing—even when there's no evidence of either perfidy. (Chapter 7, "Suspecting Victims," explores the ideology of so-called victim culture.)

- What if *she* asks for or tries to take what's meant to be *his for the taking*? In seeking masculine-coded goods in this way, I argue she is liable to be written off as greedy, corrupt, illicitly entitled, and out of order. (Chapter 8, "Losing (to) Misogynists," considers the misogynist smearing of Hillary Clinton during her unsuccessful 2016 bid for the White House.)

But before that, let me pause to consider and argue against an alternative to the account of misogyny developed in the book so far: the popular line, not always well-developed, that misogynist hostilities stem from a failure to recognize women's full humanity.

I will argue that women subject to the dynamic in this chapter are better understood as occupying a particular social position. Namely, she is positioned as a human, all too human, *giver*. And her humanity is something he, as a privileged human being, may hence feel entitled to use, exploit, or even destroy with impunity. Often, sadly and sometimes shamefully, we let him.

Chapter 5

Humanizing Hatred

You know what pisses me off, Benny? These f*cking bitches look at me like I'm some goddamn piece of meat, you know? Like a f*cking sex toy. But I'm a human being, man! I'm a person, you know, with feelings and emotions . . . I'm sitting here, right? Yeah, I exist! They think I'm so tall, my feelings don't get hurt.

George "Pornstache" Mendez, *Orange Is the New Black*,
season 1, episode 11, "Tall Men with Feelings"

I often cannot discern the humanity in a man.

Ludwig Wittgenstein, *Culture and Value*

There's a very common reflex in contemporary moral discourse, evident both inside and outside philosophy. It shows up in numerous discussions of the moral psychology of racist brutality, as well as in discussions of misogynist threats and violence. "The overall problem is one of a culture where instead of seeing women as, you know, people, protagonists of their own stories just like we are of ours, men are taught that women are things to 'earn,' to 'win'"—trophies. So wrote cultural commentator Arthur Chu (2014) after the Isla Vista killings.[1] Describing her experiences confronting "her cruelest troll" on the Internet, feminist writer Lindy West (2015) similarly wondered: "What made women easy targets? Why was it so satisfying to hurt us? Why didn't he automatically see us as human beings?" West's troll repented after she confronted him, and apologized for his misogynist

---

1. Compare the idea mooted in the previous chapter that she is tasked with being a "help meet" to her husband in the core case of patriarchal social relations (cf. the opening epigraphs).

behavior—much to her amazement (recalling West's interview with this man, discussed in chapter 1 here). But this was the one question West reports asking him that he could not answer, despite his best efforts to.

In this chapter, I argue that such questions—for example, "Why didn't he automatically see us as human beings?"—rest on a common mistake: reflexively attributing "man's inhumanity to men"[2] to some sort of dehumanizing psychological attitude. I'll call this the "humanist" explanation for interpersonal conduct of the kind that is naturally described as *inhumane*, in being not only morally objectionable, but also somehow cruel, brutal, humiliating, or degrading.[3] And on the view in moral psychology I'll subsequently call "humanism," such dehumanization is held to be the best explanation of such inhumane conduct relatively frequently (although not necessarily always). In other words, on the humanist view, such behavior often stems from people's failure to recognize some of their fellows *as* fellow human beings. The former may instead see the latter as subhuman creatures, nonhuman animals, supernatural beings (e.g., demons, witches), or even as mere things (i.e., mindless objects). If people could only appreciate their shared or common humanity, then they would have a hard time mistreating other members of the species.

Humanism in the intended sense is a popular, familiar, and in many ways tempting view. In spite of this, however—or, perhaps, because of it—it is not always clearly formulated and defended against rival explanatory models. Nor has it been much criticized—with notable, but brief, exceptions; see note 24.)[4] I have doubts about

2. This famous phrase was coined by the poet Robert Burns, who penned more than one Enlightenment anthem. Burns may in turn have adapted the expression from a line by Samuel von Pufendorf, an important forebear of Enlightenment thinking.

3. Admittedly, the word "humanist" and its cognates can mean different things to different people—but I can think of no better term that conveys something of the flavor of the view I'll be discussing.

4. The main set of extended critiques of broadly humanist thought in analytic philosophy comes from those who have argued that such views are objectionably "speciesist." I am increasingly sympathetic to the substance of these criticisms, although I have

its tenability as a general thesis about prejudice, however. This is especially so when it comes to misogyny. But, in the end, I will tentatively moot a surprising conclusion: namely, it is not clear that the humanist line works in many of the cases for which it might seem tailor-made, where people participate in mass atrocities under the influence of dehumanizing propaganda. Their actions often betray the fact that their victims must seem human, all too human, to the perpetrators. We notice this when we remember to pay attention to man's inhumanity to *women*, in particular—who are often brutally raped en masse during genocide.

HUMANIST THOUGHT IN ACTION

In Rae Langton's (2009) treatment of women's sexual oppression, the idea of "sexual solipsism" plays a central role. Whereas solipsism in the classic sense consists in skepticism about (or perhaps the sheer denial of) the existence of other minds of *any* kind, sexual solipsism regards the only human minds as male ones. Women are viewed and treated as "mere things," or objects, in contrast. And in Langton's view, this is closely connected with the moral ills of pornography. Here is Langton introducing her views, via her readings of Simone de Beauvoir and Catharine MacKinnon:

> In the company of a creature stabilized "as an object," [Beauvoir] said, "man remains alone." Sexual oppression is a solipsism made real . . . [Beauvoir] thought it was, for many, "a more attractive experience than an authentic relationship with a human being." A distinctive way of treating someone "as an object" is to be

questions about how best to understand them in relation to other liberatory political movements. But in any event, criticisms of this kind are largely orthogonal to those I am developing in this chapter, since humanism as I characterize it is not committed to (to my mind) dubious claims about the superior value or greater rights of human beings relative to other creatures.

found in pornography, so recent feminists have added, saying that in pornography "the human becomes thing." The ambiguity of [MacKinnon's] striking phrase conveys the thought that through pornography human beings—women—are treated as things, and also that things—pornographic artifacts—are treated as human beings. (2009, 2)

Langton goes on to defend MacKinnon's view that pornography (of the violent, degrading, heterosexual kind, at least) *silences* and *subordinates* women by objectifying them in this way. This claim is meant to be not only a plausible causal (and hence empirical) claim; Langton's central thesis is rather a *constitutive* one (chap. 1).[5]

Racism often involves a similar obliviousness or imperviousness to the full inner lives of its victims or targets, according to Raimond Gaita (1998). In a chapter entitled, "Racism: The Denial of a Common Humanity," Gaita offers us an autobiographical vignette by way of illustration, involving a bereaved mother, "M," who has recently lost a child and is still deep in the throes of grief. Gaita and M are watching a documentary about the Vietnam War on television. When the program turns to an interview with a grief-stricken Vietnamese woman who had also recently lost a child to the war, M initially leans forward, as if to catch every word of someone suffering the same kind of loss. But then she promptly leans back again, saying flatly, "But it is different for them. They can simply have more" (1998, 57). Gaita makes it clear that M's remark is not intended in a merely sociological vein, that is, to mean that the Vietnamese have comparatively large families. Nor is it a remark to the effect that the Vietnamese were so devastated by war during this era that their usual capacity for grief may have been blunted by trauma. Rather, M's remark expresses her sense that there is something about the Vietnamese *as such* that

5. MacKinnon (2006) gives a stipulative definition of pornography that centrally concerns violent, degrading, heteronormative material (although the exact scope of the definition is debatable). This was useful for MacKinnon's intended purposes in drafting (together with Andrea Dworkin) an antipornography civil rights ordinance.

makes their emotional experiences incapable of "going as deep" as M's own.[6] Gaita:

> In M's eyes, the Vietnamese are not contingently unable to rise to the requirements that are inseparable from the possibility of a deepened inner life, as might happen to a people if they suffer great hardships. To her, that is how they *essentially* are. (1998, 59)

M hence "could not find it intelligible that she could converse with them and learn from them about what it means to be married, to love someone or to grieve for them" (xxxv).

Gaita goes on to argue that M's moral psychology, with her truncated sense of the human subjectivity of those whom she harbors a racist prejudice against, is characteristic of many of those in the grip of racist ideology:

> Victims of racism often say they are treated as "sub-human." In many cases—perhaps the majority—that is not even slightly an exaggeration. We can see from what I have been saying about M how radically demeaning her attitude is, how literally dehumanizing—because it denies its victims any possibility of responding with depth and lucidity to the defining features of the human condition. In a natural sense of the word "human"— when it is not used to refer simply to the species *homo sapiens*. . .—those who are deemed incapable of an inner life of any depth and complexity are rightly said to be treated as less than fully human, as subhuman. (1998, 60)

A similar line is taken by David Livingstone Smith, when it comes to the moral psychology of agents who participate in mass atrocities. Livingstone Smith (2011) takes a more explicitly political and

---

6. Unfortunately, we are not told M's own race or ethnicity, if I am not mistaken. But in the context of Gaita's discussion, it is natural to imagine her as being, like the author, a white Australian.

historical line though, and bills dehumanization—understood as the attribution of a nonhuman, animal "essence" to the relevant class of people—as a solution to the problem, as it were, of empathy in politics. For:

> To recognize someone as a person—a fellow human being—you need to have the concept of a human being. And once you categorize someone as human, this has an impact on how you respond to him. . . . Thanks to our empathetic nature, most of us find it difficult to do violence to others. These inhibitions account for the powerful social bonds that unite human communities and explain the extraordinary success story of our species. But this generates a puzzle. From time immemorial men have banded together to kill and enslave their neighbours, rape their women, [etc.]. . . How do we manage to perform these acts of atrocity? An important piece of the answer is clear. It's by recruiting the power of our conceptual imagination to picture ethnic groups as nonhuman animals. It's by doing this that we're able to release destructive forces that are normally kept in check by fellow feeling. (2011, 127)

In other words, when some people are tasked with brutalizing and persecuting others under a political regime, they will have a difficult time of it unless their natural tendency to sympathize with these others is tempered. This is where dehumanization in general, and dehumanizing propaganda in particular, may prove instrumental.

There is already something to notice about the humanist position as regards to gender here; namely, the extent to which it seems to overlook it. The fact that M is contemplating a Vietnamese person who is also a *woman* and a *mother*—and hence, a Vietnamese woman and Vietnamese mother—which is analytically trivial but may have social and psychological meaning—seems incidental to Gaita's discussion, for example. For all we are told, M might just as well have been contemplating a Vietnamese father.

And although Livingstone Smith explicitly brackets off gender oppression in his account, it's not clear how well this jives with his acknowledgment of the role of the mass rape of women in the historical atrocities his paradigm comprises. The same point carries over to the fate of the Jewish women who were consigned to sexual slavery during the Holocaust, who were until recently widely omitted from the historical record (Hedgepeth and Saidel 2010). And, in moral philosophy, discussions of the Holocaust often center on Primo Levi's brilliant but necessarily partial account in *Survival in Auschwitz* (to use its American title). The book's alternative title asks us, however inadvertently, to broaden our focus—*If This Is a Man* being its title in the United Kingdom, Australia, and Europe.

If this is the moral psychology characteristic of racism and ethnic hatred, then we would expect that some kind of *humanizing* process would be required to overcome it. A nuanced treatment of such a process can be found in Nomy Arpaly's discussion of the case of Huckleberry Finn (2003, 75–78). As the story goes, Huck and Jim have run away together and are floating down the river on a flimsy raft (a none-too-subtle metaphor, on Mark Twain's part, for their being in "the same boat").[7] And despite Huck being a white boy, and Jim being a black slave, the two have become companionable and at ease with one another. When the slave hunters approach, and Jim is in danger of being captured, Huck cleverly heads them off and thereby acts rightly. But there is a puzzle about whether and, if so, why Huck deserves moral *praise* for so doing, given that he acted contrary to his explicit, misguided moral belief that he should have handed Jim over. There is also a puzzle about why Huck did what he did at all. Arpaly argues that Huck's deed is indeed morally praiseworthy, since it stems from Huck's morally enlightened, increasingly humane *view* of Jim. Arpaly:

> [D]uring the time he spends with Jim, Huckleberry undergoes a perceptual shift . . . Talking to Jim about his hopes and fears and interacting with him extensively, Huckleberry constantly

7. In describing the case, I draw on Manne (2013, sect. 2).

perceives data (never deliberated upon) that amount to the message that Jim is a person, just like him. Twain makes it very easy for Huckleberry to perceive the similarity between himself and Jim: the two are equally ignorant, share the same language and superstitions, and all in all it does not take the genius of John Stuart Mill to see that there is no particular reason to think of one of them as inferior to the other. While Huckleberry never reflects on these facts, they do prompt him to act towards Jim, more and more, in the same way he would have acted toward any other friend. That Huckleberry begins to perceive Jim as a fellow human being becomes clear when Huckleberry finds himself, to his surprise, *apologizing* to Jim—an action unthinkable in a society that treats black men as something less than human. . . [W]hen the opportunity comes to turn Jim in and Huckleberry experiences a strong reluctance to do so, his reluctance is to a large extent the result of the fact that he has come to see Jim as a person. (2003, 76–77)

That should suffice to give a preliminary taste of humanist thinking of the kind I have in mind here.[8] What should we make of it? We can grant, I think, that it would be a serious problem to lose sight of the humanity of other human beings (at least with any consistency, or for no good reason).[9] But is seeing people *as* people, or recognizing other human beings as such, really all it is made out to be? To what extent does it dispose us to treat these others decently? And to what extent is

8. Aspects of the humanist view as I will understand it have also been defended by Christine Korsgaard, Martha Nussbaum, Stephen Darwall, and Julia Markovits, among others.

9. I say "with any consistency" because, following P. F. Strawson (and recalling the discussion in the preface), I think room must be made for intermittent "relief" or "refuge" from the "strains of involvement" with other human beings ([1962] 2008, 10, 13, 18). This may arguably involve a certain amount of detachment from these others' very humanity. And I say "for no good reason" because there may be circumstances in which such detachment is vital in order to get a certain job done—for example, as a surgeon who has to view her patients as mere bodies or complex systems when they are on the operating table.

dehumanization responsible for the most brutal forms of treatment that people visit on each other? To what extent should we take it literally qua psychological phenomenon, especially when it comes to misogyny? These are the main questions I try to answer in this chapter—but first, to clarify the key claims of humanism.

CLARIFYING HUMANISM

The term "humanism" has historically meant many things to different people, and it continues to do so today. I've already pointed in the direction of my stalking horse in giving the foregoing examples, and in identifying some of the theorists whose views would (I take it) commit them to balking at some of my eventual conclusions here. But rather than try to pin down the specifics of their different positions, it will be helpful—both for the sake of clarity and brevity—to abstract away from any particular theorist's views and try to distill the humanist position into some key commitments. These comprise descriptive claims (conceptual-cum-perceptual, moral psychological, and historical), and also a normative claim (moral-cum-political). And their conjunction represents my attempt to put together various (it seems to me) complementary humanist thoughts, as gleaned in the previous section, into a natural, attractive package. Each claim follows fairly naturally, but not deductively, from preceding ones, as will become apparent.[10] We can begin with the following:

(1) **Conceptual-cum-perceptual claim:** Human beings are capable of seeing or recognizing other human beings *as such*, in a way that goes beyond identifying them as other members of the species.[11] This

10. To be clear though, I don't mean to imply that each of the aforementioned theorists is committed to each of the above claims, let alone to precisely these versions of them.

11. I mean "see" somewhat metaphorically here, in that the distinctively visual aspect of some experiences of such recognition should not be over-generalized, partly on grounds of ableism. On the other hand, something *perceptual* or quasi-perceptual in

involves thinking about people in a way that has both perspectival and richer cognitive dimensions. It is to view them as a "*fellow* human being," as a member of one's own kind, or (similarly) as a member of "our *common* humanity." Similarly, it is to recognize them not merely as belonging to the species *Homo sapiens* (if it in fact involves this at all), but rather, as a *person*.[12]

What does this come to? Recognizing others as fellow human beings is generally supposed to comprise (inter alia) thinking of them as having, or at least as having had, the potential to[13]

- be *minded* in a similar way to oneself (cognitively, conatively, emotionally, phenomenologically, etc.);
- develop and exercise various characteristically *human capacities*, including sophisticated forms of *rationality, agency, autonomy*, and so on, as well as a capacity to *value*, and to reflectively form and revise at least some of those values;
- enter into and sustain various characteristically *human social relations*, including *marriage, parenthood, siblinghood, friendship, collegial relations* and
- be the intelligible intentional object of others' *deep emotional attachments*, perhaps including one's own, at least potentially.

With this conceptual-cum-perceptual claim in hand, the humanist can now make their second key claim, which presupposes the first (or something much like it):

terms of its *holism* often seems to be at issue. Fortunately, I can remain neutral about the appropriate story about social (so-called) perception on behalf of the humanist for my purposes in this chapter.

12. Identifying someone as a fellow member of the species of course wouldn't have been necessary before the concept of a species became salient, or in contexts in which it still isn't.

13. The clause about "potential" is included so as to allow the criteria below to encompass those human beings whose development has had, or will take, an atypical course, due to certain illnesses, injuries, disabilities, etc. Many humanists are keen not to exclude people who currently do not, and will likely never, fit the criteria below. To my mind, this is one of the most attractive (and humane) aspects of humanist thinking.

(2) *Moral psychological claim:* When we recognize another human being as such, in the sense given by claim (1), then this is not only a *necessary* condition for treating her humanely, in interpersonal contexts, but also strongly *motivates* and *disposes* us to do so.[14]

Why should this be so, though? What is the mechanism that connects the *recognition* of someone's humanity with the *motivation* to (e.g.) be kind, and the aversion to being cruel, to her? This is an especially pressing question for those of us who subscribe to what is known in moral philosophy as the Humean theory of motivation, according to which *beliefs* and other "world-guided" mental states don't motivate an agent by themselves. One also needs to posit a suitable *desire* or other "world-guiding" mental state in order to explain someone's disposition to take *action*.

A plausible account of the connection can be gleaned by considering an example from George Orwell, which more than one humanist has cited in this connection. (See Cora Diamond 1978, 477; Gaita 1998, 48.) Orwell recalls a morning in the trenches during the Spanish Civil War, trying to snipe at the Fascists, when:

> [A] man presumably carrying a message to an officer, jumped out of the trench and ran along the top of the parapet in full view. He was half-dressed and was holding up his trousers with both hands as he ran. I refrained from shooting at him. It is true that I am a poor shot and unlikely to hit a running man at a hundred yards, and also that I was thinking chiefly about getting back to our trench while the Fascists had their attention fixed on the aeroplanes. Still, I did not shoot partly because of that detail about the trousers. I had come here to shoot at "Fascists"; but a

14. I'll accept the necessity claim contained in (2) for the sake of argument. Given the deep human desire for interpersonal recognition, it is prima facie plausible, and nothing hangs on rejecting this claim for my purposes. However, I intend it to be fully compatible with holding that there is nothing *special* about being human, in the sense that nonhuman animals are just as valuable as human beings. (Although one may still hold that there are deep differences between different kinds of animals, including between human and non-human, and between different non-human, species.)

man who is holding up his trousers isn't a "Fascist," he is visibly a fellow-creature, similar to yourself, and you don't feel like shooting at him. (1981, 194)

Orwell speaks of the soldier as appearing on his radar as a "fellow-creature," rather than a "fellow human being," as Cora acknowledges. But she nevertheless argues that a humanizing vision of a would-be target is especially prone to engender *pity*, and hence make an agent in Orwell's position reluctant to pull the trigger.[15]

We can generalize. The most promising route from claim (1) to claim (2) will plausibly invoke a concept like *empathy, sympathy, compassion*, or *fellow feeling*. And the thought would then be that, in view of our recognition of someone's similarity to ourselves, we will be able and inclined to *identify* with her, or (somewhat more modestly) to take her *perspective*. We will subsequently often feel what we imagine she feels, or at least experience congruent pro-social, "helper" emotions (pity being one such).[16] This being the case, we will tend to want to be kind, rather than cruel, to her—or even to help, not to hurt, her more broadly. The conclusion that we will be disposed to treat her in humane ways in interpersonal contexts is thereby significantly helped along. She will now be not only recognized but *embraced* as a member of our common humanity, an object of moral concern, reciprocity, or similar. Recognizing someone as a fellow human being can hence now be said to have a *motivational* upshot, at least in typical cases (e.g., absent certain psychological profiles).[17]

15. Orwell, for his part, was more circumspect. Before recounting this incident, he warns the reader that it does "not prove anything in particular." And immediately afterward, he reiterates: "What does this incident demonstrate? Nothing very much, because it is the kind of thing that happens all the time in all wars" (1981, 194).

16. See Nichols (2004, chap. 2) for a discussion of the role of perspective-taking in various candidate forms of empathy, and homologous versus non-homologous forms of distress and concern.

17. These being, for example, psychopathy, sociopathy, autism, depression . . .? This is a delicate issue, which I don't want to speculate about here. There is too little time to do it justice, and too much risk of perpetuating stigma—not to mention reifying concepts that wrongly pathologize certain people.

So claim (2) follows naturally, if not inevitably, from claim (1), together with additional claims about a subsequent capacity for empathy or something like it, and the altruistic dispositions that characteristically follow.[18]

A number of claims now become plausible on the basis of claim (2) without, again, being logically entailed by them.

(3) *Quasi-contrapositive moral psychological claim:* In order for people to mistreat others in the most morally egregious ways (e.g., to murder, rape, or torture them with relative impunity), a failure to see them as fellow human beings is a powerful, and perhaps even necessary, psychological lubricant.[19]

(4) *Historical claim:* When a class of historically oppressed people comes to be seen as fellow human beings by most members of dominant social groups, and in society as a whole, moral and social progress becomes much more likely, perhaps even virtually inevitable.[20] Relatedly (or again, quasi-contrapositively), when people who belong to certain social groups are the targets of the most morally egregious forms of widespread or weaponized mistreatment (e.g., genocide, massacre, mass rape, systematic torture), then this is typically due to their *not* being seen as full human beings in the first place, or dehumanized shortly thereafter, often due to the influence of dehumanizing propaganda.

---

18. An alternative route from claim (1) to claim (2) would involve construing the notion of a fellow human being as an essentially *moralized* concept—for example, very roughly, as someone who one ought to treat with the same kind of respect, kindness, and care that would be reasonable to claim for oneself and one's intimates—and then to endorse some version of *motivational internalism*. In this context, however, this would be question-begging without an independent account of *why* the concept of a human being has this moral content. In other words, this alternative would simply build in the altruistic dispositions the above line of thinking makes a (defeasible) case for.

19. I say "quasi-contrapositive" because neither of the relevant claims is meant to be a genuine conditional. They are rather generalizations along the lines of "if *p*, then probably *q*."

20. For particularly strong historical-cum-teleological claims along these lines, see Pinker (2012, chap. 7).

(5) *Moral-cum-political claim:* when the members of certain social groups are mistreated in the above ways, then one of the most crucial immediate political goals should be to make their humanity visible to other people (whatever that involves, exactly). And this would also constitute a crucial form of individual moral progress for the people whose outlooks are transformed in the process.

THE TROUBLE WITH HUMANISM

What should we make of humanism, understood as the conjunction of the preceding five claims? How well does the humanist diagnosis capture the moral-cum-social outlook of those in the grip of various oppressive ideologies, especially racist and misogynist ones?

It might look as if humanism is in pretty fatal trouble already when it comes to misogyny, based on the following hypothesis (which chapter 8 will serve to confirm): women as well as men can practice it. If this is right, then internalized misogyny would either go so deep as to make a woman less than human to herself—and hence undermine the "identification" basis for membership in the class of one's fellow human beings—or she must regard other women as fundamentally different sorts of creatures from herself. And neither possibility seems plausible, on the face of it.

However, it's not clear that this objection to the humanist account of misogyny in particular is as fatal as it initially appears to be, owing to the following possibility. It could be that dominant men's attitudes to women are dehumanizing in the above way, but that their views spawn an *ideology* about certain women that others then pick up on. Indeed, although I disagree with the first of the conjuncts here (i.e., that dominant men's misogyny typically consists in dehumanizing women) I will eventually propose something like that "ideological contagion" mechanism myself (in chapter 8). Women's role as givers, and privileged men's as takers, is internalized by women as well as men; so women who are fully paid-up members in the club of femininity are no less prone to enforce such norms, at least in certain contexts. Indeed, when it comes to third-personal moralism, as opposed to second-personal reactive attitudes, they may be *more* prone to do so, because women who appear to be shirking their duties, in being, for example, careless, selfish, or negligent, make more work for others who are "good" or conscientious. Moreover, such women threaten to undermine the system on which many women have staked their futures, identities, sense of self-worth, etc. I'll moot that view in chapter 8 and come back to it during the conclusion as well. But I anticipate. In the meantime, having staved off disaster on behalf of the humanist position applied specifically to misogyny, we should look at more general problems the position may encounter.

We can start by considering claim (1) above—that is, that there is a way of seeing people that goes beyond identifying them as another member of the species. It instead involves a sense of *commonality* with them sufficient to give rise to something like empathy: which, as we saw, is one concept of the kind that it would be natural to invoke to make the transition from claim (1) to claim (2). I think that claim (1) is quite plausible in some version, and I'll accept it for the sake of argument in what follows. The trouble is that it is radically incomplete. For a fellow human being is not just an intelligible *spouse, parent, child, sibling, friend, colleague,* etc., in relation to you and yours. They are also an intelligible *rival, enemy, usurper, insubordinate, betrayer,* etc. Moreover, in being capable of rationality, agency, autonomy, and judgment, they are also someone who could coerce, manipulate, humiliate, or shame you. In being capable of abstract relational thought and congruent moral emotions, they are capable of thinking ill of you and regarding you contemptuously. In being capable of forming complex desires and intentions, they are capable of harboring malice and plotting against you. In being capable of valuing, they may value what you abhor and abhor what you value. They may hence be a threat to all that you cherish. And you may be a threat to all that *they* cherish in turn—as you may realize. This provides all the more reason to worry about others' capacity for cruelty, contempt, malice, and so forth.

The basic upshot is this: under even moderately non-ideal conditions, involving, for example, exhaustible material resources, limited sought-after social positions, or clashing moral and social ideals, the humanity of some is likely to represent a double-edged sword to others. So, when it comes to recognizing someone as a fellow human being, the characteristic human capacities that you share don't just make her *relatable*; they make her potentially *dangerous* and *threatening* in ways only a human being can be—at least relative to our own, distinctively human sensibilities. She may, for example, threaten to undermine you.[21]

What follows from this? In view of the radical incompleteness of claim (1)—and thus, on the whole, the half-truth it represents—claim (2) can now be seen to be problematic. The capacity for empathy and the associated tendency to form altruistic dispositions can still be allowed to hold. But these dispositions will have to *compete* with, and may arguably be *canceled* by, the dispositions associated with various hostile stances.[22] For example: the stance toward one's purported enemies, which comes with a disposition to try to *destroy* them; the stance toward one's seeming rivals, which comes with a disposition to try to *defeat* them; the stance toward one's recent usurpers, which comes with a disposition to try to *turn the tables*—that is, to

21. See Lynne Tirrell (2012), for an illuminating account of the way the Tutsi were represented as *threatening* (among other things) by the Hutu in the lead-up to the Rwandan genocide, owing partly to new forms of dehumanizing hate speech. The Tutsi were called *inyenzi* (cockroaches) and *inzoka* (snakes) by the Hutu, terms that Tirrell plausibly argues had an *action-engendering* function, since there are characteristic actions one takes toward such creatures—namely, destructive ones. Tirrell also insightfully emphasizes the embeddedness in oppressive social contexts that make these deeply derogatory terms (as she calls them) much more pernicious than ad hoc terms like "sausage face" (an example Tirrell gives of a term spontaneously made up by some children during a game they were playing).

22. If we allow for the latter possibility—which is something like John McDowell's (1995) idea of motivating reasons being "silenced"—then claim (1) will be positively false, in being subject to an important range of counter-examples. But even if not, i.e., if we insist on taking the former view, claim (1) will leave out half of the story—a half that the humanist would need in order to make the crucial transition from claim (1) to claim (2) licit.

undermine and again surpass them; the stance toward those perceived as insubordinate, which comes with a disposition to try to *put them in their place again*; and the stance toward someone perceived as a traitor, which comes with a disposition to try to *punish them for desertion*. Many of these number among misogyny's most characteristic maneuvers, tellingly.

So much for claim (2), understood as a claim about an agent's motivational profile on balance. Claim (3), in being close to the contra-positive of claim (2), will plausibly be undermined along with it. And the remaining claims, (4) and (5), now lack their hitherto justification. (Technically, it remains to be seen if these claims could be furnished with an independent warrant but, for my own part, I am doubtful they have alternative justifications.)

So far in this section, my criticisms of the key claims of humanism have been largely conceptual in nature. But a glance at concrete examples serves to underline their pertinence. Many of the nastiest things that people do to each other seem to proceed in full view of, and are in fact plausibly *triggered* by, these others' manifestations of their shared or common humanity.[23]

Take Elliot Rodger, who (recalling chapter 1) declared his intention to wreak vengeance on the "hot blonde sluts" of the Alpha Phi Sorority House at the University of California, Santa Barbara, their having failed to give him the love, sex, affection, and attention he craved so sorely. Indeed, they had failed to notice him at all, so preoccupied were they, Rodger complained, with "throwing themselves" at the "obnoxious brutes" they preferred to him, "the supreme gentleman." "What don't they see in me?" Rodger wondered, self-pityingly, in his self-recorded video. Recall the mood then shifting, both emotionally and grammatically. "I will punish you all for it," Rodger assured these women. He was now speaking *to*, not *of*, them, second-personally.

---

23. In addition to the triggers being odd, the *symptoms* of a supposed failure to recognize others as fellow human beings often seem wrong as well. For, they often consist in the manifestations of characteristically *interpersonal* "reactive attitudes," in P. F. Strawson's ([1962] 2008) sense. I introduced this point in the preface, and I'll return to it later on in this chapter.

What is striking about these sentiments is that they not only pre-suppose but seem to *hinge* on the women's presumed humanity in the sense canvassed earlier (see claim (1) above, in the section "Clarifying Humanism"). Rodger ascribes to these women subjectivity, prefer-ences, and a capacity to form deep emotional attachments (love, as well as affection). And he attributes to them agency, autonomy, and the capacity to be *addressed* by him. But far from being a panacea for his misogyny, such recognition in fact seems to have been its very precondition.[24] Rodger wanted what these women were not giving him; they subsequently had a *hold* over him. He did not deny women's power, independence, or the reality of their minds. Rather, he hated and sought to punish them for evincing these capacities in ways that frustrated him, given his sense of entitlement to their benefit.

A SOCIALLY SITUATED ALTERNATIVE

But if the humanist explanation does not work all that well in some of the cases in which it tends to be invoked, what might we put in its

24. Similar points have been made by Adam Gopnik (2006) and Kwame Anthony Appiah (2006; 2008), in relation to genocide. Appiah (2008) writes:

> At their worst [conflicts between groups] can lead to genocidal massacres. How? The familiar answer is: by persuading us that members of some out-group aren't really human at all. That's not quite right: it doesn't explain the immense cruelty—the abominable cruelty, I'm tempted to say—that are their characteristic feature. The persecutors may liken the objects of their enmity to cockroaches or germs, but they acknowledge their victims' humanity in the very act of humiliating, stigmatizing, reviling, and tor-turing them. Such treatments—and the voluble justifications the perse-cutors invariably offer for such treatment—is reserved for creatures we recognize to have intentions, and desires, and projects. (144)

In a subsequent footnote, Appiah (2008) also points out that *génocidaires* will often "tell you why their victims—Jews or Tutsi—*deserve* what's being done to them" (247n25). Elsewhere, Appiah (2006) offers a slightly different take on things (151–153). He writes there that the problem is not that marginalized people are not held to matter at all; it is that they are held to matter *less* than dominant group members, on the basis of *ad hoc* rationalizations.

place? What else could explain the inhumane forms of treatment that people visit on each other, generalizing or extending from my foregoing analysis of misogyny?

We can make a start here by taking a closer look at the puzzle that the humanist takes himself to be addressing. If a human agent A understands that a human subject S is much like A, then how can A so mistreat S—or, alternatively, ignore or turn away from S in her suffering?

A's *lack* of recognition of S's common humanity is one potential explanation that would negate the antecedent of the opening conditional. This would block the supposedly far-fetched possibility that someone could brutally mistreat other human beings while representing them as such. But another, equally sensible place to look, structurally speaking, for an explanation of people's inhumanity to each other is for some *additional* representation—that is, a way of envisaging people that gives rise to motivations that *compete* with or even *cancel* the incipient altruistic ones. They may be mediated by political ideologies, hierarchies, and the associated sense of entitlement—and hence subsequent needs and aggression when these needs are thwarted. This would open up the possibility that seeing others as fellow human beings, while treating them abominably, is *not* in fact far-fetched; it is merely in need of some kind of backstory, without which the assertion of the conjunction would be pragmatically anomalous.

What could these additional ways of seeing people be? We have already encountered some of them. Seeing someone as one's *enemy* engenders a motivation to try to destroy that person, and seeing someone as one's *rival* engenders a motivation to try to defeat them, for example.[25] I'll continue to focus on these concepts in what follows,

---

25. What is the connection between the relevant representation and motivation here? This is an especially important question for me, given that I outed myself earlier as a proponent of the Humean theory of motivation, at least in some version. I think the crucial observation here is that the world-guided or "mind-to-world" representations in question aim to fit a state of the world that is *itself* world-guiding or "world-to-mind." For, your enemy is (among other things) a minded creature in the world in

along with that of a *usurper*, an *insubordinate*, and a *betrayer*, to keep the discussion focused. But it would not be difficult to extend this list of (more or less covertly) hostile *socially situated stances*—that is, stances that are taken toward people *from* somewhere specific in the social world—more or less indefinitely. Think of the terms "thug," "welfare queen," "urban youth," or even "looter," as they figure in current political discourse in the United States. These are all primarily terms used by whites to refer disparagingly to black Americans. This is why these terms can all serve as effective racist "dog-whistles," as Jason Stanley (2015, 158–160) has argued. Yet none of the concepts these terms express seems, on the face of it, well-described as dehumanizing. True, some reflect and help to shape a sort of "us" and "them" mentality. But the "us" in question need not be human beings *writ large*; it may be human beings in a *particular social position* or who occupy a certain *rank* in one of many potential intra-human hierarchies (including those that have their basis in supposed moral values).[26]

The motivations associated with hostile stances can result in some very ugly behavior (although of course this will vary widely).

---

a world-to-mind state of mind, that is, who wants to *destroy* you. Similarly, your rival is a minded creature in the world in a (different) world-to-mind state of mind, i.e., who wants to *defeat* you. Representing someone as your enemy or as a rival hence has accuracy conditions *about* others' desires where you are concerned. And this will naturally elicit a certain response from you. Namely, it is very natural to respond to these (purported) desires on the part of the other by *responding in kind*—at least, under the (typically safe) assumption that you do not *want* to be destroyed or bested by the agent in question. In other cases, the response called for is not symmetrical; but there is still a natural progression from representing someone as insubordinate (say) to being motivated to try to regain the upper hand over that person. Again, this has to do with the fact that an insubordinate is represented as a minded creature with "ideas beyond her station" or as someone trying to undermine your authority. If you don't want that to happen, then you will need to take *action*.

26. Like Strawsonian stances, these stances should be seen, I think, as a holistic overall "take" one can have on a person, encompassing affective dimensions and constraining and enabling what one may do with, to, and for her, in addition to the aforementioned motivational upshots. Although the latter are most relevant for my purposes here, I don't mean to suggest that this is their only extracognitive dimension.

They often bring with them a temptation to lash out, put people down, or otherwise try to (re-)establish dominance. And these ways of envisaging people need not be blocked by a sense of the humanity one shares with them; indeed, they plausibly depend on that very recognition. For only another human being can sensibly *be* conceived as an enemy, a rival, a usurper, an insubordinate, a traitor, and the like, at least in the fullest sense of these terms.[27] Nonhuman animals to whom human beings do violence are, rather, envisioned as *prey*, as *game*, or as predators, that is, wild and a danger to *us*. Or, alternatively, they are viewed as *disobedient*, in the case of domesticated animals who can be taught to respond to complex commands. But wayward dogs and horses are held to be *insurgents*. The different terminology that we reach for when it comes to human versus nonhuman animals is suggestive. Namely, it suggests that there are distinctively interpersonal, yet distinctly hostile, postures that we typically only take toward recognized human beings. (Whether or not we *ought* to—recalling this is an exercise in descriptive moral psychology, not a normative one.)

It is worth pausing over the notion of an *enemy* for a moment, since the claim that it is sustained by the recognition of shared humanity seems to have been rejected by some humanists.[28] Cora Diamond (1978) writes, for example, that the notion of an enemy and the notion of a "fellow human being" "are there in a kind of tension," in connection with the Orwell passage quoted earlier (477).[29] But what kind of tension is this? And why think that it is operative,

27. "Sensibly" might either be construed as "intelligibly" or "reasonably" here, depending on how one construes the folly of a Captain Ahab, vis-à-vis his white whale. But I don't need to choose between them in this context.

28. I owe this helpful way of putting my views to David Livingstone Smith (2016).

29. In a previous draft of the paper this chapter is based on, I mistakenly implied that Diamond holds that these concepts are inevitably in tension. I now take it that Diamond only means to be committed to the view that they "are *there* in a kind of tension" (my emphasis). It's not obvious to me why these concepts would be in tension here and not elsewhere; but I leave further discussion of this nuance for a future occasion. Thanks to Professor Diamond for helpful correspondence about her views here.

in this case or elsewhere? It's true that the latter *expression* has a friendly sound that the former manifestly lacks. But this may be just pragmatics. The task is to give some kind of determinate content to the thought that there is something in the similarity of others to ourselves the perception of which can make it hard to treat them as an enemy combatant. And this I do not see. If anything, the more similar these others are to ourselves, the more one may have to watch out for them, in the case of competing claims or interests.[30]

I do not claim that this is the end of the argument, of course. Perhaps there is some meaning in the notion of a "fellow" that I have not gleaned that could do the necessary work here, without simply begging the question—or omitting "fellow" women. But more would need to be said than I think *has* been said in the literature to date (at least to the best of my knowledge) in order to be convincing. And the argumentative burden falls on the humanist in the meantime.

To make matters worse for the humanist at this juncture, there is a competing explanation of what made the soldier's enemy status fade from salience for Orwell. This has to do, again, with *hierarchical relations*. When Orwell saw the enemy soldier running across the battlefield holding up his trousers, it did not merely underline the

---

30. A similar thought applies to the idea that there is a fundamental tension between seeing someone as a person and seeing them as a piece of property. Pace the remark of Arthur Chu's that I quoted in opening, this can't simply be assumed; it needs to be argued for. Admittedly, on some conceptions (e.g., some Kantian ones), seeing someone as a person encompasses seeing them as a morally autonomous being who cannot be bought, sold, or owned and is just as morally valuable as any other person, has equal rights to them, etc. But humanism as I understand it here needs to walk a certain tightrope in order to make good on its explanatory ambitions. If the idea of recognizing someone as a fellow human being packs in all this moral content, then it is hard to see how it could be the promised *explanans* in moral psychology. (Attributions of such recognition to an agent come precariously close to saying approvingly, "She gets it!" where the referent of "it" has been given a substantive characterization.) On the other hand, if the idea of recognizing someone as a fellow human being is thinned down to the point of being a suitable potential *explanans*, then it is not clear that it will provide the most plausible explanations of the target *explananda* all that frequently. Thanks to Nomy Arpaly for pushing me on this point, as well as for valuable discussion and comments here generally.

soldier's similarly human, or perhaps simply vulnerable, creaturely body. Rather, or in addition to this, Orwell caught a glimpse of the man at his most *ridiculous*. And this would plausibly have altered Orwell's perception of their relative social positions for a moment. It became natural to view him, as Orwell did, with pity—a kindly attitude, but one that nevertheless involves stooping downward, sometimes condescendingly. It is hard to see a "fellow-creature" in such an abject position as *fair game*, or hence as an *enemy* at all, in the sense of the former that matters for the latter. Although those engaged in battle may be confident of winning, the enemy is not typically conceived as so helpless and defenseless as to make it an *ambush*.

These socially situated ways of envisaging people—that is, as enemies, rivals, usurpers, insubordinates, traitors, and so on—seem clearly ripe to do useful work in explaining inhumane behavior. Why, then, aren't they called upon to do this work more often in this context in philosophy? One reason for this, I suspect, is that the position of the agent is often underdescribed in setting up the problem. For often, the agent is not depicted as firmly *situated* in the human world, embroiled in complex social practices, roles, institutions, and (in this context, crucially) oppressive hierarchical relations. The agent is instead depicted merely as trying to *assess* other people and evaluate their merits, rather as a god might; whereas all five stances mentioned above are essentially *positional*, and many of them *hierarchical*, in nature. They involve dispositions to try to protect, improve, or regain one's social standing relative to other people. They involve (in that useful phrase) "jostling for position."

In addition to enmity, many of these forms of jostling involve some kind of *rivalry*. And one need not think *poorly* of one's rival in order to regard him as a rival, or even a nemesis. Indeed, quite the contrary—if one did not have some appreciation of his merits in the relevant domain, then competing with him would tend to lose much of its intrinsic (if not extrinsic) interest. And while competition can be healthy, it can also be vicious. Rivalry can be friendly, but also, bitter. It can lead us to be resentful and hostile toward our rivals, to think of them uncharitably (because of the effects of motivated reasoning, among other things), and to subsequently treat them poorly. So the inference from an agent A's thinking highly of a subject S's abilities, at least deep down, to A's being disposed to treat S kindly is simply not a good one (nor conversely, importantly; see note 13).

But why was this inference thought to be plausible in the first place? In particular, why think that the recognition of the humanity of members of historically *subordinate social classes*—in a sense that involves recognizing their equal capacity for human excellence—would come as uniformly good news to hitherto dominant group members? On reflection, this seems unduly optimistic. The recent ingress of (e.g.) nonwhites and white women to the most prestigious positions in contemporary Western societies has meant that white men now have serious *competition*. Add to this the fact that the competition will often result in the hitherto dominant being surpassed by those they tacitly expected to be in social positions beneath them, and you have a recipe for resentment and a sense of "aggrieved entitlement," to invoke sociologist Michael Kimmel's notion (2013, 18–25, chap. 1).[31]

This becomes clear when we are careful to picture the agent as *embedded* in the social world, rather than merely trying to form a "view from nowhere" about other people's merits. Even so, we will have to be careful to picture the social landscape properly. Another common way of (in my view) underdoing the set-up is to place comparatively privileged agents at the center of what Peter Singer (2011) calls "the circle of concern," such that their main moral task in the struggle to end oppression is simply to open their arms and embrace the humanity, or perhaps just the sentience, of the rest of us. This picture situates the (supposedly relevant) agent *in* the world, but forgets all of the *vertical structure* the world contains—that is, the bastions of privilege that would need to be dismantled in order to achieve social justice. These bastions are often well-defended and difficult to challenge. For people are often, unsurprisingly, deeply invested in their continuation. To make matters worse, these structures are often quite invisible to the people whose privileged social positions they serve to

31. I draw in this paragraph on a previously published work of mine (Manne 2014b), as well as in this chapter as a whole (see the preface).

uphold and buttress. So dismantling them may feel not only like a *comedown*, but also an *injustice*, to the privileged. They will tend to feel *flattened*, rather than merely *leveled*, in the process.

I would hence suggest, on the strength of this, that the mistreatment of historically subordinated people who are perceived as threatening the status quo often needs no special psychological story, such as dehumanization, to account for it. It can rather be explained in terms of current and historical social structures, hierarchical relations, and norms and expectations, together with the fact that they are widely internalized and difficult to eradicate. As with the analysis of misogyny I developed, we won't then need the supplementation of the dehumanization paradigm. Rather, the psychological story can be seen as the upshot of the internalization of ideology and features of the (unjust but all too real) moral-cum-social landscape.

The humanist sense that something *is* needed by way of a special psychological story here is, as we have seen, premised on the idea that it will typically be difficult for an agent to commit acts of violence or otherwise aggress against vulnerable and innocent parties. So something has to be done to alter the agent's perception of his soon-to-be victim. But this misses the fact that agents in a dominant social position often don't start out with such a neutral or salutary view of things. They are perpetually mired in certain kinds of *delusions* about their own social positions relative to other people, and their respective obligations, permissions, and entitlements. So, from the perspective of the dominant, the people they mistreat are often far from innocent. On the contrary, they are often tacitly—and falsely—held to be deeply guilty.[32] We have seen this time after time when it comes to misogyny, in particular. But I believe the point generalizes—as indeed it must, in some sense, in order to do justice to the intersections of racism and misogyny, as in misogynoir, for example.

32. Specifically, nonwhites and white women are often held to have committed acts of gross disrespect, intimidation, insubordination, negligence, etc., by the lights of patriarchal and white supremacist ideologies. And the mere presence of these historically subordinated people in prestigious social roles may constitute highway robbery by the lights of these deeply unjust, but deeply internalized, social orders.

Michael Kimmel reports, on the basis of his extensive interviews with white men that, when a black woman is hired over a white man with similar qualifications, the latter is prone to complain that the former took his job. Kimmel asks: why *his* job, not *a* job? (2003, chap. 1). I think the answer is relatively straightforward. This woman *has* taken his job, relative to unjust patriarchal and white supremacist hierarchies, and a sense of entitlement that is in urgent need of redress. The illusion is not a psychological matter that gives rise to moral mistakes down the line and would cease to do so if bigots could just get perceptually clearer on who is there before them. Rather, what is in question is a pervasive and an inherently *moral* delusion, born of the toxic ongoing legacy of a white hetero-patriarchal order.

DOMINATING PEOPLE

Where does all this leave us, then? I've argued that an agent's recognition of a human subject as such may fail to dispose her strongly on balance—or, arguably, at all—to treat this subject humanely (i.e., with due consideration, respect, care, and moral concern, in interpersonal contexts). This is not because I think the humanist is wrong that the recognition of someone's humanity will tend to motivate humane conduct, all else being equal. It is rather that all else is often *not* equal; indeed, it may be as unequal as can be. Relatedly, I think the humanist has taken insufficient account of the fact that such recognition may be overlaid, and the altruistic disposition outweighed or even canceled, by *competing* representations and the dispositions they give rise to. For we may see others as *rivals, insubordinates, usurpers, betrayers*, and *enemies* (inter alia), without ever losing sight of these people's full humanity. And we may subsequently be disposed to try to defeat, chastise, trounce, punish, destroy, and permanently close the eyes of those we know full well are people like us.

With that in mind, let us return to the opening examples, and see what might be made of them now that the socially situated view is on the table alongside the humanist position. Which of these models, if any, is more explanatory in some of the main cases that humanists take as paradigms?

Arpaly interprets Huck's morally good deed (and, in her view, his morally praiseworthy action) as the product of his burgeoning recognition of Jim's fellow humanity. Elsewhere, I have argued that what is crucial in bringing about Huck's moral turnaround is something Arpaly mentions only in passing: Huck's having formed a genuine *friendship* with Jim (Manne 2013). This makes sense of the fact that, at this point in the story, Huck is actually seething with anger at Jim for having *ideas beyond his station*—his station as a slave, that is, and hence his master's property. Mired in his enduringly, resentfully racist conception, Huck fumes:

> Jim talked out loud all the time while I was talking to myself. He was saying how the first thing he would do when he got to a free State he would go to saving up money and never spend a single cent, and when he got enough he would buy his wife, which was owned on a farm close to where Miss Watson lived; and then they would both work to buy the two children, and if their master wouldn't sell them, they'd get an Ab'litionist to go and steal them. It most froze me to hear such talk. He wouldn't ever dared to talk such talk in his life before. Just see what a difference it made in him the minute he judged he was about free. It was according to the old saying, "Give a n—— an inch and he'll take an ell." Thinks I, this is what comes of my not thinking. Here was this n—— which I had as good as helped to run away, coming right out flat-footed and saying he would steal his children—children that belonged to a man I didn't even know; a man that hadn't done me no harm. I was sorry to hear Jim say that, it was such a lowering of him. (Twain 2010, 99–100)

Huck subsequently decides to right these supposed wrongs, as well as vent his spleen, by snitching:

> My conscience got to stirring me up hotter than ever, until at last I says to it, "Let up on me—it ain't too late, yet—I'll paddle

ashore at the first light, and tell." I felt easy, and happy, and light
as a feather, right off. All my troubles was gone. (2010, 100)

So Huck's plan to turn Jim in isn't simply borne of a genuine sense
of duty, tempered by sympathy or conscience, which eventually wins
out. It is at least as much an expression of Huck's resentful, self-righteous desire to teach Jim a lesson, and to put him in his place again.
For, Jim had been getting "uppity."[33]

What happens in the story to change Huck's mind, then? Just as
Huck makes off in the direction of the slave hunters who have (coin-
cidentally) turned up, Jim comes out with this:

Pooty soon I'll be a shout'n for joy, en I'll say, it's all on account o'
Huck; I's a free man, en I couldn't ever ben free ef it hadn't been
for Huck; Huck done it. Jim won't ever forgit you, Huck; you's de
bes' fren' Jim's ever had; en you's de only fren' ole Jim's got now.
(2010, 100)

Huck resumes as the narrator:

I was paddling off, all in a sweat to tell on him; but when he says
this, it seemed to kind of take the tuck all out of me. (2010, 100)

33. Pace Jonathan Bennett's (1974) original discussion of the case. My reading of the case also runs counter to Arpaly's (2003) claim that Huck initially "hopes
against hope to find some excuse not to turn Jim in . . . [but] fails to find a loophole"
(75). However, Arpaly's instructive account of the role of *motivated reasoning* in certain
instances of racism and sexism means that she (unlike many other theorists) plausibly
has the resources to accommodate my point here (98–114). And, as she points out, the
correct interpretation of the episode in the novel isn't terribly important for philosophical purposes (76). A remaining question is how to assess a volte-face based on sympathy like Huck's would be on Bennett's and Arpaly's reading, given that Huck never
questions his racist conscience—and in fact feels deeply guilty for helping Jim—in
the aftermath (Manne 2013). Would this show his moral compass to be more or less
broken? Or would it suggest there is more than one dimension of moral assessment
in play here? Interesting as these questions are, they are orthogonal for my purposes.

So I suggest it is primarily Huck's recognition of his *friendship* with Jim, and his background awareness that *one does not turn in one's friends*, which trumps his explicit belief that one ought to return stolen property, runaway slaves like Jim included. I am happy to agree with Arpaly that recognizing Jim's humanity does play an important role here, in the sense that it is plausibly this recognition that allows Huck to enter into the friendship with Jim in the first place. But this just goes toward my point in this context (which matters less for the point Arpaly uses the case to make). Recognizing Jim's humanity does little to block Huck's intention to cruelly betray him. Rather, this recognition conditions the sense of *friendship* that ultimately does the conceptual-cum-psychological heavy lifting. Huck undergoes a kind of gestalt shift from representing Jim as an "insubordinate" and as "uppity" to a "friend" at the crucial moment. And this is what seems to "take the tuck" out of the dispositions that flow from the former set of perceptions. Huck's basic grasp of Jim's humanity remains a constant throughout the episode.

What about the case of Gaita's character, M? Suppose we accept Gaita's view of M as ascribing only a truncated inner life to the Vietnamese woman in the documentary. This form of racism seems possible, indeed common. But Gaita seems to assume that this is M's view of Vietnamese people quite generally—that she consistently attributes to them a certain *nature* or essence. This is one possibility, but it is surely not the only one. For one thing, the Vietnamese had been considered the *enemy* by many Australians for many years, in living memory. And the fact that the documentary was about the Vietnam War would also presumably have served to bring up the association. So it seems like an open question, for all that has been said, whether M would have had the same reaction to a Vietnamese person in a different social context, where their nationality and ethnicity were known to M, but their erstwhile enemy status was rendered much less salient.

Then there are specifically gendered possibilities to consider. Social norms permitting or encouraging "leaning down" on the caregiving and domestic labor of nonwhite women are unfortunately as much a legacy of racist white Australian culture as they remain prevalent in certain sectors of the United States. And at roughly this time, the relatively high percentage of Vietnamese immigrants (often, refugees) made them particularly vulnerable to such exploitation. So again, it may have been ideologically and psychologically expedient to mentally bracket this woman's capacity to feel resentful of such treatment. The capacity for empathy with other human beings can be confronting, even overwhelming, and dispose us to turn away from them.

This raises a possibility that Gaita (1998) dismisses rather summarily in developing his overall account of racism (62–66)—namely, that the tendency of a person like M to minimize the subjectivity of out-group members (at least in certain cases) is something like wishful thinking or, rather, willful denial. This need not be a straightforward belief, or even an implicit representation, of the relevant people's nature, at least in the first instance. Whatever representations are in play may instead be the result of something like motivated reasoning, stemming from an inchoate *desire* to minimize these people's subjectivity. And such a desire might in turn owe to the risk of guilt and shame otherwise, or the possibility of being flooded with debilitating compassion. Alternatively, and less flatteringly, it might owe to the (again, often inchoate) yen to hang onto the kind of privilege that relies on taking out-group members' preferences and plans less seriously than those of in-group members.

The upshot is that there are possible ways of filling out M's story that would make her denial of the full human subjectivity of the Vietnamese relatively superficial and, ultimately, dependent on her uncomfortable awareness that they are of course equally capable of being as wounded and grief-stricken as she is. It would then be greater emotional strength and moral lucidity, not a humanizing experience, separating M from a less racist outlook.

What, now, of Langton's views about the nature of pornography? In some sense, Langton is clearly right that there is a genre of heterosexual pornography that depicts women as blank, staring, comparatively mindless creatures. (The female lead always wants what he has to give her, and breathy affirmations more or less exhaust her vocabulary.) But I think it is a mistake to suppose that pornography of this kind engenders or reflects this literal *view* of women. I find it more plausible to think it is, rather, a marketable fantasy, in offering an escape from more painful and confronting realities. Women's subjectivity and autonomous sexuality is increasingly difficult to deny, for anyone not utterly delusional and endowed with an Internet connection (ironically). For, women's voices ring too loud and clear in cyberspace.[34] Hence, from the perspective of patriarchal values, women may be human—all too human, sometimes. Pornography may provide a welcome relief from realities that are difficult to bear in being apprehended. It may soothe by imaginatively defusing the psychic threat women's humanity can pose, inasmuch as she has the capacity to reduce men to shame or humiliate them sexually. This is as opposed to expressing or even shaping men's literal view of women. (See Bauer 2015 for illuminating discussion.)

So far, the socially situated model has been faring pretty well. But it faces an obvious challenge to extending it much further. What should be said about the moral psychology of agents in the grip of explicitly dehumanizing ideologies because of the influence of dehumanizing propaganda, in particular? If this cannot be explained on the situated approach, then it would serve to delineate an important arena in which the humanist model is clearly superior.

I am not convinced that the situated approach should be set aside so hastily even here, though. This is obviously a large issue, with a rich and growing literature that bears on it directly. (See, e.g., Tirrell [2012] and Stanley [2015], as well as David Livingstone Smith [2016].) So I will just try to say something preliminary about the subject here, leaving a fuller discussion for a future occasion.

One simple point is that dehumanizing speech can function to *intimidate, insult, demean, belittle,* and so on (Manne 2014b), since it helps itself to certain powerfully encoded *social meanings*. And given

---

34. The obvious irony of this being that the rise of Internet pornography seems not unconnected with the advent of the platform for the expression of women's subjectivity that the Internet as a whole has provided. Hence, backlash and silencing.

that human beings are widely (if erroneously) held to be *superior* to nonhuman animals, denying someone's humanity can serve as a particularly humiliating kind of *put-down*. When a white police officer in Ferguson called a group of black political protesters "fucking animals" (following the police shooting of Michael Brown, which I discuss in chapter 7), he was using this trope to demean and degrade the protesters and reassert his own dominance. White supremacist ideology benefits from having a ready stock of put-downs of this kind to draw from. Such put-downs would hardly be apropos when it comes to *actual* nonhuman animals, who could neither comprehend the insult nor *be* successfully put down by having their nonhuman status correctly identified. This requires human comprehension, not to mention an incipient human status to be degraded *from*. There is nothing to object to in being called a rat if, in fact, you are one.[35]

One might retreat to the view that dehumanizing ideologies are best suited to explaining the moral outlook of agents who participate in mass atrocities, as per David Livingstone Smith's focus. But even here, there are grounds to worry about reading the moral psychology off the literal content of dehumanizing propaganda (or people's

35. Since members of in-groups also speak of out-group members in these ways among themselves, Livingstone Smith (2016) points out that dehumanizing speech cannot serve *simply* to dominate, intimidate, insult, and so on. This is clearly right. However, there is also the simple point that in-group members can egg each other on and sanction certain previously proscribed behaviors toward out-group members by reiterating the terms in question, whose central purpose may still be to humiliate out-group members in other contexts.

See also Tirrell (2012) for a discussion of a case in which the derogatory terms (as described in note 21) were initially used primarily by in-group members among themselves in a similarly *action-engendering way*, and only later leveled derisively *toward* out-group members (175). Tirrell also points to the ways in which derogatory terms can function to *police* out-group members, by threatening the "good ones" who are privy to the insult (while the "bad ones" being insulted are not) with being similarly disparaged if they do not toe the line (192). These possibilities vis-à-vis dehumanizing speech are all fully compatible with the socially situated model, I take it, and are useful to bear in mind in understanding certain manifestations of misogyny, in particular.

subsequent parroting of it).[36] It remains possible that the uptake of dehumanizing propaganda amounts to false consciousness, at least in many instances. I suspect this is the case more often than is recognized.

Why think this? It is significant in this context that war, genocide, and so-called ethnic cleansing often encompass the mass rape of women. This seems to me to raise an important question for the humanist to answer: viz., if the perpetrators of mass atrocities often dehumanize their victims, then why do the perpetrators so frequently rape the female ones? It is not just that sex between human beings and nonhuman animals is generally taboo, and relatively unusual, presumably partly because of this.[37] It is also that the *spirit* in which mass rapes tend to be committed is typically vindictive, punitive, triumphalist, and domineering. These acts hence bear all of the hallmarks of *interpersonal* violence, which is expressive of and gives vent to paradigmatically interpersonal reactive attitudes—such as resentment, righteous anger, jealousy, and so on.[38]

How might the humanist deal with this challenge? One interesting possibility, which Livingstone Smith (2016) pursues, is that the victims of dehumanization are represented as *both* human and subhuman. Specifically, they are held to have the outer appearance of a human being, but to share an essence with some kind of nonhuman animal that often represents a threat or hazard to humankind (e.g., snakes, rats, cockroaches). The victims of mass atrocities hence tend to be perceived as "uncanny" and monstrous, he argues.

---

36. Compare Jason Stanley (2015, chap. 2), for an instructive discussion of what he calls "the sincerity condition," which can hold despite the fact that dehumanizing rhetoric is, in his view, often clearly metaphorical.

37. Compare Bernard Williams's remark: "Take the case of the slave-owners who drafted the Bill of Rights. There was a great deal of false consciousness there, since when these slave owners took advantage of their women slaves, they didn't actually think they were engaged in bestiality. They were well aware that they were fucking a human being!" Williams, interview by Alex Voorhoeve, uncorrected proofs, December 2002, circulated posthumously.

38. As Livingstone Smith (2016) himself points out, when it comes to the humiliating nature of the rape of women during the Rwandan genocide.

I think Livingstone Smith is onto something important here when it comes to the gestalt shifts in perception and the subsequent ambivalence that often mark an agent's stance toward the people they are tasked with persecuting or destroying. But I worry that his specific story makes mass rape even *harder* to explain, if anything. Sexual liaisons with those who are perceived as uncanny, and subsequently inspire horror and revulsion, ought to be at least as aversive as any other interaction with them, if not more so.

The notorious Soviet minister of propaganda during World War II, Ilya Ehrenburg, was confident of this himself. According to a recent account by historian Antony Beevor (2003), the German propaganda ministry charged Ehrenburg with inciting the Red Army to rape German women while they occupied Berlin (25). Ehrenburg, hardly one to shrink from charges of viciousness and ruthlessness, nevertheless held that the Soviet soldiers "were not interested in Gretchens but in those Fritzes who had insulted our women." The Soviet political department echoed Ehrenburg's sentiment, saying, "When we breed a true feeling of hatred in a soldier, the soldier will not try to have sex with a German woman, because he will be repulsed."

Ehrenburg's propaganda contained a classic mixture of dehumanizing tropes and the reification of enmity. The former aspect of it is particularly striking in the context of this chapter. It features prominently in the pamphlet *Kill!* (1942), distributed to over a million Red Army soldiers, which opens with the statement, "The Germans are not human beings." It is also central to the more searching "The Justification of Hatred" (1942), in which Ehrenburg takes pains to emphasize the sympathetic nature of the Soviet people, as was supposedly evident from their conduct during World War I. This leaves him with the following puzzle, not to mention justificatory burden:

> How did it come to happen, then, that the Soviet people came to abhor the Nazis with so implacable a hatred?
>
> Hatred was never one of the traits of the Russians. It did not drop from the skies. No, this hatred our people now evince has been born of suffering. At first many of us thought that this war

was like other wars, that pitted against us mere human beings dressed only in different uniforms. We were brought up on grand ideas of human fraternity and solidarity. We believed in the force of words, and many of us did not understand that opposing us were not human beings but frightful, loathsome monsters, and that the principles of human brotherhood imperatively demand that we deal ruthlessly with the Fascists . . .

The Russians have a song and in it the people have expressed their attitude towards just and unjust wars: "Wolfhounds are justified where cannibals are not." It is one thing to destroy a mad wolf; it is another thing to raise one's hand against a human being. Now every Soviet man and woman knows that we have been attacked by a pack of wolves.[39]

The rhetoric here is strikingly in line with Livingstone Smith's claim that the dehumanized are represented as wolves in sheep's clothing—or human clothing, rather. And the reference to "frightful, loathsome monsters" is equally grist for Livingstone Smith's mill. Or at least, this is so if we take this piece of propaganda to have *succeeded* in helping the Nineteenth Army soldiers to see German people in the way that it depicted them.

But the Soviet soldiers' mass rape of German women casts doubt on this hypothesis. So does the fact that they were not just following orders. Indeed, quite the contrary—there were widespread concerns, which came from as high up as Stalin himself, that the brutal behavior of the soldiers (which included looting and extensive destruction in Berlin) would undermine their military efforts—not to mention destroy valuable resources, such as factories. So the Soviet soldiers were actually being *disobedient*. Despite that, the mass rape of German women continued for several years. At least two million women were raped during this period—and many, if not a majority,

39. "The Justification of Hate," Stormfront Russia: White Nationalists in Russia, https://www.stormfront.org/forum/t107725-2/.

were raped multiple times. Gang rapes were very common. There were documented rapes of girls as young as twelve and women as old as eighty. Nobody was exempt—not nuns, not women pregnant in a hospital, not even women in the process of giving birth there. And many of these women were raped in the most brutal ways imaginable. When certain of the soldiers were too inebriated to proceed as planned, they would violate women using bottles, sometimes broken ones. Needless to say, this caused horrific injuries. Many women died as a result; and many committed suicide (Beevor 2003, 24–38).

In trying to grapple with these horrors, the questions I am left with are these: if the dehumanizing propaganda had seeped very deeply into the soldier's moral outlooks, then how could their subsequent behavior toward these women (these "she-wolves") be explained? But if it did not go deep when pushed so hard, then does it usually? Does it ever?

This leaves us with an important, albeit confronting, possibility: people may know full well that those they treat in brutally degrading and inhumane ways are fellow human beings, underneath a more or less thin veneer of false consciousness. And yet, under certain social conditions—the surface of which I've just barely scratched in this chapter—they may massacre, torture, and rape them *en masse* regardless.[40]

WOMEN, ALL TOO HUMAN

So what makes many people—including, seemingly, many propagandists—believe that humanism is correct? In the closing section

---

40. Interestingly, Beevor (2003) emphasizes the envy the Soviet soldiers felt toward the people of Berlin; for the latter lived more comfortably than the former had ever dreamed of. He gives a striking example of the enraged Soviets destroying so many pillows and mattresses—paradigmatic creature comforts—that the streets of Berlin often resembled a snowstorm, so awash were they with feathers (35). The envy of Jews is similarly an important theme in some recent historical explanations of the escalation of anti-Semitism in Germany prior to 1933. See, for example, Amos Elon's *The Pity of It All: A Portrait of the German-Jewish Epoch, 1743–1933* (2013), and Götz Aly's *Why the Germans? Why the Jews? Envy, Race Hatred, and the Prehistory of the Holocaust* (2014).

of this chapter, let me note two somewhat less obvious possibilities than those mentioned above that seem capable of giving rise to dehumanizing ways of viewing and treating women, among others. But neither threatens to undermine my suspicion that failing to recognize other people as human beings is rare, especially when it comes to women subject to the dynamic canvassed in chapter 4. On the contrary, each again presupposes her humanity.

The first point concerns the sorts of perceptions that can result from other people's anomalous behavior, because it is viewed as anomalous *simpliciter*: it involves a reversal of their usual human, all too human, social roles, relations, or obligations. The second involves giving a woman "a taste of her own medicine," that is, seeking *vengeance* against her, on the part of those who feel *treated* by her or her ilk as *personae non gratae*, or even as subhuman—often falsely and unfairly. For his wounds may be due to an illicit sense of entitlement to be the subject of her gaze, the focus of her attention, or the beneficiary of her tender ministrations. He feels less human or perhaps better, less *humanized*, than he believes he deserves, and was expecting, to be made to feel. And so he (more than) returns the (non-)favor, as payback.

I'll take these points in order.

Regarding the first: part of being recognized as human involves the potential to be cast in social scripts in specific roles and relations, in virtue (among other things) of one's group memberships or identities.[41] We've seen how this can give rise to brutal forms of (mis)treatment. But a *failure* to play one's assigned part in the script, or to attempt some kind of role *reversal*, is prone to give rise to *startled* reactions—a sense of being "taken aback." The person may then be perceived as "off," off-putting, peculiar, and creepy. They may even be perceived as uncanny or robotic: as if they are an imposter in the role, merely "going through the motions." This doesn't mean they are perceived as less than fully human, though. It means they are being viewed with the kind of *suspicion* and even disgust or horror liable to

---

41. Thanks to Joel Sati for his valuable insights in this connection, during a talk I gave at the University of California, Berkeley.

arise when someone's behavior seems socially anomalous. She is not playing her part in the script. And so we have grave doubts about her character or persona—or even doubt she *has* one.

Consider, for example, the "little robot woman" Meursault encounters in two different contexts in Albert Camus's *The Stranger* (1946). The first time he sees her, she is ordering a meal at a restaurant. She acts very deliberately. Her agency is striking to him. And it may be striking to us, too, as readers, that she is engaged in a very human act—and a very social one. She is doing the same thing Meursault is, having a meal out on her own. Here is how he describes her:

> The waiter brought the hors d'oeuvre, which she proceeded to wolf down voraciously. While waiting for the next course, she produced another pencil, this time a blue one, from her bag, and the radio magazine for the coming week, and started making ticks against almost all the items of the daily programs. There were a dozen pages in the magazine, and she continued studying them closely throughout the meal. When I'd finished mine she was still ticking off items with the same meticulous attention. Then she rose, put on her jacket again with the same abrupt, robot-like gestures, and walked briskly out of the restaurant. Having nothing better to do, I followed her for a short distance. Keeping on the curb of the pavement, she walked straight ahead, never swerving or looking back, and it was extraordinary how fast she covered the ground, considering her smallness. In fact, the pace was too much for me, and I soon lost sight of her and turned back homeward. For a moment the "little robot" (as I thought of her) had much impressed me, but I soon forgot about her. (1946, 30)

The woman is not only interacting with her waiter, in an interpersonal exchange, but evincing myriad other powers of mind and autonomous agency: she has preferences, orders accordingly, reads her magazine, plans (it being a radio schedule), writes, calculates, and walks with an "extraordinary speed," such as to outpace Meursault. The two of them are playing essentially the same part in the same social script, in tandem. But on a woman, the behavior seems odd, even funny. She subsequently seems out of place—her place—and somehow unconvincing, fake, even veritably robotic, in this role. Much the same (including the "robotic" charge) was said of Hillary Clinton when she was running for president in 2016 (see chapter 8). And here, too, Clinton was playing a role historically exclusively reserved for men—and asking for that which she might have been expected to *give* to him. To wit: support and attention, which many people who might otherwise have been expected to give to her (in being strongly opposed to Trump, among other things) withheld in her case.

The next time Meursault encounters the "little robot woman" is in court. By that time, he has shot and killed "the Arab" who stared daggers in his direction, and who made *him* feel inhuman, like a mere object or impediment. Like a rock or a tree, specifically; a movable object with no will of its own. Meursault is out and about with his friend Raymond, when they first encounter "the Arabs," whose gaze is described as having a withering, petrifying, even dehumanizing effect on our narrator—in his mind, that is—simply by looking in his direction in a way he finds inscrutable. To wit:

> They stared at us silently, in the special way these people have—
> as if we were blocks of stone or dead trees. Raymond whispered
> that the second Arab from the left was "his man," and I thought
> he looked rather worried. However, he assured me that all that
> was ancient history . . . There was no point in hanging about here.
> Halfway to the bus stop he glanced back over his shoulder and
> said the Arabs weren't following. I, too, looked back. They were
> exactly as before, gazing in the same vague way at the spot where
> we had been. (32)

Again, we see the need to consider dehumanization from the other direction to the customary one in moral philosophy: as a psychological manifestation of a sense of illicit *entitlement* to be the observer or the judge, or an object of care and admiration, rather than suspicion, contempt, hostility, or indifference. Such a sense can be highly dangerous for those who are held to be looking the wrong way at people in the grip of what may amount to a persecution complex. Something like this is at stake when "Raymond's man" appears again on the beach, this time alone, as if to underscore his vulnerability. Meursault, who had considered the matter settled, is taken aback. The man's face is shaded by a rock, and the haze of the heat renders him a blurry figure. Meursault pulls Raymond's revolver from his pocket, and fires at the threatening specter: he sinks four more shots into the dead body, on which they leave "no visible trace." (39) He hears the shots land as much as he sees them. So goes the undoing of a stranger in Algeria. The moment is over; Meursault's blunted, but real, sense of his own humanity returns to him in prison.

Now the "little robot" woman is at his murder trial to observe. She is described as wearing a "mannish" coat, and training her eyes upon him (54). Meursault feels acutely aware of her presence there, judging him (he fancies), though she is only one among many in the courtroom gallery. And when Meursault feels judged, the effect is always disorientation, from the beginning of the novel. He loses his sense of agency—as if faced with the behavior known as "stonewalling" (or, for that matter, the "still face" paradigm touched on in the conclusion). It may not be an accident that prior to all of this happening, Meursault had just lost his mother. When they lived together, her eyes had followed him around the room, "though they hardly ever talked." She was, he felt, "always watching," and he did not seem to mind (1946, 5). It was just the way things were, is the sense one gets. Perhaps she hence did what a mother is meant to do: she looked after him.

As well as withdrawal symptoms stemming from a lack of sympathetic oversight, a second, similarly non-obvious source of dehumanizing behavior can now be considered. There are acts of *revenge* toward women who do not play their part in the social script an agent has adopted, warping his sense of reality, as opposed to being understood as merely a wish or a fantasy. Elliot Rodger did not receive the attention, affection, admiration, and sexual favors he desired from a suitably "hot" woman, in a suitably timely fashion. His social script was so rigid, and he so thoroughly ensconced in it, that he felt the women he stalked were ignoring him—even though he never introduced himself. Their story did not include him as a character, until he forced the issue.

But as I have shown, it is not that Rodger held women to be mindless things, objects, nonhuman or subhuman creatures; nor is this true of women in general under a patriarchal order. Rather, a woman is regarded as *owing* her human capacities to particular people, often men or his children within heterosexual relationships that also uphold white supremacy, and who are in turn deemed entitled to her services. This might be envisaged as the de facto legacy of coverture law—a woman's being "spoken for" by her father, and afterward her husband, then son-in-law, and so on. And it is plausibly part of what makes women more broadly somebody's *mother, sister, daughter, grandmother*: always somebody's someone, and seldom her own person. But this is not because she's not held to be a person at all, but rather because her personhood is held to be *owed* to others, in the form of service labor, love, and loyalty.

Her personal services, moreover, have a humanizing psychological effect on those in her care orbit, to whom her attention is held to be owed. So, when she fails to give him what he's held to be entitled to, by way of various forms of nurturing, admiration, sympathy, and attention, *he* may be left feeling less than human—like "an insignificant little mouse," as Elliot Rodger described himself at one point. And his revenge may be to dehumanize *her* in turn: to give her a taste of her own medicine, when it comes to making her feel like a nonperson. Here's how Rodger opens his so-called manifesto (really more of a memoir—the character of the self being prescient, pitiable, and perpetually central):

> Humanity . . . All of my suffering on this world has been at the hands of humanity, particularly women. It has made me realize just how brutal and twisted humanity is as a species. All I ever wanted was to fit in and live a happy life amongst humanity, but

I was cast out and rejected, forced to endure an existence of loneliness and insignificance, all because the females of the human
species were incapable of seeing the value in me.

As "My Twisted World" unfolds, or rather, unravels, it becomes clear
that this battle between the sexes is more than a metaphor for Rodger.
But the enmity is borne of unmet felt need and the subsequent sense
of vulnerability that underlies, and sometimes provokes, interpersonal aggression. Rodger hates such women in much the same way
that insecurely attached children (at least in popularized attachment
theory) hate and rage at their mothers (typically, and tellingly), when
she leaves him with a stranger. He hates her for leaving him feeling
helpless and lonely. He feels entitled to her time, focus, attention,
and care and may love her intensely—but as a personal possession, who must be jealously guarded, and who must not betray him,
break her promises, or disappoint him. Something similar applies to
Rodger's hatred of the women who sexually rejected him. They make
him feel inhuman in the sense of again, perceived, social isolation
and pariahdom. He concludes:

I am not part of the human race. Humanity has rejected me. The
females of the human species have never wanted to mate with
me, so how could I possibly consider myself part of humanity?
Humanity has never accepted me among them, and now I know
why. I am more than human. I am superior to them all. I am Elliot
Rodger . . . Magnificent, glorious, supreme, eminent . . . Divine!
I am the closest thing there is to a living god. Humanity is a disgusting, depraved, and evil species. It is my purpose to punish
them all. I will purify the world of everything that is wrong with
it. On the Day of Retribution, I will truly be a powerful god, punishing everyone I deem to be impure and depraved. When I think
about the amazing and blissful life I could have lived if only
females were sexually attracted to me, my entire being burns
with hatred. They denied me a happy life, and in return I will take
away all of their lives. It is only fair.

He is not quite done. He continues in an epilogue:

> Women represent everything that is unfair with this world, and in order to make the world a fair place, they must all be eradicated. A few women would be spared, however, for the sake of reproduction. These women would be kept and bred in secret labs. There, they will be artificially inseminated with sperm samples in order to produce offspring. Their depraved nature will slowly be bred out of them in time.

This sounds like the unhappy alternative ending of the movie *Dr. Strangelove* (1964).[42] It would be hard not to laugh, but for the fact that Rodger obtained firearms—and he acted.

Rodger's sense of fairness (or lack thereof) is based on a narcissistic delusion that encapsulates some of the madness, and method, of patriarchy. Its ideology often positions women as human *givers* in moral and social life, which does not cut against, and indeed often presupposes, her humanity. But it also results in bids for her attention, grabs for her body parts, and put-downs (or worse) if she demurs or refuses to oblige him. These moves may or may not have a dehumanizing quality in terms of their social meaning, or the way they "come across" to the women on their receiving end. Whatever the case, I believe they stem, most fundamentally, from a sense of what she's (there) *for* as a woman, and hence often socially situated as a provider of moral goods and resources (to him, first and foremost).

---

42. Recalling Dr. Strangelove's plan to set up an underground breeding lab in a mineshaft:

> TURGIDSON: Doctor, you mentioned the ratio of ten women to each man. Now, wouldn't that necessitate the abandonment of the so-called monogamous sexual relationship, I mean, as far as men were concerned?
>
> STRANGELOVE: Regrettably, yes. But it is, you know, a sacrifice required for the future of the human race. I hasten to add that since each man will be required to do prodigious . . . *service* along these lines, the women will have to be selected for their sexual characteristics which will have to be of a highly stimulating nature.

It makes sense that we would see symptoms of deprivation mind-set in this regard following the advent of feminist social progress in supposedly post-patriarchal settings. When demand for her attention exceeds supply on a grand scale, it is not surprising to find practices of men trying to turn the heads of women previously unknown to them—via catcalling and wolf-whistling and various forms of online trolling (from the patently abusive to ostensibly reasonable demands for rational debate, which unfortunately sometimes result in her being belittled, insulted, or mansplained to). In public settings, she is told to smile or asked what she's thinking by many a (male) stranger—especially when she appears to be "deep inside her own head" or "off in her own little world," i.e., appearing to think her own thoughts, her attention inwardly, rather than outwardly, focused. These gestures are then supposed to either *make her look*, or else force her to stonewall—a withholding, rather than sheer absence, of reaction. So her silence is icy; her neutral expression, sullen. Her not looking is snubbing; her passivity, aggression.

But an ice queen, a bitch, a temptress—or an angel, for that matter—each has something in common: they are human, all too human, female characters.

Chapter 6

Exonerating Men

The noble Brutus
Hath told you Caesar was ambitious:
If it were so, it was a grievous fault,
And grievously hath Caesar answer'd it.
Here, under leave of Brutus and the rest—
For Brutus is an honourable man;
So are they all, all honourable men—
Come I to speak in Caesar's funeral.
He was my friend, faithful and just to me:
But Brutus says he was ambitious;
And Brutus is an honourable man.
He hath brought many captives home to Rome
Whose ransoms did the general coffers fill:
Did this in Caesar seem ambitious?
When that the poor have cried, Caesar hath wept:
Ambition should be made of sterner stuff:
Yet Brutus says he was ambitious;
And Brutus is an honourable man.
You all did see that on the Lupercal
I thrice presented him a kingly crown,
Which he did thrice refuse: was this ambition?
Yet Brutus says he was ambitious;
And, sure, he is an honourable man.
I speak not to disprove what Brutus spoke,
But here I am to speak what I do know.
You all did love him once, not without cause:

What cause withholds you then, to mourn for him?
O judgment! thou art fled to brutish beasts,
And men have lost their reason.
. . .
But yesterday the word of Caesar might
Have stood against the world; now lies he there.
And none so poor to do him reverence.
O masters, if I were disposed to stir
Your hearts and minds to mutiny and rage,
I should do Brutus wrong, and Cassius wrong,
Who, you all know, are honourable men:
I will not do them wrong; I rather choose
To wrong the dead, to wrong myself and you,
Than I will wrong such honourable men.

Marc Antony in Shakespeare, *Julius Caesar*, Act III, Scene II

HOW TO GET AWAY WITH MURDER

In this chapter, I begin with the story of two murders. Both of the victims were women. Both of the prime suspects were men with whom the victims had been intimate. And in both cases, the man's story got rewritten—to the point where one of the seeming murders became her elaborate attempt to frame him. In one of the two cases, he turned out to be innocent. In the second, the plot is driven by the question: Will he get away with it? (cross fingers).

Both stories are fictional. But they are nevertheless instances of a prevalent cultural narrative to which we ought to pay close attention. Said narrative reflects and perpetuates a strenuous collective effort, yet to be fully acknowledged—namely, trying to uphold certain men's innocence, to defend their honor, and to grant them a pardon prematurely, or without the proper authority to do so. In many cases, this initially involves extending the benefit of the doubt to the alleged perpetrator over his accuser-cum-victim, no matter how thin the basis for doubting her word may be. I hence go on to connect these "exonerating narratives" (as I call them) to the concept of testimonial injustice as theorized by Miranda Fricker (2007), José Medina (2011), and Gaile Pohlhaus Jr. (2012). Later, I draw further insights from work by Kristie Dotson and Marita Gilbert (2014) on the "curious disappearances" and attendant invisibility of certain subjects within public discourse.

In making my argument, I restrict myself to men who enjoy most, if not all, major forms of privilege.[1] And the degree to which this can distract us from the erasure of women from the story is quite something to behold. Think of it as a dark art, as magic: the disappearing woman trick.

But it's also important to acknowledge, in saying this, that less privileged men are typically vulnerable to the dynamics in question here too. Indeed, that is part of the point. The "bad guys" are liable to be distinguished from the "good guys" in excessively Manichean (i.e., black and white) terms by being cast as monsters, psychopaths, sexual predators, and pedophiles—in ways ranging from the basically accurate, if lacking in nuance, to deep and systematic forms of injustice. Again, this is part of the same interlocking and dynamic set of social mechanisms: for the advent of these monsters makes for a highly flattering contrast with our privileged would-be heroes.

The examples I cite are contemporary, since my method in this chapter and the next is that of a philosophical bowerbird, a collector

---

1. Although, ultimately, I would want to explore a standard complication by showing how important moral and political concerns can be co-opted as part of a problematic bid for male redemption. Compare the role of concerns about implicit bias in what I suspect (but lack sufficient space to argue) was an exonerating narrative promulgated by the hit podcast *Serial* (hosted by Sarah Koenig, produced in collaboration with WBEZ Chicago, Season 1, 2014, https://serialpodcast.org/season-one).

I restrict myself here to the point that the ostensible concerns about such biases did little to justify the evident sympathy with, and sometimes explicit desire to exonerate, Adnan Syed, who was convicted of the murder of his ex-girlfriend Hae Min Lee, some fifteen years earlier, when the two were in high school. Although racial biases would have been operative against Adnan, who is Muslim, they would also have worked against the main witness who testified against him—Adnan's friend Jay, an African of shiny bits and pieces, which it uses to make a nest for itself. In what follows, I draw my examples from TV, politics, news stories, novels, social science, and ethnographies that have come out at roughly the same time and place, and hence form part of a cultural moment that I've lived through. But the dynamic in this chapter is as old as the patriarchy itself. The good guy can do no wrong; so we won't hear a bad word said against him. I call this the "honorable Brutus" problem. To abridge and adapt the relevant lines:

> She was my friend, faithful and just to me—at least, to the best of my knowledge. But Brutus says she's lying. And Brutus is a good guy.

The implicit *modus ponens* here is too seldom *tollens*ed. In other words, in such "he said"/"she said" or "her word against his" scenarios, we move from the premise that he's an "honorable man" or "good guy" to the conclusion that she must be lying or hysterical, instead of responding properly to the stronger evidence that *she's* the one telling the truth. And we subsequently fail to question the collective presumption that he is trustworthy after all—let alone with the bitter fury evinced by a Marc Antony over Brutus's cruel betrayal.

Marc Antony breaks down at the end of his famous speech, having exposed the "honorable Brutus" as a traitor and a fraud. "Bear with me," he says, "my heart is in the coffin there with Caesar; and I must pause till it come back to me." Writing in the immediate aftermath of the 2016 presidential election, I have to say: I know the feeling.

American man of the same age. Then there was the narrative erasure of Hae Min Lee— this being a form of misogyny to which Asian American women seem disproportionately vulnerable, as I suggested in chapter 3. This chapter takes up another general problem plausibly illustrated by the podcast: exonerating and excusing "golden boys" and "good guys." Both labels were applied to Adnan during *Serial* by people who knew him at the time of the murder.

Also notable: Hae Min Lee was murdered by strangulation, which significantly raises the likelihood that the homicide was committed by a male intimate partner, as discussed in the introduction.

BOY KILLS GIRL

Gillian Flynn's best-selling novel *Gone Girl* (2012) begins and ends with the good guy's side of the story. Nick and Amy, who have been married for five years, are unhappy in a routine way, pace Tolstoy. (Perhaps the tropes for the unhappy couple were a product of the sitcom.) They were both laid off from their jobs in Manhattan during the recession. They've since moved to the generic Midwestern town where Nick grew up to care for his ailing father. Amy is still unemployed; she is bored, miffed, and lonely. Nick has opened a bar and begun an affair with one of his writing students. He spends the rest of his time playing video games and brooding.

I'll cut to the chase. Here's the structure of the story: boy meets girl; boy and girl get married; boy fails girl; girl feels let down by him. Boy kills girl—or seems to, anyway. But it turns out to be a trick: the girl in this case is *crazy*.

She set him up, creating a faux diary of their five-year-long relationship. She went to the lengths of procuring blood and faking a positive pregnancy test. After she runs away, into the arms of a rich ex-lover, girl changes her mind (being fickle as well as conniving). Boy wasn't so bad, she decides. She murders the controlling ex, during sex, like a praying mantis. Girl and boy are reunited.

The 2012 book was a *New York Times* bestseller, and the 2014 feature film based on it did well at the box office too. Flynn (who also wrote the screenplay) was widely criticized for the misogyny in her depiction of her leading lady, Amy. Flynn writes that after the film came out:

> I had about 24 hours where I hovered under my covers and was like: "I killed feminism. Why did I do that? Rats. I did not mean to do that." And then I very quickly kind of felt comfortable with what I had written.[2]

2. Cara Buckley, "Gone Girls, Found," *New York Times*, November 19, 2014, https://www.nytimes.com/2014/11/23/arts/talking-with-the-authors-of-gone-girl-and-wild.html.

Rats indeed—however briefly. But Flynn is hardly alone in not rec-ognizing the connections here. Given our collective overinvestment in upholding male dominance, we tend not to notice the extreme lengths to which we're willing to go in so doing. While the center holds, we notice neither the fulcrum nor the fallout.

Part of the initial impetus for writing this book was my frustration with myself for having so little to say regarding the second of the murder cases I want you to consider. The show in question was the premiere of the 2014 TV adaptation of the Coen brothers' 1996 film *Fargo*; the Coen brothers were also listed as coproducers of the series. However, unlike the main character in the film version, his updated counterpart—the conspicuously renamed Lester Nygaard—has no plans to kidnap his wife, rechristened Pearl (from "Jean" in the origi-nal, film version). What happens is all his doing. It was a long time coming; but, at the same time, it's spontaneous. It's a violent out-burst borne of the shame of emasculation.

The story begins when Lester encounters his old nemesis, the bully from his high school class, Sam Hess, who humiliates Lester just like in the old days, now with Hess's laddish offspring acting as onlookers. Hess tells Lester he got a hand job from Pearl in high school. Hess has Lester off balance, metaphorically and literally. Lester stumbles and falls into a glass window, face first, so hard that his nose breaks.

In the ER waiting room, Lester meets a mysterious stranger—or rather, his id incarnate, in the form of Billy Bob Thornton—Lorne Malvo. When Lester tells him what has happened, Malvo offers to have Hess killed as vengeance. Lester is bewildered by the offer at first and tries to refuse it—though not quickly enough to be convinc-ing. So Malvo decides to go ahead and do it anyway. He goes to Hess's strip club and takes Hess out from behind, with a screwdriver to the back of the skull, as Hess is grunting his way through doggy-style intercourse with one of the dancers. We see Hess's blood spattering and painting the nameless woman's shoulders and neck, a kind of premature ejaculation, before we see Hess slump and collapse heavily on top of her. As the camera pans away, she's howling, screaming.

When Lester learns that his Goliath has been slain for him, he is both unnerved and emboldened. He resolves to fix the washing machine at home, whose off spin-cycle has long been a point of contention in his marriage—along with Lester's lackluster career and meager paycheck compared with his go-getting brother. To make matters worse, it turns out that Lester is a let-down in the bedroom as well. He has failed to father a child, and Pearl is sexually dissatisfied. She begins to taunt Lester about his inability to look her in the eye while having sex, during the argument that follows.

The scene begins with Lester proudly leading Pearl down to the basement to show her that he has managed to fix the washing machine. But Lester's moment of triumph is not to be—quite the opposite, in fact. The spin cycle goes out more wildly than ever before. Pearl smirks at his failure. Still worse, she is not surprised by it.

The structure of their story: boy fails girl; girl sneers at boy; boy feels wounded; boy gets angry; boy smashes girl's face in repeatedly with a hammer.[3]

A woman who nagged and emasculated her husband (some may be inclined to interject the adjective "poor") was hence shut up for good. We watch her face grow bloodier and bloodier until, before our presumptively unflinching eyes, it ceases to be a face at all—turning into a featureless mass of ragged, raw-meat tissue. Pearl's own eyes are no longer there—or at least, they're not visible. Shame "wants to destroy the eyes of the world," according to Erik Erikson (1963), as I noted in chapter 4. But as I then went on to argue, this only seems true of those among the shamefaced who felt entitled to more or

---

3. There are no comparable events in the film version, and the story is quite different. Lester's cinematic counterpart, Jerry Lundegaard, desperate for cash, tries to arrange to have his wife kidnapped so that he can pocket most of the ransom money. But one of the hit men he has paid to do the deed reverts to type and kills Jean instead. His rationale being, she was too noisy.

better—that is, to the admiration and approval of the subjects they want to destroy for looking at them the wrong way, or failing to look at them at all. The rest of us will rest content with hiding our faces, fleeing, or freezing.

As Lester looks up, shocked, realizing what he has done, his gaze lands on a (now conspicuously blood-spattered) motivational poster taped up on the wall. It features a school of blue fish, and a lone red fish, swimming against the tide. The caption reads, "What if you're right and they're wrong?" It's not exactly subtle. The poster was such a big hit with viewers that it was reproduced and sold on Amazon by an entrepreneurial type. The product description there reads:

> The reoccurring fish theme throughout Fargo's first season begins with this poster found in Nygaard's basement. This adorable cartoonish poster was meant to inspire, but after killing his wife, it soon became Lester Nygaard's new mantra. Much like Lester we too found inspiration in this blood splattered poster, but unlike him, managed to resist our dark urges . . . hopefully you can too!

Adorable; hopefully: a real inspiration.

What does it say about us, and the zeitgeist, that viewers in some sense wanted to watch this in 2014? What does it say that when I watched it with a friend and her husband while staying with them as a houseguest, it didn't ostensibly register with any of us as noteworthy or disturbing? (Should we make some popcorn? Want to watch another episode?) The whole series is premised on the assumption that the viewer will sympathize with Lester and want him to get away with it, at least initially. If you think that doesn't say anything about our tendency to pardon the hitherto historically dominant, especially when they're currently down on their luck, then try reversing the genders. Not that there are no cases of gender role reversals like this, but they seem comparative rarities, and they have a more shocking quality in proportion to their degree of violence. *Thelma and Louise* of course springs to mind, but it came out over twenty-five years ago.[4]

When it comes to a "he said"/"she said," "her word against his" scenario, there are obvious reasons to give him testimonial priority, from the point of view of upholding patriarchal order. For what if *she* is right? Then he would stand to be proven wrong. She would have the power to take him down with her word, when she is the more credible. And that power does not tend to be granted to historically subordinate people vis-à-vis the dominant without a fight. Such flipping of gendered hierarchies is part of what misogyny is effectively meant to prevent from happening.

This brings into view the connection between misogyny and testimonial injustice.

TESTIMONIAL INJUSTICE AS HIERARCHY PRESERVATION

Testimonial injustice has been a prominent and fruitful topic in recent analytic philosophy. The phenomenon was brought to the attention of analytic philosophers under that description by Miranda Fricker, and it has also been theorized (under various descriptions) by Patricia Hill Collins, Charles W. Mills, Karen Jones, José Medina, Gaile Pohlhaus Jr., Kristie Dotson, and Rachel V. McKinnon, among others.

Testimonial injustice arises due to systematic biases in the "economy of credibility," as Fricker (2007) aptly calls it. It afflicts members of a certain social group, most notably when the group has historically been and to some extent remains unjustly socially subordinate.[5]

---

4. Two other examples, courtesy of my editor, Peter Ohlin: Jennifer Lopez's character in the movie *Enough* and Jody Foster's character in *The Brave One*.

5. Fricker (2007) speaks of "social identity power" instead, and allows that there are forms of testimonial injustice that are more local and less historicized, for example, where proponents of a particular methodology or discipline are negatively stereotyped (28–29). But like Fricker, I concentrate here on more systematic forms, such as testimonial injustice based on race, gender, class, disability, age, sexual history (including being a sex worker), and their attendant intersections.

Testimonial injustice then paradigmatically consists in subordinate group members tending to be regarded as less credible when they make claims about certain matters, or against certain people, hence being denied the epistemic status of *knowers*, in a way that is explained by their subordinate group membership.

Fricker's (2007) opening example of testimonial injustice in *Epistemic Injustice* is Marge Sherwood's dismissal by the father of her fiancé, Dickie Greenleaf, in *The Talented Mr. Ripley*. When Marge airs her concerns that Dickie may have been done a mischief by his best friend, the eponymous antihero Tom Ripley, Mr. Greenleaf doesn't want to hear it. "Marge, there's female intuition, and then there's facts," he says matter-of-factly, dismissing both the legitimacy of Marge's fears and her standing to air them (2007, 9–17) She is just a woman being irrational and hysterical, according to the proper (read: sexist) standards of objectivity in play in that era (namely, the 1950s).

There are two different ways in which a person may be subject to testimonial injustice, according to Fricker's framework. First, she may be taken to be less *competent* than she ought to be—that is, as less likely to know of what she speaks, or be justified in believing it, than is warranted. Secondly, a person may be taken to be less *trustworthy* than she ought to be—that is, as less likely to be sincere or honest in her claims than (again) is warranted, from the perspective of the listener. On the face of it, Mr. Greenleaf appears to dismiss Marge's suspicions about foul play in this instance because he underestimates her *competence*. However, we can easily imagine that this is really just window dressing (or, alternatively, unconscious rationalization) for what is going on beneath the social surface. Perhaps Greenleaf Senior habitually suspects women of being controlling and manipulative, and liable to don a mask of concern in order to prevent boys from being boys, and enjoying the fun to which they are entitled. For example, he might be imagining that his son Dickie is enjoying a last hurrah of bachelorhood with his best friend, Tom, prior to "tying the knot." Marge is just spouting concern in an attempt to spoil their fun, he thinks. Everybody lies; but women are the *liars*.

Although the example of Marge Sherwood provides a vivid illustration of testimonial injustice, this phenomenon is often subtler and hence more insidious. It is important for my purposes that people can be unjustly dismissed as less credible than they are without any explicit thought, let alone mention, of the relevant social category. Rather, the fact that they are *interpreted* as a woman or nonwhite man *predicts* and *explains* how they are viewed and treated, even though their social identity does not loom large in the consciousness of the listener—who may unwittingly come up with post-hoc rationalizations, or have no conscious reason at all, for finding their testimony suspect or their arguments unpersuasive.

So that is the phenomenon of testimonial injustice. But why does it persist? What is its social and psychological basis? When, where, and why is it likeliest to be operative?

To be more precise here, we should distinguish four questions:

1. *When* do historically subordinate group members tend to suffer from credibility deficits?
2. *Why* do historically subordinate group members tend to suffer from credibility deficits?
3. *Do* historically subordinate group members tend, in fact, to suffer from credibility deficits across the board? Or are these deficits more domain- or context-specific, sometimes resulting in attendant credibility *surpluses*?
4. What are the ideological *functions*, if any, of such credibility deficits—and surpluses?

Let me say something about each of these questions in turn.

1. *When do historically subordinate group members tend to suffer from credibility deficits?*

Answering such fine-grained questions about statistical prevalence in any detail is clearly beyond my pay grade as a philosopher; Fricker doesn't tackle these sorts of questions either. What one *can* say is that testimonial injustice is either clearly or very plausibly at issue in many of the fictional cases that I've given—and taken from her—in this chapter, along with other, real-life cases to follow. Even if one disagrees with my analysis of some of them, all need not be lost, in view of my primary purposes. The main point is to glean the shape of the phenomenon, in order to be able to have fruitful disagreements of this very nature, about whether or not some candidate example is an instance. Similarly, the idea is to be able to recognize types of cases and their prevalence as they arise, not to decide on their prevalence a priori.

2. *Why do historically subordinate group members tend to suffer from credibility deficits?*

Fricker's answer to this question is that there are "negative identity-prejudicial stereotypes," which she describes as "widely held disparaging associations between a social group and one or more attributes, where this association embodies a generalization that displays some (typically epistemically culpable) resistance to counter-evidence owing to an ethically bad affective investment" (2007, 35).

This seems plausible. But Fricker doesn't say very much about the nature of the affective investment here. (A similar lacuna is sometimes evident in the implicit bias literature.) Further questions about these stereotypes remain, including why they tend to be resistant to relevant counterevidence. We might also wonder why subordinate group members are often held to be both incompetent *and* untrustworthy. These two stereotypes are often at cross-purposes, yet comorbidity in terms of these perceptions is certainly not unheard of; indeed, it seems common, as empirical evidence discussed in chapter 8 will confirm. What explains this?

3. *Do historically subordinate group members tend, in fact, to suffer from credibility deficits across the board?*

As Fricker herself briefly acknowledges in relation to one of her examples—Harper Lee's novel *To Kill a Mockingbird* (1960), wherein a black man, Tom Robinson, is falsely accused of raping a white woman, Mayella Ewell—the answer is surely no. Fricker:

> We have already remarked on the context dependence of the sort of prejudice that leads to testimonial injustice: the jurors of Maycomb County would have trusted Tom Robinson on many an issue relating to the harvest he was working on, and Herbert Greenleaf would have been ready to trust Marge on many a matter less apparently susceptible to distortion by her female intuitiveness than the question of her lover's disappearance. (2007, 135)

Fricker doesn't offer an explicit explanation for this. But she had suggested just prior that

> Tom Robinson might have been relied on and trusted epistemically on certain matters even by the more thoroughly racist white citizens of Maycomb County—matters relating to his daily work, no doubt, and indeed many everyday matters of practical import, so long as there was no challenge to a white person's word, no perceived implication of non-inferiority of intellect, nothing about the subject matter that might be seen to imply that this Negro was getting above himself. The tendency for incoherence in human prejudice, sustained through mechanisms of psychological compartmentalization, is such that significant pockets of epistemic trust can remain relatively untouched, even by a powerful racist ideology that corrupts that same trust in countless other contexts. (2007, 131)

So we see Fricker point to the roles of both hierarchy and ideology here. And, although she doesn't elaborate on these points, and I don't want to put words in her mouth, I believe they are crucial—and crucially connected. They enable us to get a grip on a plausible *political* basis for the affective investments in question: for example, those that underpin the relevant social stereotypes that testimonial injustice partly sustains, and is sustained by.

José Medina (2011) brings the role of hierarchy into clearer view here, in arguing that the surplus credibility enjoyed by dominant group members results in testimonial injustice for subordinate group members, given the comparative and contrastive—as well as temporally extended—nature of epistemic assessment. Medina:

> [In] the trial proceedings of *To Kill a Mockingbird* there is an entire hierarchy of credibility presumptions at play: white women are more credible than Negroes; and white men are more credible than white women: both [Atticus] Finch and the prosecutor are depicted as speaking for Mayella in a more credible voice than she can muster. The comparative and contrastive character of credibility assessments can also be appreciated in the audience's perceptions of the defendant and his interrogator as they interact, for their authority and credibility shrink and grow simultaneously and in tandem as they go back and forth . . . The discrediting of Tom's testimony does not happen in a vacuum; his credibility is not undermined independently of the credibility of those around him, but in fact the diminishing of his testimonial authority is achieved through the epistemic authority implicitly given to his questioner: the prosecutor is assumed to be a better evaluator of sentiments and their plausibility than the witness. (2011, 23–24)

The relationship between social hierarchies and testimonial injustice—in particular, the way the two are connected by ideology and what Charles W. Mills (1997) has called "the epistemology of ignorance"—is further illuminated by Gaile Pohlhaus Jr.'s (2012) discussion of this example. Pohlhaus points out that Tom Robinson's case goes beyond failing to glean who is trustworthy, and hence what really transpired between Tom and Mayella (namely, she made sexual advances on him, which he rebuffed: and her father was the one who beat her). Rather, there is a *refusal* to acknowledge what is revealed by the evidence. This is "systematic and coordinated misinterpretation of the world" and ignorance of the *willful* variety (731).[6]

Why this refusal? For one thing, as Medina argues above, acquitting Tom Robinson would require taking a black man's testimony over that of a white woman, which would run counter to existing social hierarchies (even in view of the Ewell's extreme poverty and lowly status compared with other whites). For another thing, as Pohlhaus's discussion helps crystallize, buying Tom Robinson's story would require conceiving of a white woman as capable of sexually *desiring* a black man, which is anathema to a white hetero-patriarchal order. White women's gaze is owed to white men; so black men who attract such attention are therefore conceived as threatening—and threatened, bodily—within a white supremacy.

Tom Robinson's disability makes it clear that he could not have attacked Mayella, but it also makes his body the more expendable or disposable for the purposes of upholding the existing racial order. It is not that Mayella and her father are trusted, or their story believed: indeed, the pair is thoroughly discredited in the town, to the great humiliation of the latter (consider how the novel ends—which I won't spoil for first-time readers). But the Ewell's lies conceal a truth that many are determined not to acknowledge: namely, that a white woman might be attracted to a black man, who merely felt sorry for her. The price of maintaining this ignorance is convicting a man who is clearly innocent—like the mockingbird that does no harm and simply gives pleasure with its song. Tom Robinson is not misunderstood: he is hunted, shot down, sacrificed.

6. Pohlhaus gives two reasons why such ignorance is especially insidious: "First, in moral and political discourse it blocks the transmission of knowledge that ought to make a normative claim on those for whom the knowledge is intended, presenting instead a distorted picture resulting from faulty epistemic resources. Second, it allows for a coordinated experiencing of the world that is determined by knowers themselves without their realizing it, because epistemic resources can become second nature once one has developed a facility in using them, and because epistemic resources work to coordinate knowers in relation to the world and one another" (2012, 731).

All told, the resources Medina and Pohlhaus bring to Fricker's framework suggest a way of thinking about testimonial injustice that fits naturally with my account of the nature of misogyny. Let me pause to explain why, and to do a little housekeeping.

Throughout the book so far, I've primarily been focused on the hostile reactions women face. (As might seem fitting, indeed mandatory, for a book on misogyny—what else would it concern, you might wonder?) But recall my point, from chapter 2, that we need to remember the flipside of the coin here. Or, indeed, the two distinct coins my account of misogyny suggests we should turn over—that of negativity, but also that of gender.

On my analysis, misogyny's primary function and constitutive manifestation is the punishment of "bad" women, and policing of women's behavior. But systems of punishment and reward—and conviction and exoneration—tend to work together, holistically. So, the overall structural features of the account predict that misogyny as I've analyzed it is likely to work alongside other systems and mechanisms to enforce gender conformity.[7] And a little reflection on current social realities encourages pursuing this line of thinking, which would take the hostility women face to be the pointy, protruding tip of a larger patriarchal iceberg. We should also be concerned with the rewarding and valorizing of women who *conform* to gendered norms and expectations, enforce the "good" behavior of others, and engage in certain common forms of patriarchal virtue-signaling—by, for example, participating in slut-shaming, victim-blaming, or the Internet analog of witch-burning practices. Another locus of concern

7. Note that I prefer not to include their non-hostile manifestations, for example, the rewarding and incentivizing of "good" women by the lights of patriarchal ideology, under the heading of misogyny, lest the label lose its affective connotations. "Soft misogyny" would be better; but I continue to hanker for a pithier, distinctive label. "Pedestalling" is one possibility, and I like that it draws attention to the fact that women deemed Madonnas and angels are in a *precarious* position—liable to be brought crashing down to earth when they make the slightest mistake. On the downside though, this label doesn't encompass forward-looking mechanisms, for example, incentives for good behavior, and the siphoning of women's energy in ways that suit patriarchal interests.

is the punishment and policing of men who flout the norms of masculinity—a point that is fairly well-recognized and, up to a point, well-taken. Least widely discussed by far are the *positive* and *exonerating* attitudes and practices of which the men who dominate women tend to be the beneficiaries. This is the system working in conjunction with misogyny I am highlighting in this chapter.

Before continuing, let me also return for a moment to the Isla Vista killings committed by Elliot Rodger, discussed in the opening chapters. I can now substantiate some hunches as to why there was so much resistance to the feminist diagnosis of misogyny—which, even if you disagreed with, shouldn't have received as much *hostility* as it garnered. I suggest that two factors were playing a role here: Elliot Rodger's "softness" and vulnerability and our disposition to sympathize with men's pain over women's, unless and until a privileged man can be cast in the role of hero or savior. As will be evident in the next chapter, these two points are closely connected. The tendency to forgive privileged men their sins—on the ostensible grounds of either his vulnerability to us, or ours to him, putting him in a no-lose position—is connected with our hostility to female victims. We are protective on his behalf and hence suspicious of her, as well as jealous on behalf of those in her care orbit—which some dominant men are typically encompassed by. (Jealousy with respect to what? Being the center of sympathetic moral attention in the eyes of a real or nominal audience, to telegraphically indicate the thrust of what is coming.)

Of the questions I distinguished earlier about testimonial injustice, only one remains, namely:

4. *What are the ideological functions, if any, of such credibility deficits? (And surpluses?)*

Notice that many of the examples of testimonial injustice above have an interesting feature in common. They involve someone's word being pitted *against someone else's*. Specifically, they all involve a historically *subordinate group member* trying to testify against a *dominant social actor*, in the relevant social context. Or, more subtly, they involve a subordinate group member trying to assert themselves in a domain in which dominant group members have traditionally been held to have all the answers, and have been free to talk among themselves, for the most part.

Hence my suggestion that credibility deficits—and surpluses as well—often serve the function of *buttressing dominant group members' current social position*, and protecting them from *downfall* in the existing social hierarchy: by being, for example, accused, impugned, convicted, corrected, diminished or, alternatively, simply outperformed, by those over whom they have historically been dominant. If this hypothesis is on the right track, then we would predict that historically subordinate group members will tend to suffer from credibility deficits relative to the historically dominant in situations of *conflict*, for example, "he said" / "she said" scenarios, and situations where people's agreement or attention is a sought-after and finite commodity (whether or not it is a zero-sum game, in addition to this).[8]

8. Here, I follow José Medina (2011), who offers a nuanced critique of Fricker's views when she writes:

> On the face of it, one might think that both credibility deficit and credibility excess are cases of testimonial injustice. Certainly, there is a sense of "injustice" that might naturally and quite properly be applied to cases of credibility excess, as when one might complain at the injustice of someone receiving unduly high credibility in what he said just because he spoke with a certain accent. At a stretch, this could be cast as a case of injustice as distributive unfairness—someone has got more than his fair share of a good—but that would be straining the idiom, for credibility is not a good that belongs with the distributive model of justice . . . those goods best suited to the distributive model are so suited principally because they are finite and at least potentially in short supply . . . Such goods are those for which there is, or may soon be, a certain competition . . . By contrast, credibility is not generally finite in this way, and so there is no analogous demand to invite the distributive treatment." (Fricker 2007, 19–20)

Thanks to Rachel V. McKinnon for drawing Medina's important work to my attention.

This prediction is borne out by many of the examples in this chapter, and some canvassed in others too. To wit:

- *Gone Girl*—what he said in his defense was hard to believe. Until she turned out to be incredibly conniving;
- Marge Sherwood—she was attempting to inform *on* the talented Mr. Ripley;
- Tom Robinson—a black man's word was levelled to no avail against a white woman's, among other factors just mentioned;
- Gamergate—the conflagration was sparked when indie game designer Zoë Quinn was the target of a bitter rant posted by her ex-boyfriend on his blog, accusing her of cheating on him. The fuel for the ensuing fire were allegations (false, as it turned out) that Quinn had leveraged sex with a journalist in exchange for a positive review of her video game, Depression Quest. Quinn's incursion into the male-dominated world of gaming, while she was also perceived as wronging and double-crossing particular men within it, resulted in a tsunami of misogynist abuse hurled in her direction. Quinn was subject to many death threats, rape threats, and messages encouraging her to commit suicide (see chapter 4, note 12);[9]
- Julia Gillard—having toppled former Australian prime minister Kevin Rudd, Gillard was accused shortly afterward of having reneged on her deal to let Rudd remain leader, as well as of being a traitor and dishonest, in breaking an election promise.

9. It should be noted that abuse along these lines is unfortunately disproportionately common for women who have any kind of online presence, especially if they offend against patriarchal values (now often minimally repackaged under the heading of the "men's rights," MRA, or "alt-right" movements). However, Quinn was also "doxxed," that is, her home address was published online. So those threatening to kneecap her could actually get to her. An injury designed to make her fear them; whereas a brain injury might render her insensible, it was pointed out by one forum poster. Quinn was eventually forced her out of her home as a result of this: none-too-subtle revenge for costing certain male gamers their hallowed and, again, dare I say, safe spaces. Simon Parkin, "Zoë Quinn's Depression Quest," *The New Yorker*, September 9, 2014, http://www.newyorker.com/tech/elements/zoe-quinns-depression-quest.

Gillard was nicknamed "Ju-liar," and never shook the moniker. Her ratings for trustworthiness were also historically low, which was not justified by her record. (I return to Gillard's case in chapter 8, along with the similar—and similarly outsize—suspicions leveled at Hillary Clinton.);

- Women's word against men's in cases of sexual assault—who do we *want* to believe (in)?

This last question is not a rhetorical one, unfortunately. With a heavy heart, I now turn to it, by way of a recent case that received a lot of attention in the media—and that people seemed to think more soundly about than usual. So, one might have hoped this would have been a watershed moment for combating rape culture. No such luck, however, on grounds I'll get into after canvassing the incident. This raises the possibility that a fair number of people had the right reaction to the following case, but for the wrong reasons.

HIMPATHY

In June 2016, Stanford University student Brock Turner, age twenty, was tried for treating a young woman, age twenty-two, like a proverbial piece of meat—sexually assaulting her behind a dumpster, after a party on campus. The woman he assaulted, who had been visiting her sister, was discovered unconscious. Among his father's chief concerns after Brock's arrest and during his subsequent trial was that his son could no longer enjoy a nice rib-eye steak fresh off the grill, having lost his appetite. Many of us lost ours, reading Dan Turner's letter to the judge, in which he lamented his son's no longer being the "happy-go-lucky self" and "easy going" college athlete he once was. Should he have been?[10]

10. WITW Staff, "Victim's and Father's Statements in Campus Sexual Assault Case Draw Strong Reactions Online," *New York Times*, June 6, 2016, http://nytlive. nytimes.com/womenintheworld/2016/06/06/victims-and-fathers-statements-in-campus-sexual-assault-case-draw-strong-reactions-online/.

The judge in this case, Aaron Persky, similarly worried about "the severe impact" of the conviction on Turner's future and gave him what was, by the relevant standards, a very lenient sentence (six months in county jail—of which he served just three—and three years' probation). Much was made throughout the trial and sentencing of Brock Turner's swimming prowess. And Dan Turner was still not satisfied, believing his son shouldn't do any time whatsoever. He described his son's crime as a mere "twenty minutes of action," out of twenty years of good behavior (WTIW Staff 2016; see note 10 here.).

But just as the murderer can't claim credit for all of the people he didn't kill, Turner was no less a rapist for all of the women he didn't violate. And when there is one victim, it must be said: there are often others. So his father's estimated ratio may have been on the low side.[11]

This case vividly illustrates the often overlooked mirror image of misogyny: *himpathy*, as I'll call it. It is so overlooked that it is a "problem with no name," to use Betty Friedan's famous phrase from *The Feminine Mystique* (1963). But this isn't because the problem of himpathy is rare. On the contrary—it's so common that we regard it as business as usual. (See Manne 2016f, where I also suggested the label "androphilia.")

The specific form of himpathy on display here is the excessive sympathy sometimes shown toward male perpetrators of sexual violence. It is frequently extended in contemporary America to men who are white, nondisabled, and otherwise privileged "golden boys" such as Turner, the recipient of a Stanford swimming scholarship. There is a subsequent reluctance to believe the women who testify against these men, or even to punish the golden boys whose guilt has been firmly established—as, again, Turner's was.

11. Specific evidence subsequently emerged that Brock Turner's past behavior with women had at least been less than stellar: "Members of Stanford Swim Team Not Surprised by Brock Turner Arrest," *Inside Edition*, June 16, 2016, http://www.insideedition.com/headlines/17021-members-of-stanford-womens-swim-team-not-surprised-by-brock-turner-arrest.

One reason for this denialism is a mistaken idea about what rapists must be like: creepy, uncanny, and wearing their lack of humanity on their sleeve. Brock Turner is not a *monster*, wrote one of his female friends, in a letter blaming his conviction on political correctness. He was the victim of a "camp-like university environment," in which things "get out of hand" due to alcohol and "clouded judgment." Turner's crime was "completely different from a woman getting kidnapped and raped as she is walking to her car in a parking lot." "That is a rapist," she wrote. "I know for a fact that Brock is not one of these people."[12]

She had known Brock for a long time, she added. And he had always been caring, respectful, and sweet to her. So Brock was not a rapist, his friend again insisted. The judge, Persky, concurred with her assessment. "To me that just rings true. It sort of corroborates the evidence of his character up until the night of this incident, which has been positive."

Both Brock's friend and the judge in this case seemed to be reasoning in accordance with the following inference pattern: a golden boy is not a rapist. So-and-so is a golden boy. Therefore, so-and-so is not a rapist. This is the honorable Brutus problem.

It is high time to give up the myth of the golden boy, to reject the major premise, and learn to *tollens* the *ponens* when appropriate. Turner was found actively violating his victim, who was unconscious and intoxicated, in an alley behind that dumpster. That is rape. Someone who rapes is a rapist. So Turner is a rapist—as well as a golden boy. Therefore . . .

---

12. Compare Pete Rose, the Brooklyn precinct commander, who opined in January 2017 that the majority of rapes in the district were "not total abomination rapes where strangers are being dragged off the streets." Rose continued: "If there's a true stranger rape, a random guy picks up a stranger off the street, those are the troubling ones. That person has, like, no moral standards." Rose apologized afterwards, following a widespread public outcry. Graham Rayman, "Certain Sexual Assaults Are 'Not Total Abomination Rapes,' Brooklyn NYPD Commander Reportedly Claims," *New York Daily News*, January 6, 2017, http://www.nydailynews.com/new-york/nypd-commander-sex-assaults-not-total-abomination-rapes-article-1.2938227.

Too often, we avert our eyes and refuse to face the prevalence and character of sexual assault in the United States in general and on college campuses in particular. We assure ourselves that real rapists will appear on our radars either as devils, decked out with horns and pitchforks, or else as monsters—that is, as creepy and ghoulish creatures. Monsters are unintelligible, uncanny, and they are outwardly frightening. What is frightening about rapists is partly the lack of identifying marks and features, beyond the fact that they are by far most likely to be men. Rapists are human, all too human, and they are very much among us. The idea of rapists as monsters exonerates by caricature.[13]

Another, related, myth is that rapists are psychopaths, pictured as ruthless, unfeeling, and sadistic. This is accurate about neither group (which is not to say there is no overlap between the two, as they are in reality). But many sexual assaults are committed not because the assailant lacks any concern for or awareness of other people, but because of aggression, frustration, a desire for control, and again, a sense of entitlement—be it aggrieved or still expectant. This also means that while factors like alcohol and other intoxicating substances, as well as frat house culture, undoubtedly contribute to the prevalence of sexual assault, they are more a matter of enablement than motive.

Even among those who are prepared to acknowledge the prevalence of sexual assault, and the myths above as such, there is a subtler form of wishful thinking that is also very common: the idea that sexual violence on college campuses occurs primarily due to youthful inexperience and ignorance, to the exclusion of misogynist aggression, serial

13. For a compelling first-personal account of one of the comparatively rare instances of sexual assault that did have many of the features of a "monster in the bushes" narrative, see Susan Brison's *Aftermath: Violence and the Remaking of a Self* (2002, chap. 1). And compare Brison's subsequent account of the different—and in some ways even greater—challenges she faced in speaking out about a sexual assault committed by an acquaintance: Susan Brison, "Why I Spoke Out about One Rape but Stayed Silent about Another," *Time*, December 1, 2014, http://time.com/3612283/why-i-spoke-out-about-one-rape-but-stayed-silent-about-another/.

sexual predation, and norms that enable and protect the perpetrators: that is, rape culture. Dan Turner said his son is fully committed to educating others about "the dangers of alcohol consumption and sexual promiscuity." Judge Persky referred to this plan approvingly. But so-called promiscuity is not the issue: violence is. And the suggestion that Brock Turner might be an appropriate spokesperson against sexual violence at this juncture is, to say the least, galling. He would need a moral education before presuming to provide one. And his being so eager to adopt the moral high ground, after having seized the upper hand via sexual violence, strongly suggests that the crucial lesson here has yet to be learned—viz., that a preeminent position in any given hierarchy is not his moral birthright.

But it is easy to be angry with the father, the judge, and the friend. It is also fitting, up to a point. Yet it would be a mistake to view them as on a different plane of moral obtuseness, as opposed to merely being on the extreme end of a himpathetic spectrum on which many of us lie. Brock Turner's defenders exhibited forgiving tendencies, and spun exonerating narratives, that are all too commonly extended to men in his position. And such tendencies stem largely from capacities and qualities of which we're rarely critical: such as sympathy, empathy, trust in one's friends, devotion to one's children, and having as much faith in someone's good character as is compatible with the evidence.[14]

These are all important capacities and qualities, all else being equal. But they can also have a downside, when all else is *not* equal: for example, when social inequality remains widespread. Their naïve deployment will tend to further privilege those already unjustly privileged over others. And this may come at the expense of unfairly impugning, blaming, shaming, further endangering, and erasing the

---

14. See Paul Bloom (2016) for a critique of empathy as a moral panacea that I'm sympathetic to—on the above grounds, among others. That is, empathy can make us take sides with the historically dominant, against the less privileged, in consequence. Bloom also rightly points out that lionizing empathy can ask for and extract too much from women. This resonates with my diagnosis of much of the *substance* of misogyny in allegedly post-patriarchal contexts, which I advanced in chapter 4. I return to similar themes in my conclusion, "The Giving She."

less privileged among their victims. In some cases, the perpetrators, knowing this, select their victims on this basis. I will come back to this point at the end of the chapter, in connection with the form of misogynoir evident in the case of Daniel Holtzclaw.

The excessive sympathy that flows to perpetrators like Brock Turner both owes and contributes to insufficient concern for the harm, humiliation, and (more or less lasting) trauma they may bring to their victims. And it both owes to and contributes to a tendency to let historically dominant agents get away with murder—proverbially and otherwise—vis-à-vis their historical subordinates. In the case of male dominance, we sympathize with him first, effectively making him into the victim of his own crimes. For, if someone sympathizes with the rapist initially, insofar as he loses his appetite or swimming scholarship, then *he* will come to figure as the victim in the story. And a victim narrative needs a villain, or victimizer (at least in the absence of a natural disaster), as I will argue in the next chapter. Now consider: who is the "but-for" cause of the rapist ending up in this situation? None other than the person who testified against him: his victim may hence be recast as the villain.

This is one mechanism I suspect often gives rise to victim-blaming. And it is pernicious partly because of the way it turns the narrative inside out, and effects this perverse moral role reversal.[15]

15. You might wonder if these narratives are the problem. I think they are *a* problem, but I doubt that we can give them up completely. Would that we were better at recognizing that someone can be both threatened and a threat to others, both wounded and lashing out, and both vulnerable and hostile. I believe we need to think seriously about how to do justice to the duality and ambiguity of our moral roles, perhaps by dint of more nuanced alternatives to the fairly crude, Manichean moral narratives that are currently our primary cultural resource for interpreting wrongdoing. But at least as importantly, I think we need to get better at recognizing the fact that there are often multiple *overlapping* narratives that cut against each other. All action is action under a description, as G. E. M. Anscombe famously pointed out (1957). And, we may add, if there are multiple apt descriptions of some action, then it may form a part of multiple true stories, featuring different casts of characters, in different relations, to each other and us, as hearers. These are topics I plan to take up on a future occasion.

Here neither the judge nor the father blamed the victim, however. (Brock's friend did, her denials notwithstanding.) They instead made a move as, if not more, insidious: they erased the victim from the narrative entirely. She simply does not figure as a character in their stories.

In this case, however, the victim refused to go quietly. Her powerful impact statement, which she was allowed to read aloud in court, revealed with painstaking clarity what the impact of Brock Turner's crime on *her* was. And this not only in overriding her will, but in rewriting her mind in the aftermath. He super-imposed his story, with its many elisions and fabrications, over the blank spaces his actions had left in her memory. ("[A]ccording to him, I liked it. I liked it," she read, to her horrified incredulity—in the same article from which she learned how she was discovered, half-naked and unconscious.) The victim was hence robbed of her rightful authority when it came to both her body and the *story* of her body, in connection with that incursion. As she went on to explain:

> I was warned, because he now knows you don't remember, he is going to get to write the script. He can say whatever he wants and no one can contest it. I had no power, I had no voice, I was defenseless. My memory loss would be used against me. My testimony was weak, was incomplete, and I was made to believe that perhaps, I am not enough to win this. His attorney constantly reminded the jury, the only one we can believe is Brock, because she doesn't remember. That helplessness was traumatizing.
>
> Instead of taking time to heal, I was taking time to recall the night in excruciating detail, in order to prepare for the attorney's questions that would be invasive, aggressive, and designed to steer me off course, to contradict myself, my sister, phrased in ways to manipulate my answers. Instead of his attorney saying, Did you notice any abrasions? He said, You didn't notice any abrasions, right? This was a game of strategy, as if I could be tricked out of my own worth. The sexual assault had been so clear, but instead, here I was at the trial, answering questions like:

How old are you? How much do you weigh? What did you eat that day? Well what did you have for dinner? Who made dinner? Did you drink with dinner? No, not even water? When did you drink? How much did you drink? What container did you drink out of? Who gave you the drink? How much do you usually drink? Who dropped you off at this party? At what time? But where exactly? What were you wearing? Why were you going to this party? What'd you do when you got there? Are you sure you did that? But what time did you do that? What does this text mean? Who were you texting? When did you urinate? Where did you urinate? With whom did you urinate outside? Was your phone on silent when your sister called? Do you remember silencing it? Really because on page 53 I'd like to point out that you said it was set to ring. Did you drink in college? You said you were a party animal? How many times did you black out? Did you party at frats? Are you serious with your boyfriend? Are you sexually active with him? When did you start dating? Would you ever cheat? Do you have a history of cheating? What do you mean when you said you wanted to reward him? Do you remember what time you woke up? Were you wearing your cardigan? What color was your cardigan? Do you remember any more from that night? No? Okay, well, we'll let Brock fill it in.

I was pummeled with narrow, pointed questions that dissected my personal life, love life, past life, family life, inane questions, accumulating trivial details to try and find an excuse for this guy who had me half naked before even bothering to ask for my name. After a physical assault, I was assaulted with questions designed to attack me, to say see, her facts don't line up, she's out of her mind, she's practically an alcoholic, she probably wanted to hook up, he's like an athlete right, they were both drunk, whatever, the hospital stuff she remembers is after the fact, why take it into account, Brock has a lot at stake so he's having a really hard time right now.[16]

16. Katie J. M. Baker, "Here Is the Powerful Letter the Stanford Victim Read Aloud to Her Attacker," *Buzzfeed*, June 3, 2016, https://www.buzzfeed.com/katiejm-baker/heres-the-powerful-letter-the-stanford-victim-read-to-her-ra?utm_term=.uveV3VxYaM#.wrWLMLemVy.

This last line crystallizes the problem of himpathy: when our loyalties lie with the rapist, we add profound moral insult to the injuries he inflicts on his victims. We may also lose sight of the fact that, in the eyes of the law, his crimes were committed against the *people*: that is, all of us, supposedly. And with regard to the rape victim who comes forward and bears witness to his crime, the question too often becomes, what does she want out of this? She is envisaged not as playing her difficult part in a criminal proceeding, but rather as seeking personal vengeance and moral retribution. What's more, she may be seen as being unforgiving, as trying to take something *away* from her rapist, rather than as contributing to upholding law and order.[17]

When we ask, "cui bono?" and "what is the point of her pursuing this?" we undermine the standpoint from which a rape victim testifies: as the person on whose body a crime against society was wrought. And this marks a recognition that her body, though hers, and hers alone, is also that of someone whose interests we are

---

17. See John Rawls's famous paper, "Two Concepts of Rules" (1955) for the distinction between the point of view of a judge and that of a lawmaker. At the risk of oversimplifying Rawls's wonderfully subtle discussion: the judge must be concerned with upholding the law—and hence ask questions such as whether the accused actually committed the crime, their motive, *mens rea*, and whether and how they hence deserve to be punished. Whereas the lawmaker may and arguably ought to be concerned exclusively with broadly consequentialist considerations: for example, with regard to some candidate criminal statute, in terms of both its content and the specified penalties for its violation, what are the costs and benefits of its being enshrined in law, and used as the basis for (among other things) a judge or jury's verdicts and sentences? Will such means of deterrence be effective, and warranted, given the costs imposed on those who will then be punished?

I am suggesting above, in brief, that the perspective of *witnesses* to a crime ought to be conceived along similarly non-consequentialist lines as that of a judge, even if one takes the rationale and purpose of the law to be deterrence, not retribution. And although I don't take myself to have given an adequate argument to that effect, I take it to be a natural default position and generalization of Rawls's case with regard to judges and juries. And, even for those who would take a different line here, the general question remains: why should sex crimes be treated as any different in this respect from property crimes, and similar? When one is burgled, say, one's entitlement to report it is very seldom questioned.

collectively invested in protecting. Or at least, this ought to be the case: a moral aspiration.

LOCKER ROOM TALK

Many people hoped that Brock Turner's case would be a turning point in the recognition of sexual assault victims, given the heated public outcry over his light sentence and (most importantly) the reasoning that supported it. I must admit I enjoyed a brief moment of uncharacteristic optimism myself. But these hopes were soon dashed, given what happened a few months later, and then failed to happen after that. I refer to the release of the now notorious hot mic tape of Donald Trump confiding to Billy Bush:

> I'm automatically attracted to beautiful [women]—I just start kissing them. It's like a magnet. Just kiss. I don't even wait. And when you're a star they let you do it. You can do anything . . . Grab them by the pussy. You can do anything.

These and similar boasts, which were played on repeat in the media in the ensuing days and weeks, failed to sink Trump's presidential campaign. Just over a month later, he was elected president.

Why didn't the (then eleven-year-old) audiotape do Trump more damage? But, in a way, the better question to ask in the wake of its release was, why did it cost him as much as it did? Trump's words conveyed little to no new information. Trump had a long, well-known, widely-publicized history of sexual harassment and sexual assault. The myriad credible accusations against Trump included that of his ex-wife, Ivana, whose testimony regarding the alleged rape was no secret (as discussed in the introduction). And, even if we restrict the domain of iniquity to misogynist offenses against women in *other* people's families—and white women, we might add, since many of Trump's almost exclusively white supporters love their mothers, whereas Muslims and Mexicans may remain perpetually othered—there was little news on this score either. Trump's aforementioned remarks (see chapter 3) about Megyn Kelly, Rosie O'Donnell, Carly Fiorina, as well as Hillary Clinton, whose use of the restroom during a debate commercial break in December was "too disgusting to talk about" (though Trump raised the subject), were often quickly forgiven or conveniently forgotten. In truth, such misogyny was plausibly a selling point with many of Trump's fans, in evincing his total shamelessness. For Americans tired of so-called political correctness, especially those men caught between silence and shame when it comes to gendered derogations and airing their thoughts about women's bodies, watching Trump vent his vile spleen without so much as the risk of subsequent embarrassment, must have been a cathartic and sometimes emboldening spectacle.

So, why was Trump's supposed "locker room talk" (as he tried to bill it) so controversial? What was it about what he said that made some Republicans finally contemplate cutting ties with him, even if they ultimately didn't?

I suspect the main factor, which Adam Gopnik of *The New Yorker* was the first to put his finger on in the immediate aftermath, was the sheer strangeness of Trump's remarks: their discomfiting, lip-curling quality.[18] "Visceral" is the word that more than one commentator used; "sickening," said Paul Ryan. And this not so much because of the acts described—which one will know are an everyday occurrence if one is attuned to and prepared to take women's word for it—but, rather, because of the *language* Trump used, for which he subsequently apologized. "'I moved on her like a bitch!' Is that even an idiom?" Gopnik wondered. I had a similar question regarding the now infamous "Grab 'em by the pussy" comment. Gopnik thinks the former made Trump sound like a nonnative English speaker. I found myself with a ludicrous image of the latter line being scripted for an

18. Adam Gopnik, "Donald Trump: Narcissist, Creep, Loser," *The New Yorker*, October 9, 2016, http://www.newyorker.com/news/news-desk/donald-trump-narcissist-creep-loser.

alien sexual (or, as the case may be, asexual) being in a movie where it had to pose as a red-blooded American man. Men talk about grabbing breasts, tits, and cocks, too—maybe balls. But pussies? I'm doubtful, and so were my informants.

Men do sexually assault women in this way, to be sure. But do they conceive of themselves as so doing? It's an awkward place for grabbing, for lack of a handle, so to speak. Consider too that, often, sexual assault involves not just overriding the victim's will, but mentally rewriting it. ("You like that, don't you." A fake question.) This rewriting is liable to ascribe sexual prowess, not ineptitude, to the assailant. Finally, even if such assailants do inwardly admit to lunging at women's groins in this way, do they subsequently boast of it so brazenly to others? Do they pause, as Trump ostensibly did, to fastidiously pop a tic tac prior to a round of nonconsensual kissing? How considerate for one so rapey.

Then there are the echoes of other phrases audible in this one. ("I punched him right in the face" and "I fucked her right in the pussy," lately popular among pro hecklers of female journalists and sportscasters.) All told, and at the risk of giving a close reading of some of the least literate remarks in human history, the effect was inauthentic. It didn't quite add up, somehow. Trump sounded off, gross, creepy—and phony. Fake, even.

Setting aside why that might be, what does it suggest, regarding the public outcry?

Nothing good, I'm afraid, insofar as it suggested that the Republicans who moved to finally reject Trump on this basis weren't bothered by his misogyny as such, although they may have *told* themselves that that was the issue. Rather, it was the peculiar phraseology, off-putting boastfulness, and all-around social awkwardness that I suspect perturbed people more than anything—more than what there was already ample evidence Trump had routinely done to women.

And indeed, since tendering this diagnosis a few days after the tape was released (Manne 2016g), almost all of the Republicans who initially moved to reject Trump on this basis walked back their distance, inasmuch as this suited their political interests. Predictable though this was, it is no less depressing. I am all for letting go at the appropriate time, after someone has expressed genuine remorse of a kind evidently not in Trump's conceptual or moral repertoire.[19] But pardoning a presidential candidate for such behavior within the space of a month strikes me as, forgive me, unforgivably unprincipled.

Return now to the question of why the victim of Brock Turner's sexual assault was taken unusually seriously. I suggest two factors, neither very flattering to our collective moral sensibility—and one would hope not, in the interests of maintaining the depressive realism that is morally required here, given the significance of the outcome of the subsequent election:

1. Brock Turner's victim had a powerful voice, and her impact statement went viral: but it was not an *embodied* voice. She remained anonymous and faceless; she was therefore not subject to suspicion for "playing the victim." And for all we learned about her, she might have been someone to more or less anyone—any man, in particular: for example, their sister, friend, girlfriend, wife, or the (actual or future) mother of their (again, real or notional) children. Moreover;

2. She was rescued by a pair of Stanford graduate students, visiting from Sweden, who were exemplary active bystanders and morally attractive characters. These two young men behaved courageously and fittingly—as I in no way want to minimize. But, as they themselves were uncomfortably aware (hence their initial refusal to talk to the press), they were subsequently cast as the heroes in the story. And they were lauded relative to an overly entitled or even, some people implied, disgustingly "coddled" rich kid at an elite university.

19. "Trump Has a 'Great Relationship' with God," *CNN*, January 17, 2016, http://www.cnn.com/videos/politics/2016/01/17/sotu-tapper-trump-has-great-realtionship-with-god.cnn.

So, although the rage directed at Brock Turner was intense and prolonged, one subsequently has to wonder: was it about what he did, or who he was, and represented?

In the next chapter, I will explore some of these questions in connection with the idea of—and pernicious moralism over—so-called victim culture. I will argue that claiming the moral spotlight as a woman over an equally or more privileged man is about as fraught as giving testimony against him, given a tacit—and, often, mistaken competition—for sympathetic attention and moral priority. I argue that this constitutes a less recognized but no less deep source of injustice as that which applies to giving testimony. And it encompasses, without being exhausted by, victim-blaming practices.

But first, one more case study, to show how misogynist exploitation, himpathy, along with "herasure," as I will call it, can work together in sui generis ways to the detriment of black women in the American context. The resulting case is hence meant to draw attention to the operation of misogynoir, a term and concept developed by the black queer feminist, Moya Bailey.[20]

MISOGYNOIR IN ACTION: THE DANIEL HOLTZCLAW CASE

"Who is Daniel Holtzclaw?" The article answered its own question in the ensuing tagline: linebacker, as in football, at Eastern Michigan

---

20. Bailey writes that she coined the term "misogynoir" "to describe the particular brand of hatred directed at black women in American visual and popular culture." Bailey: "I was looking for precise language to describe why Renisha McBride would be shot in the face, or why *The Onion* would think it's okay to talk about Quvenzhané the way they did, or the hypervisibilty of black women on reality TV, the arrest of Shanesha Taylor, the incarceration of CeCe, Laverne and Lupita being left off the *Time* list, the continued legal actions against Marissa Alexander, the twitter dragging of black women with hateful hashtags and supposedly funny Instagram images as well as how black women are talked about in music. All these things bring to mind misogynoir and not general misogyny directed at women of color more broadly" (Bailey 2014).

University.[21] He was also a police officer in Oklahoma City, convicted of eighteen counts of sexual assault—including sexual battery, rape, and forcible oral sodomy—all against women who are African American. Holtzclaw himself is half-white (on his father's side) and half-Japanese (on his mother's). The jury that found him guilty of these crimes, while also acquitting him on eighteen other such charges, sentenced Holtzclaw to 236 years in prison. The convictions only represented eight of his thirteen accusers.

The article, by Jeff Arnold, was published on the sports journalist site SB news, on February 17, 2016. It focused almost exclusively on the perspectives of his friends and family members. Everyone named and quoted by Arnold said they couldn't believe Holtzclaw did what he was accused of. Though one former football teammate interviewed did recall the following episode:

> Holtzclaw was attempting to break the program record for squatting weight. With approximately 600 pounds on the bar, Holtzclaw completed the impressive lift and then, unsure of what to do with his pent-up emotions, began to repeatedly head butt the bar, banging his head into the metal over and over again.
> "Everyone was like, 'Holy shit, . . . this guy is fucking crazy.'"

Holtzclaw's other former teammates were more positive, however—the only caveat being unsubstantiated rumors about his steroid use. And the lone exception above only spoke to Arnold on condition of anonymity.

The first woman to come forward to report Holtzclaw was the then fifty-seven-year-old Jannie Ligons, the director of a daycare center in Oklahoma City. Ligons testified that, after stopping her for swerving in 2014, the officer patted her down for weapons, and then demanded she expose herself. After that, he forced her to perform

---

21. Jeff Arnold, "Who Is Daniel Holtzclaw?," February 17, 2016, archived at http://archive.is/O3Gub.

oral sex on him. Ligons protested, "You're not supposed to do that, sir. . . . You don't do that."

But the jury concurred with Ligons that Holtzclaw did indeed, and also found him guilty of myriad other, similar crimes that he was accused of—partly on the basis of DNA evidence that matched another of his accusers. She was only seventeen when Holtzclaw apprehended and searched her and then offered to drive her home. Holtzclaw raped her on her own front porch, before driving off again, she testified.

Holtzclaw's defenders point out that the patch of fluid discovered on the inside of his trousers containing this victim's skin cells could have been "DNA transfer," for example, from his hands, having searched her before undressing or using the restroom. Daniel's sister adds it's not clear that the fluid was vaginal, specifically.

His parents remain similarly convinced of their son's innocence, and are planning to appeal his conviction. His father, Eric:

> It's very hard, because this is not Daniel; He's just a man, and he's not the villain that they portrayed him as. It was just really, really tough to see this—them portray him like this. [To] everybody that knows him, he's just not that person.

But the trouble is, virtually no one will seem like "that person" to people who know them, especially their family members and friends. (Recall Brock Turner's friend's conviction that he was not a rapist: "I know for a fact that Brock is not one of these people.") "These people" are pictured as unlovable, invulnerable, and as having no past beyond their crimes, no life of their own to date, and no valuable future to miss out on. "That person" is not a socially situated, morally multifaceted, and sometimes talented human being. Rather, they are a caricature; or, again, a monster.

That misogynist violence and sexual assault are generally perpetrated by unremarkable, non-monstrous-seeming people must be accepted if things are to improve in this arena, among others. We must accept the *banality* of misogyny, to adapt a famous phrase of Hannah Arendt's—and an oft-maligned idea. But Arendt's basic moral point regarding the banality of evil seems to me not only correct but crucial to recognize now more than ever, whatever the wisdom of her having extrapolated it from the observation that Adolf Eichmann didn't resemble a monster either. He seemed ordinary, if rather foolish—specifically, in his case, clownish, Arendt wrote. ("Despite all the efforts of the prosecution, everybody could see that this man was not a 'monster,' but it was difficult indeed not to suspect that he was a clown" [1963, 54]). For many people (especially some American Jews) at the time, Arendt's was too anti-climactic a portrait, too coolly drawn, to face up to: would that we had done.[22]

Holtzclaw made just one strategic mistake, according to the investigating officer, Detective Kim Davis. This was targeting Ligons, who had no convictions, outstanding warrants, or anything else to make her loath to come forward, lest he hold it over her. Davis and the other investigating officers say Holtzclaw was usually careful to target those who were least likely to be believed, in having criminal records, and being drug users or sex workers, and subsequently marginalized. As Davis puts the thought she ascribes to Holtzclaw: "They're the perfect victim. Nobody's going to believe them. If you believe them, who cares? A prostitute can't be raped," she concludes her suspect's imagined line of reasoning. Resuming in her own voice: "Yes, they can.

---

22. This "clownishness" was due to Eichmann's clichéd and repetitive turns of phrase, constant bald-faced lies, meaningless declarations and subsequent volte-faces, and overall shamelessness and narcissism. Eichmann cared deeply about his career and belonging to some organization (he was very much a "joiner," Arendt observed). And, once he had joined the Nazi party, he was determined to climb in its ranks, having had a lackluster career before that. But Eichmann lacked even the faintest sense of how he must have come across, in his characteristic boastfulness and self-pity to, for example, the Jewish policeman to whom Eichmann relayed his hard-luck story about not having gotten to where he wanted to be in the Nazi Party hierarchy. It wasn't his fault, Eichmann told the increasingly incredulous officer, as he was awaiting trial in Jerusalem for his war crimes.

I will leave drawing contemporary parallels as an exercise for the reader.

Yes, they can. So that's why he was picking these kinds of women, because that's the perfect victim."

And Holtzclaw's defense indeed focused on the fact that many of his thirteen accusers were, in various ways, legally compromised—and hence superior victims from the point of view of their assailant's exoneration. Even Ligons wasn't *quite* perfect, Holtzclaw pointed out, in an interview with *20/20*, in April 2016, following his conviction. Holtzclaw:

> Let's get the factual facts out there. She's not innocent the way people think she is. She had a bust in the '80s. . . . But we couldn't present that to the jury. This is not a woman that's, you know, a soccer mom or someone that's credible in society.[23]

The charges Holtzclaw was referring to were dropped, and Ligons hasn't been arrested since the 1980s, either. In Ligons's words:

> The thing is, he'd been stopping a lot of prostitutes and drug users, and he has held something over their head, like [arrest] warrants. And I guess apparently he thought I was one of them, but big, big mistake. He just stopped the wrong lady that night. (Diaz et al. 2016)

Ligons said she is happy for herself and the other victims that justice was done. So often, in these sorts of cases, it isn't. And the fact that the jury was all-white had boded poorly.

But a year after Daniel Holtzclaw's conviction, he and his defenders received a significant source of support, as well as a morale boost: conservative journalist Michelle Malkin released a two-part documentary arguing he was innocent, and thrown under the bus, due

23. Joseph Diaz, Eric M. Strauss, Susan Welsh, Lauren Effron, and Alexa Valiente, "Ex-Oklahoma City Cop Spending 263 Years in Prison For Rape and His Accusers Share Their Stories," *ABC News*, April 21, 2016, http://abcnews.go.com/US/oklahoma-city-cop-spending-263-years-prison-rape/story?id=38517467.

to the protests going on in Ferguson, Missouri, at the time.[24] Daniel Holtzclaw concurred with this diagnosis, "If they didn't convict me, there would be the next Ferguson deal happening in Oklahoma City."

It's at least unclear this is true though. Holtzclaw's case garnered very little attention as compared with, for example, the Isla Vista shootings committed by Elliot Rodger. White feminists remained largely silent about these crimes against African American women—a painful silence, as powerfully attested to by Michelle Denise Jackson (among others) (Jackson 2014). That silence can be golden for some also makes it heedless and hostile to their victims.

The extent to which white liberals are prone to be sympathetic to women's predicament reflects our racist habits of moral attention, as Kristie Dotson and Marita Gilbert (2014) have argued, in connection with Nafissatou Diallo's sexual assault allegations against (now former) managing director of the International Monetary Fund, Dominique Strauss-Kahn. As Dotson and Gilbert (2014) point out, many of us will remember his name, and forget hers, or fail to learn it in the first place. The "affectability imbalances" they theorize hence contribute to the "curious narrative disappearances" of black women, such as Holtzclaw effectively sought to engineer and exploit to his advantage. That he might easily have succeeded in this endeavor ought to be the basis for shameful self-reflection on the part of white women like me, certainly me included, regarding our complicity with misogynoir and contribution to black women's herasure—along with "lean down" exploitation and other such racist strands in (white) feminism.

Jeff Arnold's article "Who is Daniel Holtzclaw?" explored various potential explanations that would exonerate Holtzclaw, even if his

24. The protests were initially a response to the death of Michael Brown, a black teenager, at the hands of a white police officer, Darren Wilson, who continued to shoot at Brown after he raised his hands in surrender, according to several witnesses. Wilson was not indicted by a grand jury. I discuss this case in connection with victim narratives in the next chapter. For a history of the Black Lives Matter movement, see Christopher Lebron (2017).

accusers *weren't* lying about his actions. Still, Arnold wrote, he may have suffered a brain injury acquired while playing football (common enough—but, in this case, there was no evidence of this presented at trial; and the link with reduced self-control, let alone serial sexual assault, remains fairly and highly speculative, respectively). Then again, perhaps Holtzclaw was suffering from depression, due to his not having been drafted to the NFL after college—to his bitter disappointment. Or it may have been a sexual disorder, divorced from his ordinary moral make-up, held one expert. Perhaps, when he did it, he was acting out of character.

And there we have it: a pretty full run-down of the reasons why we might take what P. F. Strawson called "the objective stance" to a person like Holtzclaw, as opposed to treating him like a responsible fellow adult, someone with whom we have ordinary interpersonal and moral relations, and hold accountable for his actions. Instead, given this shift to the objective mode, the idea is that we must refrain from blaming the agent for his actions, or even from *attributing* them to this person. "He wasn't himself" is a particularly interesting "plea," to use Strawson's terminology. Strawson suggests we take the "admirably suggestive" locution as seriously as it deserves (i.e., very), notwithstanding its "logically comic" quality ([1962] 2008), 8–9). And Holtzclaw's reputation—people's sense of who he was—had a significant effect here. Our identities partly depend on what others make of us, that is, our social reputation. As we have seen, if a man has a "good guy" persona, and enough material and social resources—or alternatively, a heart-rending "down on his luck" story—then we will often fight with all our might to defend his honor, maintain his innocence.

What evidence would have convinced Holtzclaw's supporters he was guilty? And even if his family's loyalty is understandable, and would perhaps even be considered justified by some (though not by me), why was Arnold so sympathetic to Holtzclaw that he wrote a story so one-sided that the website had to pull it some five hours after it was published? The editor called it "an utter failure," taking responsibility for the breakdown in their editorial process, to his credit. But how did the breakdown occur? As Matt Bonesteel pointed out in the *Washington Post*, it was a twelve-thousand-word essay, which must have been weeks, if not months, in the making. And at least one editor presumably worked on it extensively. It wasn't a hastily thrown-up blog post. Still, nobody seemed to anticipate the objections to a story almost exclusively devoted to the more or less implausible grounds for denying the guilt of a convicted serial rapist, who had preyed on African American women with few social or legal resources. Nor did they notice the virtual erasure of the victims—who figured in two brief paragraphs at the end of the story, using quotes from the court documents. There's no evidence that Jeff Arnold tried to speak with any of these women.

Has Arnold learned his lesson? The signs are not that promising. He subsequently tweeted (December 17, 2016) about a *"must read story,"* which just happened to be about a football player supposedly being treated unfairly because of the NFL's unduly long investigation. The player is Ezekiel Elliott, accused of domestic violence. The story, by Tim Rohan, argued that Elliott's accuser might well be lying about the lot of it.[25]

The crimes for which Daniel Holtzclaw was convicted, along with other aspects of the case, provide a powerful illustration of how misogyny works systematically, even when it *does* involve bad apples as well as social structures and practices (recalling the discussion from chapter 2). Serial sexual predators comprise a small minority of men, but the system works to shield and protect them from the law. Beyond that, there are a wide variety of social scripts, moral

---

25. Jeff Arnold @JeffArnold_17 Dec 2016
Jeff Arnold Retweeted Tim Rohan: "A must read here from @TimRohan"
https://twitter.com/JeffArnold_/status/810195406894362624.
The tweet links to Rohan's story, "The Anatomy of an NFL Domestic Violence Investigation," http://mmqb.si.com/mmqb/2016/12/14/ezekiel-elliott-domestic-violence-nfl-investigation-process.

permissions, and material deprivations that work to extract feminine-coded goods from her—for example, attention and attentiveness, among other forms of social and sexual labor—ranging from
the anti-choice movement to cat-calling to rape culture. There are
also dispositions and mechanisms that ward and warn her off from
trying to take possession of masculine-coded statuses, power, and
authority—including testimonial injustice, mansplaining, victim-
blaming and, as we will see in the next chapter, other victim-impugn-
ing methods.

Notice that we need not know what motivated a man like
Holtzclaw in order to see that the social meaning of his actions
was profoundly hostile toward his victims and contingent on their
being women, of a particular race and class, inter alia, in this case,
in a hitherto man's world. And this is so whether he was merely
"punching down" at characteristic objects of domination, or specifically resented women for being withholding, taking his place, or
had some similarly gendered grievance. When men are privileged,
or long have been, they may proceed with a sense of not only legal
impunity but also moral *entitlement*—secure in the idea that what
they seize is theirs for the taking, and sometimes trying to wreak
revenge on women who fail to uphold their end of history's bad gendered bargain.

If the women who are the victims of such crimes try to bring
their attackers to justice, they will be up against structural barriers
and roadblocks, as well as subject to suspicion, blame, resentment,
and so on. This is especially the case for women who are subject to
other forms of disadvantage—for example, racism, poverty, having
a criminal record, being a sex worker, and the non-additive results
of their various intersections. And their attacker may know this,
and select his victims cynically, to take advantage of their relative
powerlessness.

The dismissal of the victims of misogynistic violence may take
epistemic forms: where, typically, they are held to be lying—but
alternatively, they may be dismissed as stupid, crazy, or hysterical.
Or, it may take *moral* forms, where a woman's entitlement to claim

victimhood is called into question, and earns her contempt for not being more resilient—or, as the case may be, forgiving. She may even be impugned on *both* epistemic and moral grounds, for example, of being delusional and a liar. Holtzclaw made another typical discrediting move, claiming that his victims were trying to make a profit at his expense, indeed hoping to become "billionaires." This would have been a high-risk and low-reward scheme, to put it mildly.

I do not think we can solve these interconnected problems by addressing the stereotypes that are often held to underlie testimonial injustice for women and nonwhite men. The impugning and undermining of the victims of misogyny tends to be ad hoc. We can well imagine that many of the people who didn't believe or trust Holtzclaw's accusers would have trusted someone like Ligons perfectly well to care for their children at her day-care center, for instance. (Recall Fricker's similar point about Tom Robinson, in connection with testimonial injustice, discussed earlier in this chapter.) That these stereotypes are ad hoc in their nature and deployment owes to the fact that testimonial injustice is often highly *motivated*. As we have seen in this chapter, there is a strong if, typically, unwitting disposition to protect dominant men's interests and uphold their reputations. Many will hence instinctually reach, with a sense of moral necessity, for any excuse in the book as to why he's innocent, and all the women who testify against him can't be trusted. Or, in the alternative, why coming forward isn't in their interests: as if they can't be trusted to determine this in particular cases and contexts, which differ widely.

The problem hence goes beyond mistakes born of misinformation and erroneous associations picked up from the social imagination, which is the main diagnosis Fricker offers. More virtuous listening—which Fricker proposes as a helpful if partial solution to this problem—is a skill that will not motivate people to deploy it in the first place. Nor will attempts at direct structural reform necessarily suffice to solve what is clearly a structural problem. Changes in agents' attitudes, allegiances, and habits of attention are needed too, I believe.

But (how) can we make them? And (how) can enough people be pre-vailed upon to try to?

In the end, in order to address such egregious forms of injustice, it is necessary—without being remotely sufficient—to stop people siding with dominant men against the women who accuse them of acts of misogynistic violence. The nature of the problem suggests it will be sticky. It won't be easy to persuade people that they're being prejudiced in ways that are so ugly, unjust, and morally pernicious, and hence show up (only) in particular social contexts. All the more so because such prejudice affects our habits of moral attention: their operation may hence feel, from the inside, like simply being fair to the men who stand accused, rather than being *unfair* to the women who are making these accusations. She is prone to seem dishonest, an unsavory or unsympathetic character. Or, if too compelling, there may be moves made to intimidate her into silence her from bearing witness.

He, on the other hand, believes he is owed. He is wrong. Yet our loyalties often lie with him—the least deserving and most expectant. Daniel Holtzclaw:

> I absolutely 100 percent [know] in my heart, within my family, everyone was on my side. They all said, "There was no way that you should be convicted." I looked at [the jurors.] I looked in every single one of their eyes, and I told 'em, "I did not do this." And I looked at the men and I looked at those women, and I saw women crying.

The white women on the jury judged that Holtzclaw was guilty—to their credit, given the evidence. Even so, they wept for him and his bright future in law enforcement, before his victims.

Chapter 7

Suspecting Victims

> A trial resembles a play in that both focus on the doer, not on the victim. A show trial, to be effective, needs even more urgently than an ordinary trial a limited and well-defined outline of what the doer did, and how. In the center of a trial can only be the one who did—in this respect, he is like the hero in the play—and if he suffers, he must suffer for what he has done, not for what he has caused others to suffer.
>
> Hannah Arendt, *Eichmann in Jerusalem*

ON SO-CALLED VICTIM CULTURE

That we have a fraught relationship with victims, and victimhood, is not news. In her book, *The Cult of True Victimhood*, Alyson M. Cole (2006) traces the rise of anti-victim sentiment in the United States from the late 1980s up until a few years following 9/11. During that time, the figure of a victim—or rather, a self-perceived and self-appointed one, who nurses and perhaps fabricates her injuries, and demonstrates learned or feigned helplessness—has played an increasingly important role in conservative ideology. A portrait is being painted of an aggrieved, maudlin, melodramatic character, casting unfair aspersions, and demanding sympathy and attention from third parties. Its subject is disproportionately likely to be a student, a millennial, a woman, a feminist, a progressive, a sexual assault victim—or all of the above, as in the case of Emma Sulkowicz, which I'll canvass later. And, perhaps needless to say, this portrait is not a flattering one.

Although by no means a new phenomenon, the hostility shown toward victims seems to have been increasing during the past few years.[1] In "Micro-Aggression and Moral Culture," sociologists Bradley Campbell and Jason Manning (2014) contrast a new "culture of victimhood" with an older "culture of dignity" and an even older "culture of honor," with each having supposedly displaced the other in contemporary Western societies. Most of the examples they give of practices exemplifying so-called victim culture have the flavor of martyrdom—for example, the practice of cultivating personal squalor in ancient Rome, and "sitting dharna" in India (708). These are analogized to the practice of pointing out or publicizing "microaggressions," i.e., the relatively small, often unintended, slights and hostilities that can accumulate corrosively to systematically harm members of historically subordinated or marginalized social groups.[2]

Campbell and Manning (2014) claim to be engaged in an exercise in purely descriptive sociology—a claim that somewhat strains credibility, in light of their apparently morally loaded choice of terminology, as well as their habit of posing questions like the following, asked with seeming incredulity, "But why emphasize one's victimization?" (708).[3] In any event, conservatives have been quick to draw on their supposedly normatively neutral research in support

1. See the Google Trends graph, search term: "Victimhood," https://www.google.com/trends/explore#q=victimhood (last accessed October 2015).

2. Campbell and Manning (2014) begin by listing off various methods of social control, including genocide, lynching, terrorism, interpersonal violence—and publicizing microaggressions. "The publicizing of microaggressions is similarly a form of social control—a reaction to the deviant behavior of others—as well as a form of deviant behavior—a behavior that many others condemn" (693n1). The last item on this list seems impugned by such guilty companions. Consider also their remarks on "aggressive suicide," which is billed as a "method of social control" practiced by wives whose family members do not take their husbands' " 'mere' beatings" of them seriously enough, by these women's estimation (705).

3. See Conor Friedersdorf's piece, "Is 'Victimhood Culture' a Fair Description?," *The Atlantic*, September 15, 2015, http://www.theatlantic.com/politics/archive/2015/09/the-problems-with-the-term-victimhood-culture/406057/.

of moral and political conclusions. Despite the rather long history of questioning victim narratives in more tempered but similar ways—which has sometimes come from feminist and progressive as well as conservative quarters (see, e.g., Wendy Brown's *States of Injury*, 1995)—Jonathan Haidt called their paper "extraordinary" twice in a recent blog post devoted to their findings.[4] Haidt takes the idea of a culture of victimhood to go a long way toward explaining the rise (and, in his view, scourge) of trigger warnings, safe spaces, as well as the deployment of the microaggressions framework on college campuses. Clearly, the antipathy toward purportedly self-styled victims is having a moment.[5]

Campbell and Manning's question ought to be of interest to progressives now, too, however. What are the motivations for historically subordinated and marginalized people, women in particular, to come forward and draw attention to the ways in which they've been injured? As we will be seeing, the answer to this question is not obvious. There turn out to be strong reasons *not* to come forward from a subordinate social position, given the high risks of being discredited, dismissed, and subject to counteraccusations (among other possibilities). But if coming forward from such a position is liable to be futile or positively

---

4. Jonathan Haidt, "Where Microaggressions Really Come From: A Sociological Account," *Righteous Mind*, September 7, 2015, http://righteousmind.com/where-microaggressions-really-come-from/.

5. See also George Will, whose inflammatory remarks cost him his *Washington Post* column. Will wrote:

> Colleges and universities are being educated by Washington and are finding the experience excruciating. They are learning that when they say campus victimizations are ubiquitous ("micro-aggressions," often not discernible to the untutored eye, are everywhere), and that when they make victimhood a coveted status that confers privileges, victims proliferate.

George Will, "Colleges Become the Victims of Progressivism," *Washington Post*, June 6, 2014, https://www.washingtonpost.com/opinions/george-will-college-become-the-victims-of-progressivism/2014/06/06/e90e73b4-eb50-11e3-9f5c-9075d5508f0a_story.html.

For at least ostensibly more circumspect concerns about "victim-centered" handling of sexual assault cases on college campuses, see Jeannie Suk Gersen (2014) and Janet Halley (2015) (both of them being Harvard Law professors).

backfire—being a highly uncertain path to the material resources and social justice one may need and be entitled to, respectively, and at best a fraught way of attracting sympathy and attention—then, frankly, why bother? And yet women (among others) *are* increasingly coming forward to identify misogynist hostility. Why? What explains this? Is this merely the triumph of hope over experience? Or do these moves serve other purposes, be they valid or invalid? They do, I will argue—and I think they can be valid in certain contexts. For, coming forward can be an expression of agency and an act of subversion, insofar as it wrestles the moral narrative away from the dominant and default versions, and makes one's situation salient to those who would otherwise remain oblivious. Third parties may sympathize or not; they may in fact become *more*, rather than less, hostile and resentful. But at least they will be privy to the reality of the injury, or the fact of the ongoing domination. And this can matter, quite properly, to people who have been victimized.

WHAT IS A VICTIM? THE ROLE OF MORAL NARRATIVES

What is it to be a victim? And what is it to claim victimhood? These two questions are not, as we'll see, straightforward. And nor are they straightforwardly related to each other, due to what are in effect indexical or perspectival features of the notion of a victim. In virtue of these, claiming that one is a victim—often not in so many words, and even then in more or less subtle ways—goes beyond claiming that A is a victim, and that one happens to be A. It also involves a kind of *performance* or *assumption* of this role in addition to this.

But first, being a victim isn't generally just a matter of being subject to some misfortune. It is, I believe, at its heart a moral notion. The paradigm case of being a victim involves being morally wronged at the hands of another agent—and being injured, humiliated, or otherwise wounded because of it. One is typically lowered relative to one's previous moral-cum-social position. And one is typically put down relative to the agent who *made* one his victim in an act of moral wrongdoing.[6]

That is the core case of victimhood, I suggest. Is there no victim without a victimizer, a bully, an oppressor, though? This would be too strong a claim; we can and do speak intelligibly about being the victim of natural disasters and sometimes (although to my ear, slightly less naturally) diseases and illnesses. But my hunch is that these cases are *parasitic* on the core case, and owe their intelligibility to our tendency to anthropomorphize such destructive natural causes, or at least to envision them as agents. (Consider the practice of naming hurricanes, or calling cancer a "bitch," for some examples.) If that is right, then our concept of a victim depends crucially on the background availability of a certain kind of *moral narrative*, in which a subject is wronged in a humiliating or degrading way at the hands of another agent. She is the victim, and he is the bully or oppressor.

The core case of victimhood cleaves to this script, I think. And to be a victim in this paradigmatic way hence involves being *cast* into some version of this narrative, by oneself or another. Our reactions as members of the audience are somewhat scripted too. The victim is the one with whom we're supposed to sympathize. They are the focus of attention; they are the protagonist, perhaps the hero or heroine. And the bully or oppressor is supposed to be the person who we *resent* on the victim's behalf. Or, more precisely, they are the designated locus of what P. F. Strawson called "vicarious" reactive attitudes, felt on behalf of others toward others. In this context, these might include indignation, disapproval, punitive tendencies, and so on ([1962] 2008).[7]

---

6. There's a question about whether victimization is a "success" term—that is, whether an attempt on the part of B to victimize A has to be completed or come to fruition, in order for A to count as B's victim (and a victim whatsoever). I think we should probably allow this, although the paradigm case does involve a completed act, plausibly.

7. See Paul Bloom (2016) on the flipside of empathy being aggression—that is, the psychological tendency to feel aggression toward those who are perceived as opposed to a subject with whom we're predisposed to empathize.

If this is right, at least in broad outline, then it begins to explain why depicting *oneself* as a victim—or, again, being perceived to do so—is such a fraught exercise. For claiming victimhood effectively involves placing oneself at the *center of the story*. This move is even more fraught than self-casting is in general. It is liable to be perceived as at once self-dramatizing and self-important, and at the same time, wan or maudlin. There is a sense that the person is dwelling imaginatively on—and within—her own story, rather than moving on briskly. But, in order to be doing this, she cannot really be so abject, so shattered, as all that (so the thought continues). This fuels suspicions and accusations of hypocrisy, mendacity, manipulativeness, and self-centeredness.[8]

The way I've suggested thinking about victimhood, as fundamentally related to a victim/victimizer moral narrative, also helps to explain several of the ways we think and talk using these concepts. We talk of *playing* the victim, of course, as well as *casting* oneself and others in this role. More importantly, we tend to think of victims as *innocent*, blameless, and (worse) as needing to be. Often there is a subsequent reluctance or failure to recognize someone as a victim when they are, or are even suspected of being, guilty of some minor perfidy. By the same token, often we are inclined to deny the minor perfidies of someone who we take to be a genuine victim of some major offense. This makes sense if the script one is working with is

8. No wonder genuine victims are so anxious to renounce the "victim" moniker these days, and increasingly identify as "survivors" instead. The suspicion of dwelling on the past in an objectionable manner may be allayed by an upbeat focus on the present and the future—as well as taking the critical spotlight off the agents whose actions they are the survivors *of*. I worry that this may sometimes be the result of moral misdirection, and the pressure in a himpathetic culture to downplay the wrongdoing of comparatively privileged male perpetrators—exonerating them by granting them a narrative exemption, effectively. But I certainly don't mean to impugn or disdain the "survivor" label either: if it works best for certain people, then more power to them. My point is just that there is nothing inherently wrong with claiming to be a victim when you were one. So my argument aims to establish a *permission* or *entitlement* rather than a prohibition or (contrary) obligation, as is characteristic of my approach to moral philosophy generally.

essentially a simple, reductive, morality tale, which allows for little variation or nuance. You can't play the role of a cop's victim if you're a robber.[9]

The case of Michael Brown is instructive in this connection. Following Brown's death at the hands of a police officer in Ferguson, Missouri, in August 2014, the Ferguson police chief released surveillance footage of Brown apparently stealing a box of cigarillos from a convenience store a few minutes beforehand. The video also shows Brown giving the clerk a bit of a shove (as if to say "back off") before exiting the store. A few minutes later, the police officer involved, Darren Wilson, shot Brown at least six times, including twice in the crown of his skull. Brown was unarmed, and he had his hands held up in surrender as Wilson "just kept shooting," according to several witnesses. And Brown fell to the ground while facing Wilson, according to forensics reports—which would explain the two shots that entered Brown's skull at a downward angle (Manne 2014b). The police chief in Ferguson released the convenience store footage six days afterward, during the initial media furor. The ploy—and it seems likely to have been a deliberate one—worked as intended in many media outlets.[10]

Why did it work? And what did it work to *do*? The rational response was clearly that this alleged minor crime was completely irrelevant to

9. Cf. Gary Watson's (1987) famous discussion of the brutal murder committed by Robert Harris, himself a victim of terrible abuse in his childhood. This suggests that sympathetic perspective-shifts *within* such a narrative are difficult to effect—and hence so is recognizing the fact that the wrongdoer is a victim in his own right, in another context, or perhaps indeed in this one. There is nothing conceptually difficult about this idea. And the idea that wounded people wound, or that abuse begets abuse, is one that people tend to find intuitive. But these ideas are not easily incorporated into the narratives that script many of our *reactions* to wrongdoing. We only have one set of eyes, and hence can only occupy one point of view at once, plausibly. Similarly, our points of view are typically total, rather than partial. So, if empathy requires perspective-taking in a rather literal (though of course not necessarily visual) sense, this may limit the number of characters in a story who we can empathize with simultaneously—especially when they are somehow at cross purposes.

10. It is telling that the police chief was so anxious to release this footage. He justified doing so by claiming there had been a FOIA ("freedom of information act") request for it by multiple journalists. Searches of open records revealed none such, so

the question of whether Brown was the victim of an egregious civil rights violation, in the form of no less than a homicide, at the hands of a state actor. In part there was a racist tendency at work to ascribe criminality and aggression to black men, such that what transpired between Wilson and Brown ended up being distorted and misrepresented. Rather than being depicted as a typical teenage boy, as he in fact appears to have been, and is the minimally charitable default assumption under the circumstances, Brown ended up being reimagined as a "thug"—an inherently racist concept in contemporary America. And Wilson was rendered seemingly helpless by comparison.[11] But there is also a perceptual or at least quasi-perceptual block that this ideological move seems to effect. Once Brown was depicted as any kind of criminal or aggressor (in however trivial a way) via the footage of him in the convenience store, many white people couldn't or wouldn't see him as the victim of police brutality or misconduct. The two narratives—Brown as having committed a minor wrong, and Brown as the victim of a major civil rights violation, perhaps even murder—seemed to compete with each other, even though these two possibilities are of course compatible.

The narrative account of the concept of victimhood thus helps to explain why *victim-blaming* is held, and intuitively seems, to be so morally problematic. As soon as the focus shifts from what was done

it is likely (though not certain) that this claim was a fabrication. If so, why though? Among other things, releasing the footage enabled conservative pundits and politicians to then redirect attention to Brown's alleged criminality rather than his victimhood. Even the *New York Times* ran a story in which it was pointed out that "Michael Brown, 18, due to be buried on Monday, was no angel, with public records and interviews with friends and family revealing both problems and promise in his young life." John Eligon, "Michael Brown Spent Last Weeks Grappling with Life's Mysteries," *New York Times*, August 25, 2014, http://www.nytimes.com/2014/08/25/us/michael-brown-spent-last-weeks-grappling-with-lifes-mysteries.html.

11. Consider in this connection Darren Wilson's comments following Ferguson about feeling like a little boy in relation to Brown's Hulk Hogan, during the encounter. But the two of them were actually of a similar weight and height—not to mention fact that Brown was unarmed, and Wilson was a trained police officer.

to someone, to ways in which her (perhaps genuine) imprudence or even morally problematic behavior contributed causally to the wrongs done to her, her role as a victim in the narrative is liable to be compromised. It may then be difficult to see her as a victim whatsoever. (See also chapter 6: the section "Himpathy," in particular.)

The narrative account of the concept of victimhood also helps to explain the existence of the two kinds of victims distinguished by Diana Tietjens Meyers, drawing on an Amnesty International Protocol: the "pathetic" victim, on the one hand, and the "heroic" victim, on the other (2011). Both of these types of victims are recognizably *characters*: the hapless damsel in distress who needs rescuing, versus the plucky contemporary cartoon heroine. They are both, Meyers shows, held to be innocent, but for very different reasons— the pathetic victim because her passivity and total helplessness exempts her from so much as the suspicion of moral wrongdoing, and the heroic victim because her agency must be deployed in service of morally worthy goals, in order for her to qualify. She is fighting the good fight, then, by hypothesis—in other words, she is above reproach by dint of her narrative identity.[12]

(DOWN)PLAYING THE VICTIM

We can now begin to make some progress on the question of why the historically or currently marginalized or subordinate would draw attention to their moral injuries in such a way as to risk being perceived as "playing the victim." Ultimately, I will be particularly interested in this question as it pertains to women whose injuries are the result of misogynist aggression on the part of men who are no less privileged.

---

12. How many subjects of oppressive wrongdoing slip through the large cracks left by these two concepts, we might wonder? Meyers shares this worry, and discusses it in an illuminating way, using the examples of sex trafficking and the death penalty (2011; see also Meyers 2016).

It will help to begin by considering some of the reasons that are less than compelling grounds for, or positively count against, coming forward in this way from a historically or currently subordinate social position.[13] This will make the puzzle I'll be trying to solve a starker one.

Campbell and Manning suggest that emphasizing one's own victimization—or fabricating it entirely, as in the hate crime hoaxes they allude to in their paper on four separate occasions—is frequently a ploy for the "attention, sympathy, and intervention of third parties." Victims represent their "victimization as virtue," they announce in a subtitle. Moreover, "people increasingly demand help from others, and advertise their oppression as evidence that they deserve respect and assistance. Thus we might call this moral culture a culture of victimhood because the moral status of the victim, at its nadir in honor cultures, has risen to new heights," they explain. In contrast, "public complaints that advertise or even exaggerate one's own victimization and need for sympathy would be anathema to a person of honor—tantamount to showing that one had no honor at all" (2014, 714).

There is an alternative possibility, in light of the argument I've made so far in this book—in chapters 4 and 6, especially. It may be that an attempt to level the playing field where moral victims are concerned, that is, such that women in particular come forward or "speak out," throws off the default assumption about who belongs in the moral spotlight. If women are supposed to give their sympathetic attention and moral focus to dominant men, rather than ask for it on their own behalf, then women's claims to having been victimized may be especially salient, and attract jealousy or envy. These women will be

13. I'm fudging on the potentially important distinction between motivating and normative reasons here, because there is an intimate connection between the two on my way of thinking about it (which I've defended at length in other contexts; e.g., Manne 2013; 2014a). Moreover, if there are no good (normative) reasons, then I assume that, absent some special psychological story, there will be little in the way of motivating reasons with the same content. In other words, I'm assuming that women in this context are basically rational or responsive to the reasons that count for or against their taking certain courses of action.

perceived as much like the new baby competing for the attention of a parent, from the point of view of a jealous older sibling. (Consider the notion of "the new infantilism.") But in this case, the new baby and the parent are one and the same: so there may also be resentment, even rage, that a figure in *loco parentis* is betraying their role in turning the tables.

All of these perceptions stem from an illicit sense of entitlement that is the legacy of patriarchal norms and values. But because they are entrenched, indeed deeply internalized by both men and women, they often go unnoticed. What Bradley and Manning bill as a culture of honor may simply be a culture where—in the contemporary imagination, at least, brimming with nostalgia for a past that may never quite have happened—claims to being wounded were seamlessly anticipated and hence often didn't need to be made explicit. For, under a patriarchal order, a dominant man would often be soothed and patched up by his wife, mother, mistress, or some other such female figure, without having to ask for such tender ministrations. He received them from her automatically.

Whereas, if you claim victimhood, more or less explicitly, chances are (a) you're *not* automatically being given what you need, in terms of sympathy and redress for moral injuries; and (b) you're claiming to be *entitled* to the same, in ways that will be more salient for those not deemed to be so entitled, historically, but rather obligated to ensure that *others'* entitlements are satisfied.[14]

14. My sense is that, when people in subordinate social positions draw attention to their moral injuries, it tends to be more striking or salient. Whereas, when authority figures make analogous complaints, we tend not to notice—we just sympathize. It's a remarkable irony of this debate that Haidt and also Edward Schlosser—the pseudonymous author of "I'm a Liberal Professor, and My Liberal Students Terrify Me," *Vox*, June 3, 2015, https://www.vox.com/2015/6/3/8706323/college-professor-afraid—essentially claim to be increasingly the victims of students' complaints against them (on the basis of, to my mind, less than compelling evidence). This is one sense in which sympathy does resemble a commodity (an idea I generally think is insidious and wrong-headed, as will emerge in a moment). It is more likely to be enjoyed by those who are wealthier in the coin of privilege (see note 18).

It follows that, when we have a sense that a woman is "playing the victim," "pulling the gender card," or being overly dramatic, we have reasons to be critical and doubtful of our instincts (Schraub 2016). What she is doing may stand out not because she's claiming more than her due but because we're not used to women claiming their due in these contexts. Women are rather expected to provide an *audience* for dominant men's victim narratives, providing moral care, listening, sympathy, and soothing.

In other words, one of the goods women are characteristically held to owe dominant men is their moral focus and emotional energy. This may in turn be something that dominant men often feel excessively entitled to and, perhaps, needy for.

It also behooves us to consider how much less black women's mistreatment in the United States has garnered in terms of attention and moral concern, as compared with mass incarceration, often implicitly conceptualized by white liberals as more or less exclusively black men's problem. This isn't to minimize the seriousness and the magnitude of this injustice for black men, of course. But it is to say, first, that analogous forms of structural injustice for black women, such as eviction, have sometimes received comparatively short shrift in (again, white liberal) public discourse, as has been shown by the sociologist Matthew Desmond (2016). Moreover, something similar holds of police brutality toward black women versus black men, and the higher incarceration rates for black women versus white women (Crenshaw 2012). And the fact that the Black Lives Matter movement was founded by three black women often goes unrecognized in discussions of the movement by white liberal (ostensible) supporters—adding a further layer of shameful irony for people of my genre (me included) to face here.[15]

What Campbell and Manning seem not to notice, moreover, is that emphasizing (or, simply, stating) one's victimization is often at best an uncertain means of gaining the sympathetic attention of third parties.

---

15. See Kristie Dotson (2016) and Christopher Lebron (2016; 2017) for important discussions on this subject.

Indeed, their very article provides evidence of the hostility and resentment that those who draw attention to their moral injuries are liable to encounter (see note 2). This is all the more true for subordinate group members—women especially, but by no means exclusively.

Consider the experiences of D'Arcee Neal, a black gay man with cerebral palsy, who did not receive the wheelchair assistance he needed in order to deplane, following a five-hour flight from San Francisco to Washington DC, where he lives. He repeatedly asked the flight attendants for help, only to be told that he should be patient, that they were "just doing their jobs." Neal needed to use the restroom, having had to wait for the duration of the flight—the one on the plane not being wheelchair accessible—and spent an additional forty-five minutes waiting for the narrower, airplane wheelchair to arrive (standard wheelchairs don't fit in the aisle). Finally, unwilling to wait any longer, Neal crawled off the plane on his elbows, to the shock of the flight attendants assembled. He retrieved his own wheelchair, which was waiting for him planeside, used the airport bathroom, and went home, telling no one about what had happened. The incident was, however, reported by one of the flight attendants, who was concerned by the way Neal had been treated. This is how the news story started making headlines.

Neal was the perfect victim in almost every respect—he didn't complain himself, since he "didn't want to make an issue of it." He said that the incident was "annoying," "frustrating," and made him "angry," but also that he "was used to it." After all, this had happened to him on three or four prior separate occasions. Furthermore, the incident was publicly acknowledged by the airline, in a press release to CNN; Neal accepted their apology graciously.

Campbell and Manning's account would surely predict that a case as clear-cut as Neal's—and involving a bad guy as unsympathetic as United Airlines, it might be added—would garner near-universal sympathy from the sources they take to have incentivized airing one's grievances online. But this was not the case; far from it, in fact. While many people did express sympathy, there were also so many negative, victim-blaming responses that a journalist wrote a story detailing Neal's second humiliation via emails and online comments. (This was the most-read story in the *Washington Post* on October 28, 2015.) Neal was accused of faking his disability (if he couldn't walk, how could he crawl?), and trying to get attention for Black Lives Matter (a movement that Neal supports, but was not personally involved with). He was also accused of being a narcissist, and of having an illicit sense of entitlement to assistance. Some choice remarks from the comments sections on various news websites included:

"How much money are you looking for? How funny you need to go to the bathroom when [the] plane lands and everyone is looking to run off the plane."

"How long did he have to wait? 5 minutes? 10 minutes? Half an hour? We all have to wait for things[,] it's what makes us equal. So he just happened to be returning from a speaking engagement about accessible transportation. Isn't that just ironic. I'm willing to bet he has the Me-first attitude! I'm more valuable than you! Can't you see that I'm special!"

"Why is the airline responsible for helping him to and from the plane or bathroom? He knew he was disabled BEFORE he got on the plane. Why did he not have a nursing assistant with him to help him in such matters or a family member? In today's world, we must plan ahead and accordingly [sic] to our needs. We should not expect others to provide for our needs."

"Thank God the airplane did not crash land! I bet he would have expected the flight attendants to carry him off the airplane. Whatever happened to being self-sufficient? Next, will the elderly who lost their choppers expect the flight attendant to chew their food, or the blind to be read too [sic]? If you know that you will be traveling by airplane, as we already know that there are certain size luggage that is allowed as carry-ons. If you know the isle [sic] will be narrow, then it might be time to invest in a travel size wheel chair, where it can navigate thru narrow isles [*sic*]. That is the price of independence. It is NOT my responsibility to be my brother's keeper!"[16]

As well as being deeply, indeed comically, mean-spirited, the emphasis on who comes *first*, and who is responsible for whom, evinced by these comments is revealing. There is a prevalent sense that one needs to "get in line" or queue up for *something*. And there is a tangible frisson around the idea that someone is unfairly *cutting* in line—in particular, immigrants, both in the United States, and in Australia, a bias that has a considerably longer history of irrational moral panic about asylum seekers or so-called queue-jumpers.[17]

What is the line *for*, though? My suspicion is, among other things: women's emotional and social labor, which is now in increasingly short supply. This would explain the jealous hoarding of this moral resource,

16. The above comments are quoted in Michael E. Miller, "D'Arcee Neal: Disabled Activist Who Had to Crawl Off United Airlines Flight Reveals the Humiliation That Followed," *The Independent*, October 28, 2015, http://www.independent.co.uk/ news/ world/americas/the-disabled-gay-activist-who-had-to-crawl-off-his-united-airlines-flight-and-into-even-more-a6711626.html. An excerpt from the story:

> What you probably haven't heard, however, is what happened afterward: the ignorance, the Internet comments, the wild accusations and the humiliation of crawling on one's hands in public—relived over and over online.
>
> "There is a contingent of the Internet [that] thinks that I'm faking or I'm opportunistic and I just want to get paid," Neal said. "Somebody even said that I was doing it to raise the profile of Black Lives Matter, which I was really offended by."
>
> The first thing you should know about Neal is that his life has been pretty darn tough. The D.C. native is African American, openly gay and disabled—a triple minority.
>
> "I was born with cerebral palsy. . ."
>
> But the second thing you should know about him is that he definitely doesn't want to be pitied. . . .

17. Cf. Arlie Russell Hochschild's notion of a "deep story," which also invokes the "line" metaphor and is intended crystallize the political worldview of the subjects of her recent ethnographic study, *Strangers in Their Own Land* (2016). Hochschild spent five years with white conservatives in small-town and rural Louisiana, originally

the deep resentment of women who withhold what they are supposed to give to dominant men, or—still worse—ask for it on their own behalf, and the rage directed at those who, like Neal, are perfect victims and also have a multiply marginalized social status, in being black, disabled, and gay, in his case. The sentiment "get in line" thus tempted many people, despite clearly being grossly wrong-headed. But one left-wing woman's perfect victim—or, rather, moral priority among victims, in being particularly vulnerable—will be some right-wing men's worst nightmare. The latter may miss their default prior claim to being ministered to as victims, which was bequeathed to them by patriarchy. And they defend it fiercely, if not always by name, but partly by denying victim status to others—while simultaneously *playing* the victim, in some cases.

The journalist who wrote about Neal's double humiliation was anxious to tell the reader "two things we should know" before we judge Neal harshly: that he has had a difficult life, and that he doesn't want to be pitied. If he *had* had this desire, he would have been sorely

---

members of the Tea Party, who for the most part became Trump supporters following the Republican primaries. Hochschild writes that, in these communities,

> the scene had been set for Trump's rise, like kindling before a match is lit. Three elements had come together. Since 1980, virtually all those I talked with felt on shaky economic ground, a fact that made them brace at the very idea of "redistribution." They also felt culturally marginalized: their views about abortion, gay marriage, gender roles, race, guns, and the Confederate flag all were held up to ridicule in the national media as backward. And they felt part of a demographic decline; "there are fewer and fewer white Christians like us," Madonna had told me. They'd begun to feel like a besieged minority. And to these feelings they added the cultural tendency—described by W. J. Cash in The Mind of the South, though shared in milder form outside the South—to identify "up" the social ladder with the planter, the oil magnate, and to feel detached from those further down the ladder.
>
> All this was part of the "deep story." In that story, strangers step ahead of you in line, making you anxious, resentful, and afraid. A president allies with the line cutters, making you feel distrustful, betrayed. A person ahead of you in line insults you as an ignorant redneck, making you feel humiliated and mad. Economically, culturally, demographically, politically, you are suddenly a stranger in your own land. The whole context of Louisiana—its companies, its government, its church and media—reinforces that deep story. So this—the deep story—was in place before the match was struck. (221–222)

disappointed by many people's reactions.[18] Neal expressed disbelief and hurt regarding the accusations leveled toward him. "How could you make this story into a negative?" he wondered. "I didn't do anything wrong, especially when United openly admitted that this was all them. They have already issued an apology and a statement and the whole nine [yards]." (Miller 2015)

I hope to have gone some way here to answering Neal's good question.

So drawing attention to one's moral injuries in a public forum does *not* seem an especially good way to attract sympathetic attention, as a subordinate group member. It seems liable to provoke hostility in many people even in the most straightforward cases, such as Neal's— all the more so, presumably, in cases where the victim is imperfect.

What about other reasons to go public with one's grievances? Here again, the obvious answers aren't clearly sufficient to explain women's increasing willingness to come forward. It is striking how many structural barriers subordinate group members are liable to face, if they press such claims in the hopes of getting justice and recognition. For example, for a woman trying to press charges (literally or figuratively) against a dominant man for injuring them in morally

18. It's a truism that sympathy and empathy are central moral capacities, perhaps even the core ones (although I myself would hesitate to go that far). And yet, when people ask for sympathy and empathy, it is often liable to engender hostility and resentment. These points are likely closely connected—perhaps the desire for sympathy reads as emotional blackmail, or the affective analogue of moralism. And, to generalize, I think we often implicitly view sympathy as a commodity for which one needs to get in line, in proportion to one's injuries, as opposed to the extent to which one is blocking triage for other, needier people, or burdening the providers. But this is just a mistake. There is no central repository for sympathy, and no way of distributing it fairly to everyone in need of it. Moreover, sympathy is not a strictly bounded resource. Nor is it infinite, of course. But, in theory, we could all be more sympathetic to each other, in a way that is reciprocal, at least diachronically. (See Manne 2016c for more on this.)

culpable and recognizably misogynistic ways, there will be a higher risk of

- not being believed in the first place, and being suspected of being duplicitous or "crazy," hysterical, etc. (as in testimonial injustice; for example, the idea of women as relentlessly vindictive, as exemplified by the character of Amy in *Gone Girl*);
- being blamed for what happened (as in the concept of victim-blaming generally; the question of what she was wearing; the concept of provocation in both domestic violence and sexual assault cases);
- having the crime not investigated properly (as in a plethora of cases involving famous sports players; and some police officers' failure to take domestic violence and/or sexual assault seriously);
- having evidence of the crime destroyed (e.g., the destruction of rape kits, among other documented instances of systematic police negligence and/or cover-ups);
- having the charges minimized or treated dismissively (e.g., the practice of persuading women not to bring charges of domestic violence against their partners and ex-partners; charging male college students with less serious offenses than those they have been accused of, often without the victim's consent or prior knowledge);
- having the crime held to be random and inexplicable, rather than admitted to be part of a larger pattern of misogynist aggression, or the charges dropped entirely, by positing supposedly individual and idiosyncratic factors in its causal aetiology, such as mental illness (consider formal and informal "pleas of insanity," as in many recent mass shootings committed by white men);
- being subject to counteraccusations of selfishness, aggression, mendacity, and manipulativeness (often mooted as grounds for particular concern about false rape allegations, despite there

being little evidence of a particular actual, as opposed to hypothetical, problem here; consider also the concept of a "social justice warrior");

- being belittled (e.g., being held to be "infantile," oversensitive, unable to deal with one's own problems in a mature, adult manner); and

- being harassed, threatened, and possibly (re-)injured by the accused's fans and defenders (as in the cross-examination of women prior to "rape shield" laws).

Given the ready-to-hand examples in brackets, and the paucity of analogues running in the other direction, gender-wise, such predictions—that is, that women trying to bring dominant men to justice will face a higher risk of encountering such barriers—have considerable prima facie plausibility. I have pointed to further evidence of the following thesis in chapter 6 as well: men who dominate women are not only privileged, but unusually well-insulated from *losing* their privileged social position, at least in many cases.

So, as we can see, there are many potential stumbling blocks for women coming forward and attempting to press charges against men who enjoy social dominance over them for misogynistic behavior. And there are reasons that positively count *against* doing so as well in evidence above. What about cases in which there are no legal or civil remedies on the table, as with microaggressions, for example? It is even more difficult to see why someone would bother then, if anything.

Hence if one thinks of the goal as bringing the perpetrator to justice, and gaining material resources and benefits, let alone attracting sympathy and attention, Campbell and Manning's question remains on the table. Women's coming forward does not seem rational or even readily intelligible, if these are assumed to be the hopes motivating them.

But they may not be. Regina Rini has argued that drawing attention to the ways in which one has been wronged as a subordinate group member may sometimes be the best, or even the only viable, way to foster *solidarity* with other people in a similar position.[19] One may thus be able to get one's injuries taken seriously, or at least gain the solace of having them recognized by others who are similarly vulnerable.[20] Of course, if systems of social sanctions, formal and informal alike, are geared toward upholding patriarchal values and interests, then it's not always true that strength is to be found in numbers per se. But sometimes, "crowdsourcing power" (as it were) in this way does seem effective. And this is increasingly possible in the age of social media.

Admittedly, as the crowdsourced power increases, so may the countervailing aggression and attempt to minimize and discredit the people who are wielding it. But there is also significant value in the social support itself, as well as the prospect of enhanced pattern recognition. For women, being forewarned about how misogyny works is to be forearmed against gaslighting, among other things (recalling the introduction).

So I am in complete agreement with Rini's explanation of the value of publicizing micro-aggressions, say, in order to foster solidarity. But I think there is plausibly another piece of the puzzle to be added, quite different in nature. And what follows will also give the lie to the charge—which has come not only from the right but sometimes from the left—that claiming victimhood involves accepting *present* and *future* passivity, as opposed to recognizing past or present disempowerment and humiliation, in a way that often requires and evinces agency and courage.[21] Or so I will argue, by way of the

19. Regina Rini, "Microaggression, Macro Harm," *LA Times*, October 12, 2015, http://www.latimes.com/opinion/op-ed/la-oe-1012-rini-microaggression-solidarity-20151012-story.html.

20. For one thing, there can be a visceral sense of relief in knowing that you are not alone in having had experiences that may be difficult to categorize, but clearly count as some kind of abuse, exploitation, or made for an intimate relationship with too great a power differential; see Manne (2017) for discussion.

21. I have benefited here from discussions with Quitterie Gounot and reading her developing work about "instrumentalized agency" in connection with sexual assault cases.

following case study. It also shows that the relevant tendencies and motives are evident outside the US context and long predate the Internet, social media, etc. Finally, it shows that semi-deliberately playing the victim in some contexts, after push has come to shove, is not incompatible with valuing self-sufficiency and independence. On the contrary, the former can demonstrate the latter.

INDEPENDENT PEOPLE: A CASE STUDY

In the novel *Independent People* by Nobel Laureate Halldór Laxness ([1934] 1997), the protagonist is a recently liberated peasant, Bjartur, trying to make a living as an independent man, farming sheep on a small, inhospitable patch of land in Iceland. (Bjartur renames the property "Summerhouses," an optimistic variant on its previous name, "Winterhouses.") There is a memorable scene early in the novel in which Bjartur's new wife, Rosa, pregnant with another man's child, is left alone with a ewe for company while Bjartur is away on a round-up. Famished and half-crazy with loneliness, Rosa convinces herself that the ewe is possessed. She unceremoniously slits its throat and makes a fatty sausage out of it, grilling it over the fire, before gorging herself insensible.

When Bjartur returns home, Rosa is predictably vague about the ewe's whereabouts. So Bjartur sets off into the mountains to search for the missing member of his flock. Meanwhile, Rosa goes into labor and subsequently dies in childbirth. Bjartur returns home to find his new bride's stiffened corpse, and his dog, Titla, curling her "lousy body" around a newborn girl, to foster it as well as she could with the warmth of her belly. Bjartur is left to try to keep the infant alive, a task he sees as of "the greatest importance," feeling noble. (He intends to raise the child as his own, despite her biological paternity, which he is at this point resigned to.) But he also finds himself with a terrible problem, given the supreme value he places on maintaining his independence. "Must he then ask help of other people?" he asks himself. "The last thing that he had impressed upon his wife was not to ask help of other people—an independent man who resorts to other people for help gives himself over to the power of the arch-fiend; and now this same humiliation was to be pronounced on him, on Bjartur of Summerhouses; but he was determined to pay whatever was asked of him" (1997, 100—101).

Presently Bjartur ventures—miserably, uneasily—to the house of the Bailiff and his wife, a poetess, to ask for some milk to keep the baby alive. Once there, he is determined to vaunt his liberated status. To the housekeeper who inquires about Rosa's health, while he is eating a bowl of porridge she provides him with: "I please myself, Gunsa lass. I'm my own boss these days, you know, and need give account to no one, you least of all." He throws his precious horsemeat to the dogs, defiantly, despite his hunger.

The Bailiff's wife, a poetess, comes "sailing in, high of head and full of bosom." Bjartur tells her he is ashamed to ask, but needs a little help with something—"nothing important, of course;" "a trifle" that would surely not be upsetting to the Bailiff. Upon entering the parlor where the three of them are to talk, the narrator characteristically echoes Bjartur's own reflections: "In clothing and general appearance Bjartur of Summerhouses was far superior to this tramplike Bailiff." And yet "no one could doubt, even at first sight, that this must be a man who ruled over others, and held their fate in his hands; his lips wrinkled about the quid of tobacco as an unconscious symbol that he released nothing before he had sucked everything of value out of it" (1997, 104).

Bjartur tries again and again, using every means at his disposal, to assert his independence in relation to the Bailiff and the poetess. He refuses to be seated. He makes extensive, prideful small talk. He tries to be magnanimous, offering the Bailiff some hay for the winter, should he need it. (To no avail, alas: "Look after your own self, my lad" the Bailiff replies, in a "complacent, commiserating tone" that, "though never definitely insulting, unconditionally relegated other people to the category of pitiable rubbish."[22]) Bjartur clarifies he is

22. "This always reacted upon Bjartur as if some criminal tendency were imputed. It fostered the aggression in his nature all these years, his passion for freedom and independence" (104).

only there for "a little information." He waxes philosophical about death. He communicates Rosa's untimely demise in the most round-about of ways—via a cryptic verse—as if to demonstrate not only his wit, but also his ability to compete with, if not beat, the poetess at her own game. He insinuates that the pair ought to help him not out of charity or benevolence, but because the infant is their grand-child. (This is true enough. Rosa was impregnated by their son, as they know—and although the pair was fond of her, Rosa is socially beneath them. Hence their hasty arrangement of her marriage to Bjartur.)

Bjartur does not feel inferior to these people by the lights of his own values. On the contrary, his attitude toward the Bailiff and his wife is utterly contemptuous. Nor does he envy their social position; he wants independence, not to displace them.[23] But he deeply resents the power they have over him, and the way that they wield it—the former being high-handed and condescending, the latter petty and controlling.[24]

But when Bjartur's hand is forced, he finally kowtows. The poet-ess cuts him off, and demands to know in "plain English" (an unfor-tunate translation) if Rosa has died in childbirth. When he confirms this, she says:

> "Probably we'll try to help you, as we've helped many another before you, with no thought of repayment. But one thing we do demand, that is neither you nor anyone else should come here with veiled insinuations about me or my household." (1997, 108)

---

23. Laxness's novel as a whole is in many ways a testament to the sincerity and depth of Bjartur's desire for independence, even though others might merely be evinc-ing hubris in professing it. I have heard it remarked that Bjartur is one of the most stubborn, bloody-minded, infuriating characters in twentieth-century literature.

24. This is a brilliant—and hence rare—depiction of something like Nietzschean *ressentiment* from the inside. But, on closer inspection, we find that Bjartur's attitude toward the Bailiff and the poetess differs in numerous ways from classic Nietzschean *ressentiment* shown by the weak toward the strong. It might be construed as the *res-sentiment* Nietzsche allowed that the strong might occasionally feel toward the weak, though—for, despite the social relations between them, the pair is hardly admirable or noble. *Their* souls are the ones that are "squint-sighted," in contrast to Bjartur's high-minded fierceness.

She is not "completely mollified until Bjartur had fully and explicitly removed all suspicion that he had come with the intention of inquiring into the paternity of the child at home in Summerhouses."

That having becoming obvious, Bjartur suddenly becomes completely deferential. "My tongue, you see, is more used to talking about lambs than human beings," he says apologetically, "and the idea was simply to ask you whether you didn't think it would be worthwhile pouring a few drops of warm milk down its throat to see if it can't be kept going till morning. I'll pay you whatever you ask, of course."

At long last, Bjartur succeeds in prostrating himself sufficiently to satisfy his former mistress. And with that, the poetess declares that it is her "supreme joy" to "offer the weak her helping hand even in these difficult times; to sustain the feeble, to foster the awakening life. Her heart was all his, not only in joy, but also in sorrow" (1997, 108).

And, it is added, she meant it.

But is it clear that the Bailiff and the poetess have won in any sense that matters (or, again, by the lights of Bjartur's own values)? No. The effect of this scene is to make *them* look ridiculous. Ultimately, Bjartur performs his subordination—plays it up, if anything—in order to expose the depth of their domineering, petty, ignoble behavior, for the benefit of the reader.[25] They would be willing to let the

---

25. The performance of abjection—what a miserable condition he has been reduced to!—becomes further exaggerated, when we come to passages like the following, describing Bjartur's homecoming. While Gudny, the Bailiff's housekeeper, is attempting to revive the infant, and tells him to leave the house so she can get on with it, Bjartur reflects:

> That was the first time that Bjartur was driven out of his own house, and had the circumstances been otherwise he would most certainly have had something to say in protest against such an enormity and would have tried to drive into Gunsa's head the fact that he owed her not a cent; but as it was . . . he had been provided with a tail to trail between his legs as in utter ignominy he took the same path as the dog and crept down the stairs. . . he pulled out a truss of hay and, spreading it on the floor, lay down like a dog. (1997, 109–10)

spark of life in their grandchild go out rather than let Bjartur retain some measure of the pride and independence that bigger people (as we say) would never think to begrudge him.

And those determined to maintain the upper hand will often tend to lose their appeal to an audience in general. In humiliating others, they will tend to take on the unattractive cast of bullies. They may begin to seem pathetic. We may start rooting for the underdog.

What is to be learned from this tragi-comic episode? It points, I think, to the possibility that playing the victim—in the sense of accepting or even embracing one's status as such—can sometimes be an act of protest or resistance, rather than an act of passive resignation to one's victimization. In actively performing one's role as a victim, or trying to draw attention to it, one is *not* in fact passive.[26] On Wendy Brown's (1995) reading, those who accept victimhood in this way are in the grip of a kind of Nietzschean *ressentiment* that is "an effect of domination that reiterates impotence, a substitute for action, for power, for self-affirmation that reinscribes incapacity, powerlessness, and rejection . . . [it] is rooted in reaction—the substitution of reasons, norms, and ethics for deeds," Brown writes, disapprovingly (69). But, as a description of Bjartur, this is clearly inapt. He does not resentfully accept, but subversively performs, his own subordination in relation to his oppressors.

Bjartur is "completely exhausted," and feels "superfluous," "never less independent in his heart than that night." But the next morning, when he wakes, his child is alive. He names her Asta, and says to himself "there is much to be done." There are sheep to be tended to, a funeral for Rosa to be arranged, and a "feast" with pancakes and Christmas cake, and good coffee to be provided, for all those in attendance. "I won't stand for people drinking any old dish-wash at the funeral of a wife of mine." This is not a man who has lost his sense of pride or what matters most to him— namely, his independence. Neither is it a man opposed to life and action, or invested in his own subjugation; on the contrary. This goes toward my hunch that this is the *ressentiment* of the strong, which engenders *action*, even if only in the form of a subversive performance of the kind of deference that they are forced to demonstrate. See Stephen Darwall (2013) for instructive discussion of *ressentiment* in this connection.

26. See Judith Butler (2016) for a nuanced exploration of demonstrating bodily vulnerability and (or, almost, as) an act of political resistance.

I suggest that, under circumstances such as these, such performances may be justified and valuable, normatively speaking. Although Bjartur may be playing a part, more or less deliberately, his performance is a dramatic re-enactment of the actual social relations between them. (He merely gives the Bailiff and his wife enough rope, so to speak.) Moreover, as discussed above, this is an act of resistance of the last resort, since he has exhausted all other viable options when it comes to self-assertion. His approach suggests ways similarly cornered and powerless agents might practice a productive form of passive aggression, effectively. If we read the scene this way, it has something of the flavor of civil—social?—disobedience, by means of passive resistance. The characteristic thought being something like: Fine. I will let you humiliate me, as a form of protest against the social norms and power relations that together make this possible. Go ahead and bully me: expose yourself; people are watching, and have long memories.

If there is some truth to this, then it explains why this move on the part of subordinated people is liable to drive conservatives (in particular) to distraction. It has the potential to expose unjust power relations in a way that leaves the powers-that-be looking ridiculous, threatened, and petty.

We saw this kind of anger on display in the reaction to Hillary Clinton's testimony before the Select Committee on Benghazi in 2015. *New York Times* columnist Maureen Dowd—whose long, hostile relationship with the Clintons is well-documented, but also largely beside the point here—wrote:

Nobody plays the victim like Hillary.

She can wield that label like a wrecking ball.

If her husband humiliates her with a girlfriend in the Oval Office, Hillary turns around and uses the sympathy engendered to launch a political career. If her Republican opponent gets in her space in an overbearing way during a debate, she turns around and uses the sympathy engendered to win a Senate seat. If conservatives hold a Salem witch trial under the guise of a House select committee hearing, she turns around and uses the sympathy engendered to slip into the H.O.V. lane of a superhighway to the presidency.[27]

Dowd's hostility was striking here. What had Hillary done to deserve it? Nothing, when it came down to it; she was just impressive under trying circumstances. "Hillary Clinton is never more alluring than when a bunch of pasty-faced, nasty-tongued white men bully her," Dowd complained, immediately following the above passage. Continuing: "And she was plenty alluring during her marathon session on Thursday with Republican Lilliputians, who were completely oblivious to the fact that Hillary is always at her most potent when some Neanderthal is trying to put her in her place." This may be an accurate description, on the basis of which Dowd's tone drips with disapproval. But, again, there seems a leap of logic; one wants to be shown the problem. Clinton exposed their mean-minded and domineering behavior by behaving in a morally better fashion, or being "the adult in the room." Rather than calling this "playing the victim," we might just as well call this "exposing the bully." Yes, it may alter the audience's sympathies. But the question is: why shouldn't it?

Letting oneself be perceived in this way can be overdone, of course. It can be too protracted, too defeatist, too masochistic, or manipulative. It can also be unfair, or done for the wrong reasons. There is no point denying these are genuine possibilities. But it can also be a powerful manoeuver and, I suggest, a legitimate one. For those who think it cannot be, they need to say why not. And what is the alternative supposed to be, for people who have exhausted the other potential avenues for bringing bullies and oppressors to justice?

One person who recently found herself in such a predicament is Emma Sulkowicz, then an undergraduate at Columbia University.

27. Maureen Dowd, "The Empire Strikes Back," *New York Times Sunday Review*, October 24, 2015, https://www.nytimes.com/2015/10/25/opinion/sunday/the-empire-strikes-back.html.

Sulkowicz tried to bring charges of sexual assault against her alleged attacker, without success. Following what she held to be the failure of the campus police and the NYPD to prosecute the case properly, she crafted a performance art piece, "Carry That Weight," around her experience: dragging her fifty-pound standard-issue twin mattress wherever she went on campus. She actively lugged around the visual reminder of the way in which she had been wrongly deprived of her agency during the attack, as well as afterwards. This clearly took strength—not only emotional, but physical.

A subsequent piece of Sulkowicz's is at least as interesting for my purposes. She recorded a performance of an initially consensual sexual encounter that subsequently turned violent, in which she herself played the victim—literally. The actor who played her assailant has his faced blurred out. The video is called, "Ceci n'est pas un viol." This is not a rape. It is an artistic representation of one that transforms the experience of being rendered passive and humiliated into an act of agency by dint of its very performance and presentation. Its creative deed seems to be to say: *these things happen*. They happened to the artist. Hence, the artwork.

On the website for Sulkowicz's project (http://www.cecinestpasunviol.com/), she asks potential viewers to reflect on some questions before they scroll down to the video—questions about "searching," "desiring," and about Sulkowicz herself ("me"):

- How well do you think you know me? Have we ever met?
- Do you think I'm the perfect victim or the world's worst victim?
- Do you refuse to see me as either a human being or a victim? If so, why? Is it to deny me agency and thus further victimize me? If so, what do you think of the fact that you owe your ability to do so to me, since I'm the one who took a risk and made myself vulnerable in the first place?
- Do you hate me? If so, how does it feel to hate me?"

Satisfying, among other things, is my suspicion. And this should worry us regarding the culture of so-called victim culture, i.e., resenting and blaming certain victims.

So, to return in closing to Campbell and Manning's question: why emphasize one's own victimization? Sometimes, to foster solidarity, as Regina Rini has argued. And sometimes, to make oneself the center of a narrative that one has had an active role in (re)shaping, which may compete with dominant and default versions thereof, I've argued. One thereby has an opportunity—possibly a unique one—as a subordinate group member to reveal what it is natural to call one's point of view on the matter, one's side of the story, in relation to dominant parties. One may be able to expose the people who *made* one a victim as bullies and aggressors, even if this cannot be relied on to redirect the usual flow of sympathy, which tends—like heat—to rise up the social hierarchy.

This kind of subversive maneuver is liable to make people hostile and resentful, particularly when the two parties involved are, respectively, a woman and a man who is socially dominant over her. As I've argued in several places in this book so far, asking for sympathy and attention as a woman tends to be a fraught endeavor. It can go morally wrong, as well as backfire socially, in numerous ways. But this, I'm tempted to say, is just moral life. Attempts to disrupt existing power relations are rife with moral hazards. And to those who would maintain that doing this is never a justifiable move, my question is, why not? Moreover, if "playing the victim" is inevitably deplorable, then *cui bono*? And to whose detriment? Oftentimes, the women who are subject to misogyny *ought* to draw attention to their moral injuries, in relation to the men who have made this the reality. It is no surprise the exposure may be unwelcome, and the attempt to do so, threatening.

Chapter 8

Losing (to) Misogynists

If a woman be never so comely, think her a counterfeit; if never so straight, think her crooked; if she be well set, call her a boss; if slender, a hazel twig; if brown, think her as black as a crow; if well colored, a painted wall; if sad or shamefaced, then think her a clown; if merry and pleasant, then she is the liker to be a wanton.

Joseph Swetnam, *The Arraignment of Lewde, Idle, Forward, and Unconstant Women*

She was called a witch, a bitch, a liar, and the lesser of two evils. "She has many masks but who has seen her face?" one pundit asked, rhetorically. He was thereby expressing widespread and entrenched doubts regarding her sincerity. Her ratings for trustworthiness were exceptionally low, despite her record being well above average among politicians. She was Julia Gillard, the first female prime minister of Australia, my home country.

That Gillard was subject to a vicious misogynist mobbing that eventually played a major role in her losing the leadership (following an internal party challenge) is now widely accepted, to the point of being uncontroversial.[1] The interesting issues for my purposes are why, how, and, in view of this, how we failed to learn these lessons.

---

1. See, e.g., Manne 2016a, where I discuss Gillard's case in more detail, and quote historian Marilyn Lake, who summarizes: "It is now a truism that history will prove more sympathetic to Gillard's prime ministership . . . than contemporary commentators have been. What will mostly attract historians' attention, however, will be how she was treated, the rabid misogyny, the hysteria of men who could not abide the spectacle of a woman in power, who labeled her a bitch, a witch, a liar, a usurper, an illegitimate claimant who refused to bow down before her male rivals."

For history repeated itself in America, in a strikingly similar fashion during the 2016 presidential election campaign—in terms of the rhetoric and mechanisms, despite significant differences between the targets and social contexts. And I believe these misogynistic mechanisms and broader gendered dynamics are an important part of the story of Donald Trump's upset victory over Hillary Clinton.[2] If nothing else (and I admit this is a very thin silver lining), the result gives us an opportunity to reflect on how badly misogynist forces can distort our thinking and bias our reasoning.

WHEN A MAN COMPETES WITH A WOMAN: COMPARATIVE GENDER BIASES

We often conceptualize gender biases as something like demerit points applied to individual women, whom we subsequently assess more negatively than we would otherwise, in the domains in which we're biased.[3] We tend to underestimate her, making it harder for her to compete successfully with a male counterpart, whom we are disposed to assess fairly (so the thought continues). She might have to be twice as good to beat him, say, in an extreme case.

But there's a distinct way of conceptualizing gender biases as applying to our *rankings* of men and women, and disposing us to prefer a man to his female counterpart, all else being equal—i.e., holding fixed other potentially prejudicial factors. These preferences may come out in a variety of ways: supporting, promoting, liking,

2. To be clear, the thought here isn't to give a wonkish analysis of what the most important "but-for" causes of the result were, ranked in order of their importance. Rather, it's to shed light on the more coarse-grained sociological issue that arose in the lead-up to the election, as well as in the aftermath: why was it ever even a serious competition? For although reasonable minds can of course disagree about Clinton's merits as a presidential candidate, it is difficult to doubt that (a) Clinton was a better presidential candidate than Trump, on the basis of the evidence available at the time, which has subsequently not proved misleading (on the contrary), and (b) had misogyny not been (such) a factor, this would have been (more) evident to a (much) greater number.

3. This section of the chapter draws heavily on Manne 2016i.

believing, or voting for him over her, for instance. This may result in *overestimating* him, and turning against her with hostility, as well as underestimating her merits. Regardless of how good she is, we may find something, anything, to doubt or dislike about her—again, in extreme cases, or perfect storm scenarios.

One such may have been that in which we found ourselves twice over during the election campaign: where a man and a woman were competing head-to-head for a position of historically male-dominated power and authority. Here are some of the most striking of the findings in each of the three relevant bodies of literature. Each of them points to a prevalent and strong disposition to uphold gendered social hierarchies under these conditions.

1. Researchers David Paul and Jessi Smith (2008) surveyed nearly 500 likely voters in Ohio, some two years prior to the 2008 election. Respondents were asked to assess five likely presidential candidates—three Republicans, two Democrats, and three men and two women. Voters rated the two women as the least qualified of the five, despite their both being highly qualified, objectively speaking (according to the researchers). And in each of the six head-to-head matchups that might result in the general, the male candidate beat the female one in every single contest.

Each of the men also did better against a female nominee, as opposed to another man, from the opposing party. Perhaps most tellingly of all, voters were several orders of magnitude likelier to *defect* from a female nominee from their own party to a male nominee from the opposing one, compared with vice versa. The researchers concluded that "the presence of a woman candidate opponent for president may aid the [male] competition" (2008, 466).

The three male politicians in the survey were John McCain, John Edwards, and Rudy Giuliani. One of the female politicians was Elizabeth Dole. The other woman? Hillary Clinton.

But wait, you might say: Hillary had much more political experience in 2016 than she did a decade earlier. If her qualifications were no longer in doubt, due to women in her position admittedly being held to more stringent, or double, standards, would such gender biases cease to be an issue?

No—or, at the very least, not necessarily. This in fact seems quite unlikely at the level of the general population, on the basis of studies like the following (among many congruent findings by each of the two teams of researchers). They show that, when women are not doubted as viable competitors for male-dominated roles, they are widely *disliked* and subject to social punishment and rejection.

2. The psychologist Madeline Heilman has produced a body of research geared toward answering the following question, among others: when the evidence of a woman's competence in male-dominated fields is unequivocal, are they still subject to gender discrimination?[4] It would appear so; highly successful female managers are still promoted at rates much lower than their male counterparts. Why is this?

In one particularly striking study, Heilman and her collaborators gave participants packets of information profiling two high-status employees in a male-dominated industry: assistant vice presidents (AVPs) for sales in a company manufacturing airline parts. One of the employees was male, the other female—as signaled just by their names, "James" and "Andrea," pre-tested for being similarly liked monikers on average. And which information packet was assigned to which of the pair was alternated, such that each of the employee profiles was associated with James for half the participants, and Andrea for the remaining half, within each of the two conditions.

---

4. I draw here primarily on Heilman, Wallen, Fuchs, and Tamkins (2004)—Heilman et al. (2004) hereafter—along with Heilman and Okimoto (2007) and Parks-Stamm, Heilman, and Hearns (2008).

In the "unclear success" condition, the evidence of James and Andrea both being outstanding AVPs was equivocal. For this group, the vast majority of participants (86 percent) judged James more *competent* than Andrea when asked to compare them. But the two of them came off as similarly likable.

In the "clear success" condition, the remaining half of the participants received an additional piece of information that made each employee's competence unambiguous: an annual performance review stating that each was a "stellar performer," in the top 5 percent of all AVPs at such companies. In this case, participants judged the two about equally competent, but James as more *likable* than Andrea, in a similarly large majority of cases (83 percent). Andrea was also then held to be more interpersonally *hostile* than in any other condition—a measure that encompassed being abrasive, manipulative, conniving, and untrustworthy, notably. Heilman et al. (2004) describe this effect as "dramatic."

Remember, this was based on identical (on average, since alternating packets of) information. So these radically disparate judgments had no rational basis whatsoever. Insofar as the participants *felt* themselves to have reasons, they must have employed ad hoc standards and post hoc rationalization.

Why, though? Why did they so dislike Andrea, when her competence was undeniable?

3. The psychologist L. A. Rudman has proposed the following answer: people are (often unwittingly) motivated to *maintain gender hierarchies*, by applying social penalties to women who compete for, or otherwise threaten to advance to, high-status, masculine-coded positions. This "status incongruity hypothesis" is consistent with the results of the previous study, and helps to explain them. In one recent study citing it (Rudman, Moss-Racusin, Phelan, and Nauts 2012), along with work by Heilman, Rudman and her collaborators showed that the effect is mediated by what is known as the "social dominance penalty," where women in such positions who

are *agentic* (i.e., competent, confident, assertive) are perceived as extreme in masculine-coded traits like being arrogant and aggressive. They are often described as "ballbreakers" and "castrating bitches." (Sound familiar?[5])

These also happen to be verboten traits for women (as Rudman et al. [2012] confirmed experimentally for these subjects). So agentic women competing with men for male-dominated roles are doubly likely to be punished and rejected in light of these mechanisms. They are *perceived* as having more of the qualities they are *less* permitted to have than their identically-described male counterparts (described, again, using the same textual stimuli, such as letters of recommendation with the names switched).

The explanation Rudman offers for the social dominance penalty was further confirmed by the following fascinating result: it could be augmented under a "high threat" condition where, at the beginning of the experiment, participants read an article called "America in Decline," which included the following paragraph:

> These days, many people in the United States feel disappointed with the nation's condition. Whether it stems from the economic meltdown and persistent high rates of unemployment, fatigue from fighting protracted wars in the Middle East that have cost America dearly in blood and treasure, or general anxieties regarding global and technological changes that the government seems unable to leverage to their advantage, Americans are deeply dissatisfied. Many citizens feel that the country has reached a low point in terms of social, economic, and political factors. (Rudman et al. 2012, 172)

---

5. See, for example, Tucker Carlson, who said repeatedly on his MSNBC show *Tucker* that whenever Hillary Clinton came on TV, he crossed his legs involuntarily. "She scares me," he said. "I can't help it." (Be that as it may, he didn't have to air this reaction.) Ryan Chiachiere, "Tucker Carlson on Clinton: 'When She Comes on Television I Involuntarily Cross My Legs,'" Media Matters, July 18, 2007, http://mediamatters.org/research/2007/07/18/tucker-carlson-on-clinton-when-she-comes-on-tel/139362.

In this condition, agentic female figures who aspired to high-powered positions were significantly less liked and more often turned down for a promotion than in the "low threat" and control conditions. For her agentic male counterpart, however, the threatening stimulus made no difference. The researchers explained:

Given that people under system threat tend to defend their worldviews, which include gender status differences . . . and because female agency was especially rejected by people under system threat, [these results] provide direct evidence that backlash functions to preserve the gender hierarchy. (2012, 174)

This helps to account for the otherwise surprisingly good run that Donald Trump and arguably even Bernie Sanders had against Hillary Clinton—over and above the boost Paul and Smith (2008) predict a male presidential candidate will receive when they compete against a female rival. Both Trump and Sanders told recognizable (though different) versions of an "America in decline" story. This may have placed Clinton at a further disadvantage.

Note too that the common assumption that millennials (i.e., people born after 1980) are more or less immune to such gender biases, given a tendency to identify as progressive, seems dubious at best. The second and third of the above studies involved participants primarily if not solely in this age group (their being undergraduates at the time).[6] The first at least included them. And the age of participants reportedly made no statistically significant difference here.[7] Nor, in any of

6. In Heilman et al. (2004), the participants' mean age was 20.5 years old (the range and standard deviation is not listed, unfortunately). This would make participants roughly my age, on average, i.e., on the upper end of the millennial spectrum. In Rudman et al. (2012), the study recruited college undergraduates taking an introductory psychology course. So, although no specific age information was listed, it is a safe bet that most would also be millennials. Finally, the Paul and Smith (2008) study surveyed what is described as a fairly representative sample of nearly five hundred likely voters in Ohio, including people in the 18–24 age range.

7. Moreover, another study by Smith and Paul, together with Rachel Paul (2007), explicitly studied young voters (who were then undergraduates), and found they

these studies, did participants' gender. Many people expressed shock at the number of (white) women who voted for Donald Trump over Hillary Clinton. But, given that the above comparative gender biases tend to be found in women just as much as men, it arguably shouldn't have been so surprising. I'll come back to the more complex issue of various possible *explanations* of this common bias, together with why white women were particularly susceptible to it in this case later in this chapter. But we should note in the meantime that, if misogyny is a matter more of gendered norm enforcement than seeing women as sub-human or mindless creatures, or as loathsome, fearsome, and so on, then there's an immediate explanatory payoff in this connection: for, there's no mystery (and little doubt) about the fact that women police other women, and engage in gendered norm enforcement behavior. On the view of misogyny I've developed in this book, we would expect women who channel misogynistic forces against other women to be excessively moralistic toward—for example, prone to blame and punish—those who do not adhere to gendered norms and expectations. Similarly, when it comes to *internalized* misogyny, we would expect women to be excessively prone to guilt and shame for violating feminine-coded duties, rather than necessarily harboring any global attitude of self-loathing. I'll return to these themes shortly.

SOCIAL REJECTION IS MEDIATED BY DISGUST

So dislike and hostility are relatively predictable reactions to female politicians aspiring to highest office. So is regarding her as

---

assess fictional male versus female presidential candidates' resumes differently. When there was a characteristically male name at the top of a résumé, it was significantly likelier to be held to belong to a more accomplished politician and promising presidential hopeful than when a characteristically female name was substituted. This effect did *not* hold for candidates for the Senate though, interestingly, suggesting that the effect may be limited to women competing for positions of unrivaled and/or unprecedented masculine-coded power and authority.

untrustworthy, on no ostensible basis. Where does this view of her come from, however?

Recent research on disgust helps to forge the connection. For disgust is the emotion of social rejection rather than anger, say. The philosopher Daniel Kelly (2011) has argued that our innate disgust responses—elicited both by contaminated foodstuffs and pathogen threats—were particularly well-suited, and hence recruited, to play the role of regulating people's adherence to social norms, conventions, hierarchies, and so on. For one thing, the prospect of becoming disgusted strongly motivates people to avoid those behaviors deemed to be disgusting. For another, disgust sticks, stains, seeps, and catches; disgust is easy to learn from others by bearing witness to their disgusted reactions to people and objects. Moreover, once learned, it is hard to undo disgust-based associations.

As the psychologists Yoel Inbar and David Pizarro (2014) have pointed out, disgust also has the advantage of *spreading* by association. Those who tangle with what disgusts us may become disgusting to us too. So the risk of becoming disgusting to others by engaging in socially taboo behavior acts as a further motivator, given a more or less universal aversion to shunning, shaming, and being ousted from one's community. Historically, this would often have been a death knell. And ostracism and isolation can be emotional wrenching, indeed tortuous in extreme cases, even absent material deprivation and the vulnerability or precarity that comes with losing people.

Disgust is also a *moralizing* influence that intensifies and even drives novel moral judgments—in some cases, powerfully.[8] It turns out that even mild "pangs" of disgust can cause some people to judge that someone is *suspicious* and *up to no good*, even when such judgments clearly have no rational basis—when what the person was doing was entirely innocent, even praiseworthy.

---

8. I owe the original connection here to Tali Mendelberg (2016). In her excellent commentary on my essay, "The Logic of Misogyny" (Manne 2016d), Mendelberg pointed out that Trump's expressions of non-moral disgust will be prone to give rise to moral judgments among his followers.

In a particularly striking study by Thalia Wheatley and Jonathan Haidt (2005), participants susceptible to post-hypnotic suggestion were hypnotized to feel a pang of disgust upon reading either the word "often" or the word "take." Participants then read vignettes featuring people committing conventional moral transgressions. For example, in a "bribery" scenario:

> Congressman Arnold Paxton frequently gives speeches condemning corruption and arguing for campaign finance reform. But he is just trying to cover up the fact that he himself [will *take* bribes from/is *often* bribed by] the tobacco lobby, and other special interests, to promote their legislation. (781)

Participants who read a version of this vignette containing the word that matched their post-hypnotic suggestion, and hence experienced artificially heightened visceral disgust upon reading it, tended to judge the relevant acts significantly more harshly, that is, as *more morally wrong*, than those who read a semantically identical vignette without the disgust elicitor.

In a follow-up study, the experimenters included another vignette as a control, describing a student council representative named Dan who [tries to *take*/*often* picks] topics of widespread mutual interest for discussion at their meetings. Perfectly innocuous behavior, right? Good behavior, even. But some of the participants who read the version of the vignette containing the disgust-inducing word begged to differ, to the initial surprise of the researchers. "It just seems like he's up to something," said one participant, vaguely. Dan seemed like "a popularity-seeking snob" to another. His behavior "seems so weird and disgusting," a third reported, helplessly. "I don't know [why it's wrong], it just is," they concluded (2005, 783).

The first suggested lesson: disgust reactions can make us harsher moral critics and may even prompt some people to read moral offenses into entirely, and obviously, innocent actions. The second: as moral critics, we don't always deliver our verdicts based on moral reasons and arguments. Sometimes, we *reach* for these reasons and arguments to rationalize a verdict already rendered. We unwittingly concoct a post hoc case on this basis.[9]

EXPRESSIONS OF DISGUST TOWARD HILLARY

Cut now to Hillary Clinton, whom many people not only disliked and mistrusted but also expressed visceral disgust for during her 2016 presidential campaign. One such was Donald Trump, who didn't want to "even think" about Clinton using the restroom during a debate commercial break in December 2015 (though he was the one to raise the subject).

Some of this disgust involved a fixation with Clinton's health, which served as a pretext for misrepresenting her as weak, frail, aging if not dying, and lacking in the necessary presidential (read: masculine) stamina—in short, as an old lady, now presumptively useless except for providing caregiving labor. There was also a striking fixation with Hillary's bodily secretions, and the possibility of her contaminating others—for example, the risk of her infecting people she shook hands with during a bout of mild pneumonia in September 2016. Phlegm or no, her cough due to a dry throat and seasonal allergies was an outsize source of controversy. Even Clinton's signature laugh—where she tilts her head back, and opens her mouth to laugh with an abandon that ought to have been evidence against the common perception she isn't genuine—prompted disgust reactions. The "envelope" of her body seemed too loosely sealed for many people's comfort.

---

9. It's worth noting that not everyone is equally prone to having disgust reactions. But Inbar and Pizarro, together with Paul Bloom (among others) have shown that people who *are* easily disgusted are much more likely to be socially conservative—a finding that is important to bear in mind in other contexts. But given the way disgust seems prone to proliferate via public discourse (of which more shortly), it's not clear that its explanatory purchase is so limited in the case of Clinton that follows.

A Trump supporter interviewed on Samantha Bee before the first presidential debate opined that he expected Clinton to be using a catheter on stage, because of her many health problems. I looked it up; somehow, this had become a popular Internet conspiracy theory. The interviewee added he was trying to be empathetic—to which the interviewer responded, aptly, that he might need to try harder. And, ironically, it was Trump who was rumored to have wet his pants at a debate back in February—an insinuation of Marco Rubio's that seemed almost too strange and socially awkward to be fabricated. But it was conveniently forgotten soon afterward. When it comes to structural amnesia, that is, collective forgetting mediated by social privilege and dominance, one could scarcely hope for a better example. We drag her name through the mud; we uphold his dignity almost primly.

Meanwhile, a small dark patch on Clinton's jacket at the first debate was said to be a drool spot—another symptom of her inability to keep her mouth shut, all evidence to the contrary notwithstanding, given Trump's menacing stance and threat to throw her in prison for her emails. (In reality, the mark was a shadow cast by Clinton's lapel mic.)

When people chanted of Clinton, "lock her up," at Trump's rallies, it obviously expressed a desire to see her punished. But it also went beyond that and seemed to express a desire for her *containment*. When a Republican New Hampshire representative and Trump delegate called for Clinton to be shot for treason in July 2016 over her emails and Benghazi, he framed his remarks as follows: "Something's wrong there. . . . This whole thing disgusts me. Hillary Clinton should be put in the firing line and shot for treason." Later, he also called her a "piece of garbage."

So I don't think it's a stretch to suggest that Clinton was subject to a striking number and intensity of disgust reactions as her campaign wore on, just as the empirical evidence canvassed above would predict. And, as we've seen, this plausibly would have led to their mistrusting her, and may also have increased the severity of their moral disapproval of her actions. It might also have led to the conviction that Clinton was guilty of *something*, even absent specific charges, or strong counterevidence against charges previously leveled. The attempt to clear her of false accusations and poorly evidenced myths and rumors hence often resembled a game of whack-a-mole. This too can be explained in terms of general features of disgust I take up in next two sections: the way it sticks, and the way it makes us want to keep our distance from its object.[10]

HOW DISGUST STICKS

In a number of places in the lead-up to the election, I explored the strikingly similar moral suspicions leveled at Hillary Clinton and Julia Gillard. Both were branded liars—as discussed in previous chapters, "Ju-Liar" became the latter's standard nickname among her detractors, both in the media and Australian households—and accused of corruption on a manifestly thin basis. The charges, in each case, ultimately came to nothing. But the sense of suspicion never abated. Even when no evidence to warrant such suspicions came to light, and the absence of such evidence might have been thought strong evidence of its absence, some people publicly maintained their suspicions without embarrassment.[11]

Nor are such episodes restricted to politics. Consider the "trial of Alice Goffman" in the media, which was subsequently deemed a

10. It's also worth remembering how recently Clinton had been much more popular, e.g., when she left her position as secretary of state. And then she asked for a "promotion" and was perceived by many as greedy and grasping, as several pieces on her political trajectory argued persuasively. See, e.g., Sady Doyle, "America Loves Women Like Hillary Clinton—As Long as They're Not Asking for a Promotion," *Quartz*, February 25, 2016, https://qz.com/624346/america-loves-women-like-hillary-clinton-as-long-as-theyre-not-asking-for-a-promotion, and Michael Arnovitz, "Thinking about Hillary: A Plea for Reason," *Medium*, June 12, 2016, https://thepolicy.us/thinking-about-hillary-a-plea-for-reason-308fce6d187c.

11. See, e.g., Callum Borchers, "A Former Top New York Times Editor Says Clinton Is 'Fundamentally Honest.' So . . ." *Washington Post*, March 30, 2016, https://www.washingtonpost.com/news/the-fix/wp/2016/03/30/a-former-top-new-york-times-editor-says-hillary-clinton-is-fundamentally-honest-and-trustworthy-so-what/.

witch hunt by one of her more conscientious commentators (Singal 2016)—and where none of the charges stuck, despite the convictions and commentary of the Internet. Goffman, a young, prize-winning sociologist and writer was accused of everything under the sun, from academic misconduct (based on a widely circulated, anonymous, sixty-page document purporting to reveal inconsistencies in her account—which Goffman subsequently accounted for; see Singal 2015), to sheer fabrication to "driving the getaway car in a murder plot." It's not that Goffman was immune from certain valid criticisms. But she alone was not their proper target. Most of the valid criticisms were ones that could be leveled at many if not most ethnographers, who were by and large spared this kind of public shaming. Hence my sense that the suspicions were excessive or singled Goffman out to the point of crying out for explanation; the gendered pattern in question seems to me to provide the best or, at the very least, a plausible one.

To be sure, not every female politician or prominent public figure is subject to such suspicion, condemnation, and the desire to see them punished. But, when the mud-slinging does begin, it quickly tends to escalate. And there tends to be not only a pile-on (common enough on the Internet), but an "oozing" effect—where the suspicion and criticism encompasses every possible grounds for doubt about her competence, character, and accomplishments. Clinton, Gillard, and Goffman were all suspected of myriad distinct offenses. And this suggests a conviction they're guilty of *something*.

Even among those who don't share this conviction, it may have an impact on their thinking indirectly. My sense is that people in liberal and progressive circles were not generally as proud to vote for Clinton as President Obama, despite their very similar policies and politics, and the fact that each was or would have been (respectively) a history-making president, from the point of view of so-called identity politics. More than that, I think there was an atmosphere on the left that led to moral defensiveness about a vote for Clinton—as if voting for her meant complicity or complacency vis-à-vis the admittedly terrible effects of some of her (I agree) misguided foreign policies. But most of these policies were also Obama's. Yet, somehow, they often seemed to do less to damage his reputation—and didn't turn a vote for him into a moral liability on the left, was my impression.

The problem here is exacerbated by the way moral criticisms become personal and go to a woman's *character* especially quickly and cut especially deep. It also says something about the way misogyny works to disrupt female solidarity, especially among white women. In the next section, I'll take up these points in reverse order.

KEEPING ONE'S DISTANCE

Recall from chapter 3 that misogyny often involves distinguishing between "good" and "bad" women, by the lights of their conformity to patriarchal norms and values. So, at the highest level of generality, it's not surprising that women who aspire to be "good" have social incentives to distance themselves from a woman deemed "bad," as Clinton often was, and to publicly participate when she was ostracized and punished for supposed moral crimes and misdemeanors.

Another study coauthored by Madeline Heilman (Parks-Stamm, Heilman, and Hearns [2008])—sheds some light on why over half the white women who voted in the general in 2016 cast their ballots for Donald Trump over Clinton. It turns out that women penalize highly successful women just as much as men do, as indicated earlier in this chapter, but for seemingly different reasons. The researchers had male and female participants rate a newly appointed female vice president, described in a personnel file, on measures of hostility, antisocial traits, and overall likability. Both male and female participants were prone to punish her, socially, by inferring norm violations—for example, manipulativeness, coldness, aggression—unless given specific information about her feminine virtues and good behavior. In which case, the "social punishment" effect was blocked for male and female participants. However, crucially, only the female participants then had more negative *self-evaluations*. This supported the researchers' hypothesis that penalizing successful women serves an ego-protective function (only) for other women. It defuses the threatening sense that a similar—and similarly good, decent, and/ or "real" woman—is more competent or accomplished than they are. And, tellingly, it appears that this is linked to a lack of self-belief that can be assuaged by positive feedback.

In the first experiment, the researchers blocked women's punishment of other women by describing the subject as having feminine-coded, prosocial tendencies. In the second experiment in the same research paper, they achieved a similar magnitude of the same effect by priming participants (all of whom were women) in the experimental condition with positive feedback about their own exceptional business acumen. They were no longer motivated to penalize the female high achiever.

In the days following the election, it was common for those of us grieving the result to judge the white women who voted for Donald Trump even more harshly than their white male counterparts. I was guilty of this myself. But, in view of these results, I subsequently came to redirect a good portion of my anger toward the patriarchal system that makes even young women believe—noting that, again, participants in this study were college undergraduates—that they are unlikely to succeed in high-powered, male-dominated roles. And, judging by both the outcome of the election, and the strength of the above mechanisms, they may very well be right. It is wrong but natural to protect oneself from the prospect of threatening others who challenge one's extant sense that one couldn't have been the president (say), notwithstanding one's best efforts. A way to do this is to hold that these women are *different* and in some way inferior or objectionable or otherwise suspect. They are, say, ruthless, callous, or uncaring. Or their success makes them witches; their power is black magic.

Among the questions to ask, following on from this research, is the effect of race. For almost no black women and relatively few Latina women voted for Trump over Clinton. Is racial difference part of what makes for psychological self-differentiation from Clinton?

Or was the obvious fact that these women had more to lose in having a white supremacist-friendly president rather an *overriding* factor in blocking the underlying dispositions that might otherwise have been operative? Since the above study doesn't mention the race of participants, unfortunately, there's no indication of the answers. It's also not clear whether or not the subject of assessment in the above studies was envisaged as being white by the participants.

Whatever the case, it seems plausible that white women had *additional* psychological and social incentives to support Trump and forgive him his misogyny (among other things). Such incentives are due to the fact that (1) on average, white women are considerably likelier than their nonwhite counterparts to be partnered with a Trump supporter, and (2) again, on average, relatedly in some cases, white women would generally have greater incentives, and hence corresponding dispositions, to try to get or stay on the good side of powerful white men of Trump's genre. The thought being that it is virtually only a white woman who stands a fighting chance of being regarded by men like Trump as a "good girl," if she plays her cards right; whereas, such men's treatment of black and Latina women was frequently erasing or derogatory.

Kimberlé W. Crenshaw's (2016) conversations with sixteen social justice leaders in the wake of the election highlighted the need for intersectional thinking about social relations as well as social identities here. In dialogue with Crenshaw, critical race theorist and feminist Sumi Cho pointed out that "instead of actually voting on the basis of the interest of individual [white] women . . . instead, you heard this narrative of, 'But I'm concerned about what it will do to my son, my brother, my husband,' etc. You have this concept of family that's highly racialized, that overwhelmed and supplanted the common rational voter approach." Cho thereby shows how himpathy for the "little guy" may be part of the story as well. Within American society, where a nominally monogamous intimate relationship between one man and one woman is the statistical norm—and remains the more or less explicit *moral* norm in many communities, for example, many conservative ones—women's first loyalty is often to her male intimate partner, rather than other women. If there are subtle patterns of male dominance and other forms of misogynistic behavior on the part of the male partner, then there are also fairly powerful psychological incentives for the female partner to deny, minimize, and overlook their prevalence and importance. These include the possibility that, in voting for Trump, he was effectively shrugging about a counterpart's sexual misconduct and misogyny.

The point can be extended. As white women, we are habitually loyal to powerful white men in our vicinity (e.g., those who outrank us in our workplaces, communities, and other social institutions, including the academy). We keep dominant men's secrets as a default matter—including when it comes to their sexually predatory behavior. My choice of the inclusive plural pronoun here is deliberate. White liberal and progressive women are not reliably willing to break the habits of a lifetime in this respect either. Consider the amount of time it has taken for multiple credible reports of sexual harassment and assault in academia—philosophy included, which remains one of the least diverse disciplines—to lead to any action against certain prominent male perpetrators. This is a symptom of our collective tendency to keep silent, to be a "good one." This requires being loyal to dominant men—and caring for anyone and everyone in the vicinity, additionally.

In chapter 4, I suggested that women are supposed to give everyone around them personal care and attention, or else they risk seeming nasty, mean, unfair, and callous. But, of course, that's an impossible mandate when you're running for president. And, in general, the larger and more diverse a woman's audience or constituency, the more she will tend to be perceived as cold, distant, "out of touch," negligent, careless, and selfish, in view of these norms of feminine attentiveness. No such listening skills need be demonstrated by her male counterparts, however. Indeed, when it came to Trump, they could hardly have been less so.

This suggests that we need to move beyond simply thinking about higher and lower standards for men and women. Rather, we often take men and women to have fundamentally different, and nominally complementary, responsibilities. I will now canvass some evidence of two mechanisms that helps to bear this out: what I call "care-mongering," on the one hand, and gendered "split perception," on the other.

CARE-MONGERING

Evidence of the way women are disproportionately required to be caring, even by young adults, comes from the well-known effects of gender biases on student evaluations of their professors. This evidence is also worth considering in this context because, when you think about it, there are a considerable number of parallels between politicians and professors—not just in terms of the authority figure you tacitly have to represent yourself as being (this would apply to many other professions too), but also in their embodied and performative dimensions. As a professor, you have to stand before a crowd and ask them to invest in your words in the coin of trust, respect, and attention. And it turns out that gender has a significant impact both on how, and how well, you are subsequently evaluated—in the latter case at least, and hence the former as well, plausibly.

It's not just that many students—again, male and female alike—tend to prefer their intellectual and moral authority figures to come in a cis male body, either. (Although that is what studies consistently show; some recent results regarding race are more promising.[12]) It's also that the perceptions of women versus men tend to be very different; and, relatedly, they tend to be punished for different shortcomings. Joey Sprague and Kelley Massoni (2005) showed that male professors are penalized more for being boring, and female professors for seeming cold, uncaring, or not developing a personal relationship with each and every student. They also found that, in students' descriptions of their best and worst teachers:

12. E.g., according to one recent study, students of *all* races prefer nonwhite professors. Anya Kamenetz, "Study Finds Students of All Races Prefer Teachers of Color," NPR, October 7, 2016, http://www.npr.org/sections/ed/2016/10/07/496717541/study-finds-students-of-all-races-prefer-teachers-of-color.

[T]he most hostile words are saved for women teachers. The worst women teachers are sometimes explicitly indicted for being bad women through the use of words like "bitch" and "witch." Students may not like their arrogant, boring and disengaged men teachers, but they may hate their mean, unfair, rigid, cold, and "psychotic" women teachers. These findings are substantiated by . . . reported incidents of student hostility toward women instructors who are perceived as not properly enacting their gender role or who present material that challenges gender inequality. (2005, 791)

The researchers concluded that, though both male and female professors had to make special efforts due to their gender, women's efforts were likely to be especially effortful. For, while a man's not being boring will scale with relative ease to a larger audience, a woman's developing a relationship with each student obviously won't. And, beyond a certain point, it will simply not be feasible.

The advent of "care-mongering" or, for another term I like, a (gendered) tyranny of vulnerability, played an important role in attacks on Julia Gillard in Australia. When Kevin Rudd, the former leader Gillard succeeded in an internal leadership challenge, wanted to get his own back, he knew just what to do. First he alleged to a journalist, Laurie Oakes, that Gillard had reneged on a deal giving give him more time to improve his performance as prime minister before issuing her challenge. Rudd then seems to have leaked reports to Oakes of cabinet meetings where Gillard opposed a proposal to increase spending on pensions for senior citizens and paid parental leave, due to a budgetary deficit. Although Gillard explained she supported these measures after the budget had been balanced, her popularity plummeted, and she nearly lost the ensuing election. She was not to be trusted, and she was callous.

One Australian journalist viewed Rudd and Oakes as behaving badly enough to raise the following question:

Would this have happened if this competition were between two men? I'm not sure. I think we have to unpack this and see what we are actually seeing with our own eyes, which is a lot of blokes trying to monster up a woman.

Unfortunately, George Megalogenis's appeal to Australians went largely unheeded.[13]

I suspect a similar tactic did Clinton a lot of damage too. She was held not just to more stringent standards but also very different ones, as compared with her male counterparts. The question being: was there any vulnerable person in her care orbit over time to whom she was or had been insufficiently giving, caring, or attentive? The answer was, but almost inevitably would be, "yes," given that her care orbit as an experienced politician and the former secretary of state was indefinitely extensible, that is, to pretty much anyone. In contrast, Donald Trump held that he could stand in the middle of Fifth Avenue and shoot someone, and still not lose voters.[14] Many people were outraged by his remarks. Yet he still won the election.

GENDERED SPLIT PERCEPTION

The common focus on gendered double standards may be unduly narrow in another respect as well. The notion encompasses cases where women are judged more harshly than their male counterparts on the basis of what we take to be the same actions, on the assumption that these perceptions are more or less morally neutral common ground here. But evidence suggests that the same actions performed by a man versus a woman may be viewed differently *in the first place*— where a lens of differential prior suspicion or a gendered division

---

13. On Gillard's (2014) own account: "Oakes's story had been devastating in its electoral impact. It had played to questions voters were already thinking about in relation to me: if I was unmarried, childless, could I really understand the pressures and concerns of families?" (40).

14. Jeremy Diamond, "Trump: I Could 'Shoot Somebody and I Wouldn't Lose Voters,'" CNN, January 24, 2016, http://www.cnn.com/2016/01/23/politics/donald-trump-shoot-somebody-support/index.html.

of labor makes the very same actions performed by her versus him seem different. *His* behavior seems normal, unremarkable, business as usual, nothing to see here. Her doing the same thing makes us wonder: what's she hiding?

This suggests it's not just a matter of gendered double standards, then; gender biases in politics encompass this "split" in social perception.

The evidence I refer to here comes from a recent study in social psychology, and it is still early days for this hypothesis. It is nonetheless so explanatory of otherwise bewildering impasses as to be worth canvassing with this caveat. Participants in the study read anecdotes about parents who left their young children home alone, for a variety of reasons. The participants were then asked to assess the degree of *risk* or danger to which the children had been exposed. The parents who left to play Pokemon Go were judged to have put their children at greater risk than those who left them to go to work. And crucially, for my purposes, the woman's behavior was judged riskier than the man's, all else being equal (i.e., holding fixed the reasons why they left, for how long, the children's age, etc.) (Thomas, Stanford, and Sarnecka 2016).

These results are admittedly preliminary (indeed, cutting edge at the time of writing—August 2016), and there's more work to be done on the effects of gender here in particular (as the researchers acknowledge). Still, they would explain a lot that cries out for explanation. It's natural to hypothesize a mechanism roughly like the following: we see people doing something that strikes us as morally better or worse, for example, more or less worthy of outrage, moral disgust, or indignation. We then match the *description of what they did*, for example, how risky their actions were, to the prior intensity and valence of our spontaneous moral reactions. Such moral reactions or judgments about someone may hence be a significant factor in how we view or describe their actions, at what is supposed to be a purely factual, non-moral, level. What one would have hoped is, of course, the opposite—that we assess the non-moral facts, and only then pass moral judgment on their actions.

Now consider prejudice against women in certain social positions—those aspiring to masculine-coded power positions, as in politics. Part of what this may involve is moral *prejudgment* in line with widely disavowed, but not yet defunct, gendered social mores. Someone like Hillary Clinton is frequently cast in the moral role of usurper. And unsurprisingly so (which is of course not to say justifiably); she threatens to take men's historical place or steal their thunder. If she wins, the game is rigged. She could not have won it fairly. And her behavior and she herself seems to be careless, shady, and crooked (so the thought continues).

Women in positions of unprecedented political power, or right on its cusp, are also prone to be perceived as *rule-breakers* generally. They are not to be trusted to stay in line, or respect law and order. These perceptions are understandable, because they're not baseless so much as defunct: these women *are* breaking the rules of an unjust patriarchal system that is still in the process of being dismantled. Someone like Clinton *was* breaking rank; she was out of order relative to nominally passé, but entrenched, social hierarchies wherein only men could aspire to highest political office. And women were expected to defer to and support, not compete with, them. Her defection from this role may hence seem like treason or betrayal—and reacted to in ways both bewildered and bewildering, both threatened and threatening (recalling the preface).

In view of this, a woman who has done nothing wrong in moral and social reality (i.e., relative to fair and egalitarian standards) may be subject to moral suspicion and consternation for violating edicts of the patriarchal rulebook. And her *behavior* may then be cast as dangerous, suspicious, risky, or deceptive, in line with moral verdicts already rendered. The latter judgments drive the former, rather than the reverse. It just seems like she's up to something; *what* being a matter for discovery—or invention.

This may be all very well in theory, as a speculative hypothesis, but (how) does it work in practice? Is there evidence this actually happens?

I believe so. Take the glut of news stories about Hillary's staff-ers destroying her electronic devices and what this might mean. Take—again, for an example outside of politics—the suspicion to which Alice Goffman was subject when she burned her field notes after publishing *On the Run* (2014). She was subsequently accused of fabricating much of her research by numerous pundits and scholars, on bases as thin as the fact that she documented police misconduct of a sort the author's lawyer friend in the relevant city (Philadelphia) happened not to have heard of. Numerous other allegations cast a long shadow over Goffman's achievements. There were allegations of academic misconduct, and even a fantastic bid to have her indicted for conspiring to commit homicide. This for offering a vivid account of briefly entering into a revenge fantasy with a friend after a close mutual friend was murdered.[15]

But wasn't it fair to be suspicious when someone destroys evidence as Clinton and Goffman did? No; these were both completely standard practices in the relevant domains. The above description—and associated image of the furtive disposal of a blackberry, as if it were a dead body in a movie—is tendentious and misleading. In the case of Clinton's staff, they weren't destroying evidence; they were following a protocol for protecting classified information. And Goffman was similarly following ethnographic best practices.

When men engage in these actions, it is unremarkable, and hence tends to go unremarked on. But when a woman encroaching on men's turf does the same thing, her actions—and she—may seem decep-tive or negligent.

Consider then FBI director James Comey's remark that Clinton was "extremely careless" in her handling of her emails, and that she exposed the American people to serious risks from "hostile actors" while traveling overseas. Both the description itself and its subse-quent uptake were clearly inflated. The idea that Clinton was so care-less as compared to other politicians seems driven by a tacit moral

15. Lubet 2015a.

judgment, a prior conviction that she was guilty, rather than an unbiased assessment of the evidence.

There was a somewhat similar episode in Australia, when Julia Gillard was put on trial on trumped-up charges of corruption dating back some twenty years, after she was ousted as the prime minister of Australia. The charges came to nothing, and were widely deemed a witch hunt, conducted by her old rival, by then prime minister Tony Abbott (the inspiration for her "misogyny speech," discussed in chapter 3). Nevertheless, Gillard was held not only to have shown "a lapse of judgment," but also to seem somehow "evasive," and "excessive, forced," even "dramatic and angry," in giving testimony. Despite being "an excellent witness" in tangible ways, nevertheless "there was an element of acting in her demeanor... the delivery fell flat," according to the commissioner.[16]

When it came to Bernie Sanders's controversial remarks about Clinton's being unqualified he ascribed to her "bad judgment," in reference to her voting for the war in Iraq. And Trump echoed the phrase repeatedly in subsequently debating Clinton. Donald Trump's vice president, Mike Pence, also voted for the war in Iraq. But according to Trump, Pence was entitled to make such mistakes "every once in a while." "She's not?" CBS's Lesley Stahl asked Trump, of Clinton. "No. She's not," was Trump's full answer. "Got it," Stahl blinked, and proceeded with the interview.[17]

FAKING IT

A final valuable source of evidence of the gender biases that may have been in play in the election is an interactive database of a huge

16. Matthew Knott, "Unions Royal Commission Clears Julia Gillard but Questions her Credibility as a Witness," *Sydney Morning Herald*, December 19, 2014, http://www.smh.com.au/federal-politics/political-news/unions-royal-commission-clears-julia-gillard-but-questions-her-credibility-as-a-witness-20141219-12alcd.html.

17. Tessa Berenson, "Donald Trump Says Hillary Clinton Can't Make Mistakes, but Mike Pence Can," *Time*, July 17, 2016, http://time.com/4409827/donald-trump-mike-pence-hillary-clinton-iraq/.

number of student evaluations (some fourteen million) from rate-myprofessor.com, designed by Benjamin Schmidt, which shows the frequency of word use therein, broken down by subject area and the gender of the professor. Not all gendered descriptions are as obvious as "witch" and "bitch." On a hunch, I typed in the word "fake," and the results were striking (see figure 8.1).

The results suggest that female professors were more often described as "fake"—sometimes by many orders of magnitude—in all but two subjects. On the flipside, male professors were likelier to inspire students to use the word "genuine," although by a somewhat

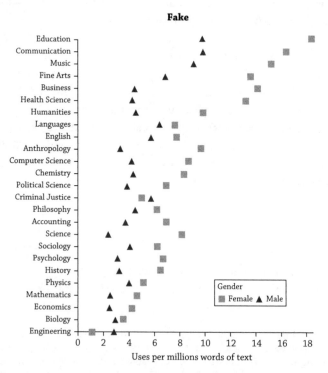

Figure 8.1 Frequency of the term "fake" in student evaluations of male vs. female professors in different academic fields (based on data and graphics accessed via http://benschmidt.org/profGender/#fake, accessed September 2016).

smaller margin. (This time, in all but one subject; a different one, not obviously suggestive of a pattern.) The results for "cold," "mean," "nasty," and—again, strikingly—"unfair" also showed dramatic gender distributions. Namely, women appear to be perceived as mean, nasty, cold, unfair, and above all *fake* as opposed to genuine, much more often than their male colleagues.

You might wonder whether male and female professors just have different teaching styles and so are subject to different kinds of assessment and criticism. Fortunately, Sprague and Massoni address this point in the aforementioned paper (2005), and argue this is unlikely: male teachers often receive comments along the same dimensions, but with the opposite polarity. This suggests they are not evincing incommensurably different qualities, so much as being held to more or less stringent standards.

Assume (as I think is safe—though, again, defeasibly) that it's not that female professors *deserve* these unflattering perceptions— by genuinely seeming "fake," somehow, whatever that might look like. This suggests that people are more inclined to see women in positions of authority as posers and imposters compared with their male counterparts.

Suppose that this is true: that so-called imposter syndrome is sometimes in the eye of the beholder of female as compared with male professors, in their positions as moral and intellectual authority figures. This hypothesis could help to explain why Bernie Sanders was preferred by many millennials to Hillary Clinton by such a large margin, in no small part due to differential perceptions of their integrity, sincerity, and authenticity, and seemingly in excess of the political and moral differences between the two of them—especially after it was clear that the insinuations about Clinton's dishonesty and untrustworthiness came to essentially nothing (Abramson 2016).

It would also help to explain some of the bizarre conspiracy theories to the effect that Hillary's health concerns were much more serious than was reported—which resulted, two months out from the election, in the preposterous rumor that Hillary had a "body double." Or, alternatively, that Clinton had died and been replaced by this doppelganger-cum-puppet. (*Weekend at Bernie's*, meet Hillary's September.)

Clinton is not the first to suffer from these kinds of perceptions among female politicians, either. Julia Gillard was slated as inauthentic to the point where her first election campaign tried to undo the damage by presenting the Australian public with "the real Julia." This effort was, however, spectacularly unsuccessful: Gillard was mercilessly mocked and depicted as a Russian-doll-like figure—layer on superficial layer, with no substantial core of values.

Recall the pundit's remark with which I opened: "She has many masks but who has seen her face?" He quotes an unnamed friend of his saying: "She is either very conservative or she believes in nothing. We better hope she's conservative." At least with her opponents, you know what you are getting; "whereas with her there is the strongest risk of dissembling." There is a "Machiavellianism just short of mendacity" visible in her demeanor. In lacking an authentic political vision, her policies are based merely on "apprehension of what the electorate might like." And if she "believes in nothing but power," and ruthlessly thirsts to obtain it, then "doesn't this raise the specter, all but unthinkable in left liberal circles," that you should just vote for the right-wing candidate—who "however much you disagree with him, might make the better leader because at least he stands for something?" (Craven 2010).

If you didn't know any better, you'd likely assume that these fairly distinctive—and vivid—images in the above paragraph were of Hillary Clinton, not Julia Gillard. The two were consistently described in a strikingly similar way, especially given the differences between them in appearance, age, and history (though not their center-left politics, notably).

The belief in female leaders in politics seems to founder even at the level of visual perception. They look hollow, stiff, wooden, robotic, as well as fake and inauthentic. Their energy doesn't appear to come from inside them; nor, it appears, do their values—which are subsequently held to be merely a product of mercurial, outward social forces.

When Clinton called Trump a puppet of Putin during the third debate, Trump's immediate instincts were interesting to behold: "No . . . no puppet . . . You're the puppet!" he spluttered. Unusually for him, he seemed to believe what he was saying. She was the marionette; he was the master.

Trump's supporters were wont to say, approvingly, that he tells it like it is. I think it's fair to say that the power of the man's ability to convey the impression of authenticity without its substance was underestimated by many liberals—on the grounds that much of what Trump says is false, indeed an outrageous lie, incoherent, self-contradictory, or a reversal of previous statements made by him. But we should ask ourselves if ascriptions of authenticity or genuineness to prospective leaders in politics and beyond has much if anything to do with the belief that they tell truths as opposed to falsehoods, versus their seeming right for the role somehow, perhaps by dint of telling a good story while looking like a natural, unlike Clinton, for reasons that may have had little to do with her in particular, when it came down to it. (Compare the fundamental attribution error of preferring explanations that cite particular over general information.)

Partly in view of that, I believe there were serious grounds to worry about Trump's winning the election, and in particular to fear that low voter turn-out for Clinton might cost her dearly, given a small but predictable and potentially significant turn-off effect mediated in large part by gender. Or at any rate, rightly or wrongly (i.e., justifiably or no), I am on the record as having fretted about that beforehand.[18] And whatever the case, the politics of authenticity and

18. Lest I be accused of wisdom in hindsight (i.e., lying)—and bearing in mind that having one's claims match reality seems like so last season's bragging right in the era Trump has ushered in of alt-facts and fake news (strikingly)—I wrote about this worry in March and May, leading to the tentative prediction I made in print in a piece published on July 11 (Manne 2016d), and reiterated on October 19 (Manne 2016i), despite Hillary's healthy lead in the polls then, and subsequently began to explain and defend in Twitter conversations.

the aesthetics of truthfulness of character can and do work strongly against women in politics inter alia. When she doesn't seem as if she quite belongs up there on the podium, or behind the desk of the oval office, she may seem untrustworthy, dishonest, an impostor, and even viscerally and then morally disgusting. We tend to be much too quick to trust our feelings of being unsettled as probative evidence of bad character. Meanwhile, Trump seemed like the sort of man you expect to be in a position of power, a leader, if not in politics, then in something. So many were prepared to follow him on Twitter and beyond that—and now to where, at what cost, heaven help us.

E.g., I tweeted on October 19:

@kate_ manne "When a Man Competes with a Woman -- research in social psychology helps explain why Trump still has ~38% of voters," and linked to my piece in *Huffington Post*, which the first section of this chapter was based on (Manne 2016i). https://twitter.com/kate_manne/status/788798586268057600

I added @kate_ manne "Despite the polls, these studies made me pessimistic about HRC winning. Supporting a woman over a man for POTUS goes deeply against t/grain." https://twitter.com/kate_manne/status/788874657319546888 In response to pushback based on the evidence that the polls are rarely wrong at this stage, I explained to @bweatherson and @FiveThirtyEight, that I was "skeptical about induction from past elections due to gender dynamics this time." https://twitter.com/kate_manne/status/788875451779407872

And, finally, I added (again, to @bweatherson and @FiveThirtyEight) that the "strong gender biases in match-ups may keep some HRC voters from the polls." https://twitter.com/kate_manne/status/788883913557078016. Of course, this is a far cry from the truly impressive prescience of Michael Moore, who predicted which *states* would be responsible for Trump's victory. See Michael Moore, "5 Reasons Why Trump Will Win," MichaelMoore.com, July 21, 2016, http://michaelmoore.com/trumpwillwin/; Matthew Sheffield, "Michael Moore: People Will Vote for Trump as a Giant "F**k You"—and He'll Win," Salon, October 26, 2016, http://www.salon.com/2016/10/26/michael-moore-people-will-vote-for-donald-trump-as-a-giant-fk-you-and-hell-win/.

Conclusion

The Giving She

Once there was a tree . . . and she loved a little boy. And every day the boy would come and he would gather her leaves and make them into crowns and play king of the forest.

He would climb up her trunk and swing from her branches and eat apples. And they would play hide-and-go-seek. And when he was tired, he would sleep in her shade.

And the boy loved the tree. . . . very much. And the tree was happy. But time went by. And the boy grew older. And the tree was often alone.

Shel Silverstein, *The Giving Tree*

So goes the opening of *The Giving Tree*, a famous children's book by Shel Silverstein. Originally published in 1964, *The Giving Tree* is still in print, and still selling.[1] The book gets four and a half stars on Amazon. Some parents say their kids love it, and regard it as an endlessly touching portrait of unconditional love: the tree, a pretty transparent mother figure, gives everything she has for her beloved only son. Others worry that she doesn't set firm boundaries, even when the boy starts asking for more than is reasonable. Also, he sounds pretty ungrateful. For example:

"I am too big to climb and play" said the boy. "I want to buy things and have fun. I want some money!" "I'm sorry," said the tree, "but

1. Silverstein's menacing-looking dust jacket photograph even made a cameo appearance in *The Wimpy Kid*: its role was scaring children.

I have no money. I have only leaves and apples. Take my apples, Boy, and sell them in the city. Then you will have money and you will be happy."

The boy comes back, asking for yet more—he needs a place to live, he blithely announces. So the tree offers him her branches, which he takes, and builds a house with them. Then the boy wants a boat, so she offers him her trunk, which he takes and uses for that purpose. He goes off and has adventures. Meanwhile, as for the tree, she is happy: " . . . but not really." The last line of the penultimate stanza jars you; and eerily, conspicuously, it never gets expanded on.

And so, naturally, one is left with questions. For example: was the tree really happy all those other times? And if not, does it matter? Does the boy ever give her anything in return—or, indeed, anything whatsoever?

In any case, it's too late for her to recoup her losses. She has been reduced to nothing; the boy took all of her. When he returns from his great voyage, feeling tired, she has nothing left to offer him but the amputated stump he has made of her. That is where the boy lays his head to rest. And that is where the story leaves them.

During the time I was researching this book, I became less optimistic about the prospects of getting people to take misogyny seriously—including treating it as a moral priority, when it is—unless they already do so. And there are fewer people in this category than I had been hoping. I have found it much easier to get people interested in trigger warnings, a relatively minor topic, as compared with misogyny. The fact that misogyny is killing girls and women, literally and metaphorically, clearly isn't enough to grip that many people.[2]

---

2. From October to December 2016, I attempted to keep a record of cases in the United States of women murdered by male family members or intimate partners only reported in local news outlets (as best I could tell). There were still so many of these cases that I couldn't keep up with my Google alerts. To narrow it down further, I

I shouldn't have been surprised by this. It has always been killing girls and women, literally and metaphorically—especially those who step out of line. So it goes. It is a bitterly sad state of affairs, but it is hard to see what would change it. Misogyny is a self-masking problem. Trying to draw attention to it is illicit by the lights of the

focused on murders by stabbing. The reporting of these murders was often revealing, both insofar as the victims were almost invariably depicted as somebody's someone— for example, partner, mother, daughter, or grandmother—and also insofar as there was often a reluctance to blame the male perpetrator. The news stories on the murders of Shanai Marshall, Amanda Williams, Rebecca Hodges, and Dorothy Bradshaw were cases in point, as the following excerpts serve to show. Each of these victims was, notably, a woman of color.

Excerpt from a news story on the fatal stabbing of Shanai Marshall, allegedly by her ex-boyfriend:

> Shanai Marshall, a 37-year-old mother of three, was a loving, fiercely loyal woman who was not afraid to speak her mind, her friends said. Marshall had recently broken up with her allegedly abusive boyfriend again, but this time it looked like the break-up was permanent, they said. "She was done with the guy. . . . You could see the glow in her," Nicole Vieira, 42, of Lumberton, said. "She was serious, and he knew it."

Rebecca Everett, "Slain Mount Holly Mom Recalled as Loving Woman Who Spoke Her Mind," *NJ.com*, November 19, 2016, http://www.nj.com/burlington/index.ssf/2016/11/slain_mount_holly_mom_recalled_as_loving_woman_who.html.

Excerpt from a news story on Amanda Williams, a victim of a fatal stabbing by her boyfriend:

> The family of a Fayetteville woman who was stabbed to death by her boyfriend Wednesday night said Friday that they don't blame him for the attack, and they hope police video of the crime scene, including officers fatally shooting the boyfriend, is never released.
>
> Amanda Williams was killed in her Bedrock Drive home by Mark Hicks, whom police found standing over her body with a knife when they responded to a 911 call from her two sons. Officers shot Hicks when he refused to drop the knife and then lunged at them with it as they tried to take him into custody, police said.
>
> "We are all struggling to try to come to terms with it," said Williams' aunt, Lawanda Barnwell . . . Williams suffered from mental health problems for years, Barnwell said, adding that no one should point fingers in how Williams and Hicks died. "I believe he cared about Mandy, and things got kind of out of hand when he could have walked away. I am not going to excuse him, nor are we trying to excuse her," Barnwell said. "Who was right, who was wrong doesn't matter anymore. We lost two young souls."

phenomenon itself, since women are supposed to minister to others, rather than solicit moral attention and concern on their own behalf.

But then 2016 happened: Donald Trump was elected president. It surely cannot be doubted that, among the factors that account for this largely unforeseen and disastrous outcome, misogyny is one of the most important. And, for those who think misogyny and racism are not connected here, I would beg to differ. This is due not only to the intersecting systems of oppression that can compound vulnerabilities, but also because some hitherto dominant social actors, e.g., disappointed white men, will punch down fairly indiscriminately—for example, to nonwhites and immigrants, as well as white women—when

> Mark Hicks apologized for killing Williams in a 911 call, and Barnwell said the family takes him at his word. "I just killed somebody," he told a dispatcher. "She's gone. I'm sorry. I killed her."
> "We heard him say he's killed somebody and he's sorry, and he meant it," she said. "You could feel it. So, we are sorry that he's gone."

Adam Owens, "Family of Fayetteville Domestic Violence Victim: Who Was Right, Wrong Doesn't Matter," WRAL.com, December 9, 2016, http://www.wral.com/family-of-fayetteville-domestic-violence-victim-who-was-right-wrong-doesn-t-matter-/16325581/.

Excerpt from a news story on the fatal stabbings of Rebecca Hodges and Dorothy Bradshaw, by their son and grandson (respectively):

> Friends, family, and strangers alike are still trying to piece together what happened Monday night inside a Randolph Avenue apartment where two women were viciously stabbed to death. Authorities say Kevin Hodges, 36, killed his mother, 56-year-old Rebecca Hodges, and grandmother, 76-year-old Dorothy Bradshaw, with a sword and meat cleaver.
> . . . Monday's brutal killing stunned the community and family that said Kevin Hodges loved his mother and grandmother. "His mother, grandmother and him were the dynamic trio," family member Lamar Scott said in a statement to *The Jersey Journal*. "They loved one another and shared a bond outsiders hoped for. He and his family deserves this time to mourn and grieve."

This is a remarkable quote to be included without further comment. To reiterate: Kevin Hodges deserves time to mourn the female family members whom he loved, lived with, and brutally murdered.

Caitlin Mota, "Mother, Grandmother, the Latest to Die in Alleged Domestic Violence Incidents in Hudson," *Jersey Journal*, December 7, 2016, http://www.nj.com/hudson/index.ssf/2016/12/on_heels_of_gruesome_double_murder_hudson_sees_spi.html.

they develop withdrawal symptoms or a deprivation mind-set vis-à-vis women's social and emotional labor.

Given the likely impact of misogyny on the outcome of the election, you might think people across the political spectrum who likewise lament the result would now be waking up to the power of misogyny to distort our moral and rational judgments. You might think they would be willing to say mea culpa, inasmuch as many attacked Hillary Clinton relentlessly, viciously, disproportionately, misleadingly, moralistically, and sometimes, in my view, self-indulgently. But you would be wrong: this has largely not happened. Notice too that those who mounted these attacks thereby neglected to listen to women well-positioned to judge telling them that the build-up of toxic sentiment could cost Clinton the election. And even now, nobody seems to look back at the people who, whether or not they supported Clinton politically, defended her against a sustained misogynistic smear campaign, or pointed out notable double standards as well as those she was held to more stringently. There are notable commonalities among those who did—who included Brittney Cooper, Joan Walsh, Amanda Marcotte, Michelle Goldberg, Lindy West, and Rebecca Solnit, among others.[3] They're all feminist writers who are prominent online and also happen to be women. So it's safe to say that they are all familiar with the flavor of misogynistic backlash—not least because they likely receive a disproportionately large amount of hate mail themselves, if recent studies are indicative.[4]

3. See also Danielle Allen's explanation of why she came to admire Clinton over the course of the last campaign year—particularly after reading her e-mails. "I've Come to Admire Hillary Clinton: What on Earth Happened?" *Washington Post*, September 30, 2016, https://www.washingtonpost.com/opinions/ive-come-to-admire-hillary-clinton-what-on-earth-happened/2016/09/30/4a3a92a8-85c3-11e6-92c2-14b64f3d453f_story.

4. See, for example, the study showing that eight of the ten writers for *The Guardian* to get the most hate mail are women; the other two being nonwhite men. Becky Gardiner, Mahana Mansfield, Ian Anderson, Josh Holder, Daan Louter, and Monica Ulmanu, "The Dark Side of the Guardian Comments," *The Guardian*, April 12, 2016, https://www.theguardian.com/technology/2016/apr/12/the-dark-side-of-guardian-comments.

So you might think they'd be treated as authorities, as knowing of what they speak, when they testified that the treatment of Clinton had the feeling of a witch hunt. But that was not the case either: there was a general sense that the women who said as much were overreacting, as opposed to picking up on the social equivalent of risk factors for a bush-fire (e.g., heat, wind, drought conditions). If you have lived in regions prone to them, you tend to be more skilled—though of course not infal-lible—at anticipating days when fire is highly likely to break out. It is then mostly a question of whether the fire can be brought under control before it becomes an inferno and does terrible damage.

If this seems epistemically suspect, even spooky, consider the following anecdote. When multiple commentators called Clinton's voice "shrill" in late March (after she gave a victory speech the night she effectively became the presumptive nominee for the Democratic Party), there was an intense, week-long debate about whether it was about the quality and timbre of her voice. Or could it possibly, rather, be sexism? My own willingness to bet "yes" was based partly on having seen Gillard subject to the very same criticism on becom-ing prime minister of Australia. One vocal coach opined that her voice had changed somewhat in quality (slowing down, deepening and becoming more "twangy," throaty, and grating) and that Gillard needed to lift her vocal game to keep pace with voters' preferences.[5] There was also the fact that, as a quick rifle through my ample stock of hate mail confirmed, people call *my* voice shrill without having

---

5. "How can she improve?" Dean Frenkel asked, unsolicited, and then went on to answer his own question. He advised Gillard to work on her:

> "Vowel articulation—"e", "i" and "o" should be exercised in a far more understated way. No over-articulating of vowels. She should consciously decide to drop the "Gillard twang". This may well be the biggest-impact change she could make.
>
> More lightness—there's too much gravity in her voice. Add some occa-sional lightness that taps into a greater range of melody and more frequent higher melody. This would raise her energy and sound more natural . . .
>
> Energy/tone—it's time to think about the colour in her voice. Her tone is heavy and earthy. But she could do with some lighter and brighter tones that introduce more melodious qualities.

heard it.[6] That's surely good evidence that we should be suspicious when someone raises this aural specter regarding a woman's voice. Instead though, we often let them air their impressions uncontested, as if their desire to do so when there's any room for doubt that it's due to gender biases trumps our collective interest in not perpetuating them in the discourse. "I, and many other people, do find Hillary Clinton's voice to be shrill. In fact, it sounds like a cat being dragged across a blackboard a lot of the time," said one guest on Fox, during a debate in March about whether there was sexism in the "shrillness"

> Vocally—she appears to have little experience of singing and has not developed some vocal subtlety skills that pass across to speech. Singing could greatly help—but not the gung-ho footy anthem type."

Suggestion noted. The prime minister should surely have time to take singing lessons for the sake of more pleasing vocals.

Dean Frenkel, "Drop the Gillard Twang: It's Beginning to Annoy," *Sydney Morning Herald*, April 21, 2011, http://www.smh.com.au/federal-politics/political-opinion/drop-the-gillard-twang-its-beginning-to-annoy-20110420-1dosf.html.

6. Here is the email reproduced in full, with the signature line redacted. For the record, it was sent to me in October 2014, before I'd been on the radio a few times. So it seems safe to say his use of the term "shrill" wasn't based on my voice's actual acoustic properties.

> Ms. Manne,
> I was surprised and irritated by your recent article in the [*New York*] *Times*, deriding American white men across the board . . . amazing you would write such a thing. You must have a lot of hate stored up in you to denounce an entire class of people like that, when any fair-minded person would pull back from such a sweeping claim . . . quite sexist and racist really. As a white, American man, I took serious offense at it and found your logic not so much worthy of a philosophy professor at one of the country's best schools but more of a snotty 15 year old girl, filled with resentment and narcissism. Sorry if your dad may have been a raging alcoholic who beat your mom, but that's no excuse to hate all men, and spin pseudo-science to justify it.
> Many of my bosses over time have been women and I got along with most all of them, and never have been accused by anyone I worked with or socialized with of being chauvinistic or sexist, but I'm beginning to feel more like it these days . . . keep calling a dog a cat and pretty soon you may have a dog who thinks he's a cat . . . or just very confused—so by obsessing on the things you hate, you are in fact bringing them about and becoming them yourself . . . probably not logical or moral?
> There is a great deal of 'white man hate' out there these days and a lot of angry, unhappy looking women too . . . who are quite unpleasant to be around,

complaints leveled against Clinton. (And when it comes to noises that many people find it more or less literally painful to hear, such as fingernails on a chalkboard or the high-pitched wailing of a cat, why settle for just one metaphor when you can mix them?) Chris Plante had just been shown footage of many male politicians yelling without garnering similar (or similarly widespread) reactions regarding their vocal qualities.[7] Yes, but there was a difference, Plante explained: his

and far more judgmental and chauvinistic than many men I run into. Being a hate monger might be a fun way to get attention for yourself or make you the darling of the militant feminist set, but you're really just bringing more sadness and hurt into the world and leaving it a poorer place for it. Well done.

If American white maledom isn't working out for you, go ahead and try tribal Pakistan or Yemen for size . . . I hear the guys there are really terrific to women. And of course, no, they are not the standard for anyone, but a little perspective is probably called for . . . and perhaps instead of spite and egoism, a little grace.

Maybe you could use all that terrific education you've been blessed to have to help bring people closer together instead of fomenting ill will and shrillness . . . we definitely have enough of that already.

~Signature

Of course, it's possible this particular correspondent uses "shrill" for men just as much as women. But the term nevertheless has a long and gendered history. See William Cheng, "The Long, Sexist History of 'Shrill' Women," *Time*, March 23, 2016, http://time.com/4268325/history-calling-women-shrill.

7. This is not to say that male politicians' voices are never called "shrill" and similar: obviously, they have been, as in the infamous Howard Dean scream. But, as the piece by Cheng (2016) referenced in the previous note shows, this is not plausibly nearly so common or as much a "go-to" reaction to men's ordinary speaking voices as compared with women's. There is a simple explanation for such gendered differences on my account of misogyny, in light of the discussion in chapter 8. I argued on the basis of several bodies of empirical evidence (drawn from political science and social psychology) that, when a woman competes for unprecedentedly high positions of male-dominated leadership or authority, particularly at the expense of an actual male rival, people tend to be biased in his favor, *toward* him. That is, there will be a general tendency, all else being equal, to be on his side, willing him to power. And this in turn predictably leads to biases against her (so my argument continued). So, when she speaks against or over him—by disagreeing with him, interrupting him, laughing at his expense, or declaring victory over him—it would be natural for her voice to be heard as grating, raspy, shrill, or otherwise painful sounding. We do not want to hear her say a word against him, so she becomes hard to listen to. Another natural conjecture is that she will tend to be to be perceived as abrasive, nasty, disagreeable, or otherwise unpleasant in her general demeanor. We might call such impressions

impressions. He was just reporting the facts, which had spoken to him—or caterwauled.[8]

As I wrote in the introduction, and have tried to keep it clear throughout, my concern here has been chiefly with moral diagnosis, not condemnation. Individual agents' guilt or innocence is not the main issue. But the above remark is just one among many examples of the kind we might try to render socially unacceptable, moving forward from this point onward. The same goes for blaming Clinton for everything under the sun that might have led to her defeat, instead of taking responsibility for it ourselves, as would be fitting in many cases. (As Trump said during the first debate, why not blame her for everything? It turned out, in retrospect, not to have been a rhetorical question—and certainly not a humorous one. Its answer was "no reason," because we, the public, gave him none.)

Similarly pernicious is the under-recognized tendency to speculate idly in damaging ways about women's motives (another common aspect of misogynistic portrait-painting), for example, calling Clinton selfish, ungrateful, narcissistic, malevolent, a "taker," entitled, as well as a liar, corrupt, hypocritical, excessively privileged, and a member of the establishment.

"aversive audition" and "painful beholding" (or some such) on the model of idioms like "wishful thinking" and "willful denial." And they would be the result of what the great eighteenth-century Scottish philosopher David Hume called "gilding and staining" the world with our subjective impressions, that is, projecting such properties as would cause these impressions onto their objects, and regarding them as inherent properties thereof. A good deal of subsequent empirical evidence has confirmed Hume's hypothesis that we are prone to projective errors of this kind. So a plausible specific conjecture would be that pain like Chris Plante's in listening to Hillary Clinton's victory speech over Bernie Sanders will often originate in the biased ears of the listener. This is particularly likely when many other perceivers regard the relevant stimulus as unremarkable or unobjectionable, for example, as just the voice of a woman speaking, or the voice of one who had given many speeches on the campaign trail, and whose throat was hence sore, unsurprisingly.

8. So the obvious possibility that gender biases can affect our very aesthetic impressions was clearly less than salient to Plante. And the possibility that such impressions are differentially *harmful* to women, who are then envisaged as shrews, harpies, or fishwives, also tends to be overlooked or shrugged about. Alex Griswold, "Male Fox Guest: Hillary Sounds 'Shrill,' 'Like a Cat Being Dragged Across a

These criticisms were invariably taken seriously and more or less at face value. But, again, many of the same criticisms (including that *I'm* a member of an unspecified "establishment") were tweeted at me last week, at the time of writing.[9] And this on no legitimate, nor even readily intelligible, basis I could discern—save for the fact that I had the temerity to suggest (in a single tweet replying to a friendly stranger) that white women may have voted for Trump despite his sexual misconduct because of strong norms of loyalty on their part to the white men they are typically partnered with (due to heteronormative as well as racist statistical and social norms governing romantic relationships). This was enough to not only garner the usual rapey, misspelled, and lately anti-Semitic, bilge water thrown in my direction but, more interestingly in this context, insults of the same general kind as were often levelled at Clinton.

These experiences are so far from unique to me that they are only worth mentioning insofar as I'm a nobody. I'm not famous, nor

---

Blackboard,'" *Mediaite*, March 16, 2016, http://www.mediaite.com/tv/male-fox-guest-hillary-sounds-shrill-like-a-cat-being-dragged-across-a-blackboard/.

9. Some of the more eyebrow-raising tweets included, for example:

> @kate_manne Hey ugly hoe I hope you never get aids or raped that would be horrible
>
> @kate_manne A Purge is needed
>
> @kate_manne shut the fuck up already
>
> @kate_manne I dont care if it changes her mind she is my enemy and hopefully the day will come when she has her lying mouth shut for her

Other tweets, like this last one, accused me of hypocrisy and lying—again, on no discernible basis—as well as being "banal," unoriginal, money-hungry, and an establishment "Jewess." E.g.:

> @kate_manne [Your] Double-standard is old and ppl see through it.
>
> @kate_manne Hypocrisy & stupidity coming from the Left is unending boring & embarrassing. Like a river in Egypt De Nile.
>
> @kate_manne Not surprising given her "kind's" loyalty extends only so far as the cash register.
>
> @kate_manne It is you who is the trite, predictable, kiss-ass establishment cog jewess—so very sad!
>
> @kate_manne If you think you're anything other than a pretentious dullard, you're very wrong.

I asked what one of the tweeters meant by "hypocrisy." They didn't answer, and blocked me.

married to Bill Clinton, nor a politician, nor monied. All I am and all it takes to garner these kinds of moral reactions, seemingly, is being a woman who is perceived as taking up male-dominated space without pandering to patriarchal interests and vanities. That's enough, as best I can tell, to get the kind of moral reaction one might expect if one had trespassed on someone's property: because, in a way, one has done.

So why not shame this unacceptable behavior? Why not call it out, if people refuse to learn from their mistakes, and continue to blame Clinton for the effects of their own participation in a misogynist mobbing of her, which continues even to this day?[10]

That brings me to another reason I suspect misogyny is so persistent. As has emerged over the course of discussing various cases in this book, it often seems to be a *shame*-based phenomenon, at the level of the moral psychology of individual agents. Within a misogynistic worldview, women's admiration and approval, among other things, confers status on men relative to one another within intra-masculine hierarchies. And erstwhile or aspiring alphas often become pathologically ashamed when such attentions are withheld or unforthcoming. So it's dangerous to try to call out such misogyny, even if the shame is only a by-product of trying to get someone to think before he speaks the next time. This is particularly true for women who dare to complain or even name instances of misogyny

---

The tweets flooded in following this one, which came out of the blue some days after the exchange mentioned above:

> RorschachRockwell¶@False_Nobody She's (@kate_manne) a Jewish professor at Cornell. Her nose-trunk finds white loyalty & familial values offensive.

10. See, for example, Shaun King's "Will Hillary Clinton Join the Long Line of Democrats Who Bail on Their Promises after a Presidential Election?" *New York Daily News*, December 27, 2016, http://www.nydailynews.com/news/politics/king-hillary-join-crowd-democrats-bail-promises-article-1.2925441. For an excellent reply, see Oliver Chinyere's "Dear Shaun: Hillary Clinton Lost but So Did Bernie Sanders," ExtraNewsfeed, December 28, 2016, https://extranewsfeed.com/dear-shaun-hillary-clinton-lost-and-so-did-bernie-sanders-trumps-your-president-7bf923406c37#.79e96gh44.

that are remotely controversial. Our designated role is that of being moral listeners, not critics or censors. In the meantime, we ourselves may elect to hold our tongues, given the likely social penalties for defending imperfect victims of misogynistic vitriol—moral disgust, counter-shaming, and ostracism.

But shame—especially of the entitled variety—doesn't make for the kind of pain you can pander to, productively. That's the mistake that some people on the left, including some of the most intelligent and sensitive commentators, such as Arlie Russell Hochschild, seem to me to be making at the moment. (See, e.g., the "open letter" to her fellow liberals at the end of *Strangers*; 2016.) Listening and offering sympathy to those who are prone to shame-based misogynistic as well as racist outbursts is feeding the very need and sense of entitlement that drives them in the first place, when they go unmet. In other words, it's adding fuel to the fire, at least in the long term. You can't do much to *help* or *give* to someone who, yes, is in genuine pain and lashing out— but only because they feel too needy and illicitly entitled to getting such moral attentions to begin with. The liberal impulse is therefore misplaced here, unless we want to get stuck feeding the need-monster forever. As many white women indeed appear to be committed to doing, when it comes to the white men they'll remain loyal to notwithstanding their sexual misconduct (among other things).

All of this is to say that misogyny makes people so irrational, so inclined to engage in post hoc rationalization, and so lacking in that thing that many tout and purport to think crucial, namely personal responsibility (a tricky philosophical concept, but the point here is one of consistency) that this has made me pretty pessimistic about reasoning with people to get them to take misogyny seriously. And I suspect that, for many readers who have made it this far, you may be of a similar mind to mine and feel similarly frustrated by the apathy, indifference, and pernicious ignorance of most people. So maybe the thing to say, somewhat reluctantly, is—fuck 'em, in the limited sense of ceasing to even try to catch the moderate with mild honey. Perhaps we should just start with more radical, if acerbic, but I now think more accurate, default assumptions. These being?

We're often expected to depart from a paradigm that remains pointedly neutral on men's and women's capacities for various kinds of human excellence, including the capacity to nurture. But we are meant to agree that we are generally treated as moral equals now, full persons, socially and politically, at this point in human history. Sexism and misogyny are rare, and progress will continue, more or less inevitably. The Enlightenment has worked, the odd blip notwithstanding.

That's the preferred combination of null and non-null hypotheses. There is, however, a viable alternative. We're just not accustomed to considering it: it's simply the opposite. It involves granting the null hypothesis regarding people's abilities and capacities for human excellence whatever their gender, unless there is persuasive evidence to the contrary. And this is generally lacking at this historical juncture, for lack of a control group: i.e., a society in which people have lived for some time under genuinely egalitarian conditions. Of course such evidence *may* emerge to cover the residual small gaps in achievement that have been rapidly dwindling in many areas that have historically been and continue to be male-dominated, e.g., mathematics, STEM fields, or philosophy, for that matter. We simply don't know yet, though we may have our hunches (à la Larry Summers).

But instead of arguing over sexist hypotheses, I have come to feel liberated to point out the obvious: a good portion of the dominant social class have a vested interest in maintaining men's superiority. An apt response may be, are you really just curious about the truth of this hypothesis, which has attracted quite a lot of attention for one that is not yet falsifiable? Or are you, rather, inchoately worried about it being false indeed, i.e., women being every bit men's equals? Are you looking to form a justified belief, or driven by a misogynistic desire to keep women out, or not to have to make an effort to cease to exclude us?

The tacit misogyny hypothesis may make some people uncomfortable, it's true: different ones. The hypothesis that women just aren't as prone as men to be brilliant has been making others of us uncomfortable in academia for as long as we've been in it. For those of us who make it through, and plenty who don't, turning the tables is our prerogative. You speculated we didn't belong in the room, while we were in it. We are within our rights, having stayed, to posit theories that you may find discomfiting.

The non-null hypothesis applied to gender may take various forms. But the dynamic I have focused on in the second half of this book would see the people embroiled in it slotted into one of two moral-cum-social categories—givers and takers, respectively—with regards to feminine-coded goods and services, on the one hand, and masculine-coded privileges and perks, on the other. There is some evidence that this process starts early on: that infant boys are soothed more than infant girls, who are talked to more (or, rather, talked *at* more, since they can't talk back). Not that this is necessarily a bad thing for girls: it may help their language development.[11] The point is just that, from the outset, we may already be dividing up social roles in this way on the basis of sex/gender assignments.

What evidence is there of such giver/taker differentiation as children grow older? For a smattering: when boys and girls go to school, and raise their hands to answer questions, boys get called on more than girls by a factor of at least eight, perhaps more. Girls get called on less, but corrected more—not only proportionally but absolutely—as compared with their male counterparts.[12] Which makes sense on this model because the epistemic high ground is his territory. So is airtime. So is priority. He comes first in the kinds of spoils that empower.

11. See, for example, Braungart-Rieker et al. (1999) for a demonstration of infant sex differences in the "still face" paradigm. For an overview of the literature on this classic research paradigm, see: https://sites.duke.edu/flaubertsbrain/files/2012/08/Mesman-The-Many-Faces-of-the-Still-Face-Paradigm.pdf

12. The classic study on these differences found that "sitting in the same classroom, reading the same textbook, listening to the same teacher, boys and girls receive very different educations" (Sadker and Sadker 1995). An updated, book-length treatment explains that significantly less has changed than the two researchers had originally hoped (Sadker and Zittleman 2009). In an article summarizing ten of the updated findings of the former monograph, David Sadker (coauthor of both works) writes:

> Classroom interactions between teachers and students put males in the spotlight, and relegate females to the sidelines. Studies of teacher discourse underscore male dominance in the classroom. Teachers unconsciously

At age five, girls and boys are equally confident that people of the same gender as them would be "really, really smart." During the ensuing few years, boys appear to maintain their faith in their own gender; girls, however, do not. Six- and seven year-old girls' belief in female brilliance drops off rapidly, in contrast. By age six, girls are "already losing their belief in female brilliance." And the girls who lose this belief tend to steer themselves away from games that are earmarked for "really, really smart" kids. (Bian, Leslie, and Cimpian 2017)

This isn't to say, again, that boys get all the advantages. Now he has to wait his turn for others too (other boys, typically) he may grow frustrated, having had little need for patience.[13] He may fall behind and, in some cases, get false diagnoses or be overmedicated. Which is just to say, too much advantage may be a *disadvantage* in ways that are unfair to him in the end too: but back to her, nevertheless, as she grows older.

She gets catcalled by certain men, who take her mind off her own thoughts, get (or grab) her attention, and inform her of what she'd give them in terms of conferred social value in dating them (her ranking).

He gets catcalled by her comparatively seldom.

She has sex taken from her, stolen, with some frequency, by some men (perhaps only a very small minority). He too may be raped, which is of course just as terrible a wrong when it occurs. However, it is also much less common. She takes sex from him in this way not never,

make males the focus of instruction, giving them more frequent and more precise attention. . . . [T]he impact can be costly. Increased teacher attention contributes to enhanced student performance. Girls lose out in this equation. African-American girls, for example, enter school assertive and outgoing, yet grow more passive and quiet through the school years. The power of the teacher's time and attention means that boys reap the benefits of a more intense educational climate. (Sadker 1999, 24)

13. This model also raises serious concerns about how non-binary children (as well as some trans children who do not "pass") will be treated. The more social scripts not only reify, but depend on, the gender binary, the more one worries that those who do not fit the false either/or of sex and gender will be caught in a kind of social limbo with some educators (among others). But I leave this important subject for other theorists better qualified to speak to it.

but far more rarely. He may rape her without ever having to face it. "Not rape, not quite that, but undesired nevertheless, undesired to the core," as the character of David admits to himself in passing, in J. M. Coetzee's *Disgrace* (1999). She may participate in unwanted sex because that is what she is meant to do. Or, he tells her she liked it: a pronouncement, not a conjecture.

If he loses exclusive access to old or all-boys' clubs, or schools as the case may be, and so she deprives him of a certain freedom from shame in her eyes, among other things, then he may drive her out determinedly, by any means necessary. We saw this both with Gamergate, and Susan Faludi's example of the Citadel.[14]

When they compete against each other for masculine-coded roles, studies suggest that the vast majority of people (both men and women) will prefer him for the job, all else being equal. And this includes cases where this has no rational basis whatsoever (e.g., with the same applicant files being alternated, as in the first study canvassed in chapter 8 by Heilman et al. [2004]).

The picture could also be filled in with comparative statistics about who gives more when it comes to domestic labor (her; see Hochschild and Machung [(1989) 2012] on "the second shift" problem); who is more likely to inflict more intimidating, injurious, and ongoing forms of violence on whom within a heterosexual household (he and her, respectively),[15] as well as who is more likely to rape and to be raped (likewise).

14. Faludi's account recalls my own experience in certain ways, as one of three girls at a previously all-boys' high school the year that it integrated. I suspect that some of my interest in the topic has its basis in these experiences, along with the subsequent predictable survivor's guilt.

15. Marianne Hester, a researcher and professor based in the United Kingdom, summarizes her findings thus: "The vast majority of domestic violence perpetrators recorded by the police were found to be men (92%) and their victims mainly female (91%). Many more repeat incidents were also recorded for male than for female perpetrators (Hester et al. 2006). This pattern has been found to be typical in police records across many areas of England and reflects the greater impact on women of such abuse" (2013). Hester also found, on the basis of analyzing police records, that men accused of domestic violence were more likely to be controlling, use more serious and harmful forms of violence, and to have instilled fear in a female victim, as compared with vice versa.

Who mansplains to whom? My sense is that men do this more frequently to women than vice versa. I hear you want hard data; call it an intuition. (Rebecca Solnit [2014a] being the foremother of the concept, if not the term here.)

Her vocal characteristics (e.g., vocal "fry") are grating; meanwhile, these same qualities in his voice are simply not noticed.[16]

Elizabeth Warren moves to read a letter by Coretta Scott King testifying to Jeff Sessions's racism; her male colleagues, Bernie Sanders and Sherrod Brown, do the same. Sanders and Brown read from the letter unhindered. Warren tries to do so and is silenced by Senate Majority Leader Mitch McConnell, invoking an arcane rule of senate proceedings. One is not to impugn the character of a fellow senator, even if he is on the cusp of becoming attorney general. McConnell: "She had appeared to violate the rule. She was warned. She was given an explanation. Nevertheless, she persisted"—until he made sure she couldn't. ("In an extremely rare rebuke, she was instructed by the presiding officer to take her seat," it was reported.)[17]

In the workplace, he can ask for a raise and may get it. If she asks, she will often be denied, even punished, for lack of politesse. Women therefore tend not to negotiate. She is advised to be more like a man, and to do so with vigor. Meanwhile, studies reveal that she knows what she's doing, given the risks and rewards to which she is subject. (See Exley, Niederle, and Vesterlund 2016.)

What if she threatens to take masculine-coded privileges and perks away from him, in the way of moral resources, sympathy, the attention and approval of an audience, or the votes of citizens? Consider she who claims victimhood, she who writes, teaches,

16. See, e.g., "From Upspeak To Vocal Fry: Are We 'Policing' Young Women's Voices?" NPR, July 23, 2015, http://www.npr.org/2015/07/23/425608745/from-upspeak-to-vocal-fry-are-we-policing-young-womens-voices.

17. Eugene Scott, "Warren's Male Senate Colleagues Read King Letter Uninterrupted," CNN, February 8, 2017, http://www.cnn.com/2017/02/08/politics/jeff-merkley-mark-udall-elizabeth-warren/.

professes, or tries to become a comedian, politician, or athlete. It just so happens that these are some of the figures who garner the most in the way of misogynist vitriol.

What about the times when she fails to provide feminine-coded goods and services, in the right way, at the right time? Withholding sympathy makes her a bitch; looking inward makes her cold or selfish; being ambitious makes her hostile and anti-social, as well as untrustworthy (Heilman et al. 2004); giving sexual attention to the wrong person makes her a slut—or a dyke, an unsexy lesbian; if she was wearing the wrong thing, or drunk, she was asking for it. Or, she led him on. She prevailed on him to take what was promised to him, sexually: what he had coming.

She wants not to go through with a pregnancy. Increasingly, it's enforced—even if it was the result of sex illicitly taken from her, where she was robbed of her sexual autonomy, as in rape or incest. More broadly, she withholds a certain amount of care within the family, by historical standards: and male politicians and others in power more than return the (non-)favor. She is deemed a host for the fetus by one lawmaker.[18] Others campaign for more parental rights for rapists. Still others try to mandate cremation or burial for fetal tissue, whether due to abortion or miscarriage (see chapter 3, note 16). Current vice president Mike Pence was a pioneer of this push for "fetal dignity" (Grant 2016). Other states have followed. The forefather of these laws? None other than Andrew Puzder, in Missouri, who featured in the introduction. Apparently disparate dispositions that tend to coalesce, individually and politically, are unified by misogyny on my analysis.

She is among the politicians who lies the least, and has never assaulted anyone; nor is there any evidence of her corruption or fraudulence (Abramson 2016). But she has that reputation, perhaps because she took the payment for a speech in the handsome sum offered.

18. Prachi Gupta, "Oklahoma Lawmaker: Pregnant Women Are 'Hosts' Whose Bodies Don't belong to Them," *Jezebel*, February 13, 2017, http://theslot.jezebel.com/oklahoma-lawmaker-pregnant-women-are-hosts-whose-bodie-1792303950.

He "grabs pussies," and takes advantage of many women, sexually. Yet despite this, he goes on to take the presidency. She's forced to concede to him. She is badgered by his lackeys to concede to him sooner (Baragona 2016). Such is the state of the art of male dominance—and heteropatriarchy, more broadly—upheld by misogynist threats and violence. And, to remind you, this is to consider comparatively privileged women. None of this should obscure the fact that others have less, and worse, and face sui generis problems. Rather, it is to highlight how unequal are even the most equal women.

That we often expect such women to give so much is clearly connected our being highly moralistic about their perceived failures to serve others selflessly. This was surely a factor in the animosity that developed toward Clinton during her latest bid for the White House— i.e., the fact that she was perceived as putting herself first, or being "self-serving," being a common theme among her critics.

Then there was the fact that she was portrayed as corrupt, "on the take," and "in bed" with Wall Street.

And she was also portrayed as illicitly *entitled*. Regarding the prospects of her eventual Democratic Party nomination, people spoke with palpable contempt and resentment about her "coronation."

But entitlements can be valid, genuine, or real. They are also, it should be added, contrastive or comparative: often, nobody is entitled to something *simpliciter*; but X is *more* entitled to Y, rather clearly.

I will leave devising an example as an exercise for the reader.

There's no question that Clinton was subject to frequent, vicious attacks for being too self-focused during her campaign for president. And many of these attacks were not only unfair, by evincing double and differential standards, but seemed more or less unfounded and immune to counterevidence. It was not clear what, if anything, might have allayed these suspicions. When it was pointed out that Clinton had a distinguished career in public service, David French wrote in *The National Review*:

> Let's be clear. Hillary Clinton hasn't sacrificed—she's lived the progressive dream. And she's certainly not a "public servant"—she's a

cynical, grasping, and ambitious politician. Her accomplishments are meagre, and her one guiding star is her own self-advancement.

Hillary Clinton has mainly been a destructive force in American life. Her zealous defense of abortion-on-demand has helped maintain a culture of death that has cost millions of young lives. Her foreign-policy missteps have helped turn Libya into an ISIS playground and assisted in squandering American victories in Iraq and Afghanistan. Her Russian "reset" merely lulled Americans into believing the Russian bear was benign. Her unrelenting personal corruption has helped degrade American politics. She serves mainly herself.

A nation founded by great men—and that has spawned many great presidents—still yearns to look up to its leaders. And so we commence the selling of a president. A real-estate developer develops his own strongman cult, and a glorified political wife tries to transform herself into a heroic trailblazer. But in the end we're left with nothing but grasping cynicism and petty personal corruption. Neither candidate sacrifices for this nation.[19]

Strong words: but drawing such false equivalences was— disgracefully—all too common. And the idea that Clinton only served herself in an objectionable way was, of course, everywhere.

I didn't grow up with *The Giving Tree*; I just stumbled across it recently. But several friends who had it read to them as a bedtime story said they'd found it horrifying. (Others still read it to their children and think it's a beautiful story.) So, even though my use of it was mostly

---

19. David French, "Dear Hillary Clinton Fans, Ambition Isn't 'Sacrifice'—It's Not Even 'Service,'" *National Review*, August 1, 2016, http://www.nationalreview.com/article/438568/hillary-clintons-public-service-donald-trumps-sacrifice-are-empty-words.
For some other examples in the same vein, see:
Roger L. Simon, "Hillary Clinton's Real Sickness Is Not Physical," PJ Media, September 12, 2016, https://pjmedia.com/diaryofamadvoter/2016/09/12/hillary-clintons-real-sickness-is-not-physical/.

allegorical, I wondered if perhaps I had been uncharitable. Perhaps Silverstein had intended his tale to be a modern parable for children: don't ask for too much. Your tree might get exhausted.

But I don't think so. Here's a poem of Silverstein's that was particularly controversial—so much so that the book in which it was published, his *The Light in the Attic* (1981), was banned from some schools. On an unrelated note (sincerely) it might remind you of someone—or rather, the way she was depicted in the media:

"Ladies First"
Pamela Purse yelled, *"Ladies first,"*
Pushing in front of the ice cream line.
Pamela Purse yelled, *"Ladies first,"*
Grabbing the ketchup at dinnertime.
Climbing on the morning bus
She'd shove right by all of us
And there'd be a tiff or a fight or a fuss
When Pamela Purse yelled, *"Ladies first."*
Pamela Purse screamed, *"Ladies first,"*
When we went off on our jungle trip.
Pamela Purse said her thirst was worse
And guzzled our water, every sip.
And when we got grabbed by that wild savage band,
Who tied us together and made us all stand
In a long line in front of the King of the land—
A cannibal known as Fry-'Em-Up Dan,
Who sat on his throne in a bib so grand

Jonah Goldberg, "Selfishness, Not Incompetence, Explains Hillary's E-mail Scandal," *National Review*, July 9, 2016, http://www.nationalreview.com/g-file/437640/hillary-clinton-email-scandal-selfishness-not-incompetence-behind-it.

For a useful history of hostility to Hillary, and its highly varied content over time, see: Michelle Goldberg, "The Hillary Haters," *Slate*, July 24, 2016, http://www.slate.com/articles/news_and_politics/cover_story/2016/07/the_people_who_hate_hillary_clinton_the_most.html.

With a lick of his lips and a fork in his hand,
As he tried to decide who'd be first in the pan—From back of the
    line, in that shrill voice of hers,
Pamela Purse yelled, "*Ladies first.*"[20]

Reading Silverstein's words, I feel truly defeated: one of the chief dynamics underlying misogyny has been disseminated by means of popular children's poems and beloved bedtime stories. It has been dignified before children are even in preschool. And many people seem not to have noticed the gender dynamics at work here, even though they genuinely care about (not) instilling these biases.[21] Yet if the boy may take everything his giving tree/she has to offer, and we think it is lovely, and the girl cannot even eat, drink, and enjoy condiments with impunity, then what am I doing here? What could possibly change any of this? Even *trying* is liable to make me seem nasty, abrasive, and pushy (dare I say, shrilly) and give rise to the sort of resistance that, in being aesthetic as well as moral, tends to be fatal. Or, if one does manage to sugar-coat it, it becomes self-defeating.

So I give up. I wish I could offer a more hopeful message. Let me close just by offering a postmortem.

---

20. A recent blog post about the poem, in honor of "Banned Book" week, reads:

> Silverstein's work tends to rile up the book banning types because of its "dangerous" ideas (defiant children, general nonsense, etc.), but the poem "Ladies First" met ire for its "promotion of cannibalism" (seriously). Of course anyone with a reasonably perceptive mind could deduce that the poem is actually a warning against greed, but a closed mind is often an ignorant one. Enjoy the poem and share it with your child if you have one.

If you follow this advice, one small suggestion: for the sake of variety, and to err on the side of caution vis-à-vis misogyny, try switching up the genders. E.g., *Masters first*; "Cameron Coin" gets cannibalized.

If the original poem isn't gendered, then it shouldn't be a problem.

21. For those who still think I'm reading too much into Silverstein's stories and poems, I subsequently discovered he also wrote stories for grown-ups (in addition to writing for *Playboy* magazine, as is well-known). One such story is "Going Once." Read it and then get back to me.

As I've observed throughout this book, we often contrast recognized *human beings* with those conceptualized as *objects*, as in sexual objectification, or sub-human creatures, or supernatural beings, or nonhuman animals. But instead of placing the emphasis on recognizing someone's *humanity* (or failing to), I have explored shifting the contrast to the second part of the idiom. In many of the cases considered in the last half of this book, we can distinguish between a (self-)recognized *human being*—e.g., white men who are otherwise privileged in most if not all major respects—versus a *human giver*, a woman who is held to owe many if not most of her distinctively human capacities to a suitable boy or man, ideally, and his children, as applicable. (Variants may be tolerated to varying degrees; wholesale alternatives or critical stances toward the nuclear heteropatriarchal family, much less so.) A giver is then obligated to offer love, sex, attention, affection, and admiration, as well as other forms of emotional, social, reproductive, and caregiving labor, in accordance with social norms that govern and structure the relevant roles and relations.

The human being/giver distinction is of course far from exhaustive. But I think it is important. And, according to my argument, it underlies and gives rise to many (though by no means all) of the forms of misogyny discussed in these chapters, where the privileged and powerful enforce their will, either enabled by or directly by means of social institutions. Such misogyny is then what happens when she *errs* as a giver—including by refusing to be one whatsoever—or he is dissatisfied as a customer, not least because a personalized giver fails to materialize whatsoever.

A human giver was evidently what Elliot Rodger wanted and felt entitled to, partly insofar as having one, in the form of a high-status girlfriend, would in turn confer on him the higher social status he so coveted. It might even have gone further than that and been bound up with his own sense of *humanity*, if his "manifesto" and other, similar sentiments, like that of George "Pornstache" Mendez of *Orange Is the New Black*, are indicative. (See chapter 5's opening epigraph and the last section, "Women, All Too Human.")

Rodger complained that he no longer felt like a human being toward the end of his downward spiral; he was in the grip of an ideology according to which a woman's humanizing gaze—not to mention touch—was an existential necessity for him. Something similar held for the family annihilator, Chris Foster, of chapter 4. On Jon Ronson's account, he could not abide the possibility of losing his wife's and daughter's *admiring* gaze up at him as a successful entrepreneur, after he ceased to be one. At that point, each man sought to destroy she who did not, or could no longer, provide him with the existential moral support he required by holding a flattering image of him in her eyes and beaming it back to him. So giving him his sense of self effectively became *her* existential mandate, too—unbeknownst to her, tragically, and often unforeseeably.

That we do not always think of the toxic masculine violence of family annihilation or strangulation as misogynistic, even though they are typically faced by women and committed by men due to patriarchal forces that serve and reflect gender roles and relations, is testament to the fact that we think of hostility in an excessively psychologistic way. Shame is not in itself a hostile emotion—or at least, not necessarily. But its manifestations certainly can be, from the point of view of its victims. Such is the case here, all too clearly.

One frightening aspect of such violence is how easily one could miss its incipient possibility, beneath the smooth surface of ordinary social relations. But when these eruptions occur, they give us important insights into what may be lurking darkly in many other cases: e.g., absolute, entitled, asymmetrical demands on his part, rather than looser social norms, expectations, and reciprocal obligations between social equals.

White men privileged in most if not all relevant respects, and who are aggrieved about the lack or loss of a human giver, are disappointed about a *state of affairs* (or its not obtaining). So how and why does this turn *personal* in many cases of misogyny? I suggested in chapter 1 that this is due to the specific *nature* of the felt deprivation in these cases. In light of the "human giver" or "giving she" dynamic since explored, we can say more about this. If each of the women in the relevant social class (e.g., in this case, those who Rodger wanted to "see" him) were meant to *give*, then why not to him? What, in their view, was wrong with him, exactly? Recall his wan question: "What don't they see in me?" This was as he was planning to annihilate a large swath of them. Again, his words were so lacking in self-aware-ness that they might almost be funny had he not acted. These women became to him an undifferentiated mass of withholding, stuck-up bitches. Given she was bound to give to *someone*, she was rejecting him: her not materializing was personally wounding.

I also considered cases where a woman in the relevant (i.e., human giver) class, relative to the target audience, asks for the sorts of goods, benefits, services, and support that are characteristically *hers* to give to him and his to get (or else *take*) from her. She will then seem entitled and ungrateful, as if she is demanding more than her due. She will also seem to have ideas beyond her station, or to be reneging on her end of history's gendered bargain—especially inas-much as she wants these benefits in order to *avoid* becoming a human giver (e.g., a wife and mother). This held, as we saw in chapter 2, in the case of Rush Limbaugh, as he conceived of Sandra Fluke. She was also "typical" of the kind of liberal woman who wants access to abortion providers, as chapter 3 demonstrated. And we can now make sense of contraception coverage having become a common point of conten-tion, too. She is asking to be *provided* with an *antidote* to human giv-ing—and in a way that often highlights her human capacities being deployed in self-development or geared toward financial success, that is, his province. The latter also threatens to turn her into a *usurper*.

As we saw in chapter 8, and earlier in this conclusion, these women may be perceived as greedy, grasping, and domineering; shrill and abrasive; corrupt and untrustworthy; or, wooden, stiff, and robotic. She is not providing the sorts of goods she ought to be giving up. She is negligent, irresponsible, careless, and callous. She may not even *have* such resources in the first place: being shriveled up, dried up, desiccated, or barren. She is also suspect at the level of supposed (i.e., cis) female embodiment and sexuality. And she is *demanding* some of the resources that her male rival is owed, by trying to drum up support, appeal to donors, and win over voters (say). Since the office belongs to men, historically, this makes her scheming, ruthless, and crooked: she is threatening to steal the election. She is an embezzler of power and money—what's his for the taking, by the lights of misogyny.

There are the men (or, as the case may be, boys) to whom women are under pressure to give her all—including, nay especially, human attention and affirmation and interest in his story. Himpathy and mansplaining are closely related phenomena. Women in the designated "giver" class may be prone to see a privileged man's side of the story first, and then last, without being asked to. This emerged in chapter 6 in particular, during the course of discussing himpathy. By much the same token, and as mentioned in chapter 4, some privileged men may feel entitled to hold forth to her without asking; she is expected to give him an attentive, absorbed audience. Mansplaining may then be the exception to the rule, where the inversion of the epistemic hierarchy is so stark that she notices, and protests, at least inwardly. Hence, it is called mansplaining and not simply a conversation.

There are the men who take from the most vulnerable women without asking, under the assumption that, once exploited, she will have no legal recourse. Sadly, it is a matter of happenstance that, in the case of Daniel Holtzclaw, this assumption was disrupted. And, in such cases, white women's sympathy—or himpathy—may lie with the rapist, and not with his victims, who were African American. Such was the upshot of the discussion of this case in chapter 6, which I suggested illustrated certain features of misogynoir in America.

There are the women who ask for sympathy on their own behalf, as discussed in chapter 7. But that is tantamount to the server asking for service, the giver expecting to receive. In other words, it is withholding a resource *and* simultaneously demanding it—a resource of the kind she ought to give to *him*, to add insult to injury (or, rather, embezzlement to begging).

One way of looking at the idea of so-called victim culture is that it trades on the trope of a passive female victim, the princess in the castle, waiting to be rescued by a princely hero. It is not controversial that the princess is a poor role model. But the critics of the "culture of victimhood" then effectively (if unwittingly) engage in concern trolling about women being able to retain a sense of agency on this basis. The resemblances between speaking out and behaving like a passive princess are slight, on closer inspection. Agency is not lacking when a woman is taking it upon herself to tell her story, or play her current part, in a manner that may be subversive or expose the bully using nothing other than his own behavior to embarrass him. This remains the case, indeed is doubly so, in a story in which she *was* made passive or, more commonly, her hand was forced (as in coercion) or she was taken advantage of (as in sexual predation, involving the exploitation of power relations and the associated social scripts; see Manne 2017). Acknowledging this may say: it happened to me as an agent, wrongfully and without adequate legal redress. I will enact it, and you, audience member—or, as the case may be, reader—will bear witness to the crime, provide the necessary moral judgment. Justice was not done: so, you be the jury.

Or you may be called upon to play this role for the sake of women no longer able to tell their stories, or testify in their own defense, when it comes to misogynist crimes and misdemeanors—having been charged, tried, convicted, and locked up or sent down, for real or nominal violations of patriarchal law and order. Often your focus should then be less on prosecuting suspected misogynists, or even agents held to have channeled misogynist social forces to her detriment. Rather, it should primarily be to set the record straight, render a "not guilty" verdict for what she has done, for the ages.

One more poem by Shel Silverstein will serve as illustration. It will also go some way toward addressing the natural question of whether men in other of his work ever give anything to girls and women. The answer is yes, but the effect here at least is mixed at best. Written for adults, this little-known piece appeared in a collection of poems and stories, called *Murder for Love* (1996, edited by Otto Penzler). Silverstein's contribution therein is titled and opens thus:

"For What She Had Done"
She had to die.
This Omoo knew.
He also knew he could not kill her.
Not even try to kill her.
Those eyes. Would look at him. Not even try.
So, what to do?
There was one Ung. Who lived in a cave.
Beyond the hard mountain. A foul cave.
Far from the village.
Ung, who hunted with stones.
Who killed with his hands.
Who had killed two saber-tooths.
And one great bear, whose skin he now wore hanging from his hairy shoulders.
And Ung had killed men. Many men.
And, it was said, a woman.

The poem concludes with the two men working out how the hit man might recognize his target. The first man tells the second he will know her by her long hair and dark eyes, very dark, "like the pool of night." Also, she will be bathing, washing her hair under the water-fall. The hit man is not satisfied: that could be any number of women, he points out. And he doesn't want to kill the wrong one, lest he not receive his payment: her weight in bear meat or lizard skins. ("An equal weight for an equal weight," as per their agreement.)

The first man thinks for a minute and comes up with a plan: he will give the woman who has to die for what she has done flowers to carry—

Bright hill flowers, that I shall gather and place in her hands,
  before she goes to bathe at the falling water.
Then you will know her.
Then you will kill her.[22]

And then, perhaps, he will be happy—or not really. Whatever the case, the point remains that she will be finished, silenced, forever silent. We never hear from her. She never has the chance to tell us what she did or didn't do to not deserve it. Perhaps no more than failing to be like the giving tree and loving the man as the tree loved the boy, "very, very much, even more than she loved herself." Her lack or loss of such love may be a capital offense, as far as he is concerned. One woman's misogyny is thus some men's poetic justice.

22. The next lines read:

For equal weight, said Ung.
Yes, said Omoo, for equal weight.
And so was begun the custom
Of giving bouquets and corsages.

And thus it ends. The poem is reproduced, along with others by Silverstein, at this website: https://m.poemhunter.com/poem/for-what-she-had-done/.

BIBLIOGRAPHY

Abramson, Jill. 2016. "This May Shock You: Hillary Clinton is Fundamentally Honest." *The Guardian*, March 28. https://www. theguardian.com/commentisfree/2016/mar/28/hillary-clinton-honest-transparency-jill-abramson.

Abramson, Kate. 2014. "Turning Up the Lights on Gaslighting." *Philosophical Perspectives* 28, no. 1: 1–30.

Alcoff, Linda Martín. 1991–92. "The Problem of Speaking for Others." *Cultural Critique* 20 (Winter): 5–32.

———. 2009. "Discourses of Sexual Violence in a Global Framework." *Philosophical Topics* 37, no. 2: 123–39.

Aly, Götz. 2014. *Why the Germans? Why the Jews?: Envy, Race Hatred, and the Prehistory of the Holocaust*. New York: Metropolitan Books.

Anderson, Kristin J. 2014. *Modern Misogyny*. New York: Oxford University Press.

Anscombe, G. E. M. 1957. *Intention*. Oxford: Basil Blackwell.

Appiah, Kwame Anthony. 2006. *Cosmopolitanism: Ethics in a World of Strangers*. New York: W. W. Norton.

———. 2008. *Experiments in Ethics*. Cambridge, MA: Harvard University Press.

Archer, John. 2000. "Sex Differences in Physically Aggressive Acts between Heterosexual Partners: A Meta-Analytic Review." *Psychological Bulletin* 126, no. 5: 651–80.

Arendt, Hannah. 1963. *Eichmann in Jerusalem*. London: Penguin.

Arpaly, Nomy. 2003. *Unprincipled Virtue: An Inquiry into Moral Agency*. Oxford: Oxford University Press.

———. 2011. "Open-Mindedness as a Moral Virtue." *American Philosophical Quarterly* 48, no. 1: 75–85.

Ashwell, Lauren. 2016. "Gendered Slurs." *Social Theory and Practice* 42, no. 2: 228–39.

Bailey, Moya. 2014. "More on the Origin of Misogynoir," *Tumblr*, April 27, http://moyazb.tumblr.com/post/84048113369/more-on-the-origin-of-misogynoir.

Bandyopadhyay, Mridula, and M. R. Khan. 2013. "Loss of Face: Violence against Women in South Asia." In *Violence against Women in Asian Societies*, edited by Lenore Manderson and Linda Rae Bennett, 61–75. London: Routledge.

Baragona, Justin. 2016. "'Corey, You're Being a Horrible Person': Van Jones and Lewandowski Battle Over Hillary's No Show," *Mediaite*, November 9. http://www.mediaite.com/online/corey-youre-being-a-horrible-person-van-jones-and-lewandowski-battle-over-hillarys-no-show/.

Barnes, Elizabeth. 2016. *The Minority Body*. New York: Oxford University Press.

Bauer, Nancy. 2015. *How to Do Things with Pornography*. Cambridge, MA: Harvard University Press.

Beeghly, Erin. 2015. "What Is a Stereotype? What Is Stereotyping?" *Hypatia* 30, no. 4: 675–91.

Beevor, Antony. 2003. *The Fall of Berlin 1945*. New York: Penguin Books.

Bennett, Jonathan. 1974. "The Conscience of Huckleberry Finn." *Philosophy* 49, no. 188: 123–34.

Bergoffen, Debra. 2011. *Contesting the Politics of Genocidal Rape: Affirming the Dignity of the Vulnerable Body*. London: Routledge.

Bettcher, Talia Mae. 2007. "Evil Deceivers and Make-Believers: On Transphobic Violence and the Politics of Illusion." *Hypatia* 22, no. 3: 43–65.

———. 2012. "Full-Frontal Morality: The Naked Truth about Gender." *Hypatia* 27, no. 2: 319–37.

———. 2013. "Trans Women and the Meaning of 'Woman.'" In *The Philosophy of Sex,* edited by Nicholas Power, Raja Halwani, and Alan Soble, 233–49. Lanham, MD: Rowman & Littlefield.

———. 2014. "Trapped in the Wrong Theory: Re-thinking Trans Oppression and Resistance." *Signs* 39, no. 2: 383–406.

Bian, Lin, Sarah-Jane Leslie, and Andrei Cimpian. 2017. "Gender Stereotypes about Intellectual Ability Emerge Early and Influence Children's Interests." *Science* 355, no. 6323: 389–91.

Bloom, Paul. 2016. *Against Empathy: The Case for Rational Compassion*. New York: Ecco.

Bordo, Susan. 1993. *Unbearable Weight*. Berkeley: University of California Press.

Bornstein, Kate. 1994. *Gender Outlaw: On Men, Women, and the Rest of Us*. New York: Routledge.

Braungart-Rieker, J., S. Courtney, and M. M. Garwood. 1999. "Mother- and Father- Infant Attachment: Families in Context." *Journal of Family Psychology* 13: 535–53.

Brison, Susan, J. 2002. *Aftermath: Violence and the Remaking of a Self*. Princeton, NJ: Princeton University Press.

———. 2006. "Contentious Freedom: Sex Work and Social Construction." *Hypatia* 21, no. 4: 192–200.

———. 2008. "Everyday Atrocities and Ordinary Miracles, or Why I (still) Bear Witness to Sexual Violence (but Not Too Often)." *Women's Studies Quarterly* 36, no. 1: 188–98.

———. 2014. "Why I Spoke Out about One Rape but Stayed Silent about Another." *Time*, December 1, http://time.com/3612283/why-i-spoke-out-about-one-rape-but-stayed-silent-about-another/.

———. 2016. "Forum Response to 'The Logic of Misogyny.'" *The Boston Review*, July 11. http://bostonreview.net/forum/logic-misogyny/susan-j-brison-susan-j-brison-responds-kate-manne.

Brooks, David. 2016. "The Sexual Politics of 2016." *New York Times*, March 29. https://www.nytimes.com/2016/03/29/opinion/the-sexual-politics-of-2016.html.

Brown, Wendy. 1995. *States of Injury: Power and Freedom in Late Modernity*. Princeton, NJ: Princeton University Press.

Burgess, Alexis, and David Plunkett. 2013. "Conceptual Ethics I and II." *Philosophy Compass* 8, no. 12: 1091–110.

Butler, Judith. 1990. *Gender Trouble: Feminism and the Subversion of Identity*. New York: Routledge.

———. 2015. *Senses of the Subject*. New York: Fordham University Press.

———. 2016. *Vulnerability in Resistance*. Durham, NC: Duke University Press.

Cahill, Ann J. 2001. *Rethinking Rape*. Ithaca, NY: Cornell University Press.

Calhoun, Cheshire. 2004. "An Apology for Moral Shame." *Journal of Political Philosophy* 12, no. 2: 127–46.

Calvin, John. 1999. *Calvin's Commentaries*. Edinburgh; repr. Grand Rapids, MI: Baker.

Campbell, Bradley, and Jason Manning. 2014. "Micro-Aggression and Moral Cultures." *Comparative Sociology* 13, no. 6: 692–726.

Camus, Albert. 1946. *The Stranger*. Translated by Stuart Gilbert. New York: Alfred A. Knopf. Originally published (in French) in 1942.

Card, Claudia. 2002. *The Atrocity Paradigm: A Theory of Evil*. New York: Oxford University Press.

———. 2010. *Confronting Evils: Terrorism, Torture, Genocide*. Cambridge: Cambridge University Press.

Cherry, Myisha. 2014. "What Is So Bad about Being Good?" *Huffington Post*, June 9. http://www.huffingtonpost.com/myisha-cherry/what-is-so-bad-about-being-good_b_5460564.html.

Chu, Arthur. 2014. "Your Princess Is in Another Castle: Misogyny, Entitlement, and Nerds." *Daily Beast*, May 27. http://www.thedaily-beast.com/articles/2014/05/27/your-princess-is-in-another-castle-misogyny-entitlement-and-nerds.html.

Coetzee, J.M. 1999. *Disgrace*. New York: Penguin.

Cole, Alyson M. 2006. *The Cult of True Victimhood*. Stanford, CA: Stanford University Press.

Craven, Peter. 2010. "Failing to Communicate the Campaign." *ABC News*, August 5, updated September 28. http://www.abc.net.au/news/2010-08-06/35762.

Crenshaw, Kimberlé W. 1991. "Mapping the Margins: Intersectionality, Identity Politics, and Violence Against Women of Color." *Stanford Law Review* 43: 1241–99.

———. 1993. "Beyond Race and Misogyny: Black Feminism and 2 Live Crew." In *Words That Wound*, edited by Mari J. Matsuda, Charles Lawrence III, Richard Delgado, and Kimberlé Williams Crenshaw, 111–132. Boulder: Westview Press.

———. 1997. "Intersectionality and Identity Politics: Learning from Violence against Women of Color." In *Reconstructing Political Theory: Feminist Perspectives*, edited by Mary Lyndon Shanley and Uma Narayan, 178–93. University Park: Pennsylvania State University Press.

———. 2012. "From Private Violence to Mass Incarceration: Thinking Intersectionally about Women, Race, and Social Control." *UCLA Law Review* 59: 1418–72.

Crenshaw, Kimberlé W., Julia Sharpe-Levine, and Janine Jackson. 2016. "16 Social Justice Leaders Respond to the 2016 Election." *African American Policy Forum*. November.

Cudd, Ann E. 1990. "Enforced Pregnancy, Rape, and the Image of Woman." *Philosophical Studies* 60, no. 1: 47–59.

———. 2006. *Analyzing Oppression*. New York: Oxford University Press.

Darcy, Oliver. 2015. "The 'F***ing Disgusting' Consequence Trump Lawyer Threatened Liberal News Site With for 'Rape' Story." *The Blaze*, July 27. http://www.theblaze.com/stories/2015/07/27/the-fing-disgusting-consequence-trump-lawyer-threatened-liberal-news-site-with-for-rape-story/.

Darwall, Stephen. 2006. *The Second-Person Standpoint: Morality, Respect, and Accountability*. Cambridge, MA: Harvard University Press.

———. 2013. *Honor, History, and Relationship: Essays in Second-Personal Ethics II*. Oxford: Oxford University Press.

Davis, Angela. 2003. *Are Prisons Obsolete?* New York: Seven Stories Press.

Daum, Meghan. 2014. "Misogyny and the Co-opting of the Isla Vista Tragedy." *Los Angeles Times*, June 4. http://www.latimes.com/opinion/op-ed/la-oe-daum-misogyny-isla-vista-20140605-column.html.

Dembroff, Robin A. 2016. "What Is Sexual Orientation?" *Philosophers' Imprint* 16, no. 3: 1–27. https://quod.lib.umich.edu/cgi/p/pod/dod-idx/what-is-sexual-orientation.pdf?c=phimp;idno=3521354.0016.003.

Desmond, Matthew. 2016. *Evicted: Poverty and Profit in the American City.* New York: Crown.

Diamond, Cora. 1978. "Eating Meat and Eating People." *Philosophy* 53, no. 206: 465–79.

Digby, Tom. 2003. "Male Trouble." *Social Theory and Practice* 29, no. 2: 247–73.

———. 2014. *Love and War: How Militarism Shapes Sexuality and Romance.* New York: Columbia University Press.

Dotson, Kristie. 2011. "Tracking Epistemic Violence, Tracking Practices of Silencing." *Hypatia* 26, no. 2: 236–57.

———. 2012. "A Cautionary Tale: On Limiting Epistemic Oppression." *Frontiers* 33, no. 1: 24–47.

———. 2014. "Conceptualizing Epistemic Oppression." *Social Epistemology* 28, no. 2: 115–38.

———. 2016. "Word to the Wise: Notes on a Black Feminist Metaphilosophy of Race." *Philosophy Compass* 11, no. 2: 69–74.

Dotson, Kristie, and Marita Gilbert. 2014. "Curious Disappearances: Affectability Imbalances and Process-Based Invisibility." *Hypatia* 29, no. 4: 873–88.

Du Toit, Louise. 2009. *A Philosophical Investigation of Rape: The Making and Unmaking of the Feminine Self.* New York: Routledge.

Dworkin, Andrea. 1976. *Woman Hating: A Radical Look at Sexuality.* New York: Dutton.

———. 1988. *Right-Wing Women: The Politics of Domesticated Females.* London: Women's Press.

Elon, Amos. 2013. *The Pity of It All: A Portrait of the German-Jewish Epoch, 1743–1933.* New York: Picador. Originally published in 2003.

Erikson, Erik H. 1963. *Youth: Change and Challenge.* New York: Basic Books.

Exley, Christine, Muriel Niederle, and Lise Vesterlund. 2016. "New Research: Women Who Don't Negotiate Might Have a Good Reason." *Harvard Business Review*, April 12. https://hbr.org/2016/04/women-who-dont-negotiate-their-salaries-might-have-a-good-reason.

Faludi, Susan. 2000. *Stiffed: The Betrayal of Modern Man.* London: Vintage.

———. 2006. *Backlash: The Undeclared War against American Women.* New York: Three Rivers Press. Originally published in 1991.

Fenske, Sarah. 2016. "Andrew Puzder, Trump's Pick for Labor Department, Was Accused of Abusing Wife." *Riverfront Times*, December 8. http://

www.riverfronttimes.com/newsblog/2016/12/08/andrew-puzder-trump-pick-for-labor-department-was-accused-of-abusing-wife.

Ferguson, Chris. 2014. "Misogyny Didn't Turn Elliot Rodger into a Killer." *Time*, May 25. http://time.com/114354/elliot-rodger-ucsb-misogyny/.

Floridi, Luciano. 2011. "A Defence of Constructionism: Philosophy as Conceptual Engineering." *Metaphilosophy* 42, no. 3: 282–304.

Flynn, Gillian. 2012. *Gone Girl*. New York: Crown.

Fricker, Miranda. 1999. "Epistemic Oppression and Epistemic Privilege." *Canadian Journal of Philosophy* 29 (Supplement): 191–210.

———. 2007. *Epistemic Injustice*. Oxford: Oxford University Press.

Friedan, Betty. 1963. *The Feminine Mystique*. New York: W. W. Norton.

Frost, Amber A'Lee. 2016. "Forum Response to 'The Logic of Misogyny.'" *The Boston Review*, July 11. http://bostonreview.net/forum/logic-misogyny/amber-alee-frost-amber-alee-frost-responds-kate-manne.

Frye, Marilyn. 1983. *The Politics of Reality: Essays in Feminist Theory*. Berkeley, CA: Crossing Press.

———. 1996. "The Necessity of Differences: Constructing a Positive Category of Women." *Signs* 21, vol. 3: 991–1010.

Gaita, Raimond. 1998. *A Common Humanity: Thinking about Love and Truth and Justice*. New York: Routledge.

Garcia, J. L. A. 1996. "The Heart of Racism." *Journal of Social Philosophy* 27, no. 1: 5–46.

Gillard, Julia. 2014. *My Story*. Vintage Books.

Glick, Peter, and Susan T. Fiske. 1997. "Hostile and Benevolent Sexism." *Psychology of Women Quarterly* 21: 119–35.

———. 2001. "An Ambivalent Alliance: Hostile and Benevolent Sexism as Complementary Justifications for Gender Inequality." *American Psychologist* 56, no. 2: 109–18.

Goffman, Alice. 2014. *On the Run: Fugitive Life in an American City*. New York: Picador.

Gold, Hadas, and John Bresnahan. 2016. "Trump Campaign CEO Once Charged in Domestic Violence Case." *Politico*, August 25. http://www.politico.com/story/2016/08/steve-bannon-domestic-violence-case-police-report-227432.

Gopnik, Adam. 2006. "Headless Horsemen: The Reign of Terror Revisited." *The New Yorker*, June 5. http://www.newyorker.com/magazine/2006/06/05/headless-horseman.

Gornick, Vivian. 2016. "Forum Response to 'The Logic of Misogyny.'" *The Boston Review*, July 11. http://bostonreview.net/forum/logic-misogyny/vivian-gornick-vivian-gornick-responds-kate-manne.

Grant, Rebecca. 2016. "The Latest Anti-Abortion Trend? Mandatory Funerals for Fetuses." *The Nation*, October 11. https://www.thenation.com/ article/the-latest-anti-abortion-trend-mandatory-funerals-for-fetuses/.

Greenhouse, Linda, and Reva B. Siegel. 2010. *Before Roe v. Wade : Voices That Shaped the Abortion Debate before the Supreme Court's Ruling*. New York: Kaplan Pub.

Halley, Janet. 2015. "Trading the Megaphone for the Gavel in Title IX Enforcement: Backing Off the Hype in Title IX Enforcement." *Harvard Law Review* 128, no. 4: 103–17.

Haslanger, Sally. 2000. "Gender and Race: (What) Are They? (What) Do We Want Them to Be?" *Noûs* 34, no. 1: 31–55.

———. 2012. *Resisting Reality*. New York: Oxford University Press.

———. 2016. "Epistemic Housekeeping and the Philosophical Canon: A Reflection on Jane Addams' 'Women and Public Housekeeping.'" In *Ten Neglected Classics of Philosophy*, edited by Eric Schliesser, 148–76. New York: Oxford University Press.

Hay, Carol. 2013. *Kantianism, Liberalism, and Feminism: Resisting Oppression*. New York: Palgrave-Macmillan.

Hedgepeth, Sonja M., and Rochelle G. Saidel, eds. 2010. *Sexual Violence against Jewish Women during the Holocaust*. Lebanon, NH: Brandeis University Press.

Heilman, Madeline E., Aaron S. Wallen, Daniella Fuchs, and Melinda M. Tamkins. 2004. "Penalties for Success: Reactions to Women who Succeed at Male Tasks." *Journal of Applied Psychology* 89, no. 3: 416–27.

Heilman, Madeline E., and Tyler G. Okimoto. 2007. "Why Are Women Penalized for Success at Male Tasks?: The Implied Communality Deficit." *Journal of Applied Psychology* 92, no. 1: 81–92.

Held, Virginia. 1987. "Feminism and Moral Theory." In *Women and Moral Theory*, edited by Eva Feder Kittay and Diana Tietjens Meyers, 111–28. Totowa, NJ: Rowman & Littlefield.

———. 2006. *The Ethics of Care*. Oxford: Oxford University Press.

Henwood, Doug. 2016. "Forum Response to 'The Logic of Misogyny.'" *The Boston Review*, July 11. http://bostonreview.net/forum/logic-misogyny/ doug-henwood-doug-henwood-responds-kate-manne.

Hester, Mariane. 2013. "Who Does What to Whom? Gender and Domestic Violence Perpetrators in English Police Records." *European Journal of Criminology* 10, no. 5: 623–37.

Heyes, Cressida. 2007. *Self-Transformations: Foucault, Ethics, and Normalized Bodies*. Oxford: Oxford University Press.

Hill Collins, Patricia. 1998. "It's All in the Family: Intersections of Gender, Race, and Nation." *Hypatia* 13, no. 3: 62–82.

———. 2000. *Black Feminist Thought: Knowledge, Consciousness, and the Politics of Empowerment*. 2nd ed. New York: Routledge. Originally published in 1990.

Hochschild, Arlie Russell. 2016. *Strangers in Their Own Land: Anger and Mourning on the American Right*. New York: New Press.

Hochschild, Arlie Russell, and Anne Machung. 2012. *The Second Shift: Working Parents and the Revolution at Home*. New York: Penguin. Originally pubished in 1989.

Hoff Sommers, Christina. 2016. "Forum Response to 'The Logic of Misogyny.'" *The Boston Review*, July 11. http://bostonreview.net/forum/logic-misogyny/christina-hoff-sommers-christina-hoff-sommers-responds-kate-manne.

hooks, bell. 2000. *Feminist Theory: From Margins to Center*. 2nd ed. London: Pluto Press. Originally published in 1984.

Hurt, Harry, III. 1993. *The Lost Tycoon: The Many Lives of Donald J. Trump*. Kindle ed. Echo Point: Brattleboro, VT.

Inbar, Yoel, and David A. Pizarro. 2016. "Pathogens and Politics: Current Research and New Questions." *Social and Personality Psychology Compass* 10, no. 6: 365–74.

Irwin, Kirk. 2016. "Trump CEO Was Charged with Choking Wife." *Daily Beast*, August 25. http://www.thedailybeast.com/trump-ceo-was-charged-with-choking-wife.

Jackson, Michelle Denise. 2014. "A Painful Silence: What Daniel Holtzclaw Teaches Us about Black Women in America." *For Harriet*, September. http://www.forharriet.com/2014/09/a-painful-silence-what-daniel-holtzclaw.html.

Jaggar, Alison M. 1983. *Feminist Politics and Human Nature*. Totowa, NJ: Rowman & Littlefield.

———. 2009. "Transnational Cycles of Gendered Vulnerability." *Philosophical Topics* 37, no. 2: 33–52.

Jenkins, Carrie. 2017. *What Love Is: And What It Could Be*. New York: Basic Books.

Jenkins, Kathryn. 2016. "Amelioration and Inclusion: Gender Identity and the Concept of Woman." *Ethics* 126, no. 2: 394–421.

Jetter, Alexis, Jennifer Braunschweiger, Natasha Lunn, and Julia Fullerton-Batten. 2014. "A Hidden Cause of Chronic Illness." Dart Center for Journalism and Trauma: A Project of the Columbia Journalism School, April 10, https://dartcenter.org/content/hidden-cause-chronic-illness.

Jones, Karen. 2002. "The Politics of Credibility." In *A Mind of One's Own: Feminist Essays on Reason and Objectivity*, edited by Louise M. Antony and Charlotte E. Witt, 154–76. Boulder, CO: Westview Press.

———. 2014. "Intersectionality and Ameliorative Analyses of Race and Gender." *Philosophical Studies* 171, no. 1: 99–107.

Kelly, Daniel. 2011. *Yuck: The Nature and Moral Significance of Disgust.* Cambridge, MA: MIT Press.

Kelly, Daniel, and Erica Roedder. 2008. "Racial Cognition and the Ethics of Implicit Bias." *Philosophy Compass* 3, no. 3: 522–40.

Khader, Serene J. 2011. *Adaptive Preferences and Women's Empowerment.* New York: Oxford University Press.

———. 2012. "Must Theorising about Adaptive Preferences Deny Women's Agency?" *Journal of Applied Philosophy* 29, no. 4: 302–17.

Kimmel, Michael. 2013. *Angry White Men: American Masculinity at the End of an Era.* New York: National Books.

King, Deborah K. 1988. "Multiple Jeopardy, Multiple Consciousness: The Context of a Black Feminist Ideology." *Signs* 14, vo. 1: 42–72.

Kittay, Eva Feder. 1999. *Love's Labor.* New York: Routledge.

———. 2013. "The Body as the Place of Care." In *Exploring the Work of Edward S. Casey*, edited by Donald A. Landes and Azucena Cruz-Pierre, 205–13. New York: Bloomsbury Publishing.

Koyama, Emi. 2003. "The Transfeminist Manifesto." In *Catching a Wave: Reclaiming Feminism for the 21st Century*, edited by Rory Dicker and Alison Piepmeier, 244–59. Boston: Northeastern University Press.

———. 2006. "Whose Feminism Is It Anyway? The Unspoken Racism of the Trans Inclusion Debate." In *The Transgender Studies Reader*, edited by Susan Stryker and Stephen Whittle, 698–705. New York: Routledge.

Kukla, Rebecca. 2005. *Mass Hysteria: Medicine, Culture, and Mothers' Bodies.* Lanham, MD: Rowman & Littlefield.

———. 2008. "Measuring Mothering." *International Journal of Feminist Approaches to Bioethics* 1, no. 1: 67–90.

———. 2014. "Performative Force, Convention, and Discursive Injustice." *Hypatia* 29, no. 2: 440–57.

Langton, Rae. 2009. *Sexual Solipsism: Philosophical Essays on Pornography and Objectification.* Oxford: Oxford University Press.

Lawrence, Charles R., III. 1987. "The Id, The Ego, and Equal Protection: Reckoning with Unconscious Racism." *Stanford Law Review* 39, no. 2: 317–88.

———. 2008. "Unconscious Racism Revisited: Reflections on the Impact and Origins of the Id, the Ego, and Equal Protection." *Connecticut Law Review* 40: 931–78.

Laxness, Halldór. 1997. *Independent People.* New York: Vintage.

Lebron, Christopher J. 2016. "The Invisibility of Black Women." *Boston Review* blog, January 15. http://bostonreview.net/blog/christopher-lebron-invisibility-black-women.

———. 2017. *The Making of Black Lives Matter: A Brief History of an Idea.* New York: Oxford University Press.

Lerner, Gerda. 1986. *The Creation of Patriarchy.* Oxford: Oxford University Press.

Lindemann, Hilde. 2014. *Holding and Letting Go: The Social Practice of Personal Identities.* Oxford: Oxford University Press.

Livingstone Smith, David. 2011. *Less Than Human: Why We Demean, Enslave, and Exterminate Others.* New York: St. Martins Press.

———. 2016. "Paradoxes of Dehumanization." *Social Theory and Practice* 42, no. 2: 416–43.

Lloyd, Genevieve. 1992. "Maleness, Metaphor, and the 'Crisis' of Reason." In *A Mind of One's Own*, edited by Louise Antony and Charlotte E. Witt, 73–92. Boulder: Westview Press.

Lorde, Audre. 2007. *Sister Outsider: Essays and Speeches.* Berkeley, CA: Crossing Press.

Lubet, Steven. 2015a. "Did This Acclaimed Sociologist Drive the Getaway Car in a Murder Plot? The Questionable Ethics of Alice Goffman's *On the Run*." *The New Republic*, May 27. https://newrepublic.com/article/121909/did-sociologist-alice-goffman-drive-getaway-car-murder-plot.

———. 2015b. "Ethnography on Trial." *The New Republic*, July 15. https://newrepublic.com/article/122303/ethnography-trial.

Lugones, María. 1987. "Playfulness, 'World'-Travelling, and Loving Perception." *Hypatia: A Journal of Feminist Philosophy* 2, no. 2: 3–19.

———. 1990. "Structure/Antistructure and Agency under Oppression." *Journal of Philosophy* 87, no. 10: 500–507.

Mac Donald, Heather. 2014. "The UCSB Solipsists." *National Review*, June 1. http://www2.nationalreview.com/article/379271/ucsb-solipsists-heather-macdonald/page/0/1 (last accessed 2015).

MacKinnon, Catharine, A. 1987. *Feminism Unmodified: Discourses on Life and Law.* Cambridge, MA: Harvard University Press.

———. 2006. *Are Women Human? And Other International Dialogues.* Cambridge, MA: Harvard University Press.

MacLachlan, Alice. 2010. "Unreasonable Resentments." *Journal of Social Philosophy* 41, no. 4: 422–41.

Maitra, Ishani. 2009. "Silencing Speech." *Canadian Journal of Philosophy* 39, no. 2: 309–38.

Maitra, Ishani, and Mary Kate McGowan. 2010. "On Silencing, Rape, and Responsibility." *Australasian Journal of Philosophy* 88, no. 1: 167–72.

Manne, Kate. 2013. "On Being Social in Metaethics." In *Oxford Studies in Metaethics*, vol. 8, edited by Russ Shafer-Landau, 50–73. Oxford: Oxford University Press.

———. 2014a. "Internalism about Reasons: Sad but True?" *Philosophical Studies* 167, no. 1: 89–117.

———. 2014b. "Punishing Humanity." Op-Ed. *New York Times*. The Stone, October 12. http://opinionator.blogs.nytimes.com/2014/10/12/in-ferguson-and-beyond-punishing-humanity/.

———. 2016a. "Before Hillary, There Was Another 'Witch' in Politics." *Huffington Post*. http://www.huffingtonpost.com/kate-manne/before-hillary-there-was-another-_b_9722158.html.

———. 2016b. "Humanism: A Critique." *Social Theory and Practice* 42, no. 2: 389–415.

———. 2016c. "Life Is Triggering: What Follows?" *The New Philosopher*, Education, August 30. http://www.newphilosopher.com/articles/3418/.

———. 2016d. "The Logic of Misogyny." *Boston Review*, July 11. http://bostonreview.net/forum/kate-manne-logic-misogyny.

———. 2016e. "Response to Forum Responses to 'The Logic of Misogyny.'" *The Boston Review*, July 11. http://bostonreview.net/forum/logic-misogyny/kate-manne-kate-manne-responds.

———. 2016f. "Sympathy for the Rapist: What the Stanford Case Teaches." *Huffington Post*, June 9. http://www.huffingtonpost.com/entry/sympathy-for-the-rapist-what-the-stanford-case-teaches_us_5758c0aae4b053e219787681.

———. 2016g. "Trumped-up Moral Outrage about Misogyny." *Huffington Post*, October 9. http://www.huffingtonpost.com/entry/trumped-up-moral-outrage-about-misogyny_us_57faa8e2e4b0d786aa52b693.

———. 2016h. "What Do We Do with Pornography?" Review of Nancy Bauer's *How to Do Things with Pornography*. *The Times Literary Supplement*, April 6. http://www.the-tls.co.uk/articles/public/where-anything-goes/.

———. 2016i. "When a Man Competes with a Woman." *Huffington Post*, October 19. http://www.huffingtonpost.com/entry/when-a-man-com-petes-with-a-woman_us_5807abc9e4b08ddf9ece1397.

———. 2017. "Good Girls: How Powerful Men Get Away with Sexual Predation." *Huffington Post*, March 24 (updated March 28). http://www.huffingtonpost.com/entry/good-girls-or-why-powerful-men-get-to-keep-on-behaving_us_58d5b420e4b0f633072b37c3.

———. Forthcoming. "Shame Faced in Shadows: On Melancholy Whiteness." Symposium piece on Judith Butler's *Senses of the Subject*. *Philosophy and Phenomenological Research*.

Marcus, Ruth Barcan. 1966. "Iterated Deontic Modalities." *Mind* 75, no. 300: 580–82.

McDowell, John. 1995. "Might There Be External Reasons?" In *World, Mind and Ethics: Essays on the Ethical Philosophy of Bernard Williams*, edited by J. E. J. Altham and Ross Harrison, 68–85. Cambridge: Cambridge University Press.

McIntosh, Peggy. 1988. "White Privilege and Male Privilege: A Personal Account of Coming to See Correspondences through Work in Women's Studies." Wellesley, MA: Wellesley College, Center for Research on Women.

McKinnon, Rachel V. 2014. "Stereotype Threat and Attributional Ambiguity for Trans Women." *Hypatia* 29, no. 4: 857–72.

———. 2015. "Trans*formative Experiences." *Res Philosophica* 92, no. 2: 419–40.

———. 2016. "Epistemic Injustice." *Philosophy Compass* 11, no. 8: 437–46.

———. 2017. "Allies Behaving Badly: Gaslighting as Epistemic Injustice." In *The Routledge Handbook of Epistemic Injustice*, edited by Gaile Polhaus Jr., Ian James Kidd, and José Medina, 167–175. New York: Routledge.

Medina, José. 2011. "The Relevance of Credibility Excess in a Proportional View of Epistemic Injustice: Differential Epistemic Authority and the Social Imaginary." *Social Epistemology* 25, no. 1: 15–35.

———. 2012. *The Epistemology of Resistance: Gender and Racial Oppression, Epistemic Injustice, and Resistant Imaginations*. Oxford: Oxford University Press.

Mendelberg, Tali. 2016. "Forum Response to 'The Logic of Misogyny.'" *The Boston Review*, July 11. http://bostonreview.net/forum/logic-misogyny/tali-mendelberg-tali-mendelberg-responds-kate-manne.

Meyers, Diana Tietjens. 2011. "Two Victim Paradigms and the Problem of 'Impure' Victims." *Humanity* 2, no. 2: 255–75.

———. 2016. *Victims' Stories and the Advancement of Human Rights*. New York: Oxford University Press.

Milgram, Stanley. 1974. *Obedience to Authority: An Experimental View*. New York: Harper & Row.

Mills, Charles W. 1997. *The Racial Contract*. Ithaca, NY: Cornell University Press.

Moi, Toril. 1999. *What Is a Woman? And Other Essays*. Oxford: Oxford University Press.

Moody-Adams, Michele. 2015. "The Enigma of Forgiveness." *Journal of Value Inquiry* 49, nos. 1–2: 161–80.

Moraga, Cherríe, and Gloría Anzaldúa. 2015. *This Bridge Called My Back: Writings by Radical Women of Color*, 4th ed. Albany: State University of New York Press. Originally published in 1981.

Nichols, Shaun. 2004. *Sentimental Rules: On the Natural Foundations of Moral Judgment*. Oxford: Oxford University Press.

Norlock, Kathryn J. 2008. *Forgiveness from a Feminist Perspective*. Lanham, MD: Lexington Books.

———. 2016. "Doctor's Orders: Menopause, Weight Change, and Feminism." *Ijfab: International Journal of Feminist Approaches to Bioethics* 9, no. 2: 190–97.

Nussbaum, Martha C. 1995. "Objectification." *Philosophy and Public Affairs* 24, no. 4: 249–91.

———. 2001. *Women and Human Development: The Capabilities Approach*. Vol. 3. Cambridge: Cambridge University Press.

———. 2004. *Hiding from Humanity: Shame, Disgust, and the Law*. Princeton, NJ: Princeton University Press.

———. 2011. "Objectification and Internet Misogyny." In *The Offensive Internet: Speech, Privacy, and Reputation*, edited by Saul Levmore and Martha Nussbaum, 68–90. Cambridge, MA: Harvard University Press.

Orwell, George. 1981. *A Collection of Essays*. New York: Harcourt.

Parks-Stamm, Elizabeth J., Madeline E. Heilman, and Krystle A. Hearns. 2008. "Motivated to Penalize: Women's Strategic Rejection of Successful Women." *Personality and Social Psychology Bulletin* 34, no. 2: 237–47. Accessed via Sage Journals, http://journals.sagepub.com/doi/pdf/10.1177/0146167207310027.

Pateman, Carole. 1988. *The Sexual Contract*. Stanford, CA: Stanford University Press.

Paul, David, and Jessi L. Smith. 2008. "Subtle Sexism? Examining Vote Preferences When Women Run against Men for the Presidency." *Journal of Women, Politics and Policy* 29, no. 4: 451–76.

Paul, L. A. 2015. *Transformative Experience*. Oxford: Oxford University Press.

Pawan, Mittal, and S. K. Dhattarwal. 2014. "Vitriolage: The Curse of Human Origin." *Medical Science* 6, no. 21: 61–64.

Penny, Laurie. 2014. "Let's Call the Isla Vista Killings What They Were: Misogynist Extremism." *New Statesman*, May 25. http://www.newstatesman.com/lifestyle/2014/05/lets-call-isla-vista-killings-what-they-were-misogynist-extremism.

Perry, Imani. 2016. "Forum Response to 'The Logic of Misogyny,'" *The Boston Review*, July 11. http://bostonreview.net/forum/logic-misogyny/imani-perry-imani-perry-responds-kate-manne.

Pinker, Steven. 2012. *The Better Angels of Our Nature: Why Violence Has Declined*. New York: Penguin.

Plattner, T., S. Bolliger, and U. Zollinger. 2005. "Forensic Assessment of Survived Strangulation." *Forensic Science International* 153: 202–7.

Pohlhaus, Gaile, Jr. 2012. "Relational Knowing and Epistemic Injustice: Toward a Theory of Willful Hermeneutical Ignorance." *Hypatia* 27, no. 4: 715–35.

Porpentine (pseud.). 2015. "Hot Allostatic Load." *The New Inquiry*, May 11 https://thenewinquiry.com/hot-allostatic-load/.

Preston-Roedder, Ryan. 2013. "Faith in Humanity." *Philosophy and Phenomenological Research* 87, no. 3: 664–87.

Rawls, John. 1955. "Two Concepts of Rules." *Philosophical Review* 64, no. 1: 3–32.

Raz, Joseph. 1989. "Liberating Duties." *Law and Philosophy* 8, no. 1: 3–21.

Resnick, Sofia. 2015. "In Sexual Assault Cases, New Laws on Strangulation Aid Prosecution." *Rewire*, April 23. https://rewire.news/article/2015/04/23/sexual-assault-cases-prosecutors-look-method-control/.

Rosenfeld, Diane L. 1994. "Why Men Beat Women: Law Enforcement Sends Mixed Signals." *Chicago Tribune*, July 29.

———. 2004. "Why Doesn't He Leave?: Restoring Liberty and Equality to Battered Women." In *Directions in Sexual Harassment Law*, vol. 535, edited by Catharine A. MacKinnon and Reva B. Siegel, 535–37. New Haven, CT: Yale University Press.

———. 2015. "Uncomfortable Conversations: Confronting the Reality of Target Rape on Campus." *Harvard Law Review* 128, no. 8: 359–80. https://harvardlawreview.org/2015/06/uncomfortable-conversations-confronting-the-reality-of-target-rape-on-campus/.

Rudman, Laurie A., Corinne A. Moss-Racusin, Julie E. Phelan, and Sanne Nauts. 2012. "Status Incongruity and Backlash Effects: Defending the Gender Hierarchy Motivates Prejudice against Female Leaders." *Journal of Experimental Social Psychology* 48: 165–79.

Sadker, David. 1999. "Gender Equity: Still Knocking at the Classroom Door." *Educational Leadership* 56, no. 7: 22–26.

Sadker, David, and Karen R. Zittleman. 2009. *Still Failing at Fairness: How Gender Bias Cheats Girls and Boys in School and What We Can Do about It.* New York: Simon and Schuster.

Sadker, Myra, and David Sadker. 1995. *Failing at Fairness: How America's Schools Cheat Girls.* New York: Touchstone Press.

Santucci, John. 2015. "Donald Trump's Ex-Wife Ivana Disavows Old 'Rape' Allegation." *ABC News*, July 28. http://abcnews.go.com/Politics/donald-trumps-wife-ivana-disavows-rape-allegation/story?id=32732204.

Saul, Jennifer. 2006. "Gender and Race." *Proceedings of the Aristotelian Society*, Supplementary Volume 80: 119–43.

Schraub, David H. 2016. "Playing with Cards: Discrimination Claims and the Charge of Bad Faith." *Social Theory and Practice* 42, no. 2: 285–303.

Serano, Julia. 2016. *Whipping Girl : A Transsexual Woman on Sexism and The Scapegoating of Femininity.* 2nd ed. Berkeley, CA: Seal Press. Originally published in 2007.

Shrage, Laurie, ed. 2009. *You've Changed: Sex Reassignment and Personal Identity.* Oxford: Oxford University Press.

Siegel, Reva B. 2014. "Abortion and the 'Woman Question': Forty Years of Debate." *Indiana Law Journal* 89, no. 4: 1365–80.

Silvermint. Daniel. 2013. "Resistance and Well-Being." *Journal of Political Philosophy* 21, no. 4: 405–25.

Silverstein, Shel. 1964. *The Giving Tree*. New York: Harper & Row.

Singal, Jesse. 2015. "The Internet Accused Alice Goffman of Faking Details in Her Study of a Black Neighborhood. I Went to Philadelphia to Check." *New York Magazine,* June 18. http://nymag.com/scienceofus/2015/06/i-fact-checked-alice-goffman-with-her-subjects.html.

Singer, Peter. 2011. *The Expanding Circle: Ethics, Evolution, and Moral Progress.* Princeton, NJ: Princeton University Press.

Solnit, Rebecca. 2014a. *Men Explain Things to Me.* Chicago, IL: Haymarket Books.

———. 2014b. "Our Words Are Our Weapons." *Guernica*, June 2. https://www.guernicamag.com/daily/rebecca-solnit-our-words-are-our-weapons-2/.

Smith, Jessi L., David Paul, and Rachel Paul. 2007. "No Place for a Woman: Evidence for Gender Bias in Evaluations of Presidential Candidates." *Basic and Applied Social Psychology* 29, no. 3: 225–33.

Snyder, Rachel Louise. 2015. "No Visible Bruises: Domestic Violence and Traumatic Brain Injury." *The New Yorker*, December 30, http://www.newyorker.com/news/news-desk/the-unseen-victims-of-traumatic-brain-injury-from-domestic-violence.

Song, Sarah. 2007. *Justice, Gender, and the Politics of Multiculturalism.* Cambridge: Cambridge University Press.

Sorenson, Susan B., Manisha Joshi, and Elizabeth Sivitz. 2014. "A Systematic Review of the Epidemiology of Nonfatal Strangulation, a Human Rights and Health Concern." *American Journal of Public Health* 104, no. 11: 54–61.

Sprague, Joey, and Kelley Massoni. 2005. "Student Evaluations and Gendered Expectations: What We Can't Count Can Hurt Us." *Sex Roles* 53, nos. 11–12: 779–93.

Stanley, Jason. 2015. *How Propaganda Works.* Princeton, NJ: Princeton University Press.

Strack, Gael B., George E. McClane, and Dean Hawley. 2001. "A Review of 300 Attempted Strangulation Cases Part I: Criminal Legal Issues." *Journal of Emergency Medicine* 21, no. 3: 303–9.

Strawson, P. F. (1962) 2008. "Freedom and Resentment." *Proceedings of the British Academy* 48: 1–25. Reprinted in *Freedom and Resentment and Other Essays*, 2nd ed., 1–28. London: Routledge. Page numbers are from the Routledge edition.

Suk Gersen, Jeannie. 2014. "The Trouble with Teaching Rape Law." *The New Yorker*, December 15, http://www.newyorker.com/news/news-desk/trouble-teaching-rape-law.

Sveinsdóttir, Ásta Kristjana. 2011. "The Metaphysics of Sex and Gender." In *Feminist Metaphysics*, edited by Charlotte E. Witt, 47–66. Dordrecht: Springer.

Swanson, Jordan. 2002. "Acid Attacks: Bangladesh's Efforts to Stop the Violence." *Harvard Health Policy Review* 3, no. 1. http://www.hcs.harvard.edu/~epihc/currentissue/spring2002/swanson.php.

Tessman, Lisa. 2005. *Burdened Virtues: Virtue Ethics for Liberatory Struggles*. New York: Oxford University Press.

———. 2016. *Moral Failure: On the Impossible Demands of Morality*. New York: Oxford University Press.

Thomas, Ashley J., P. Kyle Stanford, and Barbara W. Sarnecka. 2016. "No Child Left Alone: Moral Judgments about Parents Affect Estimates of Risk to Children." *Collabra* 2, no. 1: 10. http://doi.org/10.1525/collabra.33.

Thomas, Dexter, Jr. 2014. "Elliot Rodger Wasn't Interested in Women." *Al Jazeera*, June 7. http://www.aljazeera.com/indepth/opinion/2014/06/elliot-rodger-killing-sexism-20146219411713900.html.

Tirrell, Lynne. 2012. "Genocidal Language Games." In *Speech and Harm: Controversies over Free Speech*, edited by Ishani Maitra and Mary Kate McGowan, 174–221. Oxford: Oxford University Press.

Turkel, Allison. 2008. "'And Then He Choked Me': Understanding, Investigating, and Prosecuting Strangulation Cases." *American Prosecutors Research Institute* 2, no. 1. http://www.ndaa.org/pdf/the_voice_vol_2_no_1_08.pdf.

Twain, Mark. 2010. *The Adventures of Huckleberry Finn*. New York: Vintage Classics.

Valenti, Jessica. 2014. "Elliot Rodger's California Shooting Spree: Further Proof That Misogyny Kills." *The Guardian*, May 24. http://www.theguardian.com/commentisfree/2014/may/24/elliot-rodgers-california-shooting-mental-health-misogyny.

Valizadeh, Roosh. 2014. "Elliot Rodger Is the First Feminist Mass Murderer." *Return of Kings* blog, May 28. http://www.returnofkings.com/36397/elliot-rodger-is-the-first-male-feminist-mass-murderer.

Walker, Margaret Urban. 1998. *Moral Understandings*. New York: Routledge.

Watson, Gary. 1987. "Responsibility and the Limits of Evil: Variations on a Strawsonian Theme." In *Responsibility, Character, and the Emotions: Essays in Moral Psychology*, edited by F. Schoeman, 256–86. Cambridge: Cambridge University Press.

Websdale, Neil. 2010. *Familicidal Hearts*. Oxford: Oxford University Press.

West, Lindy. 2015. "What Happened When I Confronted My Cruellest Troll." *The Guardian*, February 2. http://www.theguardian.com/society/2015/feb/02/what-happened-confronted-cruellest-troll-lindy-west.

Wheatley, Thalia, and Jonathan Haidt. 2005. "Hypnotic Disgust Makes Moral Judgments More Severe." *Psychological Science* 16: 780–84.

Williams, Bernard. 1981. *Moral Luck*. Cambridge: Cambridge University Press.

Witt, Charlotte E. 2011. *The Metaphysics of Gender*. Oxford: Oxford University Press.

Woolf, Virginia. 2008. *A Room of One's Own: And, Three Guineas*. New York: Oxford University Press. Originally published in 1929.

Young, Cathy. 2014. "Elliot Rodger's 'War on Women' and Toxic Gender Warfare." *Reason*, May 29. http://reason.com/archives/2014/05/29/elliot-rodgers-war-on-women-and-toxic-ge.

Young, Iris Marion. 2004. "Five Faces of Oppression." In *Oppression, Privilege, and Resistance*, edited by Lisa Heldke and Peg O'Connor, 37–63. Boston: McGraw Hill.

Zheng, Robin. 2016. "Attributability, Accountability, and Implicit Bias." In *Implicit Bias and Philosophy*, vol. 2, *Moral Responsibility, Structural Injustice, and Ethics*, edited by Jennifer Saul and Michael Brownstein, 62–89. New York: Oxford University Press.

Zadrozny, Brandy and Tim Mak. 2015. "Ex-Wife: Donald Trump Made Me Feel 'Violated' During Sex." *Daily Beast*, July 7. http://www.thedailybeast.com/articles/2015/07/27/ex-wife-donald-trump-made-feel-violated-during-sex.

INDEX

and loyalty to powerful white
   men, 265–66
in mass atrocities, 165–68
Trump and, 5–7, 205–7
Rawls, John, 204n17
reactive attitudes, xv–xvii, 58–59, 60,
   129, 149n23, 165, 224
recognition of humanity, xix,
   151–56, 158–71
representative targets, 35, 58–59, 68,
   86, 108–9
reproductive rights. *See* abortion;
   contraception
resentment
   and claiming victimhood, 229
   of Rodger, 50
   and sexual objectification, 85–86
   and social progress of women and
     nonwhites, 77, 156–58
   in Strawson's treatment of reactive
     attitudes, xvii
resistance, playing victim as act of, 244
ressentiment, 86, 242n24, 244
revenge, dehumanization and acts of,
   169, 172–76. *See also* Isla Vista
   killings; Rodger, Elliot
right-wing women, 115
Rini, Regina, 238–39
rivals, 151–53, 155
Rodger, Elliot. *See also* Isla Vista killings
   entitlement of, 106, 108–9
   and events and reactions to Isla Vista
     killings, 34–41
   and exoneration of men, 193
   and feminist diagnosis of Isla Vista
     shootings, 54
   and human being/giver distinction,
     301, 302–3
   and interpersonal reactive
     attitudes, 58–59
   as misogynist, 48, 74, 87
   and revenge as source of
     dehumanizing behavior, 172–75
   as triggered by others' manifestations
     of common humanity, 149–50
Rohan, Tim, 216

Ronson, Jon, 123, 302
Room of One's Own, A (Woolf), xi,
   xvii, 86n5
Rose, Pete, 198n12
Rubio, Marco, 260
Rudd, Kevin, 195, 268
Rudman, L. A., 253–54
Russians, 166–68
Rwandan genocide, 148n21
Ryan, Paul, 206

Sadker, David, 292–93n12
Sanders, Bernie, 255, 273, 275, 295
Sarkeesian, Anita, 120n12
scapegoat. *See* representative targets
Schlosser, Edward, 230n14
Schonfeld, Zach, 41n12
self-righteous family annihilators, 124
Serial podcast, 179–80n1
Sessions, Jeff, 295
sex assignments, social roles based
   on, 292–94
sexism, versus misogyny, 20, 44,
   78–84, 88–90
sexual assault. *See* rape and sexual
   assault
sexual desire, 50
sexual jealousy, 109–10n3
sexual solipsism, 135
shame, 120–28, 183, 289–90, 302
Siegel, Reva B., 93
silencing, 4–7, 18, 214
Silverstein, Shel, 279–80,
   298–300, 305–7
sincerity condition, 165n36
Singer, Peter, 156
Skipp, Catharine, 125
slaves/slavery, 139, 159–61, 165n37
smackdown, 86–90
Smith, Jessi, 251
Snyder, Rachel Louise, 17
social dominance penalty, 253–54
socially situated model, 151–58, 163
social progress, xii, 77, 114–15
social rejection, mediated by
   disgust, 256–59